Preschool
Appropriate
Practices

Third Edition

Join us on the web at

EarlyChildEd.delmar.com

Third Edition

Preschool Appropriate Practices

Janice J. Beaty

Professor Emerita,
Elmira College

DELMAR
CENGAGE Learning

Australia Brazil Japan Korea Mexico Singapore Spain United Kingdom United States

Preschool Appropriate Practices, Third Edition

Janice J. Beaty

Vice President,
Career Education Strategic
Business Unit: Dawn Gerrain

Director of Learning Solutions:
John Fedor

Acquisitions Editor: Christopher
Shortt

Product Manager: Philip Mandl

Director of Production: Wendy A.
Troeger

Production Manager: Mark Bernard

Content Project Manager: Angela
Iula

Director of Marketing: Wendy
Mapstone

Senior Channel Manager: Kristin
McNary

Marketing Coordinator: Scott
Chrysler

Art Director: Dave Arsenault

For product information and technology assistance, contact us at
Professional & Career Group Customer Support, 1-800-648-7450
For permission to use material from this text or product, submit all requests
online at **www.cengage.com/permissions**
Further permissions questions can be emailed to
permissionrequest@cengage.com

ExamView® and ExamView Pro® are registered trademarks of FSCreations, Inc. Windows is a registered trademark of the Microsoft Corporation used herein under license. Macintosh and Power Macintosh are registered trademarks of Apple Computer, Inc. used herein under license.

© 2008 Cengage Learning. All Rights Reserved. Cengage Learning WebTutor™ is a trademark of Cengage Learning.

Library of Congress Control Number: 2007943394

ISBN-13: 978-1-4283-0448-2

ISBN-10: 1-4283-0448-7

Delmar Cengage Learning
5 Maxwell Drive
Clifton Park, NY 12065-2919
USA

Cengage Learning products are represented in Canada by Nelson Education, Ltd.

For your lifelong learning solutions, visit delmar.cengage.com

Visit our corporate website at www.cengage.com

Notice to the Reader
Publisher does not warrant or guarantee any of the products described herein or perform any independent analysis in connection with any of the product information contained herein. Publisher does not assume, and expressly disclaims, any obligation to obtain and include information other than that provided to it by the manufacturer. The reader is expressly warned to consider and adopt all safety precautions that might be indicated by the activities described herein and to avoid all potential hazards. By following the instructions contained herein, the reader willingly assumes all risks in connection with such instructions. The publisher makes no representations or warranties of any kind, including but not limited to, the warranties of fitness for particular purpose or merchantability, nor are any such representations implied with respect to the material set forth herein, and the publisher takes no responsibility with respect to such material. The publisher shall not be liable for any special, consequential, or exemplary damages resulting, in whole or part, from the readers' use of, or reliance upon, this material.

Printed in the United States of America
2 3 4 5 x x x 10 09

To a special friend, colleague, and early childhood advocate

MARY KLEIN MAPLES

BRIEF CONTENTS

CONTENTS

CHAPTER 2
THE TEACHER'S ROLE • 23

CHAPTER 3
BLOCK CENTER • 47

CHAPTER 6
BOOK CENTER • 135

CHAPTER 7
WRITING CENTER • 162

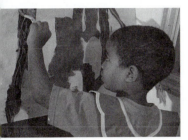

CHAPTER 8
ART CENTER • 185

CHAPTER 9
MUSIC CENTER • 210

CHAPTER 10
SCIENCE CENTER • 238

CHAPTER 11
DRAMATIC PLAY CENTER • 266

CHAPTER 12
LARGE-MOTOR CENTER • 292

CHAPTER 13
SAND/WATER/WOOD • 316

CHAPTER 14
CURRICULUM PLANNING • 333

APPENDIX

PREFACE

Let the learning environment do the teaching is the overall theme of *Preschool Appropriate Practices, Third Edition*. Because research shows us that the preschool child learns best through playful exploration of the environment, this book proposes a curriculum that addresses children's interests and needs as well as the teacher's task of choosing appropriate activities for children's development. Readers will learn how to arrange the physical environment of a preschool classroom in order for children ages 3 to 5 to become deeply involved in their own learning through a "self-directed learning environment."

Let the teacher be a facilitator of learning is a second theme that helps teachers understand how to set up learning centers, how to serve as behavior models in these centers, how to observe children's developmental levels, and then how best to support children in each of the centers. Readers will learn how to determine children's developmental levels of manipulation, mastery, and meaning by observing children's interactions with materials and with each other.

The textbook is organized into chapters based on 13 learning centers within today's preschool classroom: the block, computer, manipulative/math, book, writing, art, music, science, dramatic play, large-motor, and sand, water, and wood centers. Each chapter discusses how to set up the center so that children can use it on their own, what activities to provide in order to support specific development in children, and how to observe in order to determine an individual child's level of development and needs.

NEW FEATURES IN THE THIRD EDITION

This new edition continues its use of children's picture books in every chapter as lead-ins to the learning centers and to integrating new activities based on the books themselves. Over 200 books are included in this edition, with 100 of them having been published since 2000 and 80 of them containing multicultural characters.

Discussion of developmentally appropriate practice (DAP) as defined by the National Association for the Education of Young Children(NAEYC) has been updated to include *culturally appropriate* as an additional element of which to be aware when making sure a practice is developmentally appropriate.

New information in every chapter includes chapter 4, Computer Center, rewritten to bring it up-to-date and in line with the latest computer technology and with 20 new CD-ROM programs for children. Other changes or additions include: math concepts of classification; ordering, patterning, and numbering in chapter 5; making young children's emergence into math more understandable; and English-Spanish books for reading at home in chapter 6; along with books that feature "pattern play," an important key to emergent literacy. A new chapter 13 has been added to this edition: "Sand/Water/Wood," which includes activities for sand tables (e.g., creating miniature dramatic play episodes with block people), water tables (e.g., squeezing away bad feelings with sponges), and a Woodworking Center that uses tree stumps for hammering.

The strength of each learning center chapter continues to be its description of the role of the teacher/facilitator in this self-directed environment. To set up activities that are developmentally appropriate for every child, the teacher learns to use a unique observation tool, the Child Interaction Form. Finally, to plan an overall curriculum the teaching staff learns the approach of using curriculum webs.

ANCILLARIES

Online Instructor's Manual

There is an electronic Instructor's Manual that contains:

- an outline of the essential contents of the text;
- recommended activities;
- discussion questions;
- audiovisual resources;
- recommended readings; and
- a list of children's books.

The instructor's manual is located on the instructor lounge section found at www.earlychilded.delmar.com.

ACKNOWLEDGMENTS

My thanks go especially to my colleague Bonny Helm, who read the original manuscript and offered many meaningful suggestions; to Donna Zeigler for writing the original music to my action chants; to Mary Maples and Winona Sample for their support of the text in Indian Head Starts; to Sue Bredekamp of the National Association for the Education of Young Children for her work in developing and promoting "developmentally appropriate practice" in classrooms for young children; and to editor Philip Mandl for helping me get this new edition off the ground. Finally, I would like to thank the reviewers of this text:

- ◯ Priscilla Smith, PhD, Program Director, Early Childhood Care and Education, Gwinnett Technical College, Georgia

- ◯ Tracy Keys, MS, Assistant Professor, Kutztown University, Pennsylvania

- ◯ Pamela Davis, PhD, Professor of Early Childhood Education and Director of the HSU Child Service Center, Henderson State University, Arkansas

- ◯ Kathleen T. Cummings, MS, Assistant Professor, Suffolk County Community College, New York

- ◯ Debby Everett, MA, Early Childhood Education Instructor, Yuba College, California

- ◯ Jorja Davis, MA, Child Development Instructor, Blinn College, Texas

- ◯ Dorothy Justus Sluss, PhD, Associate Dean, School of Education, The College of William & Mary, Virginia

- Tracey Bennett, MA, Professor, Vance-Granville Community College, North Carolina
- Martha T. Dever, EdD, Professor, Utah State University, Logan, Utah
- Linda Capone Claussen, MS, Professor, New River Community College, Virginia
- Frances G. Langan, EdD, Professor and Chair, Keystone College, Pennsylvania

CHAPTER 1   THE SELF-DIRECTED LEARNING ENVIRONMENT

EXPECTATIONS OF STUDENTS AND TEACHERS

As students and teachers in the field of early childhood education, we are all engaged in a remarkable endeavor: that of guiding young children through their very first group learning experience. We want desperately to succeed. We want children to come into our classrooms with delight on their faces and excitement in their eyes. We want to be excellent teachers who offer outstanding education to the 3-year-olds, 4-year-olds, and 5-year-olds who come into our programs. We want to be able to help solve all their problems and meet all their needs.

It is such a new experience for them. They come into our classrooms with such high anticipation, with such great expectations. Will we like them? Will they be able to do what we expect of them? Will they like school? Will they find a friend?

It is such an important experience for us. Will we be able to provide the quality programs their parents expect of us and we expect of ourselves? Will we be able to handle an entire class full of some 20 lively youngsters? Will we be able to reach and satisfy those children with special needs?

This textbook offers *ideas* that can make such a learning experience happen for teachers and children. It discusses the how's and why's of learning psychology in terms teachers can relate to. It offers ideas for converting the classroom into an active and attractive learning environment with freedom for teachers to direct and support and for children to choose and accomplish the learning tasks necessary for both to succeed. It gives suggestions for providing appropriate activities and materials for the age level and learning stage level of every child in your class.

COME IN

ACTION CHANT

Walk up the sidewalk,
(march in place throughout)

Knock at the door,
(knock with hand)

Peek through the window,
(hand over eyes)

Gaze at the floor,
(look down)

Hand on the doorknob,
(turn with hand)

Should you begin?
(stop all motion)

Open the door wide!
(pull "door" open)

COME RIGHT IN!
(jump forward)

As you read this textbook, try to put yourself in the place of the children in your classroom. What would make the environment comfortable for you? What kinds of activities would you choose to be involved with? What kind of support would you appreciate receiving from those in charge? Use the answers to these questions as guidelines for your work with young children. They will appreciate this concern on your part, and they will respond in the way you hoped they would.

WHAT WE KNOW ABOUT TEACHING AND LEARNING

Research has shown us that the more direct involvement young children have with learning activities, the more effectively they learn. The studies of Swiss psychologist Jean Piaget and the cognitive pyschologists who followed him all point to the fact that young children learn best when they are actively involved in playful sensory exploration of materials and activities (Piaget, 1962). Teachers of young children agree. Whenever they set up their classrooms so that the children can become directly involved with materials, all kinds of exciting interactions take place. So intensely do young children interact with their favorite materials and activities, in fact, that it is difficult to pull them away.

You may well agree with this observation, but you may also wonder: "Is this really teaching? If I set up the classroom environment so that the children get deeply involved in the activities, then what am I supposed to do? Isn't a teacher supposed to teach?"

"Yes, of course," is the answer. But *teaching* in an early childhood classroom is a very special skill, performed for a very special audience. The teacher in an early

The teacher must observe how individuals interact with materials.

childhood classroom is a guide or facilitator of learning. This means the teacher sets up the classroom so that the children can teach themselves. Children younger than age 7, we have learned, create their own knowledge by direct hands-on interaction with the materials, activities, and people in their environment. Thus, such children, if they are to learn, must have an especially rich environment full of materials, activities, and people who relate well to children's cultures as well as their ages and stages of development.

Then the teacher must observe how individuals interact with the materials: what they do with them, how they use or misuse them, which materials are the favorites, which are ignored, and how she/he can best help and support the children in their learning. The teacher becomes a side-by-side facilitator of learning rather than a sage-on-the-stage in front of the class.

EARLY CHILDHOOD RESEARCH BASE

Piaget's studies concerning how children acquire knowledge led him to differentiate three distinct kinds of knowledge:

1. *Physical knowledge* (external reality as observed and experienced in a sensory-motor way by children)

2. *Logical-mathematical knowledge* (mental constructs of relationships such as classifying by size or shape that occurs in the child's brain)

3. *Social-conventional knowledge* (agreed-upon conventions of society, such as the names given to numerals, alphabet letters, and so forth) (Kamii, 1990)

Children acquire all three types of knowledge, first by interacting physically with the objects and people in their environment and then by mentally processing this knowledge; at the same time they test new information against their previous knowledge, resulting in new or revised mental constructs. All young children everywhere go through this natural process of constructing knowledge during their early cognitive development.

The research of Russian psychologist Lev Vygotsky adds important details to this new view of the child's acquisition of knowledge. He distinguishes children's *spontaneous concepts* acquired through direct experience from their *scientific or school-learned concepts* acquired in the social context of school. Instruction by adults can be helpful to children, but it is contingent upon the children's own development of skills in "a zone of proximal development." This "zone" represents the distance between what children can do by themselves and what they can do with assistance. But before children can benefit from instruction, they must have reached some specific level of functioning in order to incorporate any learning from their environment.

Children acquire this first knowledge through play. Play is the young child's method of thinking through things and solving problems. As Vygotsky notes: "In play a child always behaves beyond his average age, above his daily behavior; in play it is as though he were a head taller than himself. As in the focus of a magnifying glass, play contains all developmental tendencies in a condensed form and is itself a major source of development" (Vygotsky, 1978, p. 102).

From these developmental theories, cognitive psychologist Jerome Bruner went on to construct a learning theory (Bruner, 1966). His research with infants and young children demonstrated the importance not only of early learning, but also of a caregiver to provide "a social scaffold for the acquisition of skills." A caregiver is necessary to help the child participate and respond in games and activities.

Children constructing their own knowledge, an environment conducive to children's exploratory play, and a caregiver as an enabler to help children acquire skills: these are the ingredients for successful early childhood programs.

This textbook bases its approach on the findings of these cognitive-interactionist theorists, as well as on those of other important researchers and practitioners in the field: Maria Montessori from Italy at the turn of the century; the Reggio Emilia schools from Italy in the 1990s; and the Americans—Carolyn Pratt in the 1920s, Mildred Parten in the 1930s, David Weikert and his High/Scope program in the 1960s and 1970s, Barbara Biber and the Bank Street College of Education in the 1970s and 1980s; and the brain-imaging technology of neuroscientists in the 1990s and into the 21st century.

DEVELOPMENTALLY APPROPRIATE PRACTICE

In 1986 the National Association for the Education of Young Children (NAEYC), early childhood's principal professional organization, issued a position statement on developmentally appropriate practice in early childhood programs based on a two-year study of relevant research in the field. The statement provides a framework for the appropriateness of curriculum, learning activities, adult-child interaction, home-program relations, and the evaluation of child development. It includes guidelines concerning the appropriateness or inappropriateness of curriculum goals, teaching strategies, guidance, language, and cognitive, physical, and aesthetic development for 4- and 5-year-old children.

The rationale for developing a national position statement stems from the trend in recent years toward increased formal instruction of academic skills in early childhood programs. Worksheets and workbooks were beginning to appear first in kindergartens, then in preschools. Teacher-directed activities were beginning to replace children's free play in many programs.

Someone with authority and supportive research needed to take a stand against these inappropriate practices; the NAEYC stepped forward. "This trend toward formal academic instruction seems to be based on misconceptions about early learning," the NAEYC's study concluded (Bredekamp, 1987, p. 4).

The position outlined by the NAEYC in its first, and later revised, publication, *Developmentally Appropriate Practice in Early Childhood Programs Serving Children from Birth through Age 8,* makes it clear that although the quality of an early childhood program may be affected by many factors, a major determinant of program quality is the extent to which knowledge of child development is applied in program practice—the degree to which the program is *developmentally appropriate* (Bredekamp & Copple, 1997).

Continued revisions of this position emphasize that to be developmentally appropriate, an early childhood program should be:

1. *age appropriate,* that is, it should show awareness and understanding of the predictable sequences of growth and change in the children it serves;

2. *individually appropriate,* that is, it should be aware of and respond to individual differences in young children, matching children's developing abilities with appropriate materials and activities, while challenging them to develop further; and

3. *culturally appropriate,* that is, it should recognize the influence of group cultural differences on each child's development (Copple & Bredekamp, 2006, pp. 49–50).

In the chapters to follow, *Preschool Appropriate Practices* presents ideas and activities that support the "Guidelines for Developmentally Appropriate Practice" as outlined by the NAEYC.

When teachers set up classrooms so that children can become involved on their own, they are free to work with individual children, observing them and taking note of those who need special help and support. They can then provide this help to individuals or small groups. That is the appropriate practice for preschool teachers.

When young children are given a free choice of activities to pursue on their own, they become deeply and happily involved in their learning. Although they will sit still and listen when the teacher talks to the entire class, preschool children do not develop cognitively, physically, socially, or emotionally in this manner. To grow in understanding the world around them and their part in it, these children need hands-on interaction with materials and equipment on their own as individuals or in small groups. That is the appropriate practice for preschool children.

CREATING A SELF-DIRECTED LEARNING ENVIRONMENT

In order to provide a curriculum that addresses the needs of individual youngsters in this appropriate manner, we can create a self-directed learning environment within our program. That is, we can provide, assemble, and arrange a physical classroom environment that allows children to:

1. perceive what activities are available

2. make their own choices of activities to pursue

3. get deeply involved in their own learning

It is the learning environment itself that is the curriculum in the preschool classroom. The choice and arrangement of the equipment and materials we provide set the stage for whatever is to happen. Wise teachers who understand how young children learn, arrange the environment so that the children can direct their energies into the learning areas of greatest interest to them. Then teachers let the learning environment do the teaching through the children's playful exploration of materials and activities.

We must arrange this environment carefully so that individual children can use it on their own without much direction on our part. We must ensure that it contains materials and activities appropriate for the wide range of individual children's interests and abilities. And we must make sure that although each learning area stands on its own, each one is also integrated in an appropriate manner into the total curriculum.

PROVIDING LEARNING CENTERS

Dividing the classroom into specific areas known as "learning centers" is the most efficient and effective way to arrange a classroom. When set up appropriately, the centers speak to the children with materials and activities that let them know the purpose for each center and how they can go about using it.

Teachers who have worked in classrooms with and without such centers have this to say about them: "Learning centers not only provide children with opportunities to explore, experiment, and construct their own knowledge, they also provide opportunities for movement, socialization, choice making, responsibility, and problem solving" (Bottini & Grossman, 2005, p. 277).

Your first appropriate task, then, is to set up such self-directed learning centers. How will you do it? First you must become aware of the curriculum areas your particular program supports. They are often described in terms of topics: language arts, social studies, science, mathematics, physical activities, art, and music. Sometimes they are described in terms of child-development aspects: social, emotional, physical, cognitive, language, and creative.

Next you must convert these curriculum or child-development topics into the learning centers. That is, you must plan physical space for each of the curriculum topics your program includes. Because the classroom arrangement and all that happens within it make up the curriculum in an early childhood program, this text is arranged by chapters that have converted the curriculum topics into the following classroom centers (Table 1-1).

In this text, the six major aspects of child development are treated in each of the 13 learning center chapters. For example, chapter 3, "Block Center," discusses social, emotional, physical, cognitive, language, and creative growth of children through self-exploratory interaction with blocks.

Table 1-1 Learning Centers in an Appropriate Practices Classroom

Curriculum Topic	Learning Center
Language Arts	Book Center Writing Center Computer Center
Social Studies	Block Center Dramatic Play Center
Science	Science Center Computer Center Sand/Water Center
Mathematics	Manipulative/Math Center Computer Center Block Center
Physical Activities	Large-Motor Center Manipulative/Math Center Block Center Woodworking Center
Art	Art Center Writing Center Computer Center
Music	Music Center Large-Motor Center Computer Center Woodworking Center

LOCATING AND SPACING LEARNING CENTERS

Once you know which learning centers your classroom should include, you can begin to plan your locating and spacing of them. It was once believed that early childhood classrooms should be arranged so that active or noisy activities would not be near passive or quiet activities. The Appropriate Practices Curriculum takes a different point of view. Because many classrooms are not large enough for the noisy/quiet theory to make a difference, the arrangement of learning centers can be based on other concerns, for example, how learning centers relate to one another.

Children will be moving from one activity to another. They may be engaged in block building, but they may want to see the photos of the field trip taken at the bridge construction site last week. Those photos happen to be displayed in the Writing Center because other children are writing spontaneous stories in personal script about their field trip experience. Or the children may want to move from the Block Center to the Dramatic Play Center because the children there are pretending to be construction workers building a bridge.

Thirteen curriculum areas are described in this text: blocks, computer, manipulative/math, book, writing, art, music, science, dramatic play, large motor, sand, water, and woodworking, and cooking. To **arrange a classroom based on these 13 areas** it is important to **consider how each of them relates to the others** before a classroom can be arranged, so that it will be used most appropriately.

One way to approach this task is to take one learning center at a time and jot down on paper any other center of the classroom to which it has a strong relationship. You can also rank these learning centers in an informal sort of order of their importance in the relationship. For example, Dramatic Play is first in importance in its relationship to Blocks because children often represent what they have experienced on a field trip in both the Dramatic Play and Block Centers. What might result is a list like that found in Table 1-2.

Looking at the Block Center is a case in point. At the top of its list is Dramatic Play. Dramatic Play also lists Blocks at the top of its list. Thus, you might decide to locate the Block Center and the Dramatic Play Center adjacent to one another. In

Table 1-2 Relationships among Learning Centers

Learning Center	Related Center
Blocks	Dramatic Play
	Large Motor
Computer	Writing
	Manipulative/Math
Manipulative/Math	Computer
	Science
Books	Writing
	Dramatic Play
Writing	Computer
	Books
Art	Books
	Woodworking
Music	Large Motor
	Woodworking
Science	Manipulative/Math
	Sand/Water
Dramatic Play	Blocks
	Books
Large Motor	Blocks
	Music
Woodworking	Art
	Manipulative/Math
Sand/Water	Science
	Dramatic Play
Cooking	Manipulative/Math Books

like manner, the Computer Center, which lists Writing first, and the Writing Center, which lists Computer first, might well be located near one another.

To **make arranging the centers simpler for yourself**, on 13 small squares of paper write both the name of a learning center in large letters and the name of one or two of the most important related centers in small letters. Then take a sheet of paper to represent the floor plan of the classroom and move the squares around on it, so that centers having an important relationship in your program are close to one another. Obviously, the size and shape of the classroom, the doors, the sink, and other special features must be taken into consideration as you design your self-directed learning environment (see Figure 1-1).

The space allotted to each learning center depends upon the kinds of activities that will occur in the center and the number of children expected to use the center at one time. Arrangement of a particular center will be discussed in detail in the chapter describing that center.

PERCEIVING THE ACTIVITIES AVAILABLE

In order to become self-directed in the classroom, young children need to be able to recognize what is available to them. Your spacing of activities into definite centers through use of room dividers, portable screens, shelves, tables, curtains, and other means will help them understand where certain activities are to occur. For instance, two shelves of blocks against a wall do not really define the Block Center; pulling the two shelves away from the wall and placing them at right angles to the wall and to one another mark off the area in a much more definite manner. All of the learning centers in your classroom can be defined in a similar way. The learning center chapters to follow tell how.

LEARNING CENTER LABELS

Children also recognize what is available through **picture and sign labels** . Colorful cutouts of each of your curriculum centers can be mounted at children's eye level on the wall or room divider of the center. Use construction paper of various colors to make your labels attractive. One method for making learning center labels is to trace objects from the area onto colored paper; cut out the objects and mount them on a large white backing paper with words designating the area printed at the top. For example, trace unit blocks of various types (half-unit, ramp, arch, cylinder) on paper of different colors for each block. Then cut them out and paste them on the sign like a collage of blocks. Letters indicating Block Center can be cut out of colored construction paper or can be printed with colored felt-tip markers. Labels can be in two languages whether or not your programs contain bilingual children.

Another method is to **use a logo** for each center. An orange arch can represent Block Center, a blue floppy disk can represent Computer Center, purple puzzle pieces can represent Manipulative/Math Center, and so on. The backing paper of the sign itself can represent the area better if it is cut into the shape of the area. You might want to color code each area by making the sign itself a certain color, having the objects on the sign in white. Then you can cut out smaller duplicates of the same center-shaped signs and paste them on a large floor plan chart of the room. Use both written and picture symbols for your signs, because children need to know how we express our names for things in words as well as in pictures.

You can invent your own learning center signs. For instance, **take photos** of each learning center, enlarge them, and mount them on signs. Look in your professional library for illustrated books on each of the learning centers, make a photocopy of the illustration, and then enlarge it for a sign. Or do the same with children's books showing pictures of a nursery school. The time you spend preparing the environment for the children to use is well worth your effort. Some of the most stimulating and significant hours you and your coworkers will occupy during the year can be those spent preparing the environment so that children will want to use it on their own. In making the classroom environment inviting for children, you will also make it inviting to work in for yourself.

LEARNING CENTER MAPS AND SCHEDULES

Once the centers are labeled, you can **make a large illustrated floor plan** of the classroom to be mounted near the door so that children as well as visitors can identify the various centers. Be sure to mount it at the children's eye level.

Children recognize what is available through picture and sign labels.

Children are intrigued with maps. This is a map of their classroom, and they will need to learn how to read it. Introduce it to individuals and small groups at first, explaining what it is and how you will be using it. If you have pasted small colored cutouts of the learning center signs onto this floor plan as suggested, the children will be able to match the center on the map with the center in the room designated by a similar sign. However you label your learning centers, you can use a similar label on your floor plan so that children can more easily identify the centers.

This floor plan or map is a symbol for the children: it represents or symbolizes the classroom. The children will enjoy learning to "read" this illustrated symbol of their room. They will feel proud to be able to point out to parents or visitors the various learning centers represented on it. It is only one of the many symbols they will find in a classroom following the Appropriate Practices Curriculum.

Another type of symbolization for both children and visitors is the Daily Schedule of activities. This, too, can be an **illustrated schedule chart** with the learning centers shown as small cutout signs of the center. Make this chart one that can easily be taken off the wall for discussion at morning circle time or whenever it is you bring the children together. The children can learn to "read" this chart, too. It will tell them what is happening in their classroom for the day. It is another means for making them aware of what is available for them to choose to do in their self-directed environment. Let them try to match the cutout learning center symbols on the chart with the actual labels in the various centers.

An illustrated Daily Schedule should contain what is available for children to do during each of the time slots sequenced throughout the day. The chart can be divided into sections such as: arrival, activities, snack, outdoors, lunch, nap, activities, departure. Each section of the chart will show illustrations of the centers having special activities.

If your Daily Schedule is on a bulletin board, the cutout signs for the centers can be changed or moved around from day to day as the activities change. To make the schedule more meaningful for the children, let them be the ones to move the signs on the chart. Once you begin to develop a schedule for the children to "read" daily, it will become a dynamic part of your classroom and not just a permanent list of activities tacked to the wall for your supervisor to check. See chapter 14, "Curriculum Planning," for more information on developing this moveable feast of activities.

MAKING OWN ACTIVITY CHOICES AND BECOMING DEEPLY INVOLVED

Why should children make their own choices of the activities in a classroom? Wouldn't it be simpler for the teacher to assign children to a center or to an activity? Probably. Most children would certainly accept the teacher's assignment. After all, 3-, 4-, and 5-year-olds are used to being told what to do by an adult. Why should this program be any different?

This program may be different because it is based on current research and child development theory that says young children learn most effectively when they

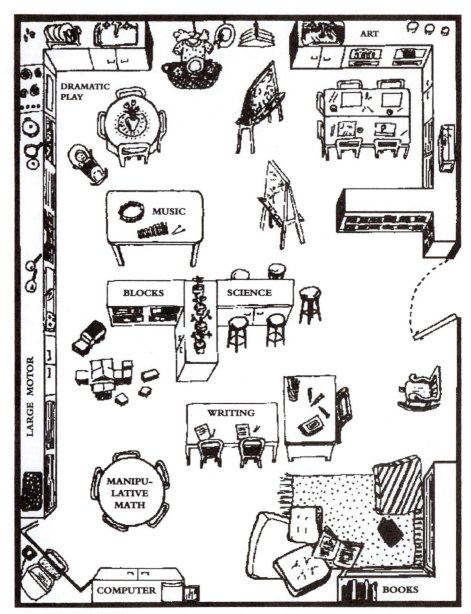

Figure 1-1 Floor Plan.

become deeply involved in their own learning. To become deeply involved means they must be interested in the activity. A teacher-assigned activity may or may not be of interest to an individual child. A child's own choice is much more likely to interest him or her deeply.

In addition, environments that support choices are crucial to a child's development of self-reliance. Children in such a child-centered classroom "have higher expectations for their own success, are less dependent on adult permission and approval, and are more willing to try challenging academic tasks" (Gestwicki, 2007, p. 18).

Children entering a preschool classroom for the first time may see a number of materials or activities that interest them. But in order for children to choose to become involved in any of them, they must first have developed a sense of trust in themselves, in the teacher, in the other children, and in the classroom itself. A new classroom, a large and lively group of peers, and new adults as teachers, can be quite overpowering for 3-year-olds who have not been out of the family circle for long.

Trust in Self

Such children need to learn, first of all, that they can trust themselves in the classroom. That is, they need to learn self-confidence. Will they know what they are supposed to do in the classroom? Will they succeed at any of the activities? Will the teacher like them? Will the other children like them? Most of your children have these questions, doubts, and even fears, whether or not they express them.

To learn self-confidence, young children need to succeed at the activities you provide. If you have been observing the developmental levels of every child, you will be providing a wide range of activities at a variety of difficulty levels. You will take into consideration children with special needs and youngsters from multi-cultural backgrounds.

Your support in helping them choose activities that interest them will send the youngsters in the right direction. Your patience in waiting for children who are not yet ready to become involved in activities will give them a chance to develop the confidence necessary to make their own choices in this fascinating new environment. And your provision of a **self-regulating method** to help them choose activities on a rotating basis, or take turns with activities when the one they want is already occupied by others, will help them to understand about others' needs.

Young children are highly egocentric or self-centered: they look at everything in terms of themselves. Yet your classroom must serve more than a dozen other children. You could spend most of your time trying to regulate individual children's behavior when more than one wants to play with a certain material or activity at the same time. On the other hand, you could set up your classroom so that the children can regulate their own behavior. Children who learn to use self-regulating devices develop trust in their own abilities and confidence to explore the classroom on their own.

You can, for instance, have **tickets** for children that are color-coded for each learning center. There would be as many colored tickets as there are children allowed in the center. The tickets can be placed in library pockets on a choice board, enough for each learning center. There might be six orange tickets for the Block Center, for example, that children would place in pockets at the entrance to the Block Center. When children are ready to leave the area, they would return the tickets to the choice board; or a child might want to trade an orange ticket with another child who has a blue ticket for the Computer Center.

Name tags are also interesting for children to use. Laminated name tags with a piece of Velcro or a hole punched in one end can be hung on a hook or fastened on a Velcro tab at the entrance to a center. The number of hooks or fasteners in a center would help to control the number of children using the center. Children can get their name tags from a hook or fastener on the choice board and hang it in the learning center of their choice. A **photo tag** of each child can also be made and laminated with clear contact paper, to be used as a self-regulating device in the same manner.

Still another popular device is a **learning center necklace:** a yarn necklace with the learning center symbol or color code that can be worn by children while they are in a particular center. When they leave the center, they take off the necklace and return it to one of the hooks at the center entrance. Color-coded clothespins, colored chips (from card games), or colored pieces (from board games) can also be selected by each child and used as a self-regulator to gain admittance to a center. Your own ingenuity and that of the children will help you to design other self-regulating devices that give children the freedom to make their own activity selections, and thus learn to trust themselves in this exciting new environment.

Trust in the Teacher

Children need to learn that they can trust the teacher to allow them to make their own choices and to support them in those choices. They need to feel secure that the teacher will not try to make them change their minds or place them somewhere else. ("Maybe those puzzles are too hard for you, Josh. Why don't you play with this table game?") Not only will the teacher support them in the choices they make, but the teacher will also support them in doing their chosen activities.

Suppose Josh has made an activity choice that is too difficult for him. The sensitive teacher will keep an eye on his progress. If he seems to need help, the teacher will offer it without intruding. If he seems to need direction, the teacher will help him to find the way himself, perhaps by offering alternatives. If Josh seems to need peer support, the teacher may suggest that he and another child work together on the activity. But if he prefers to work alone, the teacher will accept this preference as well.

Whatever Josh does in the classroom, the teacher needs to **accept him unconditionally**. She will rejoice in his successes, help him to go on to something else when his chosen task is finished, and not turn against him even when he loses self-control. She is there to support him under all conditions, and does not lose control herself when something he does annoys her. She helps him to get back on the right track without guilt or recriminations.

Another way teachers can help youngsters trust them is to **give them enough time to get involved** with the materials or activities of their choice. Too often teachers regulate classroom activity time to suit their own convenience, or their particular expectations of children. What if children need more time with an activity in order to understand and learn from it? Real learning takes time.

Is it important that everyone in the class get a turn on the computer every day, for instance, or would it be more meaningful for a few youngsters to spend an extended time with the computer in order to "construct their own knowledge" on a new program? Children will learn to trust their teachers if they see that the teachers accept their self-regulation of time in the activities they have chosen to explore.

Still another way teachers can help children trust them is through their attitudes and actions regarding each child's home and family. Does the teacher **show delight when meeting one of the child's parents?** Does he show interest when the child talks about his home? Does he **refrain from correcting the child's speech** because he realizes this is an indirect reflection on the child's family? Will he allow (and even encourage) the child to **bring a toy from home?** Helping a youngster to make the sometimes difficult transition from home to school is an important service the preschool teacher must perform for each of the children.

When children learn through experience that they can trust their teachers, they will feel free to make choices in the classroom and become deeply involved in their learning.

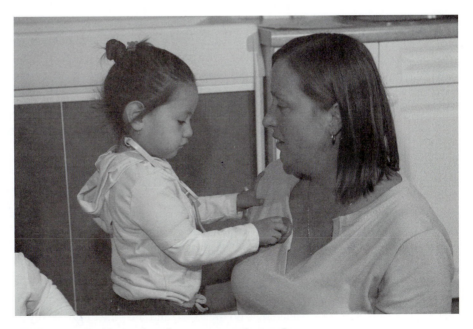

Children need to learn that they can trust the teacher.

Trust in Peers

Just as important to novice preschoolers is being able to trust their own peers. How will the other youngsters feel about them, they may wonder on the first days or first weeks in the classroom? What if the other children don't like them? What if they don't play with them? It is so difficult for some young children to let a stranger into their midst for long. As it is, many of the youngest children may relate more easily to adults than to other children, because their previous experience has principally been with adult caregivers.

What can be done? Again it is up to the teachers or other staff members to help the children become involved with peers if this is their choice. If a child is ready to build with others in the Block Center, to work with a partner on the computer, or to join the dramatic play—but doesn't know how—then it is up to the teacher to give the child assistance. **Gaining access to ongoing play** is especially difficult for some children at this age. Either they are too shy to intrude or too aggressive to be accepted by others. The sensitive teacher needs to help such a child find a middle ground (Beaty, 2008, p. 243).

Perhaps shy Marlena can do a task for the teacher with another child. If these two youngsters are compatible, then perhaps they can work together with the blocks or the computer. If Marlena is still not ready for the overpowering presence of a group, the teacher may **help her set up a similar activity parallel to the group activity**. Parallel play like this has been found to be one of the most effective ways for preschoolers to gain entrance to ongoing group activities when they are ready (Anderson & Robinson, 2006, p. 13).

On the other hand, if children are too aggressive and pushy in trying to join a group, the teacher could help them gain access by asking them to perform a task for the teacher that will include playing with the group. (Can a child count the number of items on the "grocery store" shelf and tell the "cashier"?)

Children who display self-confidence and trust in the teacher are usually ready to join a group. All they may need is your brief assistance in gaining group access. When the others see that you support them, then they may well extend their own support. Thus the children will develop trust in their peers that will eventually free them to make their own choices and become deeply involved in their own learning.

Trust in the Environment

Finally, if young children are to make choices and become deeply involved in the activities of the classroom, they must develop trust in the environment. This trust translates into: 1) an awareness of the choices available, 2) an interest in the materials, 3) freedom to explore, and 4) time to get deeply involved. Your setting up of the environment so that young children understand it and know how to use it is the first step, as already mentioned. Giving children the freedom to explore the materials on their own and the time to get deeply involved adds immeasurably to their developing of trust in the environment.

Once young children are aware of the choices available, they need to develop an interest in the materials. Are they familiar ones? Are they appropriate for the ages and developmental levels of the children? Teachers following the Appropriate Practices Curriculum will want some of the **materials** in their classroom environments to be **similar to those found in the homes** of the children.

Although many classroom activities will be new, different, and challenging to 3-, 4-, and 5-year-olds, some should also be familiar. Water play and dough-making are activities the youngsters may have first encountered at home. Native American children from the Navajo culture may be familiar with weaving. Cooking with tortillas may be familiar to Hispanic children. Teachers can set up simple examples of such commonplace activities early in the year to put the children at ease, and then add new twists in water play, yarn activities, or dough-making as the year progresses.

The dramatic play family area with its kitchen furnishings is another familiar center that should help children build trust in the classroom environment. Later, other role-play areas can be added. Home-type furnishings such as mats or rugs, wall hangings, an easy chair or rocker, pictures, and pillows are all appropriate accessories because they help young children feel at home in school.

If the children in your class have ethnic or multicultural backgrounds, your classroom furnishings can reflect this as well. A Mexican serape, a Native American blanket or rug, a Caribbean woven mat, a fishing net, or a paper lantern can also decorate the classroom walls if they seem appropriate. If children have physical disabilities, your materials may need special knobs or handholds.

Are the materials exciting ones? Put yourself in the place of a 3-, 4-, or 5-year-old child coming into a new classroom. What kinds of things would you want to play with? Your children will be attracted to colorful objects, to things that look the right size and shape, to materials that look as if you can do something "neat" with them. They love to be able to build their own huts and hideaways with card tables, cardboard packing cases, or large pieces of fabric attached to rods with clothespins or curtain rings (Curtis & Carter, 2005, p. 36).

Teachers with programs having little money for new materials can make their own. **Homemade materials** are often the best ones anyway, because they are created for particular needs, and thus are used more frequently. Bring in empty food boxes of all sizes (cereal boxes, packaged mix boxes, boxes from sugar, salt, tea, or rice, for example). Let the children paint them and then cut out pictures from magazines to glue on them. What can the boxes be used for? Science collections? Decorations in the family area? Pretend treasure boxes? Let the children decide. Table 1-3 lists some throwaway items children can bring in from home.

If the learning environment is expected to help children develop trust, then one important message it can convey at the outset is: **this classroom cares for you**. It has been arranged carefully for you to understand what is available and to choose by yourself the activities that interest you most. It will also provide materials to help you feel at home and wanted: stuffed animals for comfort while you look at a book

Table 1-3 Throwaway Items from Home

Old magazines, catalogs
Paper towel and tissue tubes
Empty boxes: cereal boxes, packaged mix boxes, tissue boxes, matchboxes, shoe boxes
Coffee tins
Seasoning jars and boxes
Clear plastic bottles and jars with tops
Plastic squeeze bottles
Margarine containers with tops
Styrofoam™ meat trays
Styrofoam packing "peanuts"
Plastic bubble wrap
Paper and plastic bags of different sizes

in the Book Center, dolls of different skin colors to care for in the Dramatic Play Center, a container of little cars and figures of people and animals to select and play with during rest time. The pictures on the wall are at your eye level, and designs in the Block Center are on the baseboard for you to see when you are playing on the floor. An **overstuffed chair in the corner is a private place** for you to go to when you are feeling out-of-sorts.

Some classrooms go a step further and offer children a basket of **tiny toys to borrow** one at a time for overnight. Other programs have a second set of children's **picture books for overnight home lending**. This is yet another way to help children trust the environment by building bridges daily from home to school. Children are encouraged to take home school material, but then they are expected to return with it the next day. Such a practice not only creates great anticipation for the day ahead, but also helps the children realize that their home and school are working together for their benefit.

SETTING THE STAGE FOR LEARNING

The self-directed learning environment is thus a dynamic setting that creates an opportunity for learning by offering appropriately arranged learning centers responsive to the individual child's interests and needs. With this setting in place the children can begin their exciting learning adventure of creating their own knowledge through interaction with the people and materials in their environment. The teachers can begin observing children in order to provide appropriate activities and support for the youngsters' continued growth and development. And the Appropriate Practices Curriculum to follow will evolve naturally as children and teachers work together in an atmosphere of trust and caring.

Children can begin their exciting learning adventure in this classroom.

IDEAS IN CHAPTER 1

1. *Arrange a classroom based on 13 centers*
   a. List each learning center along with related learning centers
   b. Make a floor plan with cutouts
2. *Help children recognize what is available*
   a. Provide picture and sign labels
   b. Use a logo
   c. Take photos for signs

    d. Make an illustrated floor plan

    e. Make an illustrated schedule chart

3. *Develop a child's self-regulating method*

    a. Use tickets

    b. Use name tags

    c. Use photo tags of each child

    d. Use learning center necklaces

4. *Develop children's trust in the teacher*

    a. Accept children unconditionally

    b. Give children enough time to get involved

    c. Show delight in meeting parents

    d. Refrain from correcting child's speech

    e. Have children bring a toy from home

5. *Develop children's trust in peers*

    a. Help children gain access to ongoing play

    b. Ask child to perform a task that will include other children

    c. Help child set up similar activity parallel to group activity

6. *Develop children's trust in the environment*

    a. Have materials similar to those in the home

    b. Make own materials

    c. Demonstrate that this classroom cares

    d. Provide tiny toys to borrow

    e. Provide picture books for home lending

    f. Place overstuffed chair in corner for private space

DISCUSSION QUESTIONS

1. How do young children gain "physical knowledge" as described by Piaget? Give examples.

2. What makes the activities and materials in a preschool program "developmentally appropriate"? How would they be inappropriate?

3. Why did the NAEYC feel the need to develop a position statement on developmentally appropriate practice in early childhood programs?

4. What makes a self-directed learning environment "developmentally appropriate"? Give examples.

5. Why is a young child's trust in self, in the teacher, in peers, and in the environment so important in a self-directed learning environment?

TRY IT YOURSELF

1. Make a classroom floor plan for your program showing learning centers arranged according to the ideas presented under "Locating and Spacing Learning Centers."

2. Design picture and sign labels for all of your learning centers according to ideas presented under "Learning Center Labels."

3. Make an illustrated schedule chart showing the daily schedule of activities in your program according to ideas under "Learning Center Maps and Schedules."

4. Provide a self-regulating method for helping children to choose activities in your classroom according to ideas discussed under "Trust in Self."

5. Carry out one of the ideas under "Trust in the Environment" that has not already been done in your classroom.

REFERENCES CITED

Anderson, G. T. & Robinson, C. C. (2006). Rethinking the dynamics of young children's play. *Dimensions of Early Childhood 34*(1), 11–16.

Beaty, J. J. (2008). *Skills for preschool teachers* (8th ed.). Upper Saddle River, NJ: Merrill/ Prentice Hall.

Bottini, M. & Grossman, S. (2005). Center-based teaching and learning: The effects of learning centers on young children's growth and development. *Childhood Education 81*, 274–277.

Bredekamp, S. (Ed.). (1987). *Developmentally appropriate practice in early childhood programs serving children from birth through age 8.* Washington, DC: NAEYC.

Bredekamp, S. & Copple, C. (Eds.). (1997). *Developmentally appropriate practice in early childhood programs* (Rev. ed.). Washington, DC: NAEYC.

Bruner, J. S. (1966). *Toward a theory of instruction.* Cambridge, MA: Harvard University Press.

Copple, C. & Bredekamp, S. (2006). *Basics of developmentally appropriate practice: An introduction for teachers of children 3 to 6.* Washington, DC: NAEYC.

Curtis, D. & Carter, M. (2005). Rethinking early childhood environments to enhance learning. *Young Children 60*(3), 34–38.

Gestwicki, C. (2007). *Developmentally appropriate practice: Curriculum and development in early education* (3rd ed.). Clifton Park, NY: Cengage Learning.

Kamii, C. (Ed.). (1990). *Achievement testing in early childhood programs: The games grown-ups play.* Washington, DC: NAEYC.

National Association for the Education of Young Children. (1986). NAEYC position statements on developmentally appropriate practice in early childhood programs. *Young Children 41*(6), 3–29.

Piaget, J. (1962). *Play, dreams, and imagination in children.* New York: Norton.

Vygotsky, L. S. (1978). *Mind in society: The development of psychological processes.* Cambridge, MA: Harvard University Press.

Other Sources

Gallagher, K. C. (2005). Brain research and early childhood development: A primer for developmentally appropriate practice. *Young Children 60*(4), 12–20.

Gallagher, K. C. & Mayer, K. (2006). Teacher-child relationships at the forefront of effective practice. *Young Children 61*(6), 44–49.

Kostelnik, M. J. (1992). MYTHS associated with developmentally appropriate programs. *Young Children 47*(4), 17–23.

Myers, B. K. & Maurer, K. (1987). Teaching with less talking: Learning centers in the kindergarten. *Young Children 42*(5), 20–27.

Neuharth-Pritchett, S., de Atiles, J. R., & Park, B. (2003). Using integrated curriculum to connect standards and developmentally appropriate practice. *Dimensions of Early Childhood 31*(3), 13–26.

Stegelin, D. A. (2005). Making the case for play policy: Research-based reasons to support play-based environments. *Young Children 60*(2), 76–85.

Swanson, L. (1994). Changes—How our nursery school replaced adult-directed art projects with child-centered experiences and changed to an accredited child-sensitive, developmentally appropriate school. *Young Children 49*(4), 69–77.

Wakefield, A. (1993). Developmentally appropriate practice: "Figuring things out." *The Educational Forum 57*, 134–143.

Read

THE TEACHER IN THE SELF-DIRECTED LEARNING ENVIRONMENT

As a teacher in a self-directed learning environment, your role is different from that of a teacher in a traditional classroom. You have already read in chapter 1 how to set up such a learning environment so that children can make choices and become deeply involved in their own learning. You have read how to help children make independent choices of activities through their development of trust in themselves, their teacher, their peers, and the environment. Now it is necessary to consider one of the most important tasks that a teacher in a self-directed learning environment must perform: that of providing appropriate curriculum materials and activities based on curriculum goals and the children's developmental levels.

These are the teacher's principal chores in a program where the learning environment does the teaching: to provide appropriate learning materials and then to support the children in their use of the materials. How does the teacher do it? The chapters to follow discuss ideas and activities for each of the classroom learning centers. This chapter discusses:

1. how teachers can determine the children's developmental stages so that the activities and materials provided will be appropriate for children at various levels of growth;

2. how teachers can support the children in their interactions with the self-directed environment.

TEACHER

ACTION CHANT

Good morning, teacher,
   (march in place throughout)

How do you do?
   (right hand wave)

Good morning, teacher,
I'm fine, too!
   (left hand pat top of head)

Good afternoon, teacher,

I want to state:
   (arms outstretched)

Good afternoon, teacher,
I feel GREAT!
   (jump!)

CHILDREN'S DEVELOPMENTAL LEVELS

We recognize that young children grow and develop physically in a well-defined chronological sequence as they mature from year to year. We also realize that children simultaneously progress through certain stages of psychological, intellectual, social, language, and creative development. Growth within these ages and stages of development is not always even. Some children progress more rapidly than others, whereas others exhibit developmental lags. How can we help them?

One 3-year-old may be speaking in expanded sentences, whereas another may be talking baby talk. How can we meet the needs of both of these children in our classrooms? Another child may be 5 years old chronologically, but only 3 years old in her social development. How will we know? And how will we know what to do about it? In order to provide appropriate materials and activities to promote the growth and learning of all the children in our classrooms, it is necessary to assess the developmental level of each child.

DETERMINING CHILDREN'S DEVELOPMENTAL LEVELS

A great deal has been written about the developmental levels of children. Researchers have examined children's physical, cognitive, social, emotional, language, and creative development, among other things. They have come up with large-motor rating scales, self-concept measures, personality projective techniques, perceptual-motor surveys, language inventories, learning profiles, observational checklists, and numerous other devices for assessing the level of the young child's development.

Many of these techniques are credible. Some are excellent, especially when used by trained people for their intended purpose. But few of them address the practical needs of the classroom teacher or the college student preparing to become a teacher.

Early childhood classroom personnel need to use tools to determine each child's developmental level in order to provide materials and activities that are appropriate for the individual. To be appropriate, such materials and activities should appeal to the child's current interest and ability level, stimulate and prolong the child's involvement, challenge the child physically and intellectually, and not be too difficult or too easy. A big bill to fill, indeed!

Lists, scales, surveys, and inventories are fine when used by the experts. But what most classroom staff members would prefer to use is a simple, surefire method for determining a child's level of development on the spot: some easy-to-see clues that can be translated immediately into curriculum ideas for that particular child; some easy-to-use observational method that takes little time but makes a great deal of sense to busy child care workers.

THE 3-M METHOD FOR OBSERVING INTERACTION

Such a method is available. It is based on the research of Piaget and Vygotsky as noted in Chapter 1. It focuses on young children's **spontaneous exploratory interactions with materials and activities** in the early childhood classroom, in other words, on their *play*. Infants, toddlers, and preschool youngsters seem to play with things not just for recreation, but in order to figure out what things are and how they work. Most researchers who have observed young children at play note how intently they pursue their chosen task. It is almost as if they are hard at work at a fascinating job. They are.

As Montessori specialist Chattin-McNichols notes: "Montessori's view of the children's free choice of activities in the prepared environment was that this was work, the proper work of the child. Constructivists would call this play, perhaps, but would also value child-chosen activities" (Chattin-McNichols, 1992, p. 160).

Take a closer look at preschool children's work/play activities, and you will note that the process seems to occur in stages of interaction with new materials. First children "fool around" with things: They manipulate them to find out how to use them or what they will do. Then they begin using them the "proper" way over and over, almost as if they are practicing how to use them. Finally, most preschoolers seem to advance to a higher level of interaction where they apply some sort of meaning or creative use to the new materials.

This text has adapted such information about children's cognitive development and translated it into an easy-to-apply observational scheme that will help students and teachers determine a child's developmental level in the activity area where the child is working or playing. We call it **the 3-M method for observing child interaction with materials: manipulation, mastery, and meaning**.

We find this method to be practical and invaluable for determining children's levels of involvement with materials and activities. It is the key to planning and setting up the self-directed learning environment so that children can choose and use the activities on their own, thus giving teachers time to work with individuals. In addition, it addresses the developmental level of individual children, giving them an opportunity to interact with materials appropriate to their own ages and stages of development.

Most psychologists and child care specialists have come to agree with the premise that children do indeed construct their own knowledge as Piaget's studies have shown us, and that they proceed through sequential stages of development as they interact with their environment and as they mature. For young children, the principal means by which they construct this knowledge is through playful interaction with the objects, activities, and people in their environment.

The important aspect of these findings for the child care practitioner is the *how*. *How* do children carry out this interaction with the objects, activities, and people in their environment that results in their acquisition of knowledge? That is the key to determining their level of development. We soon come to realize in almost every instance that children progress through certain sequential and observable interaction stages that are tied directly to their level of maturity and experience. If teachers can recognize these stages, they will know the children's levels of development.

STAGES OF INTERACTION

Children from birth to about age 7 progress through three distinct stages of playful interaction with the objects and activities they encounter in their environment. Cognitive psychologists often speak in terms of *exploratory play*, *practice play*, and

Children at the manipulation stage of interaction do not know how certain materials are to be used, so they play around with them, trying them out.

symbolic play (Van Hoorn, Nourot, Scales, & Alward, 1993). We have translated these terms into three words more meaningful for our particular use in observing children in the preschool classroom: *manipulation, mastery,* and *meaning,* the *3 M's.*

Manipulation is the earliest stage of children's playful interaction with the things in their environment. They do not yet know what the objects are for, how they are supposed to work, or what can be done with them. Young children, and even infants, begin by manipulating objects in a sensorimotor fashion. The infant picks up a rattle and puts it in his mouth. He drops it and kicks it with his feet. He picks it up again and puts it in his mouth. Then he bangs it on the crib or the floor. It makes an interesting sound, so he bangs it again. This is the manipulation stage of interaction with an object.

Cognitive psychologists sometimes call this manipulation *exploratory play* (Jones & Reynolds, 1992). Frost, Wortham, and Reifel state: "This first stage of physical play is manipulative play" (2005, p. 90). It will be known in this text as *manipulation.* All young children, regardless of their age, seem to go through this manipulation stage with new and unfamiliar materials.

Once the infant has discovered that the best thing to do with a rattle is to shake or bang it so that it will make an interesting sound, he begins shaking it over and over again. He has reached what we call the *mastery stage* of interaction. In order to master an object the infant or young child repeats the appropriate actions over and over. But in order to be able to shake the rattle in the first place, an infant must be physically mature enough to hold the rattle and shake it. In addition he must be cognitively mature enough to understand that the shaking of the rattle is what makes the noise. He must repeat the same action if he wants to hear the noise. Once he has reached this mastery stage of interaction, the infant seldom goes back to his earlier manipulation stage for long.

A preschool child at this mastery stage of interaction with materials will repeat the same scribbles in her writing over and over, the same block structures in her building, and the same dress-up role in dramatic play. It is almost as if she is spontaneously practicing her newfound skill until she gets it right. Frost et al., even mention that: "Practice play can be mental, such as repeatedly asking questions or making vocalizations" (2005, p. 95).

Why do youngsters repeat their actions over and over until it sometimes drives parents and early childhood teachers to distraction? Chattin-McNichols notes what child psychologist David Elkind has to say about children's repetition: "Both Montessori and Piaget have observed in detail the repetitive actions of the young child's motor behavior. Rather than meaningless drudgery, both feel these actions to be crucial for intellectual growth, despite how such repetition would be perceived by older children" (1992, p. 155).

Most infants do not progress beyond mastery to the meaning stage of interaction. Their cognition has not yet developed to the point where they can apply their own meaning to the object or the action. Most preschoolers, on the other hand, progress through all three stages of interaction over time while working spontaneously with materials and activities in the classroom. They may begin at the easel, for example, by smearing paint around randomly in the manipulation stage, later filling their papers over and over with lines and ovals at the mastery stage, and eventually, drawing a person at the meaning stage.

Thus, if you can identify a child's interaction stage, it is possible to recognize the youngster's level of development. Or, as noted by Johnson, Christie, and Yawkey: "Children engage in the type of play that matches their level of cognitive development" (1987, p. 8).

In that case, **by simply observing children** at work or play in one of your activity areas, you should be able to **identify which of the three interaction stages they are using**: manipulation, mastery, or meaning. This, then, will tell you what developmental level they have reached.

Does such a system really work? Can these three stages be applied to all of the many activities that occur in a busy preschool classroom? Let's try it.

Manipulation

Manipulation, the first of the interaction stages, is concerned with children's beginning explorations with unfamiliar objects or activities. Because the children do not know how these things work, they will try them out in a variety of ways until they learn what they do and how to do it.

Take block building with unit blocks, for instance. Children in the manipulation stage often fill up containers with blocks and then dump them out. They try handling blocks in all sorts of ways, but don't really build with them.

In dramatic play, children in the manipulation stage will use new implements and paraphernalia in various strange and sometimes funny ways until they figure out how the items work and what they can do with them. They may talk or shout into the "sounding" end of a doctor's stethoscope as if it were a microphone. They may use the round, silver eye examiner as a pirate's patch over an eye.

Art activities readily reveal children's manipulation stage. In the beginning they may splash one color of paint on top of another until it covers the paper, or merely swish the same color around and around in scribbles. Writing activities also begin with scribbles for children in the manipulation stage—although many children are aware of the difference between their art scribbles and their writing scribbles.

Mastery

Once children begin to control the medium they are working with, they spontaneously progress to the *mastery stage* and seldom return to manipulation. *Mastery,* often called practice play by cognitive psychologists, refers to the tendency

In block building, children in the mastery stage often stack the same kind of blocks on top of one another.

of children to repeat an action again and again, as mentioned, almost as if they are practicing or putting themselves through a drill.

Children in the mastery stage will stack one block on top of another in a tower, then knock it down and build it over, again and again. Or they may build a long line of blocks on the floor and then build a similar line parallel to the first one.

In dramatic play, the 2-year-old who has progressed through manipulation of the baby doll and the cradle may now put the baby to bed in the cradle, cover it over with the blanket, and rock the baby; then she will take everything out of the cradle and do it all over again—many times.

Once children have gained control of an art medium through manipulation, they will repeat the same operation over and over, such as painting parallel lines on one sheet of easel paper after another; or making nothing but rows and rows of cookies out of play "dough," or sticking dozens of peg "candles" in a birthday cake of dough until it can't hold another one.

Meaning

The more advanced stage of children's interactions with materials occurs when the children have finally gotten control over the medium through manipulation and have satisfied their inner impulse to practice through mastery. Now, if their cognitive development is advanced enough, they are ready to add their own *meaning* to the activity. It is fascinating to observe how children accomplish this.

More often than not, children in completely different programs who are in the *meaning stage* of interaction will spontaneously use materials in the same way.

With unit blocks children build the same kinds of buildings. In dramatic play most children play doctor by giving shots. With painting or drawing materials children around the world all draw their first spontaneous human, not as a stick person, but as a "tadpole person" with stick arms and legs attached to a big head/body. Even with computer programs, children in different preschools and kindergartens make up almost identical games after mastering a similar computer program (Beaty & Tucker, 1987). It seems as though we human beings are certainly stamped out of the same mold, doesn't it?

TIME FRAME

How long will children remain in each of these three interaction stages? "As long as is necessary" is the best answer we can give. Observe your own children and keep track of how long they do fill-and-dump manipulation-type activities in the Block Center before they begin to build the mastery stage towers or roads over and over. It may differ with every child.

It is true that the 3-M interaction stages are loosely tied to age; that is, the younger the children are, the longer they seem to stay in the earlier stages. Maturity plays an important part, but so does practice. Children need the opportunity and time to interact with both familiar and unfamiliar materials and activities. Because different children progress at differing rates through the three interaction stages, be sure to give everyone the time necessary for this spontaneous, self-taught learning to occur.

But, you may ask, would it not be more helpful for the teacher to show immature children how to build with blocks or draw with paints? They could then progress through the stages more quickly and catch up with their more advanced peers. No. **The way young children construct knowledge is through their own interaction with materials**, activities, and people in their environment. Having a teacher show them how does not really add to their understanding, and it may, in fact, detract from their accomplishments. They need to pursue the activities on their own and in their own way. That is the whole point in having a self-directed learning environment. "Telling" is not "teaching." The teacher's task is something quite different.

THE TEACHER'S TASK

The learning environment is in place. The children have chosen activities to pursue. Everyone is busily engaged. Now, what does the teacher do? The teacher or teaching team in such a classroom has four distinct tasks to perform:

1. Observe and listen to children in learning centers.

2. Record the observations.

3. Respond to individuals as they work and play.

4. Serve as a behavior model for the children.

The teacher is a facilitator of learning in a self-directed environment.

Observing Children's Interactions with Materials

While circulating around the room, the teacher will first make general observations to be sure that children are comfortable with their self-selected activities. Then the teacher will begin specific observations of particular children to see how they are getting along, to listen to what they are saying, and to determine their level of involvement.

How good is your "observer's eye"? You will need to keep it carefully focused on what children are doing with materials and with one another. In a self-directed learning environment it is this ongoing, focused observation that reveals whether the curriculum is working. The teacher who has carefully arranged the environment and supplied the materials to meet the learning and development needs of the children now needs to find out if they are really able to get involved in activities in meaningful ways.

What will you look for? First of all, try to determine whether a child is interacting with materials at the manipulative, mastery, or meaning level of involvement. When you see 3-year-old Jose pull all of the blocks off the shelf, load up the large wooden dump truck with them, and then dump them out; you will recognize that he is interacting at the manipulative stage of learning. You will want to make a note of this on the Child Interaction Form observation tool described on page 36.

When you see that Rhonda is at the easel making blue circles all over her paper, then tearing off the paper and beginning again with another page of blue circles, you will realize that she is at the mastery level of drawing skills because she is performing the same task over and over.

At a nearby table Jamal is having trouble making a puzzle on a puzzle board. He picks up a puzzle piece and tries to force it into a hole. When it doesn't fit immediately he does not rotate the piece to match it with the hole or try it in another hole. He leaves it on the board and picks up another piece to try. Soon he is frustrated, dumps all the pieces on the table, and leaves.

Because he is actually trying to make the puzzle rather than playing randomly with the pieces, you realize Jamal is past the manipulative stage of puzzle making. Had he struggled awhile until he finally got it right, you might then see him doing the puzzle over again as children often do at the mastery level. Should you intervene or not? It will depend on the circumstances, as well as on your knowledge of Jamal and the puzzle.

You might decide to sit with Jamal for a while, handing him one piece at a time and encouraging him to try each one in different ways. On the other hand, you may realize, from previous observations of Jamal and of the puzzle's use, that this particular puzzle is just too difficult for him. You may, instead, encourage him to try a simpler puzzle. Be sure to record Jamal's efforts, whatever happens.

Observing Children's Interactions with one another

In addition to observational data about the children's stages of interaction with materials, you will want to **note how children are interacting socially with one another**. Social play categories you may want to observe include some originally described by Parten (1932):

1. unoccupied behavior

2. onlooker behavior

3. solitary independent play

4. parallel activity

5. cooperative play

Children who are new to a preschool classroom sometimes begin with *unoccupied behavior* rather than getting involved with activities. They may stay in one spot, follow the teacher around, or simply wander around the room. Sensitive teachers understand that these children may need time to gain self-confidence before they become involved with classroom activities. The teachers will make a note of this on their observational records, but will not pressure children to join in.

As unoccupied children become more at ease in the classroom they may exhibit *onlooker behavior*; that is, spending time watching what other children are doing, but not joining in. If teachers realize that such behavior is the next step in the development of social skills, they will again not make an issue of it and force the children to join in, but simply encourage them to choose an activity that they might like to try on their own for a while, yet let them alone if they do not.

On the other hand, not all onlooker behavior is an indication of an immature step toward a higher level of social interaction. Anderson and Robinson have found that: "Onlooker play apparently serves a very important information-gathering function for children that has never been fully appreciated or considered" (2006, p. 13). You will need to note in your observations whether the child ever joins in any play, or spends most of the time watching others play to gain information on what they are doing.

Solitary independent play is the next level of social interaction. Many children play by themselves in the early childhood classroom, especially the younger or more inexperienced children. Even more mature youngsters at the mastery or meaning stages of art activities frequently like to paint, draw, or construct things on their own. You should make note of this and then observe to see if these children ever interact with others. Some more mature children skip this solitary play stage altogether and go directly from onlooker play (where they were gathering information) to parallel play.

As children become more aware of what others are doing, they may begin to play close to them in a *parallel activity*. A great deal of the play that goes on in an early childhood classroom is of this parallel nature. Two children may build block houses side by side, but not interact with one another in any other way. Some parallel players use this play as a means for inserting themselves into the play going on next to them. It is fascinating to watch parallel players. Keep your eyes open to what is happening with them.

Children who play together with the same materials, making or building something together, are demonstrating "cooperative play."

Cooperative play is easy for teachers to identify when they note several children playing together with the same materials, each adding to the play or following what the others have decided to do. Again, this interaction can be recorded on the Child Interaction Form. If you continue to observe, you may note that some of the players may shift back into parallel play. Anderson and Robinson discovered that play shifts may occur multiple times during the same play segment, especially into and out of parallel play (2006, p. 12).

Listening to what Children Say

How good is your "observer's ear"? You need to **keep it carefully tuned to what children are saying** as they interact with both the materials and one another. Some children may seem to be talking to themselves, saying over and over just under their breath what it is they are doing in a kind of "self-talk." Other children may talk to their neighbors, asking questions, making statements, or giving directions. Sometimes they wait for a reply, sometimes not. Some of the children may be carrying on a true conversational dialogue with another child.

In all of these situations the children's words may give you a clue to their thinking or their level of development. Their words may help you to decide whether the children need more practice in their self-selected activity, or whether they are ready to extend their learning with new materials. If you can do it unobtrusively, try to record this talk verbatim.

Observing children's actions and listening to their words is another key to the self-directed environment. Because children are in control of their own learning, teachers need to spend a great deal of time observing and listening in order to plan for individuals. From their observations teachers can find answers to these questions:

1. What is the child's interaction level (manipulation, mastery, or meaning)?

2. What is the child's social involvement (unoccupied, onlooker, solitary, parallel, or cooperative)?

3. What should the teacher do next (intervene or not, make comments or ask questions, bring in new material)?

Recording Observations

It is important that you **make on-the-spot recordings of the child observations** you are doing during the activity period. If you wait until later, you will have lost the moment. So many things occur with even one child alone that it is next to impossible to remember all you have seen and heard unless you write it down.

As a facilitator of learning in a self-directed classroom, your task is to observe and record each child as often as possible. How else will you know if your curriculum is working? How else will you discern what to arrange next for the children? You may want to repeat certain activities day after day. On the other hand, the Science Center may need expanding. Jose may need a set of table blocks and boxes to give him other manipulative experiences with blocks before he is ready for actual building. Rhonda may need a whole pad of paper and a box of watercolors to give her additional practice in her mastery of a brush and paint. Jamal may need simpler puzzles to work on, and you to sit beside him while he tries. How would you know all of this (and so much more) if you had not observed and recorded it?

As Marion tells us: "Teachers base their best curriculum decisions on what they know about the children—their experiences, what they already know, and their social history. The best way for the teacher to get this information is through observing" (2004, p. 9). Teachers in the Appropriate Practices Curriculum are not at the front of the classroom talking. They are circulating throughout the room, watching how children are interacting with the materials and activities they so carefully set up for them. And, most important, they are **writing down how each of the children is using the materials, interacting with peers, and talking about it all**.

The Child Interaction Form

Using an observation tool for data collection helps observers focus on particular aspects of child behavior. Because you will be looking for child interaction with materials in the learning centers, as well as children's interactions with one another, an observation form that features such data is especially helpful. Observers in each of the learning centers can use the one-sheet Child Interaction Form, either for individual children or for all of the children in a particular learning center on a particular day (see Table 2-1).

A number of these blank forms should be located on the tops of cabinets and shelf dividers or on clipboards in each of the learning centers. Observers can then record what individuals are doing in each of the centers on a particular day. A different sheet can be used for each child in the learning center, or one sheet can be used to record the actions of all of the children in that center at a particular time.

If the child moves on from one learning center to another, you will want to carry the form along with you to record the child's words and actions. It is also helpful for more than one observer to record data in a cumulative manner on a single form. If you are using one form to record what happens to all of the children in a particular learning center, that form will naturally be left in the center. In that case you may be evaluating the setup of a learning center to see how well it is serving the children, rather than observing a single child's interactions.

On the back of each Child Interaction Form there is space to record an individual child's *Accomplishments* and *Needs* as well as your *Plans* for the child or for the learning center. This **interpretive information can be recorded at the same time the observation is made or later on**—say, at the end of the day, if this time is more convenient. All of the data collected can then be reviewed at the end of the day to

Child _____   Observer _____

Center _____   Date _____

CHILD INTERACTION FORM
With Materials

Manipulation Level   Actions/Words

(Child moves materials around
without using them as intended.)

Mastery Level   Actions/Words

(Child uses materials
 as intended, over and over.)

Meaning Level   Actions/Words

(Child uses materials in
new and creative ways.)

With Other Children

Solitary Play   Actions/Words

(Child plays alone
with materials.)

Parallel Play   Actions/Words

(Child plays next to others with same
materials but not involved with them.)

Cooperative Play   Actions/Words

(Child plays together with
others and with same materials.)

Table 2-1 Child Interaction Form.

give you and the staff feedback about individual children and particular learning centers. In addition, **these data serve as the basis for individual planning** during weekly or monthly sessions, as discussed in chapter 14, "Curriculum Planning."

Each of the chapters that follow discusses use of the Child Interaction Form in a particular learning center. Kinds of behavior to look for as the children interact with materials and other children are presented as examples. Interpreting the observations and making plans are then featured in chapter 14.

Responding to Individual Children as they Work and Play

Not only do teachers in the self-directed learning environment observe and record child behavior, they also respond to individuals in the learning centers. The responses may be in words or in actions, but their purpose is to **give the children support, encouragement, and direction** in the activities they have chosen. Teachers remember that their role is not to "teach" in the traditional sense of the word, but to facilitate learning so that the children can learn from the environment.

This teacher–child interaction is just as important as any other feature of the classroom. It takes skill and practice on the teacher's part to respond appropriately. As Gestwicki asserts in her rebuttal to the myth that teachers don't teach in developmentally appropriate classrooms: "This misunderstanding relies on the limited view that teachers teach only by directing and controlling all learning in a classroom—instructing, assigning tasks, and correcting errors. Teachers in developmentally appropriate classrooms are in charge, but not dominating, and they use a variety of teaching strategies" (2007, p. 23). Some of the strategies she mentions include:

1. observing, planning, scheduling, arranging, and organizing;
2. commenting, asking, suggesting, and providing information and additional materials;
3. modeling, challenging, and helping children change direction;
4. collaborating with children in learning activities;
5. scaffolding children's efforts to reach greater heights;
6. helping form groups and partnerships; and
7. providing direct instruction when necessary.

She concludes by saying "Teachers [in developmentally appropriate classrooms] recognize that learning doesn't happen only when their mouths are open" (2007, p. 24).

Teachers in a private preschool for 2-year-olds also discovered with great excitement that responding to children in small groups was so much more stimulating for all than standing in front of a total group and "teaching."

To reflect a child's actions, a teacher's comments should be supportive of what she sees a child doing, and not prying or giving empty praise.

> Adults and two-year-olds seemed to be talking more. We talked about the weather, animals, moms, dads, new babies. We asked interesting questions, such as "What can we do with this?" "What else could it be?" "What do we do next?" "How does that feel?" "What else would you like to put on your bird?" We became experts at open-ended questions; the children were natural experts at finding unique things to say and solutions to problems. (Swanson, 1994, p. 70)

Because of teachers' thoughtful responses, the children's thinking should be challenged, their self-confidence should be reinforced, and their learning should be extended to new levels. It is obvious, then, that the teachers' responses to children in the Appropriate Practices Curriculum are not just small talk or empty praise. The comments, instead, are carefully thought-through statements that reflect the children's actions. Or they may be in the form of carefully worded open-ended questions that help teachers learn what the children are doing or thinking, or help the children to reformulate their own ideas.

Making Comments that Reflect the Child's Actions

As the teacher observes in the Manipulative/Math Center, for example, she notices that Adrianne is carefully lining up all the dominoes so that the dots or blanks on half of one domino match the dots or blanks on the next domino. Adrianne has to search at some length to find domino blocks whose dots match. The teacher has not seen her performing at this level before. She wonders if Adrianne has played the domino game before—at home, for instance. But before making a comment, the teacher spends more time observing and then thinks through carefully what she is going to say.

She could ask "Who taught you to play dominoes, Adrianne?" But this question assumes that Adrianne was taught by someone else, which may not be the case. What if Adrianne taught herself, for instance?

This teacher knows that her statements and questions should first of all be supportive of what children are doing, neither prying nor trying to elicit the "correct" answer. She also knows that empty praise is not really helpful in support of what children are doing. This teacher realizes that one of the best ways to support what children are doing is to **make comments that reflect specifically what the teacher sees**. Such comments usually prompt the children to reply in a way that illuminates the experience for both teacher and child: "Adrianne, I see that you are putting together dominoes that have the same number of dots. You have a long line of dominoes that match one another." Although this statement seems very matter-of-fact and not particularly full of praise, the teacher's tone of voice expresses her excitement.

Adrianne looks up with a smile and answers: "I found all the dominoes, even six. My brother can't count to six. He's only two." Then she goes back to work finding more dominoes to put at the end of her line.

The teacher's comment, reflecting what she sees the child doing, has helped in four ways:

1. It summarizes what the child is doing, which clarifies things for both teacher and child;

2. It prompts the child to respond, which gives the teacher insight into the child's thinking;

3. It lets the child know that the teacher is paying attention to her and is pleased with what she is accomplishing;

4. It indirectly encourages the child to continue.

The teacher jots down on the Child Interaction Form on top of the manipulative shelf under Mastery: "Adrianne is matching long line of dominoes accurately." On the back of the form under Accomplishments she notes: "Matching dominoes by numbers of dots; first time." Under Needs she writes: "Play with other children." Finally, under Plans she writes: "Suggest she play dominoes with someone else tomorrow."

The teacher realizes that the dominoes on the manipulative shelf have never been used as a game in the classroom; most of the children merely stack them or line them at a manipulative level. Tomorrow the teacher will set up a table for a domino game with Adrianne, if she is interested, and another child who would choose to play. This would not be a game with rules for the children to win or lose, but rather an opportunity to try out their matching skills at a mastery level.

The teacher then wonders how Adrianne will eventually "play" dominoes at the meaning level—maybe by making up her own game. This teacher knows she will need to find other number and matching games for Adrianne that will extend her learning. But she is even more excited about setting up the domino game in the Manipulative/Math Center for the next day to see who else will choose to play, and who may exhibit mastery skills in matching like Adrianne.

Another way teachers could respond to children after observing their actions is to **ask a question in a way that will elicit statements from the children about their work**: an "open-ended question." Teachers need to be careful not to ask a blunt "closed question," such as: "What are you doing, Adrianne?" Adrianne, who has been interrupted, may not even answer. Or she may reply only: "I'm playing." Far better is the open-ended question: "Why are you lining up the dominoes that way Adrianne?" Or teachers may challenge the children: "What other way can you line up those dominoes, Adrianne?"

As you note, the purpose for teachers' verbal responses to children's work in a learning center should be:

1. to give support and encouragement

2. to challenge children's thinking

3. to extend their learning

4. to help the teacher decide what to do next to support the children or extend their learning

Teachers will **avoid terms of judgment**, such as: "That's very good, Daniel," or "I like the way you did that." Instead, they will describe specifically and nonjudgmentally what children are doing: "Daniel, you are stacking the blocks up very high today! How did you get them to balance like that?"

Teachers should also avoid comparisons of one child with another, although they can compare a child's current actions with previous ones: "Daniel, you stacked your blocks more evenly today than you did yesterday." Daniel's teacher hopes he will reply to him as well, which he can then note on the observation card as an indicator of Daniel's thinking. If the teacher feels it is appropriate (based on previous observations of Daniel), he can then respond: "What other ways can you stack blocks?" Daniel may be used to this kind of challenge from his teacher and may take him up on it. On the other hand, he may not be finished building his "tower," because children in the mastery stage need a certain amount of repetition of a particular skill before they move on.

It is not necessary for teachers to respond every time they observe a child. As they circulate around the room they will be observing and recording carefully the actions and words of each child. They then need to use their good sense of timing on when to intervene with a comment or a question, and when not to intervene. With children who are deeply involved in a project, they may not want to interrupt. On the other hand, some children may need help or redirection to continue an activity or to start something new.

In reviewing recorded comments at the end of each day, teachers will have an idea about which children they need to interact with, which children they need to make a comment to, and which children may be better off not being disturbed. For Brian, who has finally stopped following the teacher around and has joined the children at the water table for the first time, it would be foolish for the teacher to make a comment that could divert Brian's attention back to her again. Experience and practice in this type of classroom interchange are the best ways for the teacher or student teacher to learn when to respond to individual children and when to leave them alone.

Serving as a Behavior Model for the Children

A fourth important task for teachers in a self-directed learning environment is to serve as behavior models for the children. For example, teachers need to be sure that their actions, words, and emotions represent the behavior they would like the children to emulate:

1. They must respond with composure when children get out of control.
2. They must exhibit curiosity about the world around them if they want the youngsters to be curious.
3. Their language must reflect the speaking habits they want the children to develop.

As Hendrick (2003) tells us: "It is important to remain in control of yourself so that you do not model such behavior for the children to copy" (p. 259).

The Appropriate Practices Curriculum presented here follows three thematic ideas intertwined throughout this textbook:

1. *Let the learning environment do the teaching* because the pre-literate child learns best through independent exploration of self-selected activities arranged by the teacher.
2. *Let the teacher be a facilitator of learning* by observing children's developmental stages in the activity areas, by supporting children's growth and learning through the teacher's responses, and by serving as a behavior model for learning in the various classroom areas.
3. *Let the children learn to care* by following the teacher's example in caring about themselves, about one another, and about their environment.

A Facilitator of Learning

To be successful facilitators of learning in such an environment, teachers need to put themselves in the place of the children as often as possible. In order to set an example as learners, they need to understand what it feels like to be learners in a self-discovery environment. They need to try out (or think how it would be to try out) the various activities from the point of view of a 3-, 4-, or 5-year-old child. What would they do with the materials upon encountering them for the first time? How would they find out how to use them? What questions would they want answered? What help would they solicit from classmates?

Teachers can discover the answers to such questions by observing what the children do or ask. Then they will know how to behave as a learning model. When someone asks a teacher how to play dominoes and he realizes he does not know how, he can respond as a child might: "Let's make up our own game. How would you like to play it?" When someone asks a math or science question with which he is unfamiliar, he can answer: "Let's see if we can find the answer together. Where shall we begin?"

The teacher in such a classroom adopts the *curiosity* of a child about finding out how things work and what they are for. The teacher's behavior serves as a model for the children to follow. Above all, the teacher takes on the *enthusiasm* of a child who has encountered a new object or a new idea for the first time. Learning is one of the great adventures of life. It should be as thrilling and exciting as you can make it!

A Model of Caring

Teachers need to **set the stage and lead the way about caring**. Children need to learn to care about themselves, about one another, and about their environment. Their behavior will reflect how they care. If they care about themselves they will show it by being self-confident, helpful, happy, and cooperative. They will help to pick up toys and clean up after they eat. They will follow health and safety practices, and not do things that are destructive to themselves, such as running down the stairs or eating without washing their hands.

If children care about one another they will work and play together co-operatively. It is the teacher, however, that often must lead the way to caring about one another. Gallagher and Mayer (2006) emphasize that: "Teachers' efforts at modeling social respect are very important. Teachers can remind children of the rules but at the same time invite them to see the perspective of another person" (p. 46).

For instance, when one child demands that the teacher help her, the teacher can tell her that she is helping a second child at the moment. When she is finished she will help the first child. Would that child like to join in helping the second child? When they are finished, both of them can help her. This is what modeling caring behavior means.

If children care about their environment they will participate in keeping both their indoor and outdoor environments in good shape, in not being destructive to materials, and in helping to pick up and clean up.

Teachers can serve as behavior models in all three of these regards, first by caring for themselves. They can **present themselves as happy, confident people** who enjoy their job. They can dress attractively; whether in jeans or dress clothing they can be neat, clean, and well groomed. Children like colorful clothing. Teachers can wear a bright top or shirt to show they like to look nice for the children. Working with active young children is physically draining for an adult. Teachers can keep themselves healthy by eating nutritiously and getting enough sleep so that they are peppy and alert for the day's activities.

Teachers also need to demonstrate their care for others: first of all, their care for the children, by **showing delight in what they are doing**, in what they are saying, in the clothes they wear, and in the interesting things that are happening in their families. Teachers also show their concern for the children's health, over the things that are bothering them, for problems facing their families. These are behaviors that help children to realize that teachers care about them. By **listening seriously** to what the children have to say, by **not "talking down"** to children but conversing with them as they would with a friend, teachers let children know they care. They can also demonstrate care for others in the classroom by **treating assistants and student interns as they would like to be treated themselves**.

Finally, teachers need to show their care for the environment of the classroom, the building, and the playground by helping to keep them clean, in order, and beautiful. What can you do to **add beauty to your learning environment?** Perhaps a plant or a picture will spruce it up. Colorful hangings on the walls or bright shelf paper on the shelves may help. During cleanup time you can lead the way by helping to pick up materials and arrange them attractively on the shelves. Perhaps the children will help you plant a tree on the playground. They could also help you frame their own artwork for display in the halls or office.

The chapters to follow are full of suggestions for caring: for yourself, for one another, and for the environment. When teachers and children work together toward these goals, an appropriate curriculum will evolve almost on its own!

IDEAS IN CHAPTER 2

1. *Determining children's developmental levels*

   a. Look for children's spontaneous exploratory interactions with materials and activities

   b. Use the 3-M method for observing child interaction: manipulation, mastery, and meaning

   c. Watch children at work or play and identify which of the three interaction stages they are using

   d. Note how children are interacting with one another

   e. Keep carefully tuned to what children are saying as they interact

2. *Recording child observations*

   a. Make on-the-spot recordings of child observations

   b. Write down how child uses materials, interacts with peers, and talks about it all

   c. Use an observation tool to help focus on particular aspects of child behavior

   d. Record interpretive information at the same time or at the end of the day

   e. Use these data as the basis for individual planning

3. *Responding to individual children*

   a. Give support, encouragement, and direction

   b. Make comments that reflect specifically what you see

   c. Ask questions in a way that will elicit a statement about child's work

   d. Avoid using terms of judgment

4. *Serving as a behavior model for the children*

   a. Put yourself in the place of the child

   b. Set the stage and lead the way about caring

   c. Present yourself as a happy, confident person

   d. Show your delight in what children are doing

   e. Listen seriously to children

   f. Avoid "talking down" to children

   g. Treat assistants and interns as you would like to be treated

   h. Add beauty to your learning environment

DISCUSSION QUESTIONS

1. How is the role of the teacher in a self-directed learning environment different from that of a teacher in a traditional classroom?

2. How can we meet the needs of each of the children in our classroom if they are all at different levels of development?

3. How can our observations of children's interactions with materials in our classroom help to determine their developmental levels?

4. Why do you think both Montessori and Piaget believed that repetitive actions are important in a young child's development?

5. Why are children's social interactions another important indicator of their development? Give examples.

TRY IT YOURSELF

1. Observe the children in your class and record (giving specific details) three different examples of children in the manipulative level of interaction. Based on your evidence, what is their level of social interaction?

2. Observe and record three different examples of children interacting at the mastery level, giving specific details; give evidence for their level of social interaction.

3. Record any children interacting at the meaning level and try to capture on paper their conversations as well as their actions. What social levels of interaction do they display?

4. How would you respond to the children you have recorded in #1 and why?

5. How can you serve as a learning model for the children recorded in #2; why?

REFERENCES CITED

Anderson, G. T. & Robinson, C. C. (2006). Rethinking the dynamics of young children's play. *Dimensions of Early Childhood 34*(1), 11–16.

Beaty, J. J. & Tucker, W. H. (1987). *The computer as a paintbrush.* Columbus, OH: Merrill.

Chattin-McNichols, J. (1992). *The Montessori controversy.* Clifton Park, NY: Cengage.

Frost, J. L., Wortham, S. C., & Reifel, S. (2005). *Play and child development.* Upper Saddle River, NJ: Merrill/Prentice Hall.

Gallagher, K. C. & Mayer, K. (2006). Teacher-child relationships at the forefront of effective practice. *Young Children 61*(6), 44–49.

Gestwicki, C. (2007). *Developmentally appropriate practice: Curriculum and development in early education* (3rd ed.). Clifton Park, NY: Cengage.

Hendrick, J. (2003). *Total learning: Developmental curriculum for the young child* (6th ed.). Upper Saddle River, NJ: Merrill/Prentice Hall.

Johnson, J. E., Christie, J. F., & Yawkey, T. D. (1987). *Play and early childhood development.* Glenview, IL: Scott, Foresman.

Jones, E. & Reynolds, G. (1992). *The play's the thing: Teachers' roles in children's play.* New York: Teachers' College Press.

Marion, M. (2004). *Using observation in early childhood education.* Upper Saddle River, NJ: Merrill/Prentice Hall.

Parten, M. B. (1932). Social participation among pre-school children. *Journal of Abnormal Social Psychology 27*, 243–269.

Swanson, L. (1994). Changes—How our nursery school replaced adult-directed art projects with child-directed experiences and changed to an accredited, child-sensitive, developmentally appropriate school. *Young Children 49*(4), 69–73.

Van Hoorn, J., Nourot, P., Scales, B., & Alward, K. (1993). *Play at the center of the curriculum.* New York: Merrill/Macmillan.

Other Sources

Beaty, J. J. (2008). *Skills for preschool teachers* (8th ed.). Upper Saddle River, NJ: Merrill/Prentice Hall.

Curtis, D. & Carter, M. (2005). Rethinking early childhood environments to enhance learning. *Young Children 60*(3), 34–38.

Myers, B. K. & Maurer, K. (1987). Teaching with less talking: Learning centers in the kindergarten. *Young Children 42*(5), 30–27.

Piaget, J. (1962). *Play, dreams, and imitation in childhood.* New York: Norton.

Rogers, D. L., Waller, C. B., & Sheerer Penn, M. (1987). Learning more about what makes a good teacher through collaborative research in the classroom. *Young Children 42*(A), 34–39.

Stegelin, D. A. (2005). Making the case for play policy: Research-based reasons to support play-based environments. *Young Children 60*(2), 76–85.

Trawick-Smith, J. (1994). *Interactions in the classroom: Facilitating play in the early years.* New York: Merrill/Macmillan.

Wellhousen, K. & Crowther, I. (2004). *Creating effective learning environments.* Clifton Park, NY: Cengage Learning.

CURRICULUM ROLE OF BLOCKS

Building with unit blocks has long been a favorite nursery school activity for both children and their teachers. Children love the feel of the smooth wood, they enjoy the clonking noise blocks make when you build with them, and they especially delight in the immensity of the buildings they can create all on their own. No teacher has to tell them what to do or how to do it. With blocks, there is no right or wrong.

Teachers, by the same token, like block-building activities because children enjoy them, and because children can do them on their own without teacher help or interference. It is a classroom activity area that, once arranged, can be left on its own—or so it used to be.

Teachers using the Appropriate Practices Curriculum realize that there is more to unit block play than meets the eye. Not only can children play with blocks on their own—the key to the construction of their knowledge, as we have learned—but also the kinds of learning that children can accomplish in the Block Center touch on every facet of their growth and development in ways that few other learning activities do. Block building can contribute to children's development in physical, cognitive, language, social, emotional, and creative areas.

Children learn the physical skills of holding, stacking, and balancing blocks. They learn the social skills of sharing and cooperation. Their language is expanded through speaking and listening to others. Their creativity is enhanced by being able to build stupendous structures of their own design. All of this activity promotes a positive feeling about themselves as worthy human beings. As for their cognitive development, almost every intellectual skill, from categorizing to counting to problem solving, is available for

BLOCKS

ACTION CHANT

Towers and tunnels,
Bridges and locks,
How do you build them?
With blocks, blocks, blocks!

A doll house, a farm house,
A road or a box,
How can you make them?
With blocks, blocks, blocks!

Some stack them gently,
Other use knocks,
Then down they tumble,
Those blocks, blocks, blocks!

Pick them up quickly,
No looking at clocks,
When you are building,
With blocks, blocks, blocks!

(March in circle for first three
lines of each verse, stop and clap
three times on last line of each verse)

children's acquisition in a Block Center arranged with care by knowledgeable teachers.

Blocks are there to be used by children every day. But it is the creative teacher who arranges the Block Center and supplies the appropriate accessories that makes sure this important curriculum area serves the needs of every child most effectively. It is the sensitive teacher who observes what children are doing with blocks and saying about blocks and who knows how to rearrange and add to this curriculum area so that exciting learning will continue on a daily basis.

THE BLOCK PLAY STORY

There is a fascinating history behind the blocks our children play with today. The history of block play, in fact, reflects the history of the early childhood movement in our country and in Europe. Started in Germany by Frederick Froebel, the "Father of the Kindergarten," block play became an integral part of his curriculum as early as the 1830s and 1840s. He believed that young children learned best through play, self-expression, and creativity with living things and moveable objects. Thus he developed a series of 20 "Gifts" and "Occupations" (i.e., educational materials and activities) for children to play with and to learn from (Provenzo & Brett, 1983).

Several of his "Gifts" were wooden cubes so split and divided that they became little table blocks with a 1-inch base and a height ranging from 1 to 12 inches. As children took them apart, reassembled them, and built with them, they learned differentiation, classification, and categorization skills, as well as numbers and counting. Thus began the use of blocks as an integral part of an early childhood curriculum wherever Froebel's ideas were adopted.

Following the Civil War in America, the Crandall family dominated the toy block industry, developing interlocking blocks and nesting blocks. Toy catalogs from that era show various types of alphabet blocks and construction blocks as well. German, and later American, companies also produced popular little cast-stone building bricks of various colors that parents bought for their children to play with during the last quarter of the 19th century and into the 20th century (Provenzo & Brett, 1983).

Structured blocks for preschool educational purposes were also used by Italian physician–educator Maria Montessori in the early childhood program she developed at the turn of the century. One of her block building exercises that is still in use consists of 10 graduated wooden cubes called the "Pink Tower." However, free play with blocks was not advocated by any of the pioneer educators until the appearance at the turn of the century of Carolyn Pratt from Fayetteville, New York (Koepke, 1989).

CAROLYN PRATT AND UNIT BLOCKS

Pratt formulated her philosophy of early childhood education by observing children playing with materials. She saw one 6-year-old boy so absorbed by his own creating with blocks that she never forgot it: "A child playing on his nursery floor, constructing an entire railroad system out of blocks and odd boxes he had salvaged from the wastepaper basket taught me that the play impulse in children is really a work impulse. Childhood's work is learning, and it is in his play that the child works at his job" (Pratt, 1948, p. 10).

From then on she was determined to develop a school for young children based on the free-play impulse, using educational toys of her own design created to meet the needs of the children she observed.

While attending Teacher's College at Columbia University in 1892, Pratt noted that Patty Hill Smith, another pioneer early childhood educator, had developed large slotted wooden blocks for the children in her laboratory kindergarten, with which they built child-sized houses in their free time. In her autobiography, *I Learn from Children,* Pratt reminisces: "Of all the materials I had seen offered to children … these blocks of Patty Hill's seemed to be best suited to children's purposes. A simple geometrical shape could become any number of things to a child. It could be a truck or a boat or the car of a train. He could build buildings with it from barns to skyscrapers, I could see the children of my yet unborn school constructing a complete community with blocks" (Pratt, 1948, p. 29).

With these ideas in mind, Pratt developed what we now call *unit blocks,* a unit being a block 5½ by 3¾ by 1⅜ inches. There were half units, double units, and quadruples, as well as curves, arches, ramps, triangles, pillars, cylinders, and switches. Figure 3-1 illustrates a sampling of these blocks, still highly valued and used by most preschool programs in the United States. Pratt's blocks were of smooth, natural finished hardwood—free from details or color. In addition, she designed unpainted wooden people, 6 inches high, in the form of family members and community workers to be used with the unit blocks. She omitted painted details on any of her "toys" because she wanted children to apply their own imaginations in their use of the materials.

Pratt also designed large hollow blocks, ladders, walking planks, platform trucks, wooden interlocking floor trains, housekeeping areas with child-sized equipment, rhythm band instruments, and on and on. Like Montessori in Italy, Pratt in the United States filled her prepared environment with materials of her own invention that are still in use in preschools today.

All of these materials evolved directly from her work with children, especially those in her own Playschool, which eventually became New York City's "City and Country School" (Caplan & Caplan, 1974). Today this equipment is such an accepted part of every preschool program that few people realize it all came from a young woman from upstate New York with a calling to teach and a vision about creating a school where children would teach themselves through play.

Another pioneer educator and coworker with Pratt, Harriet M. Johnson, validated Pratt's block play ideas with her own careful observations of children's use of unit blocks in her nursery school during the 1920s and 1930s. She published the results in 1933 as "The Art of Blockbuilding," a classic observation study

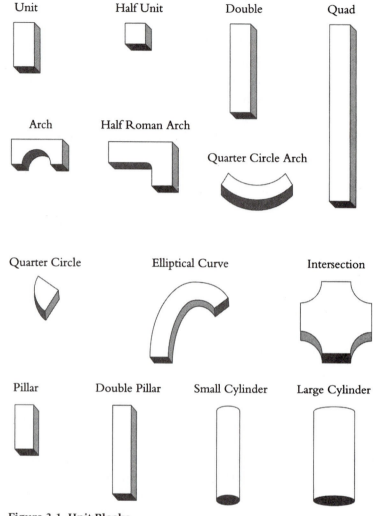

Figure 3-1 Unit Blocks

outlining universal stages of young children's block building: repetition, bridging, enclosures, patterns, and representation (Johnson, 1983). Her ideas became an integral part of the Bank Street School she helped to found. Today we accept the "block corner" as an essential learning center in preschool classrooms everywhere.

SETTING UP THE BLOCK CENTER

If your children are to choose blocks as an activity to engage in on their own, then the center needs to be arranged attractively and effectively. As with other centers in the classroom, children will choose to become involved with blocks if they can easily see what is available, if there are enough materials to make it possible to do

Pratt also designed large hollow blocks, still in use in preschools today.

an activity, and if there is space enough to use the materials effectively. It is essential that you **stock your shelves with enough unit blocks**. Many nursery school block sets are just too small to allow effective building activities for more than one or two children at a time. Instead, it is important for you to order large numbers of individual types of blocks to fit your own space and program needs.

Sets of unit blocks come in all sorts of shapes and are available from educational toy companies. For example Childcraft (1-800-631-5652) offers an Oriental Block Set, Arabian Block Set, Greek Block Set, and Thai Block Set. These tend to appeal to teachers more than children, who have their own ideas of what their buildings should look like.

You will need a large number of blocks if you expect children to build really large constructions that will teach them important skills in all the child development areas. On the other hand, it is not necessary to have every block shape available. Large numbers of blocks in a half dozen of the basic shapes are a much more sensible purchase. Although unit blocks are expensive items, they are worth every penny spent when you consider the importance of their teaching/learning benefits.

Second to numbers of blocks is the **arrangement of the blocks lengthwise on shelves at the children's height** for their easy access and return. Children should be able to see what blocks are available, choose them easily, and then return them to their proper shelves when they are finished. The reason for such an arrangement is not merely a housekeeping detail. It is an essential learning arrangement for children in a self-directed environment.

For example, block activities are an effective method for children to teach themselves the cognitive concepts of shape and size. Therefore, children need to see clearly what sizes and shapes of blocks are available. Blocks also teach categorizing and matching skills. Therefore, children need to be able to return them to their proper places by matching their shapes against the cutout block labels you have mounted on every shelf.

For the same reasons, blocks should be stored lengthwise on shelves rather than endwise or in boxes, bins, or carts. Wooden carts and bins on toy catalog pages look neat and appealing; but in actual classroom use they tend to be dumping grounds for mixed piles of blocks, after which the children cannot choose, find, or use them easily. If we want real learning to take place in our activity areas, we must arrange the materials so they are usable. If we want children to use the materials with respect, then we must show our own respect by arranging and storing them carefully.

The Block Center itself should be **spacious, with a carpet on the floor, and its borders defined by block shelves**. Most classrooms have carpeted block areas because the children sit on the floor to build. But in too many classrooms this area is not separated from the rest of the classroom with shelf dividers. Instead, their block shelves stand against the wall, leaving the area open for all kinds of traffic; walkers, runners, and even riders of large wooden vehicles.

To build in such an area, children take the chance that their buildings will be destroyed by accident or on purpose. "Oh well," you may respond, "don't children enjoy knocking down block buildings?" Yes, they do knock down their own buildings—often with relish and always with learning—but such tumbling down of the blocks should be the children's choice and not an outsider's.

Children who have constructed elaborate buildings are often given the choice to leave their building standing, rather than knock them down and put the blocks away at pickup time. In this case have them help make a sign for the building that tells others: "Please Leave Jamal's Building Standing." Although children at kindergarten age enjoy playing later with a standing block building, most preschoolers focus their attention on the construction of the building—the process—rather than the product, the building itself.

BLOCK ACCESSORIES

What should the Block Center contain other than blocks, you may wonder? The materials for this and every classroom activity area will depend upon what you want to happen in the area and what you want children to learn. Do you want children to build large and creative buildings in the Block Center? Then you will provide them with a good supply of unit blocks that they can choose and use easily. You may want to store large hollow blocks in the Large-Motor Center, because their use as a building material is entirely different from unit blocks. You may also want to store small table blocks and Lego bricks in the Manipulative/Math Center for still a different use.

Do you want children to pretend and to use their imaginations as they build? Then you will want to stock the Block Center with **accessories that support field trips and other learning center themes** to promote such creativity. Do you want children to represent in their building the field trips they have taken, the stories they have heard, or the visits from outside specialists they have had? Then you will want to stock the center with particular accessories to promote such pretending. Table 3-1 lists some of the little toys currently available from toy catalogs and stores that children enjoy using with blocks.

These block accessories come in a profusion of sizes and materials. Some are of plain wood with no details, much like Pratt's originals. Most are highly detailed in wood or plastic. Many figures of people are multiethnic, showing skin colors and features of Caucasian, Hispanic, African American, Native American, Arabic, and Asian American families. Block-play people with leg braces, forearm crutches, and wheelchairs, as well as community helpers, bring real life into the classroom. Animal sets include farm animals, forest animals, zoo animals, and dinosaurs. There are also wooden or plastic trucks and cars, construction sets, and traffic signs.

Your selection should be based on what you want to happen in the Block Center, as well as what particular skills and concepts you want children to learn. You need not have all of your accessories available at all times for your children. When you visit a fire station, for instance, you will want to put out firefighting vehicle and people accessories. Specific suggestions for use of particular accessories can be found in the "Activities" section of this chapter. If your budget does not allow so many human and animal figures, **cut them out of toy catalogs, mount them on cardboard** or foam backing, and laminate them with clear contact paper.

Table 3-1 Block Accessories

Sets of People	*Sets of Animals*
Family members	Farm animals
Community helpers	Forest animals
Children; babies	Zoo animals
Multicultural people	Dinosaurs
People with disabilities	Sea life
Construction workers	Endangered species
Hospital staff and patients	
Firefighters	*Sets of Vehicles:*
Gardeners	Cars
Westerners with horses	Trucks
Clowns	Tractors
Airport crew	Construction vehicles
Garbage squad	Emergency vehicles
Farm families	Aircraft
	Space vehicles
Other Accessories:	Boats
	Traffic signs
Dollhouse furniture	
Miniature eating, drinking, and cooking utensils	
Supermarket supplies	

BLOCK CENTER LABELS

As noted in chapter 1, learning centers should be identified with picture and word labels. The color-coded logo or picture you are using for the Block Center needs to be displayed prominently at the children's eye level at the entrance to the center. Use the name of the area often and point to the sign when discussing with the children what activities are available; they will soon be reading the words. This same sign should appear in miniature on the Pictorial Daily Schedule as well as the Pictorial Floor Plan.

In addition, you should **label every block and accessory shelf with a picture and word label** of what it contains. Trace around each block shape on colored construction paper, cut it out, and mount it on a white sign or directly onto the shelf itself. The name of the block should be labeled on the sign or on the shelf as well. Then use the names frequently when you are talking about blocks, and soon the children will be discussing "ramps," "units," and "quads" as well. Don't think these words are too difficult for children to remember. If you use the words, the children will too—and be delighted with their use.

Wooden trucks to be used with the blocks should be stored on block shelves.

As for the accessories, if you are storing sets of little cars, trucks, and planes in separate trays or baskets on a shelf, then mount the labels directly onto each basket. You can trace around each kind of toy as you did each block shape, or you may want to make a photocopy of the item and then color it in for a label; three-dimensional items like this can be copied just the same as flat materials. If you stand up your people or vehicles separately on shelves, then mount each label at the toy's location. Again, include written names of each accessory. Every accessory item on the shelves should be labeled. Children need to see words as well as pictures of the items they are playing with.

ACTIVITIES TO PROMOTE PHYSICAL DEVELOPMENT

Children's interactions with unit blocks promote both large- and small-motor development. Arms and hands are strengthened as children take blocks off the shelves and put them back. The small muscles of the fingers are strengthened as children pick up smaller items and stand them in place. Balancing the blocks in wall and tower constructions promotes eye-hand coordination, as does **placing little figures of people and equipment in precarious positions on buildings and towers**. These are spontaneous activities that children often do on their own in the Block Center. There are other ways teachers can involve children in activities that will promote physical development, especially if they have determined the children's interaction level based on observations. Table 3-2 lists actions children may be performing at the 3-M levels.

Table 3-2 Block Center Activities: Levels of Interaction

Manipulation Level
Takes most of the blocks off the shelves
Fills containers with blocks and dumps them out
Puts blocks in boxes and purses; pushes or carries them around
Pushes blocks along floor; does not build

Mastery Level
Stacks blocks in towers
Lines blocks in rows
Stands blocks up on end in rows
Makes double rows of blocks
Places second row of blocks on first row like a wall
Makes rows in patterns (short-tall, short-tall)
Learns to "bridge" one block across two standing blocks
Repeats bridge patterns
Makes enclosures: rows or walls that enclose a space

Meaning Level
Builds a construction (often names it later)
Builds roads, bridges
Builds buildings with walls in creative patterns
Builds tall buildings with blocks crisscrossed
Builds tunnels
Places figures of people, animals, or vehicles inside building
Builds named constructions: house, zoo, river bridge

Although all children seem to go through these three levels, they do it at different rates. The amount of time the youngsters remain at one level depends mainly on their age, their experience, and if they have a "breakthrough" to a new level of building. If left to pursue block building on their own, children teach themselves how to use the blocks by interacting with them as shown in Table 3-2. Many preschool children will be starting at the mastery level because of previous

How many blocks can they carry without dropping them?

experience with blocks at home. Children usually are involved in some but not all of the actions indicated under each level.

Although most block building is spontaneous on the part of the children, teachers may want to motivate or stimulate particular kinds of building through a teacher-initiated activity. Block-pickup games are excellent activities for promoting physical skills. If you want children to strengthen their hands and wrists, have them **hold one block flat** in their hands **and pile up one or two other blocks on top** for them **to carry to the block shelf**. How many can they carry this way without dropping them?

The body action chant "Blocks" at the head of this chapter is another **small-group activity** to use in the Block Center for promoting physical development. As a teacher-led activity with a small group of children, it can be done at the end of block play after pickup is completed. The motions children make as they chant can be changed every time. Maybe they would like to jump three times rather than clap when they say "blocks, blocks, blocks." Or the children can hold two blocks and clack them together three times on the last line. Ask your children what other motions they would like to make.

ACTIVITIES TO PROMOTE SOCIAL DEVELOPMENT

Social skills children need to learn in the Block Center include: gaining access to ongoing play, becoming a leader or following a leader, taking turns, playing cooperatively, and the prosocial skill of helping.

Children can learn many of these skills on their own. The Block Center is an excellent site for spontaneous experimentation regarding social skills. Some children may band together to build cooperatively. Others may try to gain access to this ongoing play, but are rejected. This is not an unusual situation in preschool programs. As noted by early childhood specialist Ramsey: "Interactions in preschool classrooms are short, so children are constantly having to gain entry into new groups. This process is made more difficult because children who are already engaged with each other tend to protect their interactive space and reject newcomers" (Ramsey, 1991, p. 27).

The teacher should not force block builders to permit other children to join them. Instead, the teacher can **help those children to gain access by having them use different strategies**. Strategies that seem to work best, according to early childhood researchers, include:

1. Hovering silently near the group (onlooker)

2. Mimicking play behavior of the group (parallel play)

3. Trying again to enter the group (Beaty, 2008, p. 245)

It is especially helpful for the outsiders to use all three strategies in this order. As they hover near the group they can better understand what the group is doing. Then they can mimic the group's behavior by building their own construction parallel to the group's. Eventually the outsiders can begin talking with their neighboring builders about what they are doing; this is often the key to gaining access. On the other hand, outsiders may be satisfied by then with their own parallel block play.

As the teacher observes what is happening, she may decide that certain children who have difficulty accepting another player may need to hear a new point of view. **At an appropriate time she can read them** *This Is Our House* (Rosen, 1996) about a cardboard carton that a group of children take out to the playground to be their house, but George claims it for his own. One after another he forces each of the children out, until at last he has to go to the bathroom, and everyone quickly squeezes into the cardboard house. When George returns he finds there is no room for him, which makes him decide that this is a house for everyone. Ask your listeners what they would have done.

ACTIVITIES TO PROMOTE EMOTIONAL DEVELOPMENT

Children can develop emotionally in the Block Center as well. Every success they experience in their building or playing with others here adds immeasurably to the good feelings they have about themselves: their positive self-images. In addition, they can learn to deal in a positive way with emotional situations if they have the experience to learn how and the support of teachers in helping them cope. Of course, when things get out of hand during block play teachers may need to **intervene with their three-part rule of helping children learn to care for themselves, to care for others, and to care for the materials**.

To help children learn how others cope in emotional situations, teachers can read *Gigi and Lulu's Gigantic Fight* (Edwards, 2004) about two little friends in school who do everything alike, until the day Gigi knocks over Lulu's block house. Then the fight begins, finally ending with each of them declaring they will never speak to the other again. Ask your small group of listeners what they think will happen; or what they would do if they were Gigi and Lulu. **Read the remainder of the story** to find out how it ends. **Would your listeners have solved the problem the same way?** What might happen if someone knocked over their block building? Wellhousen and Kieff (2001) discuss how blocks can promote children's emotional development in several ways: "The simple act of building and knocking down structures gives children a feeling of being in control. Blocks enhance self-esteem because they are an open-ended material and there is no right or wrong way to play with them. Finally, blocks allow children to translate their personal ideas and experiences into three-dimensional concrete representations" (p. 96).

ACTIVITIES TO PROMOTE COGNITIVE DEVELOPMENT

Play with unit blocks has long been associated with cognitive development in young children. In order to develop intellectually, children need to have experience with the concepts of size and shape, and with wholes and parts; they need to experiment with counting, sorting, matching, and categorizing; and they need experiences with predicting and problem solving. Block play gives them the opportunity for all of these learning experiences.

Unit blocks are especially well suited to these experiences because they have been carefully designed as fractions and multiples of a mathematical unit. Short blocks are half units. It takes two of them to make a unit. Blocks that are twice as long as a unit are called doubles. Blocks four times as long are called quadruples or quads. Children in your classroom will learn these names because they will hear you and the other teachers call the various blocks by their names. They will eventually come to understand that a unit means one, a double means two, and a quadruple means four.

Another math concept promoted by block building is one-to-one correspondence. Young children at first learn to count by rote. Later they learn the meaning of each number by using it with concrete, three-dimensional materials. Ask a child to bring you seven blocks. He or she may be able to count by rote to seven, but may not understand what seven actual items are. When you are in the Block Center with children, talk to them by **using specific names for the blocks and specific numbers for the amounts of blocks** they are using: "Luis, can you bring Tyrone five half unit blocks, please?"

As children build on their own they will also be solving the perceptual problems that all young children experience: fitting the right block to the particular space. Somehow it is difficult for youngsters to choose the right length of block to fit as a bridging block between two uprights. This problem can be solved either by finding a block long enough to reach the uprights or by moving the uprights close enough so that the child's shorter block will fit. Children solve such perceptual challenges through trial and error in the Block Center. Through such activities they learn how to judge length and width, that building problems can be solved in more than one way, and that they can solve the problems successfully.

Adults also experience such building problems. Be sure to read to your builders *Henry Builds a Cabin* (Johnson, 2002), a simple, delightful story of how Henry builds a cabin in the woods from scratch. He draws his plans, cuts down 12 trees, squares the logs into beams, fits the beams into corner posts and eventually has the outlines of a house. As he works, his friends from town come out to offer their own advice, saying how small each part of the cabin looks in one-line sentences at the bottom of each page. Henry keeps on building, telling them it's bigger than it looks until he finally finishes the cabin. What happens when he tries it out for size? Are they surprised?

Teachers can also lend their support to children's cognitive learning by leaving challenges in the Block Center for the builders to solve on their own. At the appropriate time when the children are learning about circles or squares, for example, you can make **masking tape circles or squares on the floor** of the Block Center for children to build around. Be sure to make your figures fit the size of the blocks. You can also make **contact-paper cutouts of the various blocks and stick them to the floor**; children then select the proper blocks to stack up in a tower on top of the cutout.

Children learn to choose the right length of blocks to use for bridging between two walls through trial and error.

Such activities should be done in conjunction with other classroom activities promoting the concepts of circle or square, rather than in isolation in the Block Center. Perhaps children are tracing around circles in the Writing Center, or you are reading about circles in the Book Center, or they are singing circle songs in the Music Center. A self-directed learning environment like this needs to offer an integrated curriculum, with each learning center supporting what is going on in other centers.

Block Pickup

Block pickup games are another way to help children learn sorting, categorizing, and matching skills. When you introduce a new pickup game, use the same game for a week or more until the children really understand it. If you make block pickup into a game in which you also participate, it may become one of the favorite activities of the day. Why make block pickup a drudgery? Children enjoy routines like this if teachers help them have fun with them. Following are several block pickup games that promote cognitive skills.

Sorting

Have children sort out all of the unit blocks in one pile, the half units in another pile, and the doubles in a third pile. **Pretend the long quad blocks are bulldozers** and push each of the piles over to the shelf where they go. Then have the youngsters put them on the shelf.

Matching

Have the children **find all of the blocks that match** the arch block cutout, **put them in the dump truck, and drive them over to the shelf** for placement. Next match the half arch cutout and put those blocks in a pile for the dump truck to carry.

Counting and Identifying Shapes

Put on a hand puppet (e.g., a dog) and ask the children to **feed the dog three small cylinder block "bones."** Have the children close their eyes as you put them on the wrong shelf, and then challenge the children to find where the dog hid his bones, and put them on the right shelf.

Parts and Wholes

Put on another hand puppet (an alligator) and have it pick up a double. Say to the children that the alligator will help them pick up and put away each of the double blocks if they can **find two different blocks that together make a double.** He will also help them pick up the quads if they can find two other blocks that together make a quad.

Make up your own similar pickup games. It is fun to use hand puppets or stuffed animals. Do you **have a dinosaur who eats only quads?** Put him on the block shelf and have the children feed him. How many does he eat? What other games can you or your children think of? Have a different game every few weeks.

Finally, research tells us that block building is an important brain stimulator because it involves repetition, that is, building with the same shapes over and over. As Wellhousen and Kieff (2001) point out: "Neural pathways are strengthened each time they are used. Therefore, the repetition of any experience may foster the development of more efficient neural pathways in the brain" (p. 26). In addition, the repetitive activities of stacking blocks and knocking them down help children develop concepts related to cause and effect, size, weight, and balance.

ACTIVITIES TO PROMOTE LANGUAGE DEVELOPMENT

Language development occurs in the Block Center whether you promote it or not. When children build together they tend to talk together. Listen to what they are saying. You will learn something about their social roles of leader or follower. You will learn something about their cognitive concepts of size, shape, and number. And you will certainly learn how they are handling language. Do they speak in expanded sentences? Are they asking questions with words in the right order? Are they using new vocabulary words: "arch," "quad," or "skyscraper?" Which children contribute to the conversation? Which ones seem always to be the listeners?

Wellhousen and Giles (2005/2006) report: "A research study comparing children's oral language development at the block center versus a dramatic play area revealed that children use higher quality oral language when they play with blocks" (p. 77). Perhaps the greater freedom children have in the block center to improvise settings and roles, gives them more opportunities for greater oral production. **By asking them open-ended questions such as, "What is happening here?" teachers can elicit longer descriptions with expanded vocabulary**.

If you read them stories about buildings, you can ask them to tell you stories about the structures they are building, if they care to. For instance, **ask children to dictate something about their buildings** that you will write down for them. Or you might **ask the children to tell the tape recorder about their buildings**, and then listen to it later. If you take photos of the buildings, record what the children say about them so it can be written under the photos when they are printed.

Read a Book

In order to motivate such stories by the children, you can read a book about other people's houses, such as *This House Is Made of Mud* (Buchanan, 1991), about an adobe house with the story in English and Spanish, or *Ma Dear's Old Green House* (Patrick, 2004), about grandma's wonderful old house that two African American children visit every summer. Or what about reading together the classic cumulative tale *This Is the House That Jack Built* (Taback, 2002), with its end pages showing 48 different houses and its zany illustrations of the cow with the crumpled horn, the man all tattered and torn, and the maiden all forlorn? Think of the fantastic new vocabulary words the children will soon be spouting! Leave these books in the Block Center for the children's continued perusal.

Take a Field Trip

When children go on **field trips** involving buildings, you can encourage them to **represent** such **buildings in the Block Center**. Put up pictures of the post office, fire station, or farm they have visited. Take photos of the children and buildings on the field trip. **Mount these pictures in the Block Center at the children's eye level when they are sitting** as a reminder of the trip and a stimulus for representing the trip in blocks; then they will see them when they are building. Many of your children may not be at the developmental level where they can actually represent anything in block building. For them it may be the manipulative or mastery process that counts most of all.

Children also enjoy talking about the field trips they have taken. The Block Center can extend their learning by providing pictures of trip sites and new accessories for building in the days following a trip. Teachers can mention the new accessories in the center, or they can ask the children what new things they can find. Children who choose to play with blocks may then want to build something from the trip. What they do, though, is up to them, not the teachers. Teachers can interact verbally as they observe the children during their building, to see what is happening and to help them clarify what they are doing. Table 3-3 lists ideas for field trips and block-building accessories you can provide.

Table 3-3 Field Trips to Motivate Block Building

Field Trip	Accessories
Airport	Toy planes, people, cars
Beach	People, paper umbrellas, little boxes, boats
Circus	Circus animals, horses, people, trucks, paper tent
Construction site	Construction vehicles, workers, pipe cleaners, string, aquarium tubing
Drugstore	People, little boxes, plastic bottles
Farm	Farm animals, people
Fire station	Fire truck, people, plastic tubing for hoses
Gas station	Cars, trucks, plastic tubing
Hospital	People, emergency vehicles, little stretcher
Lake	People, boats, sticks for fishing poles, string
Museum	Dinosaurs, people
Park	People, little trees, dollhouse tables
Pet store	Animals, people, little boxes
Supermarket	People, miniature food items, boxes, bottles
Restaurant	People, miniature food items, tables
Zoo	Zoo animals, people, train

ACTIVITIES TO PROMOTE CREATIVE DEVELOPMENT

Creativity in young children has to do with their imaginations and pretending. They take the information they have and use it in new and original ways. Children of preschool age are at the perfect stage for creating new forms, new ideas, new words, new block structures, new anything—because they are not bogged down with the rules and regulations like older children who conform to what adults expect of them. Therefore, they are free to experiment and find out on their own— that is, if we let them.

The Block Center is a wonderful place for creative development to occur because the materials are unstructured and available for children to use in any way they want. Your most effective intervention strategy in the Block Center, in fact, is to keep out! Let the children build on their own. Then what about all of the previously mentioned activities, you may wonder? Teacher-initiated activities should be used sparingly. Use the activities mentioned to follow up a field trip, for instance, or when other play breaks down, or especially for pickup time.

Pretend

When nothing much is happening in the Block Center, teachers may want to encourage some kind of pretending. Perhaps if the builders pretend they are someone else, they can use their blocks in imaginative ways. **To encourage pretending in the Block Center, teachers can read a book** to a small group of builders in the area, and then leave them to do some pretending on their own.

The classic book *Tar Beach* (Ringgold, 1991) can carry your children just like it did that imaginative African American girl narrator, Cassie Louise Lightfoot, up, up from the rooftop of her New York City apartment building and soaring over the George Washington Bridge that her father helped to build. The "tar beach" is the tar paper rooftop the family retreats to for an all-night picnic when the summer heat gets to be too much for them inside.

After you read the story in the Block Center, **put out a few props such as a dollhouse table and chairs, figures of people,** a square of black paper for the tar beach, and a smaller square of colored paper for the blanket Cassie lays on as she gazes at the stars and the lights of the city before she takes off on her adventure. Leave the book in the Center, too, and see what construction the story inspires. Can anyone pretend to be Cassie and tell what she sees as she floats above the city?

Another wonderful multicultural character is the Hispanic girl Rosalba who also flies above New York City—this time with her grandmother in the book *Abuela* (Dorros, 1991). They visit a park in the city to feed the pigeons, but Rosalba begins wondering what it would be like if they could fly like birds—and suddenly they do, gliding and soaring above rooftops and out to the Statue of Liberty. Abuela speaks in Spanish as she points out the wonders: "Mira!" And Rosalba translates: "Look!" **This is a book to be read after your children have built a tall building and want**

Here is a building children can make up stories about to tell to everyone.

to include it in a story. The builders can take turns being Rosalba and Abuela, flying over their classroom city and telling the others what they see. Or teachers can read the picture book *Block City* (Stevenson, 2005), based on a poem about a little boy who builds a block city and imagines it to be an old-time city with towers, palaces, and ships. The children can then try their imaginations on their own block creations. What stories can they tell about their buildings? They may want to dictate their stories to their teachers or record them on a cassette recorder. They can take photos of their constructions to be mounted in a scrapbook along with their stories for everyone to look at in the Book Center.

THE TEACHER'S ROLE IN THE BLOCK CENTER OBSERVING DEVELOPMENTAL LEVELS

As in the other learning centers, the teacher's role is to set up the center as previously described so that children can choose to become involved with blocks on their own, and so that interesting and exciting things will happen within the center. Then the teacher steps back to make observations of individual children in this and every center of the classroom during the free-choice time period. As described in chapter 2, the teacher first looks for children's developmental levels as they interact with blocks. The three levels of manipulation, mastery, and meaning play are usually highly visible in the Block Center (see Table 3-2).

Children at the manipulative level do almost everything with blocks except build with them: They take them off the shelves, carry them around, push them into piles, fill up boxes and trucks with them, dump them out, fill up containers again, and dump them out once more. These children are usually the youngest in the group or the ones with the least experience. Give them this manipulation time to get used to the blocks. The cardboard box activity from *This Is Our House* is for children at this level.

Children at the mastery level of building like to do the same building skill over and over. If they have learned to stack vertically in a tower-type structure, they will construct many, many towers. Lining up blocks horizontally in long rows, walls, or roads is another kind of mastery play. The mastery level of block play can become very elaborate as children teach themselves the skill of "bridging," that is, putting one block across the space between two other blocks. Soon they are repeating a pattern of bridging over and over in an elaborate wall or tower. The way children express their individuality with blocks is just as different as the doodling of individual adults with a pencil. The balancing and cognitive stacking activities previously described are especially appealing to children at the mastery level.

Children at the meaning level of block play apply the skills they have learned to building real buildings. They may give their constructions names at the outset or wait until they have finished before they decide what the structures are. Because preschool children are still in the "process" stage of interacting with the things in their environment, it is the doing of the thing that is important to them, rather than the final product. They soon come to realize, however, that adults seem more concerned with the final product: the building, the picture, and the story. So they will usually give a name to their building if pressed, and even make up a story about it.

Children at the meaning level of building are probably the only ones who will be skilled enough to represent in blocks the structures seen on field trips. However, even their structures will come from their own creative impulses rather than from the actual shape of a real building.

Observing Social Interaction Levels

Children in the Block Center display obvious social interaction levels in their play. Some are onlookers. Others build blocks in a solitary manner. Some build structures parallel to other children, whereas others build in cooperation with a group. As the teacher observes in the Block Center, he or she can record the actions and words of all the children involved on the Child Interaction Form, or concentrate on one particular child.

Recording on the Child Interaction Form

One teacher observed two 4-year-old boys (Rick and Edward) and two 3-year-old boys (Jake and Robbie) in the Block Center. They were engaged as follows.

Edward was near the block shelf making a square log-cabin-like building with quadruples, which he got from the shelf one at a time. Rick was lining up unit blocks in a long line parallel to the block shelf. When he came to Edward's building he started another line parallel to the first one. Rick said to Edward, "Look what I am doing!" and Edward replied, "Watch out for my building. This is a space station." Edward then got toy figures of people one at a time and stood them on top of his building.

Jake entered the Center and began pulling various blocks off a different shelf one by one, backing up a wooden dump truck, piling his blocks in it, then dumping them out, and loading it again. When Rick said, "Look what I am doing!" a second time, Jake repeated the same sentence, "Look what I am doing!" to no one in particular. Meanwhile, Robbie had followed Jake into the Center and stood watching him and the others but not playing. The teacher recorded the incident on the Child Interaction Form as shown in Table 3-4.

Interpreting the Interactions

Before she left the area, the teacher jotted down her interpretation and suggestions on the back of the form. These would be noted by other staff members at the end of the day or week, and incorporated into plans for individual children at the staff planning session. Her notes read as follows:

> **Accomplishments:**
>
> *Edward can do creative building.*
> *Rick is fine at mastery level.*
> *Jake is still at manipulation level.*
>
> **Needs:**
>
> *It would help Edward to be involved in building with others.*
> *Robbie needs to get involved with blocks.*
>
> **Plans:**
>
> *Look for another child at meaning level who could build with Edward.*
> *Have staff member try to get Robbie involved with blocks (but not force him); he is new and still unsure.*

Interacting with the Unsure Child

As teachers come to recognize individual children's developmental and social levels from their observations, they can make plans for such children. Most children handle block building well without adult intervention. However, for certain children who have not become involved, perhaps because they don't know how, teachers may decide to intervene.

Stationing themselves in the Block Center as observers **is an effective technique for enticing children into the area**. Young children often choose to work in an area where their teacher is located because they want the teacher's

Child ___Edward, Rick, Jake, Robbie___   Observer ___D.B.___

Center ___Blocks___   Date ___4/15___

CHILD INTERACTION FORM
With Materials

Manipulation Level   Actions/Words

(Child moves materials around
without using them as intended.)

Jake comes in center after other boys; takes various blocks off opposite shelf; fills and dumps dump truck.

Mastery Level   Actions/Words

(Child uses materials
as intended, over and over.)

Rick makes long line of unit blocks parallel to shelf and up to Edward's building and then makes second line parallel to first; says to Edward 2x: "Look what I am doing!"

Meaning Level   Actions/Words

(Child uses materials in
new and creative ways.)

Edward makes log-cabin-like bldg. with quads, 1 at a time off shelf; puts toy people on top; replies to Rick: "Watch out for my bldg. This is a space station."

With Other Children

Solitary Play   Actions/Words

(Child plays with
materials by self.)

Jake plays by self, not near other boys. (Robbie looks on but doesn't play.)

Parallel Play   Actions/Words

(Child next to others with same
materials but not involved with them.)

Rick and Jake play parallel, talking to one another, but not interacting with blocks.

Cooperative Play   Actions/Words

(Child plays together with
others and same materials.)

Table 3-4   Child Interaction Form: Blocks

attention. If they do not come, he can invite them. If they still refuse, the teacher should not pressure such children because they are probably not yet ready. Instead, **he may read one of the building books** previously mentioned to an individual child in the Book Center. The teacher eventually comes to realize which children need to be left entirely on their own in the beginning.

If the unsure children are girls, he may decide to read *Building a Bridge* (Begaye, 1993) about the Anglo girl Anna and the Navajo girl Juanita who are a little scared on the first day of school on the Navajo Reservation. Their teacher, Mrs. Yazzie, gives the girls a box of purple and green blocks to build with. She says the blocks are magic. At first they each build their own little purple or green bridge. But when they put the blocks together something wonderful happens: they find they can build a huge bridge. It is okay that the blocks are different colors. Differences make things magical, they agree as they ride home happily together on the school bus.

But for those who do come into the center through a teacher's invitation, the teacher can then begin to take blocks off the shelf for a building of his own. He may even start to build a simple structure. **Serving as a block-building role model** may be all that is necessary **to get some reluctant builders started**. On the other hand, a shy or unsure child may need a more direct approach. "Robbie, can you find another block like this on the shelf? That's the right one. It's called a unit block. Can you put the unit block on this building? You choose where you think it should go. That's fine. Thanks. We'll need a few more unit blocks like that one." Once the child is involved on his own, the teacher can withdraw unobtrusively from the activity.

Inclusion

If the unsure child is someone with physical difficulties or someone who does not speak English, **you may need to tailor your intervention to fit the situation**. Wellhousen and Crowther (2004) say that some children with special needs have a particular difficulty building three-dimensional structures and incorporating vehicles, animals, and people figures. You may need to take a more direct role and demonstrate specific building skills to get them started. They can try stacking blocks and knocking them down over and over at first; then lining up blocks to make a road for little cars; making a ramp for cars to roll down; or making fenced enclosures for animal figures.

A book to read that includes different children playing in harmony together is *Play Lady* (Hoffman, 1999), written in both English and Spanish, about the Hispanic boy Miguel who lives on Bay Street in a big house with a small yard and his next-door neighbor Jane Kurosawa, the Play Lady, who lives in a small house (a converted bus) in a big yard. She allows the neighborhood children to play in her yard with its flower, vegetable, and fruit gardens and "mud river." Kayla, an African American girl, finds broken dishes, dolls, and a clock that she "plants" in the garden. Mandy, a girl in a wheelchair, pounds boards to build a "power castle" hut under the pear tree.

But one day unknown strangers trash the Play Lady's place and paint "Go Home!" signs on her bus. She is devastated. The children think whoever did it never had a Play Lady of their own. When the Play Lady goes off with her brother, the children get their parents and neighborhood adults to help clean up the place, fix the broken bus windows, and paint over the offending words. Then they welcome back the Play Lady with appreciative words of their own on signs that say: "You are the Queen of the Land" and "Hurray for the Play Lady." What should they do now? "Just play," she tells them. What do your listeners say about this tale?

Interacting with Disruptive Children

Before intervening with a disruptive child, the teacher should observe to see what is happening. If the disruption is occurring because the block play has disintegrated, the teacher may decide to **redirect the activity by asking for or giving specific suggestions for a new direction**. For example, the teacher might say: "Elena and Sarah, I see that the two of you have finished building your bridge. What else can you build near the bridge? Yes. A road is a good idea. And what kinds of vehicles or people will be using your bridge and road?"

If the disruption has more to do with emotions than blocks, the teacher may ask each child to tell what is happening. **Putting emotions into words often diffuses a tense situation**. On the other hand, if the children are really out of control, the teacher needs to intervene in a firm but matter-of-fact manner. She needs to **reiterate the caring motto of the program**: "Elena and Sarah, in this classroom we care for one another. We do not push one another around. I can't let you do that. Show me that you can play without pushing."

If the disruption involves throwing blocks around, the teacher's intervention needs to stress: "Elena and Sarah, in this classroom we take care of our materials. We do not throw blocks around. Show me how you can build with the blocks." Or she may use herself as a role model: "Girls, these blocks are for building, not throwing. I am going to build with them. If you would like to build, too, you can sit right here by me and help."

If the children are totally out of control, the teacher may need to take the two children aside and sit quietly with them until they can listen and respond to her calm talk. Such an approach is much more effective than sending children to a "time-out chair," which most children view as punishment. These youngsters need to learn to control their emotions and actions, not be punished for them.

Interacting with Builders

You will learn from your observations when and if you should interact with builders. You should make it a point to interact on an individual basis with each child every day. This could occur when a child is building with blocks, but be sure it is not merely an interruption. On the other hand, if you see something you would like to comment on, this may very well be the appropriate time. As noted in chapter 2, watch and listen carefully before making your comment. Your comments can give children support, encouragement, or direction in their building. They should be specific and nonjudgmental. You may be reflecting what you see the children doing with blocks; or you may be asking a question to clarify what you see. "You're using most of the blocks on the shelf in your building today, Jasmine. How did you ever get all those cylinders to balance?"

As you observe and respond to children in the Block Center, you yourself will be learning more about: 1) the children and their wonderful inventiveness when they have the freedom to work with unstructured materials; 2) the blocks and what valuable learning opportunities they add to your program; and 3) yourself and how else you can use blocks to make your program both effective and exciting for children.

IDEAS IN CHAPTER 3

1. *Setting up the Block Center*

    a. Stock your shelves with enough unit blocks

    b. Arrange the blocks lengthwise on shelves at the children's height

    c. Have a spacious area with the floor carpeted and defined by shelves

    d. Have accessories that support field trips and other learning center themes

    e. Cut out figures of toy catalogs and mount them on cardboard

    f. Label block and accessory shelves with picture and word labels

2. *Using activities to promote physical development*

    a. Place figures of people in precarious positions on buildings and towers

    b. Hold one block flat and pile up blocks on top for pickup

    c. Do the body action chant "Blocks" at the chapter head

3. *Using stories and activities to promote social development*

    a. Help children gain access to building by using different strategies

    b. Read a book about gaining access to play

4. *Using stories and activities to promote emotional development*

    a. Use three-part rule: help children care for themselves, care for others, care for materials

    b. Read a book and then let children tell how they might solve their own building problems

5. *Using stories and activities to promote cognitive development*

    a. Use specific names for blocks and specific numbers for amounts

    b. Tape circles and squares on the floor with masking tape

    c. Stick contact-paper cutouts of blocks on the floor

6. *Using block pickup games*

    a. Pretend quad blocks are bulldozers

    b. Match blocks to label and carry in dump truck

    c. Feed "bone" blocks to a hand puppet dog

    d. Bring two blocks to a puppet to make a double

    e. Feed quad blocks to a dinosaur

7. *Using activities to promote language development*

    a. Ask open-ended questions

    b. Write down a dictated story about a child's building

    c. Have children tape-record stories about their buildings

    d. Represent field trip buildings in the Block Center

    e. Mount pictures or photos at children's eye level when they are sitting in the Block Center

8. *Using activities to promote creative development*

    a. Read a book on pretending in the Block Center

    b. Put out people and doll furniture props for pretending

    c. Read a book after your children have built a big building

9. *Interacting with children in the Block Center*

    a. Stand in Block Center to entice reluctant children

    b. Read a block story to a reluctant child

    c. Serve as block-building role model for a reluctant child

    d. Tailor intervention to fit the situation for children with special needs

    e. Redirect disintegrating activity with specific suggestions

    f. Help disruptive children put emotions into words

    g. Reiterate caring motto of the program

DISCUSSION QUESTIONS

1. What can children learn during block play, other than how to build buildings? How?

2. Why did Pratt insist that the *unit blocks* she invented be plain and without colors or designs?

3. Should young children be allowed to leave their buildings standing or should they be allowed to knock them down? Why?

4. Why should children learn the names of the different unit blocks?

5. How can reading stories to children help them in their block play? Give an example.

TRY IT YOURSELF

1. Label each type of block and each accessory with picture and word signs on your Block Center shelves.

2. Observe and record the behaviors, interactions, and talk of three different children in the Block Center for three days. Make comments on their developmental and social play levels, and how you were able to determine the levels.

3. Go on a field trip to a building or a construction site with some or all of the children. Do a follow-up activity in the Block Center by bringing in new accessories to support your trip, by mounting pictures of the building in the Block Center, or by reading a picture book about buildings or construction to a small group. Record what happens with blocks.

4. When cognitive concepts such as *circle, square, rectangle,* and *triangle* are being presented, put masking tape in the Block Center for children to build those shapes.

5. Make up a new block pickup game or use one suggested in this chapter. Use it for a week and record the results.

REFERENCES CITED

Beaty, J. J. (2008). *Skills for preschool teachers* (8th ed.). Upper Saddle River, NJ: Merrill/ Prentice Hall.

Caplan, F. & Caplan, T. (1974). *The power of play.* Garden City, NY: Anchor Press/ Doubleday.

Johnson, H. (1983). The art of blockbuilding. In E. Provenzo & A. Brett (Eds.), *The complete block book* (pp. 111–156). Syracuse, NY: Syracuse University Press.

Koepke, M. (1989). Learning by the blocks. *Teacher Magazine 1*(3), 52–60.

Pratt, C. (1948). *I learn from children.* New York: Simon & Schuster.

Provenzo, E. & Brett, A. (1983). *The complete block book.* Syracuse, NY: Syracuse University Press.

Ramsey, P. B. (1991). *Making friends in school: Promoting peer relationships in early childhood.* New York: Teachers College Press.

Wellhousen, K. & Crowther, I. (2004). *Creating effective learning environments.* Clifton Park, NY: Cengage.

Wellhousen, K. & Giles, R. M. (2005/2006). Building literacy opportunities into children's block play: What every teacher should know. *Childhood Education 82* (2), 74–78.

Wellhousen, K. & Kieff, J. (2001). *A constructivist approach to block play in early childhood.* Clifton Park, NY: Cengage Learning.

Other Sources

Beaty, J. J. (2006). *Observing development of the young child.* New York: Merrill/ Prentice Hall.

Cartwright, S. (1990). Learning with large blocks. *Young Children 45*(3), 38–41.

Chalufour, I. & Worth, K. (2004). *Building structures with young children.* St. Paul, MN: Redleaf Press.

Coughlin, P. A., Hansen, K. A., Heller, D., Kaufman, R. K., Stolberg, J. R., & Walsh, K. B. (1997). *Creating child-centered classrooms.* Washington, DC: Children's Resources International.

Frost, J. L., Wortham, S. C., & Reifel, S. (2005). *Play and child development.* Upper Saddle River, NJ: Merrill/Prentice Hall.

National Association for the Education of Young Children. *Block play: Constructing realities* (video #838). Washington, DC: Author.

Children's Books

Begaye, L. S. (1993). *Building a bridge.* Flagstaff, AZ: Northland. [*]

Buchanan, K. (1991). *This house is made of mud.* Flagstaff, AZ: Northland.

Dorros, A. (1991). *Abuela.* New York: Dutton Children's Books. [*]

Edwards, P. D. (2004). *Gigi and Lulu's gigantic fight.* New York: Katherine Tegen Books. (HarperCollins)

Hoffman, E. (1999). *Play lady.* St. Paul, MN: Redleaf Press. [*]

Johnson, D. B. (2002). *Henry builds a cabin.* Boston: Houghton Mifflin.

Patrick, D. L. (2004). *Ma Dear's old green house.* East Orange, NJ: Just Us Books. [*]

Ringgold, F. (1991). *Tar beach.* New York: Crown. [*]

Rosen, M. (1996). *This is our house.* Cambridge, MS: Candlewick Press. [*]

Stevenson, R. L. (2005). *Block city.* New York: Simon & Schuster.

Taback, S. (2002). *This is the house that Jack built.* New York: G. P. Putnam's Sons. [*]

Note: Asterisk represents multicultural book.

CHAPTER 4 COMPUTER CENTER

ROLE OF THE COMPUTER IN AN EARLY CHILDHOOD CLASSROOM

"You don't mean to say you're going to teach those little 3-, 4-, and 5-year-old children to use a computer, do you?" is the comment heard most frequently by teachers who have set up a Computer Center in their classrooms. The answer, of course, is: "No. We are not going to teach young children how to use a computer. They are going to teach themselves!"

Teachers who understand classroom computers realize that these amazing machines are not only powerful teaching/learning tools for everyone, but that they also lend themselves especially well to the self-discovery learning style of young children. Teachers who understand preschool children realize that computers do not intimidate them as they often do adults; on the contrary, the youngsters are eager to play around with the computer in order to discover how it works. Just as play with unit blocks touches every aspect of a child's development, so too can the computer make a similar contribution when set up with care and used with sensitivity.

There are many reasons for an early childhood classroom to consider including a Computer Center. The following are a some of them.

1. The Computer's Style of Interaction Favors Young Children

Young children learn best through exploratory play. They do not know what to expect from things in their environment, so they try them out playfully and keep trying them out until they finally get the things to work.

We could say they learn from their mistakes, except that for young children, there are no "mistakes"—only different kinds of responses.

Computer programs work in the same way: The users keep trying until they get the program to respond in the way it is supposed to. They are rewarded for their effort when the sought-after response appears on the monitor. Now they know what to do in order to proceed. This is how young children learn, "constructing their own knowledge" by interacting playfully with things in their environment. Because children see all computer programs as games, they are even more highly motivated to continue this exploratory play because it is fun.

In addition, computer programs are well suited to the three levels of interaction experienced by young children in their play: manipulation, mastery, and meaning. Children can manipulate keys on the keyboard or click the mouse as long as necessary until they finally extract the cause-and-effect sequence that will get the program to work. Then they can proceed through the mastery stage of repeating a sequence over and over; programs will repeat responses as long as the operator wants them to. Finally, children are able to apply their own meanings—that is, to make up their own games and express their own creativity—once they have mastered the workings of a program. This is how young children learn, and this is exactly how computer programs work.

2. The Computer's Combination of Visual and Verbal Learning Is Especially Helpful to Young Children

Computer programs respond to their users through a combination of animated visual graphics, sound, and written words on a monitor screen. Young children are in the visual stage of thinking until about age 7, when they make a transition to verbal thinking after they have learned to read and write. Thus they respond well to the visual images they have caused to appear on the screen. The words on the screen that they see (and sometimes hear) help make their transition to verbal thinking easier as they eventually learn to read and write.

This powerful combination of pictures, words, and sometimes voice has even made it possible for certain children to teach themselves to read. Although learning to read is not a goal in preschool programs, children's pre-reading skills are nevertheless enhanced whenever carefully selected computer programs are available for the youngsters to choose and use.

3. The Computer Makes It Easier to Individualize Learning

As Banet writes in his article "Computers and Early Learning," "Rather than prescribe a child's learning experience, the computer can present an inviting menu from which the child can choose, freeing him or her from adults' limited ability to prescribe optimal educational experiences" (Banet, 1978).

We already understand that the entire self-directed learning environment is set up in order for children to make choices and get deeply involved in their own learning. Now here is a learning tool designed for exactly the same purpose: to allow its users to choose from a range of activities at different levels. If they choose a program that is too difficult, they can try an easier one. When they are ready for more advanced activities, they can proceed. You provide the appropriate programs; the children themselves decide whether and how to use them.

Teachers realize how difficult it is for them to match learning activities with an individual child's level of ability. They frequently underestimate or over-estimate a youngster's abilities. Computer programs, on the other hand, present a variety of levels of activities, and through trial and error, children themselves find the level best suited to their individual capacities.

As Blagojevic (2003) points out: "When flexibility is introduced into the program by offering a variety of activity choices and adaptable learning tools like the computer, teachers are better able to design curriculum to meet the diverse needs of learners" (p. 29).

4. The Computer Serves as an Equalizer for Children from Different Backgrounds

The computer seems to have a universal appeal to children. Thus, a classroom computer can serve children of every socioeconomic level, of both genders, of every racial or ethnic group, of every ability, and even those with disabilities. Although home computers seem more in evidence among middle-class families, a computer in the classroom is available for all children no matter what their background. The so-called learning gap or "digital divide" between rich and poor, black and white, and gifted and impaired children can be reduced and even overcome through the use of a classroom computer.

The "digital divide" is a growing gap between those who have access to computers and the Internet and those who do not. Blagojevic (2003) believes the computer is an equalizer: "Considering equity issues at the center-based technology level, the computer has been called an equalizer and is a tool that brings unique qualities to the early childhood curriculum" (p. 28).

Many families cannot afford their own home computers. For those who can, their children often have a learning advantage over others. A computer in the class-room available for everyone helps to equalize such learning opportunities. Learning-impaired children can use computer programs at their own levels just as gifted children do at their levels, because computer programs work at a variety of speeds and with unlimited patience. Studies have shown that bilingual children, learning-disabled children, and children from low-income families often learn from computer programs what they had difficulty learning in regular classrooms (Lee, 1983).

Gender discrimination among elementary-aged children can be reduced and may even be eliminated if early childhood programs include this valuable tool as an integral part of their curriculum. A study by Lipinski, Nida, Shade, and Watson (1984) study showed concern over male dominance of computer use in elementary and secondary schools. One respondent stated that "among children ages 8, 9, 11, and 12, girls were never identified as computer experts" (Lipinski et al., 1984, p. 5).

Happily, this is not the case in early childhood programs. Studies of gender differences in preschool computer use do not show young boys dominating the computer or becoming more expert than girls. Lipinski's own early childhood program, in fact, showed young girls spending more time at the computer than boys.

This author's two-year study found that both preschool boys and girls demonstrated equal interest, and both became competent users. Tucker and I concluded that early childhood educators should definitely consider introducing the computer to all young children before any sort of gender stereotyping can take place. If girls become competent computer users in the preschool, they will enter elementary school with the ability and desire to continue using these valuable learning tools (Beaty & Tucker, 1987).

5. The Computer is an Effective Promoter of Young Children's Positive Self-Images

To feel good about themselves, young children need to be involved in experiences in which they are successful, and especially in activities in which they are in charge. A classroom computer lends itself especially well to the development of such

If girls become competent computer users in preschool, they will enter elementary school with the ability and desire to continue using these valuable learning tools.

positive feelings. If teachers have set up the Computer Center so that children can choose it and use it on their own, and if teachers have selected the software programs with care, then children can proceed at their own speed toward success.

As we discovered in our study of young children and computers in two preschools and a kindergarten:

> Good programs reinforce the correct responses from children. When children make mistakes, such programs ignore errors and do not respond. Thus, the young computer operators learn how to work the program as it should be done. In addition to gaining competence, they gain confidence in their ability to handle not only this adult-type tool, but also other learning activities. Success breeds success. Shy children who have held back in other classroom activities are often the ones who gain such competence, and therefore confidence from the computer. (Beaty & Tucker, 1987, p. 13)

NEGLECTING THE CLASSROOM COMPUTER

Most early childhood classrooms have at least one computer. Children sometimes wander over to it and click the mouse if a program is turned on. More often than not, the machine is not on and does not seem to be in use. The problem is not the children's lack of interest but the teacher's disregard for including computer use in the curriculum. Bewick and Kostelnik (2004) discovered: "There is strong evidence that many teachers basically ignore the computers in their classrooms or use them only in a limited fashion" (p. 26).

Why does this happen? Some teachers may have only limited experience with computers. But even those who use computers at home may not know how to involve young children in their use or how to integrate computer software into the activities available in other learning centers. Computer software is, in fact, the key to any successful use of computers by children in the early childhood classroom.

The teacher who uses it should, of course, be the one to choose the software she wants. Too often this is not the case. Either the central office has provided the software along with other supplies for the year or the previous year's teacher chose it. This software may or may not be appropriate. How will you know?

CHOOSING APPROPRIATE EARLY CHILDHOOD SOFTWARE

Your most important task is to choose appropriate software programs for 3- to 4- and 5-year-old children. There are a great many programs available from a wide range of sources. Some of these programs are excellent; others are incredibly poor. In order to choose software suitable for your children and the goals of your program, it is necessary either to **try out the software yourself and with children if possible**, to ask teachers and parents who have used such software, or to read reviews of early childhood software that you can depend on. Manufacturer's descriptions of their own software do not always give you the information you need to make a wise choice.

While a limited number of children's programs are available from office supply stores, computer stores, and discount stores, many teachers find it more efficient to order computer programs online. Type the words "children's computer software" into your search program and you will be connected to many software links. Although Web sites change and new programs are constantly added, the following are some of the Web sites many educators use. Some offer reviews of programs.

www.childrenssoftwareonline.com

www.classsource.com

www.kidsclick.com

www.superkids.com

You may be overwhelmed by the number of software programs to choose from and be uncertain how to choose the best ones. **Some teachers choose software by looking for dependable brand names** such as:

Broderbund	Fisher Price
Disney	Learning Company
Dr. Seuss	Living Books
Edmark	Sesame Street

Others choose software by characters they know children are attracted to such as:

Arthur	Little Bear
Clifford the Big Red Dog	Madeline
Curious George	Mickey Mouse
Dora the Explorer	Reader Rabbit
Elmo	Thomas the Tank Engine
Franklin the Turtle	Winnie the Pooh

Still other teachers choose software by the subject matter it contains such as: letters, numbers, sorting and matching, language arts, social studies, or thinking skill games. Be sure the word "preschool" appears on the program in order to choose the appropriate level. Several levels of activities and games from easy to difficult are usually included in each preschool program. Examples of several such programs include:

Arthur's Preschool	*Jumpstart Advanced Preschool*
Disney Learning Preschool	*Madeline Preschool*
Disney's Mickey Mouse Preschool	*Millie & Bailey Preschool*
Dr. Seuss Preschool	*Reader Rabbit's Preschool*

No matter how you choose the computer software for your children, there is one feature you must consider: how the program can be *integrated* into your self-directed learning environment. Computer programs should not stand by themselves in preschool. There should be a strong link to other activities being pursued by the children. For instance, when children are involved in learning letters by playing alphabet games, making alphabet puzzles, playing with alphabet blocks, and finding the letters of their names in various learning centers, you need to put out one of your alphabet computer games as a lead-in or follow-up to these activities. Each of your computer programs should be tied to one or more activities in the other centers. This means you must try out the programs for yourself to see what they contain.

Our use of software with young children in several classes convinced us that computer programs for preschoolers should provide:

1. ease of operation by children

2. program and its choices controlled by children

3. instructions that are clear and simple

4. exit possible at any time

5. open-ended, not drill-and-practice programs

6. problem solving and discovery emphasized

7. content bias-free and violence-free

8. content easily integrated into the curriculum

These criteria are ideals not attained by every piece of software you will purchase. Your own judgment and the goals of your program will help you to choose software that meets as many of these criteria as possible.

SETTING UP THE COMPUTER CENTER

The Computer Center in an early childhood classroom should be treated the same as any of the other learning centers. That is, **it should occupy a special space sectioned off from the other centers,** just as the Block Center does. In elementary schools, computers are sometimes placed in a computer lab separate from the regular classroom. This is not recommended for young children. A computer needs to be available in the classroom for children to choose as an activity during their free-choice periods.

A computer consists of several parts: the central processing unit (CPU) with its hard drive and disk drive, a monitor screen, a keyboard, and a mouse for moving a cursor around on the screen, as well as speakers for sound. A printer for printing out hard copy is also an important part of the equipment. Some classrooms also have a scanner for copying pictures, signs, or words onto the computer monitor to be printed out by the printer. Current software programs come on CD-ROM disks.

The center itself can contain a low table for a computer and a printer, two chairs in front of the machine for a team of users, low shelves for the software, and a table for books and activities related to the computer programs, as well as a tape recorder to record children's stories or conversations. Shelves should be pulled

The center can contain a low table for a computer and printer with two chairs in front for a team of users.

away from the walls to section off the area. **Wall space can display a rules chart, pictures that often accompany computer programs, photos of children engaged in computer activities, or book jackets** featuring books on which the computer programs currently in use are based.

Include a Typewriter

You may decide to **include a second table and chairs in the center for a typewriter** —a real one and not a child's toy typewriter. From this machine, children gain not only the experience of using a keyboard similar to the computer keyboard, but they learn that it is necessary to press only one key at a time in order to print a letter. "Piano playing" the keyboard of a typewriter will just jam the keys. This skill can be transferred to the computer, where it is also necessary to press one key at a time in order to operate computer programs using a keyboard. Having a typewriter in the center makes it a more interesting place to be than a center having one lone computer. Even more children will be attracted to the center during the free-choice period.

Read a Book

Be sure to **read a typewriter storybook to children who sign up to use this tool**. *Click, Clack, Moo Cows That Type* (Cronin, 2000) is the hilarious story about Farmer Brown's cows who find an old typewriter in their barn and type the farmer a letter demanding electric blankets because the barn is so cold. Then the ducks get into the act and demand a diving board in their pond. How do your listeners think it will all turn out? Make this a special book for users of the computer center only. Keep other special books in other centers that can be read to children using those centers.

On the other hand, some teachers prefer to locate a typewriter in the classroom Writing Center (see Chapter 7, "Writing Center") or to **combine the Computer Center with the Writing Center** if there is enough room. As children become adept at printing letters with writing tools, they enjoy practicing their newly acquired skill with all sorts of writing implements, including a typewriter and a computer.

CHILDREN CHOOSING AND USING THE COMPUTER CENTER

Whenever possible, **3-, 4-, and 5-year-old children should use the Computer Center in pairs**, not alone. Social skills, language skills, peer teaching, and even creativity will blossom when more than one young child uses the computer at the same time. This statement is contrary to adult assumptions; most adults see the computer as they do a typewriter—as a tool for a single user.

In an early childhood classroom, however, the computer is not a tool for a single child. It is an activity for a team; that is, for two children to explore, to talk about, and to take turns using. The goal for computer use in an early childhood classroom is different from that of computer use by an adult. For adults the computer is a working tool that performs a particular task. For young children the computer is a learning tool to help them develop certain skills.

As noted by early childhood computer specialists, "Not only are young children capable of working together at the computer, they prefer working with one or two partners to working alone. They seek help from each other and seem to prefer help from peers over help from the teacher" (Clements, Nastasi, & Swaminathan, 1993, p. 60).

Early childhood programs include computers in their learning centers to allow this powerful interactive learning device to promote children's development in the social, emotional, physical, cognitive, language, and creative areas. Whether children learn to use the machine itself with great efficiency is not the point. What is important is that young children improve their social skills, their language skills, their thinking and problem-solving skills, and all the rest. If the computer can help them to accomplish these goals effectively, then it is worth having in the classroom.

Computer Necklaces and Sign-Up Sheets

To choose to use the computer during the free-choice period, a child should be able to go to the Computer Center and select one of the two "computer necklaces" hanging at the entrance, or whatever other self-regulating devices you have

Two can also have fun at the computer.

arranged. If both of the necklaces have been taken already, then **the child should be able to "sign up" for the computer, or to take some kind of numbered ticket** that will give him or her a turn.

The Computer Center is often one of the more popular learning centers in your classroom if you have made it appealing. Be prepared to have a sign-up sheet or other device for children who want to take a turn. Pre-literate children can sign up by printing their names in conventional script if they are able or by scribbling their names in personal script on the sign-up sheet (see Chapter 7, "Writing Center"). If they do not get a turn on the day they sign up, then they will be first in line for the next day if they are still interested.

Helping Children Use the Computer

At the beginning of the year, you or one of your assistants should show small groups of children (four or five at a time) how the computer works. Take the children into the center and sit down at one of the two chairs in front of the computer. Invite a child to sit in the second chair. Then point out to this child and the onlookers the parts of the computer: the disk drive where the CD-ROM goes in, the keyboard, and the monitor that looks like a television (but isn't). If you are using a mouse, point that out; also show them the printer. See if the children can remember the names for all of the parts. Make a game of it; children enjoy learning new words.

Then show the children what a program disk looks like. Remove it carefully from its envelope. Show them how to hold the disk so it will not be damaged, and let them each take a turn holding the disk properly. Demonstrate how you turn on the computer, insert the CD-ROM into the disk drive, and wait for the program to appear on the monitor. (If autoplay is not operational you may need to install the program.)

Then turn off all the components and give your partner in the chair next to you a chance to try inserting the disk and turning the system on and then off. The other three or four children will be watching. Next it can be someone else's turn to try it. Have the first child show the new child how it is done.

Once they know how to turn on the system, this small group of children should have a chance to briefly operate the initial program you plan to use for the first week. Then give another small group of children the same opportunity to try the new equipment. Work with small groups like this over the next few days until everyone has had a turn. Take your time and let the children take their time. Those who are finished or are waiting can be occupied with books that relate to the program, or other free-choice activities.

If the program you plan to use is already stored on the hard drive, you can show each child how to turn on the computer and access the program, and then exit from the program and the computer. Some teachers prefer to have the computer on and the program ready to go during free-choice period. But when the period is finished the computer needs to be turned off. A computer loses its effectiveness with children if it is kept on all day long with children walking by, clicking the mouse, looking at it briefly, and leaving. It should be treated the same as other activities; that is, chosen with a necklace, being seated at its chair, and becoming involved in the program until it is finished.

RULES FOR USING THE COMPUTER

As children learn to use the computer, be sure to point out to each team the **illustrated rules chart** you have mounted nearby. It should contain only a few simple rules that everyone understands:

1. Wash hands before using.

2. Two children at a time.

3. Use only during free-choice time.

Children understand that this is a special piece of equipment if they see you treating it respectfully. Do not bring the computer into the classroom before you intend to use it, because children want to investigate and explore every new object right away. If the computer stands there unused, their temptation to touch it may be too great, and children may start playing around with the keys or trying to turn it on and off. Once you have introduced the machine and its rules, you should keep it off until free-choice time so that children are not tempted to misuse it. Then make sure children wash their hands, because sticky fingers can gum up the keys.

Computers are remarkably sturdy machines. About the only potential hazards to computers in an early childhood classroom are sticky fingers and spilled liquids. Liquids should not cause trouble unless you have inadvertently located the Computer Center near the sink. Obviously, you would not allow pounding on the keys or other destructive actions. By the time children come to use the computer, they should be well aware of the three-part classroom rule: We care for ourselves; we care for one another; and we care for the materials in our classroom.

INITIAL COMPUTER PROGRAM

In the beginning you should **use only one program for a week or so**, or until all of the children have a chance to use the program for as long as they want. **It should be a simple piece of software** that will introduce the computer. A few years ago most of the programs worked by using the keyboard. Today, most work with a mouse to move the cursor.

If you use a keyboard program, choose a program (e.g., writing program) that uses most or all of the keys. Show the children your pointer finger. Have them hold up their own pointer finger. This is **their "computer finger," which they should use to press one key** of the computer at a time. Then they should wait to see what happens on the screen before pressing another key. At first, many children cannot wait before pushing another key. They may have to learn by trial and error that only one key is necessary to make something happen on the screen.

If you use a mouse program, show the children how the mouse moves the cursor to the spot they want.

Let one of the two computer partners click the mouse once and wait to see what happens. Then let the second partner click the mouse, wait, and see what happens. The children in the small group who are watching can then have their turns. Go through the mouse program, talk about what is happening on the screen, and ask the children what they should do next. You should stay until they complete one program.

You may have to answer a few questions. But let the children try to figure out their own answers as much as possible by trying out the program and playing around with it. Then you can leave. From time to time, observe and record what the children are doing with the program. You may also want to tape-record the conversation of pairs of children when you are not in the center.

Once the children are comfortable, let them use the computer on their own. If you remain in the center, they will become dependent upon you for help in operating the program. They need to become independent in using computers just as they do with blocks and puzzles and paints. That is one of the purposes for having a computer in an early childhood classroom: to stimulate children to explore and problem solve on their own. As you circulate throughout the room during the free-choice time, keep an eye on the children in the Computer Center, dropping in from time to time to comment on what they are doing, but mainly allowing them to manage independently.

Try to integrate every computer program you use into the rest of the curriculum. Look closely at the computer program to decide in what ways the contents of a particular program can be used in other learning centers, or to see what materials from other centers can be brought into the Computer Center

Children need to become independent in using computers just as they do with blocks, puzzles, and paints.

while a certain program is being used. For instance, **children's picture books can be found that correspond to the contents of many computer programs.** Children who are **waiting for their turn at the computer can be looking at such books**.

Be sure you have previewed all the programs you use. Most young children's programs use spoken directions, but if there are any written directions on the screen, you may have to point out the meanings of the words at first. As you preview each program, be sure to write down the names of any books and any learning centers that can be integrated to any of the games.

Here is a simple program using the mouse that you might choose to start with. Many of the programs you obtain will work like this one does.

Millie & Bailey Preschool (Edmark)

(Put disk in disk drive; wait for program to boot up)

Scene appears of a room in Millie's (horse) and Bailey's (cat) house showing eight items that a child player can click on in any order (clockwise):

1. Duck looking into front door window

   Rhyming words game; choose picture of word that rhymes with last word of spoken and written verse.

2. Three pairs of shoes on floor near door

   Sizes game; choose correct size of shoes to fit Big, Middle, and Little characters from three shelves of shoes; when shelves are empty game repeats.

   Integrate:

   Dramatic Play Center—pretend shoe store

   Book or Computer Center—read shoe book:

   > *My Best Shoes* (Burton, 1994)

   > *New Shoes for Silvia* (Hurwitz, 1993)

   > *My Shoes Take Me Where I Want to Go* (Richmond, 2006)

   > *Two Pairs of Shoes* (Sanderson, 1990)

3. Pink polka-dot cartoon bug on floor

   Numbers game; make a bug

   Integrate:

   Science Center—collect bugs on field trip

4. Blue cash register on table

   Number machine game; press number key; items come out of drawer

   Integrate:

   Math Center—bring in toy cash register and play coins

5. Crayons and greeting card on floor

Card-making game; colors; words

Integrate:

Art or Writing Center—make greeting cards

6. Shelf on wall holding books

Integrate:

Book or Art Center—make a book

7. Pink computer on stand with ABC on monitor

Letter key game

Integrate:

Writing Center—play with alphabet letters

8. Mouse in mouse hole in wall

Shapes game; build a mouse house using squares, rectangles, triangles, and circles

Integrate:

Block Center: build houses for toy animal figures

ACTIVITIES TO PROMOTE SOCIAL DEVELOPMENT

The development of social skills in an early childhood classroom involves young children learning to get along with each other. This means they need to learn to share equipment and materials, to take turns using favorite toys and activities, and to work and play in cooperation with others. Such behavior is not all that easy for egocentric young 3-, 4-, or 5-year-olds to accomplish. After all, they are at the age and stage of thinking that everything revolves around them. Your classroom may be their first group learning experience outside the home.

How are they to deal with the idea that not every piece of equipment is theirs to use when they want it? How can they resolve the problem of not being first every time? And what should they do when they must share a favorite toy or activity with another child?

The Computer Center is a wonderful practice area for social skills to be worked out by the children themselves; that is why it is essential to set up the computer for two children to use at a time. Because the computer often becomes one of the favorite pieces of equipment in the classroom, there is a strong motivation on the children's part to work out the sharing and turn-taking necessary for them to use it.

Swaminathan and Wright (2003) report that "the social effects of having computers in the classroom have been strongly positive. Computers provide opportunities to build social skills, even facilitating social interaction for shy children and those who haven't found their niche" (p. 140). Other researchers have found that collaborative work on the computer can increase interaction "between children with disabilities and their typically developing peers" (Clements & Sarama, 2003, p. 35).

Turn-Taking

Your self-regulating devices at the entrance to the Computer Center can begin the process of helping children learn to take turns. A child who wants to use the computer must choose one of the two "computer necklaces." If they are already taken, the child can sign up for a turn or take a numbered ticket for a turn. In the meantime, if a child has a ticket, he can stand behind the computer operators and watch while waiting for his turn. When it is his turn, the child can put on the computer necklace and return the ticket to the ticket envelope at the entrance to the Computer Center for the next child.

Once the two children are seated in front of the computer, other social tasks await them. Who gets to turn on the machine? Who chooses the program? Who gets to click the mouse? How many clicks can one child make before the second child gets a turn? Discussion, compromise, and agreement are all part of using a classroom computer.

The computer programs you will be using are educational programs appropriate for young children. They are not arcade-type games. They are not games where the child wins or loses, nor is it really necessary to have two children using a keyboard or mouse in order for the program to work. We suggest having two children use a program as partners in order for them to learn and practice the social skills necessary for cooperative use, as well as for peer teaching.

At the outset, one of the classroom adults may need to assist the children to get them going. The adult can suggest, for example, that Sondra put the disk in and turn on the computer while Darnell clicks the mouse. The number of mouse clicks each partner gets per turn can depend upon the computer program.

On the other hand, the children themselves may want to work out their own turn-taking. If one child takes too long or makes too many mouse clicks, the other child will soon complain or step in. We were impressed with how youngsters were able to work out turn-taking in one preschool. In the beginning, certain children seemed to dominate.

We observed one girl who completely dominated her partner during her first computer experience. Even when she was waiting for her turn, she would reach over a seated child's shoulder and click the mouse to see what would happen. Imagine our surprise on the second day, after she had insisted on playing the computer game first, when she finally turned around, noticed how many children were waiting for turns, and remarked: "Well, I've been playing long enough. Let me let somebody else take a turn" (Beaty & Tucker, 1987, p. 41).

Computer specialists also note: "Teachers can expect children's interaction styles to change as they gain experience, progressing from turn-taking to peer teaching to peer collaboration. This occurs even among preschoolers, although the pattern also follows a developmental trend; preschoolers typically engage in turn taking and peer teaching, whereas primary grade children engage in more collaborative interactions" (Clements, Nastasi, & Swaminathan, 1993, p. 61).

Read a Book

For children who always rush to be the first in line or have trouble taking turns, **now is the time to read the hilarious story *Me First*** (Lester, 1992) about Pinkerton, the fat little Pig Scout who always has to be first no matter whose snout he steps on. One day, when his Scout troop takes a trip to the beach, he hears someone call "Who would care for a sandwich?" Of course he rushes ahead of everybody only to find a sand witch who makes him care for her until he learns his lesson about pushing ahead to be first.

ACTIVITIES TO PROMOTE PHYSICAL DEVELOPMENT

Although we seldom think about computers as promoters of a child's physical development, there are two important areas of such development where appropriate computer programs can contribute: eye-hand coordination and visual discrimination.

Eye-Hand Coordination

This small-motor manipulation skill is an important one for young children to develop. They must learn to control fine movements of hands and fingers according to visual clues their eyes detect. Such coordination will lead them into handling writing implements and eventually into reading.

There are a number of computer programs promoting eye-hand coordination that can be integrated into the self-directed curriculum described here. Some of the simplest ones are coloring programs that move the cursor with an external mouse. Using a mouse to move the cursor in any program gives youngsters practice in eye-hand coordination. Specific coloring programs are discussed in chapter 8.

Visual Discrimination

Discriminating shape, size, and color with the eyes can be both a physical skill and a cognitive ability. There are many computer programs designed to help children discriminate visually. Here we look at a computer program that asks children to find alphabet letters hidden within a scene.

~~~~~

Alphabet Express Preschool (School Zone)

An alligator train conductor welcomes you to the program, asking you to type in your name or three favorite letters (on the keyboard). The scene is a train at a station with icons along the side to click on with a mouse to start or stop the program or ask for help from the alligator. Of the four programs contained on this disk, you should choose the hidden letters game to test your (or your children's) visual discrimination. Colorful scenes with cartoon animals swimming in a pool, eating at a restaurant, or riding through the desert appear with three different alphabet letters at the top of each scene that the player must find imbedded in the scene. Sounds simple, but even an adult may have trouble locating each letter. Children love it.

To make the task more difficult, additional letters are added.

Integrate:

Use one particular center or the entire classroom to integrate this program by **playing find-the-hidden-object game in the classroom** or reading a book involving the listener in using the same visual discrimination skill.

~~~~~

Read a Book

Put books featuring hidden objects in the Computer Center when a program like this is being used. Children enjoy trying to find Anthony Ant in the maze of underground chambers on every page of *Find Anthony Ant* (Philpot & Philpot, 2006). An illustrated rhyme at the top of each page shows listeners three possibilities to look for. Children love to zero in closely to find the illusive bug in all the underground tunnels. A magnifying glass might help.

Finding a huge moose, on the other hand, should certainly not be difficult in *Looking for a Moose* (Root, 2006). But the four multiethnic children who traipse through the woods, the swamp, the bushes, and up the hillside miss all the signs and are ready to give up until they hear its "oo-roog" call. What about your youngsters? Can they find him before the book ends? How was he able to hide?

Large-Motor Activities

Some computer programs do, in fact, promote the large-motor aspects of physical development. In the CD-ROM Living Books in English and Spanish, *The Tortoise and the Hare* (The Learning Company), the Hare stops to show off some of his favorite moves because he is so far ahead of the Tortoise: skip, jump, hop, spring, sprint, lope. Afterwards have your children show off their own favorite moves, and reenact the story if they want. Bring in a camcorder and make a video of them. Have children tell what moves they are making, and of course let chidren and their parents view the completed video.

Integrate:

Be sure to have the book *The Tortoise and the Hare* available in the Computer Center and Book Center, as well. Children need to have hands-on experiences with actual books after seeing such stories on the computer screen.

ACTIVITIES TO PROMOTE COGNITIVE DEVELOPMENT

Most computer programs designed to promote cognitive skills are found on disks containing several games featuring a beloved character such as Mickey Mouse or Winnie the Pooh. Children find such software an appealing approach to learning shapes, sizes, colors, opposites, matching, classifying, counting, measuring, estimating, sequencing, problem solving, and memory skills.

~~~~~

Disney Learning Preschool

For example, the set *Disney Learning Preschool* (English, Spanish, & French) contains two disks with several games that promote cognitive development. On the *Winnie the Pooh* disk, "Toy Tumble" promotes categorization and deductive reasoning in its game of putting Roo's things in their proper chests. When a player clicks on the tumbled-up chests shown on the initial scene, three chests at a time appear with open covers showing various scenes: for example, winter, baseball, summer. On the ground in front of the chests are articles that need to be placed in their proper chest. Players click on an article and move it into its proper chest: for example, a baseball glove into the baseball chest. This activity is easy at first but becomes more difficult as the game progresses. Pooh makes helpful comments.

Discrimination and matching are skills promoted in the "Owl's Family Tree" game. The player must click on one of the loose photos at the right and move it to the correct blank space in the photo album next to the photo it best resembles. This is not an easy task for many preschool children because the photos are so similar. A teacher may need to "walk" the child through the game until he or she catches on.

Integrate:

Be sure to have lotto games in the Manipulative/Math Center when computer matching games are being used. Matching lotto cards with one another or with similar pictures on a lotto board are favorite activities for many children. **Make your own lotto cards** by cutting out sets of similar pictures and mounting them on cardboard cards. Catalogs from toy stores, department stores, and car dealers are good sources for lotto game pictures; or make a wonderful matching game by **printing out and laminating several digital photos of each child**. Children love to match their own photos.

When Winnie the Pooh is featured on computer games, be sure you have one or more Winnie the Pooh storybooks available in the Computer Center and Book

Center, as well as Winnie the Pooh and his friends stuffed animal dolls to go along with the stories. Children may want to make up and record their own Pooh adventures.

~~~~~

Research on the cognitive impact of computers shows specific gains. Swaminathan and Wright (2003) report: "Preschoolers who used computers with supporting activities showed significantly greater developmental gains than did those without computer experience. These children showed gains in intelligence, structural knowledge, nonverbal and verbal skills, long-term memory, and problem solving" (p. 139). Clements and Sarama (2003) believe that good software "encourages children to talk about their work as well as engage in more advanced cognitive types of play than they do in other centers" (p. 35).

ACTIVITIES TO PROMOTE LANGUAGE DEVELOPMENT

When pairs of children operate the computer together, every program they use promotes language development. Clements and Sarama (2003) found that: "Preschoolers' language activity, measured as words spoken per minute, is almost twice as high at the computer as at any other activity, including play dough, blocks, art, or games" (p. 38). We tape-recorded children's conversations as they played together with computer programs, and were impressed with the many functions they served:

1. giving information
2. giving directions
3. asking questions
4. answering questions
5. setting turn-taking rules
6. telling the partner what the operator plans to do next
7. critiquing the partner's work
8. making comments about the program
9. making up games
10. making exclamations

On the other hand, particular programs promote certain kinds of language skills. Under this heading we focus on computer software that promotes reading and listening skills. The CD-ROM Living Books series offered by The Learning Company is one of the best sets of interactive storybooks with stories in English and Spanish. The actual books are available online or at bookstores and should be placed in the Computer Center for children to look at when the computer programs are in use. Following are the programs currently available:

Arthur's Teacher Trouble	*Harry & the Haunted House*
Arthur's Birthday	*Just Grandma & Me*
Arthur's Computer Adventure	*Little Monster at School*
Arthur's Reading Race	*Ruff's Bone*
Dr. Seuss ABC's	*Stellaluna*
Dr. Seuss Cat in the Hat	*Tortoise & the Hare*
Dr. Seuss Green Eggs & Ham	

An example of one of these interactive programs is *Just Grandma and Me*, a 12-page interactive storybook by Mercer Mayer about Little Critter's adventures during a day at the beach with Grandma. After the words of the story's page are spoken, children are free to use a mouse to click on any object illustrated and watch what happens. Clicking on Little Critter on the first page, for instance, makes him say, "How much longer do we have to wait for the bus?" Clicking on the corner of the page makes it turn to the next page.

Each page has up to 20 hidden items for children to discover. Afterwards they can **make up their own stories about what they saw when they went to the beach** with Little Critter and his Grandma. It is a highly engaging program that can be used with ease by young children to explore the computer. Best of all, it comes in two languages—English and Spanish on the same disk—as do all of the Living Books, so children can hear what the same words sound like in another language.

Whatever story programs you use, be sure to integrate them into the entire curriculum. When dinosaur computer programs are in use, put up pictures and posters of dinosaurs, for instance. Play games and sing songs about these beasts. Have art projects that depict them and construction activities that build them a place. Then be sure to tape-record the children's own stories or write them down through dictation on easel paper or in personal books for them to share with others.

ACTIVITIES TO PROMOTE CREATIVE DEVELOPMENT

Can computer programs really be creative? We were at first surprised to find that young children are able to use even the most uncreative computer programs in the most imaginative ways. But then we realized that this is exactly what youngsters do with every material or piece of equipment they come across: They treat it playfully as they experiment to figure out what it can do, and then use it in all sorts of new and unexpected ways.

That is what creativity is all about: making use of ordinary things in extraordinary ways. In the hands of young children, every computer program becomes creative. They learn how it works through manipulation; they master its intricacies through repetition; and then they go on to add their own creative meanings. We watched children make up their own games, in fact, for every program they mastered.

On the other hand, there are certain pieces of software designed specifically to promote creativity. These include many of the art programs, a few of the music programs, and some of the story programs already discussed. A listing of such programs follows with more details of specific programs in the appropriate chapters.

Drawing/Coloring Programs

Millie & Bailey Preschool
 Crayons & Cards
Curious George 3-Pack Collection
 Curious George Paint & Print Studio
Disney Learning Preschool
 Winnie the Pooh Preschool
 "Piglet's Pictures"
 Mickey Mouse Preschool
 "Goofy's Body Shop"
 "Gas Pump"
Jumpstart Advanced Preschool
 Art for Fun

Music Programs

Much of the educational music software currently available is for children older than preschoolers. Some general programs, however, include music in their letters, numbers, and matching games.

Disney Learning Preschool
 Disney's Mickey Mouse Preschool
 "Tune-Up Time"
Jumpstart Advanced Preschool
 TV Game
 Music Maker

ACTIVITIES TO PROMOTE EMOTIONAL DEVELOPMENT

Being able to use the computer—this wonderful and complicated adult instrument—on their own gives young children a bigger ego boost than any single computer program could hope to do. When child operators find that computers are not merely passive television-screen-type machines, but interactive instruments with keys they can use to control what happens, then marvelous things do happen! Even learning-impaired children actually learn. Shy children blossom. All of the others have the same opportunity to work independently and to be successful in an activity of their own choosing. Swaminathan and Wright (2003) agree, reporting that "Computers can also give a sense of control and self-worth to children hitherto lacking in self-esteem" (p. 140).

Being able to use the computer on his own gives the young child a bigger ego boost than any single computer program could hope to do.

Thus teachers need not concern themselves with particular activities or software to promote the children's self-image. Instead, they should set up the Computer Center for self-directed learning to take place. The rest is up to the children.

THE TEACHER'S ROLE IN THE COMPUTER CENTER

Observing Developmental Levels

One of the great advantages of having a computer in an early childhood classroom is the ease of observation it affords the adult. When children are engrossed in operating a computer program, they are frequently oblivious to everything around them. There they are in one place, undisturbed by events swirling around them. Teachers and assistants can **make wonderful, unobtrusive observations at almost any time and for as long as necessary.** Furthermore, if the adult knows what to look for, a great deal of information on children's developmental levels can be gained. Table 4-1 shows children's levels of interaction with computer programs.

After they have finally mastered the "rules" for a program by clicking the mouse or pressing the letter keys over and over, children begin playing their own games with their favorite graphics. They have arrived at the meaning level of interaction. We watched children in four different classrooms in three different schools invent and play the identical type of meaning-level game with *Stickybear ABC.* They called it "I Caught You" or "I Stopped You." A child would press the

Table 4-1 Computer Programs: Levels of Interaction

Manipulation Level
Plays with keys, spacebar, or mouse
"Piano plays" the keys
Pushes keys or clicks mouse and laughs
May interfere with partner's turn
Makes no connection with mouse clicks and screen graphics
Clicks mouse randomly without waiting for something to happen on screen

Mastery Level
Pushes same keys or clicks mouse over and over
Makes same graphic or sound appear repeatedly
Clicks mouse on same object in graphic repeatedly
Uses same program in same way again and again

Meaning Level
Chooses favorite graphic or program and adds new meaning to it (e.g., makes a game of it)
Tells what he/she is going to do before doing it
Talks about what he/she is creating; what graphic means
Makes up story about graphic; pretends about it
Takes role involved in graphics he/she is creating
Becomes involved in peer teaching

letter either once or twice to bring up the wanted graphic, and then one or the other would try to press the space bar to stop the animation before something happened. For instance, they would watch the egg bounce but try to stop it from breaking. The one who was successful would call out, "I caught you!" and laugh. They also tried to stop the cloud in "I" for "island" from reaching the palm tree on the island; to stop the grass in "G" from growing to the top of the screen; and to stop Mama and Papa Stickybear in "K" from kissing.

It is possible to observe these levels quite clearly in all of the computer programs the children use. **Placing a tape recorder on the table next to the computer makes it possible to record children's remarks**, as well. New words and the creative use of old words are often apparent. Not every child will reach the meaning level with every program; some may not reach this level with any program. But the number of children who progress through all three levels with remarkable speed is astounding.

RECORDING ON THE CHILD INTERACTION FORM

The observer in the Computer Center can record the actions and words of each pair of children using the computer on the same Child Interaction Form. The teacher can then use this developmental information to plan activities for individual children and small groups both in the Computer Center and in the classroom at large.

For example, one teacher's observations of Maria and Rhonda playing with computer programs for about 10 minutes are as follows.

Maria and Rhonda came into the Computer Center with the two "computer necklaces" around their necks, the self-regulating method that gives children a turn in this center. Maria took the *Stickybear ABC* program off the shelf and inserted it into the disk drive. Both girls sat down in front of the computer, but it was Maria who turned on the computer. They began pressing keys one at a time and waiting for a graphic to appear on the monitor screen. Maria took charge, taking the first turn. She searched the keyboard and finally pressed *M*. A graphic showing a mountain with a floating cloud appeared. "That's me!" she said, and laughed. Rhonda pressed several keys without looking at the keyboard. Maria said, "No, you have to press one." The graphic of an octopus doing a dance came on the screen. Both girls laughed and Maria started bouncing around in her seat doing a sort of dance like the octopus. "It's an octopus," laughed Maria.

Rhonda started to press another key, but Maria held her off, saying, "It's my turn. It's my turn." She searched the keyboard for some time, finally pressing *V*. A graphic showing vegetables on a table appeared, but before any action could occur on the screen, Maria pressed *V* again, and a graphic appeared showing a volcano with a bubbling top and a cloud floating across the screen. Maria laughed and said, "That's me. That's me blowing my top!" Rhonda tried to press a key, but Maria reached over and pressed one without looking, saying, "I stopped it!" (probably meaning that she stopped the cloud from reaching the volcano).

The two girls continued pressing keys, with Maria searching for the letter key she wanted and making comments about the graphic each letter produced. Rhonda, on the other hand, pressed keys without looking or commenting. Whenever she got the chance, Maria pressed a key to stop the action of Rhonda's graphic, saying, "I stopped it again!" They finally changed programs to *Stickybear Numbers*, but neither girl could make it work, because they were not pressing the number keys. Rachel and Kurt came into the Computer Center to watch, Rachel said, "I know how to do it" and "It's our turn now," so the first two gave up their seats and their computer necklaces.

The teacher recorded on the Child Interaction Form as shown in Table 4-2. On the back of the Child Interaction Form the teacher recorded the following interpretation of her observation, as well as suggested plans for these two children.

Child __Maria, Rhonda__   Observer __D.B.__

Center __Computer__   Date __10/21__

CHILD INTERACTION FORM
With Materials

Manipulation Level   Actions/Words

(Child moves materials around
without using them as intended.)

Rhonda presses various keys for "Stickybear ABC" and "Numbers" without looking. Maria preesses 1 key at a time for "Numbers" but not a number key.

Mastery Level   Actions/Words

(Child uses materials
as intended, over and over.)

Maria has mastered "Stickybear ABC" and knows the letters A,C,D,M,O,V

Meaning Level   Actions/Words

(Child uses materials in
new and creative ways.)

Maria brings up graphics she wants by pressing proper key; then plays "I stopped it" by pressing key to stop action. She calls M her letter and identifies self as a mountain ("That's me!") and a volcano ("That's me blowing my top!").

With Other Children

Solitary Play   Actions/Words

(Child plays with
materials by self.)

Parallel Play   Actions/Words

(Child next to others with same
materials but not involved with them.)

Rhonda plays next to Maria but not with her or helping her.

Cooperative Play   Actions/Words

(Child plays together with
others and same materials.)

Maria tries to involve Rhonda in her game; she also comments on Rhonda's graphics ("It's an octopus").

Table 4-2   Child Interaction Form: Computer.

Accomplishments:

Maria knows how to insert disk and turn on computer.

Maria understands one-key pressing and cause and effect.

Maria controls the graphics on *Stickybear ABC* and plays a game with them.

Maria and Rhonda both take turns.

Needs:

Rhonda needs more time playing with one program.

Maria is ready to apply her skills to other programs.

Plans:

Encourage both girls to continue playing together as well as with others on the computer.

Encourage Rhonda to pair with another child who is working at the manipulative level (perhaps Jean?).

INTERACTING WITH COMPUTER USERS

As discussed previously, teachers should introduce a new computer program to small groups of children in the Computer Center. Talk with the children about its subject or content. Let teams of children try it out. Point out the books or activities that support the new software. Let this group of children continue working with the computer for the first day. On the next day have another group of children learn to use this program. Continue day by day until everyone who wants to has had a chance to use the program.

When introducing a new program, **it is usually best to have only this program available in the Computer Center for the first week.** Observant teachers can learn to tell when it is time to introduce a new program appropriate for current curriculum activities and the children's computer abilities. Because some programs are more complicated to use than others, it is important to begin with simpler ones.

How long at a time should a child use the computer? **It is better that two children have a long enough time** on the computer to understand what they are doing **than that everyone has equal turns** of, say, five minutes each. We have found that in classes where teachers regulate turn-taking, giving everyone equal but short amounts of time, it takes the children a great deal longer to learn how programs work. Children who have plenty of time at one sitting progress more quickly and come away with a real understanding of the programs.

One adult on the classroom team should be identified as the computer teacher. This teacher can then supervise this learning center, not necessarily closely, but with an eye to making sure all is going well. Some computer programs do not work as well as they should. Sometimes children have difficulty changing programs. The Computer Center teacher can come to the rescue when it seems necessary.

Children understand that computers are complex and expensive machines. They are excited and pleased to be allowed to use one in the classroom. But to be secure in the use of the computer, children should feel that they can turn to one of the adults when they need help. Both they and the other classroom staff can thus be assured that good things are happening with children in this new and dynamic classroom learning center as a part of the Appropriate Practices Curriculum.

IDEAS IN CHAPTER 4

1. *Choosing appropriate software*
   a. Try out the software yourself and with children if possible
   b. Choose software by a dependable brand name; by the familiar characters in it; or by the subject matter
   c. Be sure it meets specific criteria

2. *Setting up the Computer Center*
   a. Should occupy a space sectioned off from other centers
   b. Wall space can display rules chart, photos, book jackets
   c. May include typewriter and storybook
   d. May combine Computer Center with Writing Center

3. *Children choosing and using Computer Center*
   a. Use Computer Center in pairs
   b. Have waiting children "sign up" for turns
   c. Show small groups how computer works
   d. Have illustrated rules chart
   e. Use only one computer program for a week or so at first
   f. Begin with simple programs first
   g. Have child use "computer finger" to press one key at a time
   h. Have child click mouse and wait to see what happens
   i. Find picture books to correspond to computer programs
   j. Read "Me First" book for turn-taking problems
   k. Use visual discrimination programs and play find-the-hidden-object

l. Use matching programs and make lotto cards

m. Print out and laminate several photos of each child

n. Use Living Books program and later have child make up own story

4. *Teacher's role*

   a. Observe and record children using computer

   b. Put tape recorder near computer and record children's conversations

   c. Have only new program available for first week

   d. Give children enough time to understand program

   e. Have one adult designated as computer teacher

DISCUSSION QUESTIONS

1. How does the computer's style of interaction favor young children's learning style?

2. How is a computer an equalizer for children with different backgrounds?

3. What equipment should be in an early childhood computer center? Why?

4. What are the most important considerations when purchasing software for preschool children? Why?

5. How should a teacher be involved in the Computer Center?

TRY IT YOURSELF

1. Set up your computer area with interesting pictures and activities to support your latest piece of software.

2. Observe and record children using your computer games to see what developmental levels they have attained. How can you tell?

3. Use a tape recorder to record children's language at the computer. What new words or ideas are they expressing?

4. Introduce a new computer program and help children get started.

5. Read one of the suggested books to accompany a new computer program the children are using, and then set up a follow-up activity to integrate this program into another learning center.

REFERENCES CITED

Banet, B. (1978) Computers and early learning. *Creative Computing, 4*(5), 90–94.

Beaty, J. J. & Tucker, W. H. (1987). *The computer as a paintbrush.* Upper Saddle River, NJ: Merrill/Prentice Hall.

Bewick, C. J. & Kostelnik, M. (*2004*). Educating early childhood teachers about computers. *Young Children, 59*(3), 26–29.

Blagojevic, B. (2003). Funding technology: Does it make cents? *Young Children 58*(6), 28–33.

Clements, D. H., Nastasi, B. K., & Swaminathan, S. (1993). Young children and computers: Crossroads and directions from research, *Young Children, 48*(2), 56–64.

Clements, D. H. & Sarama, J. (2003). Young children and technology: What does the research say? *Young children 58*(6), 34–40.

Lee, M W. (1983). *Early childhood education and microcomputers.* ERIC Documents, ED 23150.

Lipinski, J. M., Nida, R. E., Shade, D. D., & Watson, J. A. (1984). *Competence, gender, and preschoolers' free play choices when a computer is present in the classroom.* ERIC Documents, ED 243.609.

Swaminathan, S. & Wright, J. (2003). Educational technology in the early and primary years. In J. P. Isenberg & M. R. Jalongo (Eds.), *Major trends and issues in early childhood education* (pp. 136–149). New York: Teachers College Press.

Other Sources

Fischer, M. A. & Gillespie, C. W. (2003). One Head Start Classroom's Experience: Computers and young children's development. *Young Children 58*(4), 85–91.

Frost, J. L., Wortham, S. C., & Reifel, S. (2005). *Play and child development.* Upper Saddle River, NJ: Merrill/Prentice Hall.

Hendrick, J. (2003). *Total learning: Developmental curriculum for the young child.* Upper Saddle River, NJ: Merrill/Prentice Hall.

Mulligan, S. A. (2003). Assistive technology: Supporting participation of children with disabilities. *Young Children 58*(6), 50–52.

Ray, J. A. & Shelton, D. (2004). E-pals: Connecting with families through technology. *Young Children 59*(3), 30–32.

Robinson, L. (2003). Technology as a scaffold for emergent literacy: Interactive storybooks for toddlers. *Young Children 58*(6), 42–48.

Wellhousen, K. & Crowther, I. (2004). *Creating effective learning environments*. Clifton Park, NY: Cengage Learning.

Wright, J. L. & Shade, D. D. (Eds.). (1994). *Young children: Active learners in a technological age*. Washington, DC: National Association for the Education of Young Children.

Children's Books

Burton, M. R. (1994). *My best shoes*. New York: Tambourine Books.*

Cronin, D. (2000). *Click, clack, moo, cows that type*. New York: Simon & Schuster.

Hurwitz, J. (1993). *New shoes for Silvia*. New York: Morrow Junior Books.*

Lester, H. (1992). *Me first*. Boston: Houghton Mifflin.

Philpot, L. & Philpot, G. (2006). *Find Anthony Ant*. New York: Sterling.

Richmond, M. (2006). *My shoes take me where I want to go*. Minneapolis, MN: Richmond Studios.

Root, P. (2006). *Looking for a moose*. Cambridge, MA: Candlewick.

Sanderson, E. (1990). *Two pairs of shoes*. Berkeley, CA: Oyate.*

Note: Asterisk represents multicultural book.

Children's Computer Programs

Alphabet Express Preschool

Arthur's Preschool

Curious George 3-Pack Collection

Disney Learning Preschool

Disney's Mickey Mouse Preschool

Dr. Seuss Preschool

Jumpstart Advanced Preschool

Madeline Preschool

Just Grandma and Me

Millie & Bailey Preschool

Reader Rabbits Preschool

Tortoise & the Hare

    (All computer programs from online sources)

    www.childrenssoftwareonline.com

    www.classsource.com

    www.kidsclick.com

    www.superkids.com

MATH IN PRESCHOOL PROGRAMS

"Surely preschool children do not have to learn such a difficult subject as mathematics until they are in first grade!" you may hear certain adults exclaim when you talk about your preschool math activities. "Why, I would put it off as long as I could!"

People who express such sentiments may not be familiar with math for young children. They may not realize how excited preschool children can become over numbers. And they may not know that for young children at this stage of their learning, math is manipulative.

Hirsh-Pasek and Golinkoff (2003) tell us about the surprising findings that neuroscientists have discovered about children and their math knowledge: "One of their most important findings is that the foundation for all mathematical learning takes place in infancy and early childhood, constructed by children around the world, regardless of their parentage. In fact, we believe that nature has programmed children to learn about numbers" (p. 42). They continue, telling us: "This knowledge is based on things that children like to do on their own, unsupervised, with whatever objects they can lay their hands on. In other words, children come to these principles through that magical activity we call *play*" (p. 48).

Our Self-Directed Learning Environment supports this concept precisely. Math in our preschool program involves children playing around with interesting collections of objects: sets of little toy cars and trucks; a bucketful of seashells; a basket of buttons; a box of empty plastic bottles of all kinds and the bottle tops to screw on them; a set of used-up colored markers and the colored caps that match them; a board full of bolts of all sizes and a box of nuts to fit them; a pail of smooth beach pebbles; a bunch of keys and locks; a bag of acorns, buckeyes, and hickory nuts; a set

NUMBERS

(FINGER PLAY)

One, one,
    See me run!

Two , two,
    You come too!

Three, three,
    Up a tree!

Four, four,
    Down once more!

Five, five,
    See me dive!

Six, six,
    Watch my tricks!

Seven, seven,
    Here comes Kevin!

Eight, eight,
    Don't be late!

Nine, nine,
    Just on time!

Ten, ten,
    Home again!

of colored golf tees; a pan of uncooked pasta in many shapes; and a set of miniature dinosaurs.

Our program also involves the children in playing with some fascinating games: picture dominoes, lotto cards, puzzles, color bingo, and tic-tac-toe. It involves manipulating stacking blocks, nesting cubes, shape blocks, color bricks, snap blocks, bristle blocks, parquetry blocks, slotted wheels, Peg-Boards, geoboards, an abacus, lacing dolls, dressing frames, cylinder boards, Cuisenaire™ rods, and giant dice. It involves children in reading and listening to books, using computer games, and playing with the toy cash register.

If such activities do not stimulate your children's interest in math—if such materials do not pique your own interest—then you need to learn something more about the importance of math in all of our lives, how crucial it is that young children get a good start in the basic pre-math skills, and how critical it is that young children not start out with negative attitudes toward math.

ATTITUDES ABOUT MATH

How do you feel about math? It is important to ask yourself that question—and to answer it honestly. Too many of us have to admit to a strong negative feeling about mathematics. Why is that? Is it because of unfortunate school experiences we have encountered with math? Is it because we were bored with math in school, or did poorly in math classes, or even failed? If such is the case, then we need to be sure that these attitudes are not passed on to our children. Our children should come to love math and be successful with it. They should **feel free to explore math just as they do blocks**. They should learn to **have fun with numbers**.

"Fun with numbers?" you may respond. "How can anyone have fun with numbers?" Use your imagination. At the preschool level, children can eat numbers, sing them, dance them, and build with them! They can count numbers, sort numbers, draw numbers, clap hands to numbers, fingerplay with numbers, paint numbers, weigh numbers, dissolve numbers, and pile up numbers into miniature mountains! If you provide such activities for your children, they should learn to love and not to fear mathematics. If you make math meaningful for your youngsters, they should develop a "math mania," not a math anxiety.

We desperately need young people who have grown up comfortable with math. Both the world of today and of the future depend upon young people with math ability to understand the high-tech society we have created. It starts with young children. Make math magical for them!

PRESCHOOL CHILD DEVELOPMENT

Swiss psychologist Jean Piaget spent his life observing and interviewing children to determine how they acquire knowledge. His theories have been accepted by most early childhood specialists, and refined by cognitive psychologists and modern neuroscientists specializing in information-processing skills. As previously noted, Piaget describes three kinds of knowledge: *physical knowledge* that young children build when they interact externally through their five senses with concrete objects in their environment; *logical-mathematical knowledge* that children build internally when they interpret their physical knowledge and extract relationships about the objects they have acted upon; and *social-conventional knowledge* that children learn when they come into contact with the names given to numbers by their society (Kamii, 2005).

For example, infants and young children find out physically about rubber balls by chewing on them, squeezing them, smelling them, dropping them, rolling them, hitting them, and throwing them. They process this information mentally and apply it to other round objects and other kinds of balls, making mental comparisons and noting similarities and differences. The knowledge they have thus acquired is stored in their brains to be drawn on when needed, or refined when new facts are added.

Neither physical knowledge nor logical-mathematical knowledge can really be separated in a child; they develop together and depend upon one another. Both kinds of knowledge depend upon manipulation. Children need to manipulate the objects in their environment in order to provide their brains with the sensory stimuli necessary to form logical thought. That is why the math skills promoted in your

As children handle the materials you provide, they will be strengthening their finger muscles and developing eye-hand coordination along with the logical-mathematical knowledge they will acquire.

classroom need to be manipulative. As Gellens (2005) points out: "Young children learn best through play while manipulating real objects" (p. 20).

Your Manipulative/Math Center will also help children develop good small-motor coordination. As children handle the materials and involve themselves with activities you provide, they will be strengthening their finger muscles and developing eye-hand coordination along with the logical-mathematical knowledge they will acquire.

MATH FOR PRESCHOOL CHILDREN

The particular basic pre-math concepts that preschool children need to learn involve the following four areas:

1. **Classification:** the ability to group objects that have common characteristics.
2. **Ordering:** the ability to order or arrange objects in a series by size, texture, taste, color, sound, and so on, in ascending or descending order.
3. **Patterning:** the ability to recognize and create a series of objects, words, sounds, or colors that occur in a certain order and are repeated.
4. **Numbering:** the ability to name numbers, count in a fixed sequence, and apply this ability to one object at a time, arriving at a total.

Classification

The ability to sort out one thing from another on the basis of its characteristics is one of the first skills that the human brain acquires. Classification involves visual perception. Children need to discriminate visually among various shapes, sizes, and colors. Then they need to compare one object with another. They learn that some things are alike and others are different. What makes them this way? Their brains extract this information as children handle and interact and look at the things in their environment.

To help young children develop this ability to classify, you need to **provide them with playful opportunities to practice handling, identifying, and naming sizes, shapes, and colors. Start with one concept at a time**, such as shapes—a circle, then a square, then a rectangle, and finally a triangle. Then go on to the next concept: size and, finally, color—one at a time. Later, as children develop the ability to classify, they can try applying their knowledge to sorting out items with more than one attribute alike; for instance, all of the objects that are red and at the same time are also square. These activities, you understand, are not lessons, but play activities that you set up in the Manipulative/Math Center, and that children choose to do on their own. They are the origins of geometrical thinking (i.e., geometry) for preschoolers (Seefeldt & Wasik, 2006).

For practice, put out large numbers of colored pattern blocks in squares, rectangles, triangles, and circles. Let children sort them by shape, size, and color. Let them trace their shapes and color them in the Art Center. Then they can cut them out and paste them on collages. Let them look for the various shapes around the classroom, on clothing, on food containers, and on signs outside. Make up songs about shapes and colors and sing them in the Music Center. Play a CD about shapes and colors. *Sing to Learn* (#WR203D) and *Favorite Pre-K Songs* (#FR726D) from Lakeshore (1-800-778-4456) are wonderful examples.

How long should they spend on one concept? Spend as long as it takes the children in your classroom to absorb it—at least a week at a time and maybe more for some concepts. Some children will grasp the concept of "circle" immediately. Perhaps they have already learned it at home. Others will take longer, according to their level of development. **Give them all time. There is no need to hurry**. Even those who understand the concept can have the fun of practicing and applying it over and over. Remember, mastery takes time and repetition.

Once children can recognize the basic shapes through hands-on manipulation of three-dimensional objects, put on a computer program that helps them apply this knowledge. In *Millie & Bailey Preschool*, clicking on the mouse in the hole on the menu scene brings up a shapes game where children use squares, rectangles, triangles, and circles to build a mouse house.

Read a Book

Another follow-up for shape activities is *My Painted House, My Friendly Chicken, and Me* (Angelou, 1994). It takes the reader to South Africa in glorious color photos where Thandi, a real Ndebele girl, narrates the story of her daily life in her village. All Ndebele women paint the outside walls of their houses in brilliantly colored geometric shapes and designs with chicken feather paintbrushes. Color photos of the houses show the designs and how Thandi learns to paint them. What shapes can your listeners find? Would they like to make some shapes of their own and paint them in Ndebele colors?

Ordering

This second math skill involves arranging objects in an order or a series according to a certain characteristic—say, their height, or their sound, or their color—and then placing these objects in a series from first to last, from tallest to shortest, from loudest to softest, or from darkest to lightest. This is a much more complicated math skill than the first one. Young children need a great deal more knowledge and experience in order to accomplish such a task successfully. They need to be able to discriminate between objects on the basis of the special characteristic, such as height. That is, they need to recognize that among the four toy family figures in the Block Center, they are all different in height.

How do they know this? Partly through perception. They can see and thus understand that the father figure is different in height from the mother, the son, and the daughter; that the mother is different in height from the others, and that the same is true with the son and the daughter. Some children need to line up the figures

Placing graduated cylinders in the order of their sizes is helped by the sizes of the holes in the board.

beside one another to make this determination. Other children seem to recognize this difference so quickly that they are probably using intuition as well; the ability of a person to "know" something is so, without even thinking about it. Young children do not differentiate objects in the same way that older children or adults do, that is, on the basis of logical reasoning. They have not yet reached such an abstract stage in their cognitive development. Montessori materials help the youngest children by providing clues for where to place objects in a series, such as the graduated wooden cylinders being used by the girl in the photo above.

Language also plays a part in young children's ability to differentiate sizes. They need to know and understand the vocabulary involved: tall, short, big, small, tallest, shortest, and so on. The concrete materials and activities you provide help children to understand "physically" the cognitive concept of size differences and opposites through manipulation of objects. **When you talk with them about what they doing**, or when they hear other children talking, **they begin to acquire the words** to go with their actions. As these activities are repeated, children process this information internally as logical-mathematical knowledge.

To complete the task of arranging four figures in a series from the tallest to the shortest without clues, the child must recognize that not only are all the figures of different heights, but that one is the tallest of all, a second figure is taller than two others, a third figure is taller than one other, and a fourth figure is not taller than any of the others, but is the shortest. Not all children of preschool age are able to arrange objects in a series like this with accuracy. They may be able to identify the tallest figure and the shortest one, but not the ones in the middle. This is normal for preschoolers. They will eventually acquire this skill as their cognition develops through interacting with materials.

Patterning

Young children (and all of us) are surrounded by patterns, although we seldom recognize or mention them. Daily we get up, get dressed, and eat breakfast in a repeated pattern. Songs, chants, and jump rope rhymes are repeated in patterns. We talk and even think in patterns: up-down, front-back, or yes-no. The daily schedule occurs in a pattern. Rainbows are patterns of colors. Floor tiles are often laid in patterns. Look around and you will see patterns everywhere. Copley (2000) says research tells us: "focusing on the concept of patterns effectively facilitates children's ability to make generalizations about number combinations, counting strategies, and problem solving" (p. 89).

Learning about patterns helps young children predict what will happen next in a story, or even in their daily routine. Why is it so important for children to know this? Patterns serve as the cornerstone of algebraic thinking, Taylor-Cox (2003) tells us: "algebra in the early years establishes the necessary groundwork for ongoing and future mathematics learning" (p. 14). It helps set up the brain wiring for high-level thinking and problem solving. Children have learned about the attributes of objects and how they are alike or different (e.g., their shapes, size, texture, and color), and now they can play around with these objects in an entirely different way.

Children love to make patterns. It is a wonderful new math game to engage their thinking. "Let's make a pattern out of the colored cubes. Red, blue, red, blue … and what comes next? Red … you're right!" After children have had the fun of making patterns out of colored cubes, let them try unit blocks, dolls, paint jars, and hats (e.g., hard hats, soft hats). Then see if they can add a third item to carry the concept another step. Math computer games also lead children to make patterns in this manner.

Can they find patterns in the classroom? Make it a game. Put up a chart to be used with colored stickers. Each time a child identifies a pattern, let her put a colored sticker on the chart. Someone spots the squares of window glass, others see patterns on T-shirts, napkins, cars in the parking lot, and the rainbow! Now they've got the idea. Have they put their stickers on the chart in a pattern?

For the next few days you can put out the sets of little toys on the tables in the Math Center along with a sign saying: Make a Pattern with the Dinosaurs (or Farm Animals, Cars, Block People, Snap Blocks, Lego Bricks, Stringing Beads, Color Cubes).

Keep track of children who make patterns and ask them what makes theirs a pattern or what could come next in their pattern. Take digital pictures of the patterns and their creators for a Pattern Book they can assemble for all to see. Pair children who have not made a pattern with children who have, to get them started.

Read a Book

Just as colorful as the Thandi book is *Kofi and His Magic* (Angelou, 1996). Kofi is a West African boy who has learned to weave the celebrated Kente cloth by wiggling strings attached to his toes as the book photo shows. The book itself is a bazaar of Kente cloth woven with wonderful geometric patterns shown not only on its end pages but also on the brilliant wrap-around garments everyone wears. Which patterns do the children like best? Can they color or paint similar patterns in the Art Center to be cut into small rectangles of paper to wrap around the block people as African garments?

Numbering

This skill requires children to do three different things: 1) say the number names by rote in the proper order, 2) apply the number names in order to objects to find out how many there are, and 3) use the numbers in one-to-one correspondence. To perform the first skill, rote counting, children need to know the names and order of the numbers. They quickly learn this by heart almost as a one-word litany—"onetwothreefourfivesixseveneightnineten"—and will rattle it off on any occasion. The youngest children do not realize that they are saying 10 separate number names in order. They love to count like this, nevertheless, and older preschoolers often are able to count to 20 and beyond—although they often omit or mix up a number here and there.

Counting objects, the second skill, is something altogether different. Here, as before, children need to know the names and the order of the numbers. But then they need to be able to apply one number to one object when they count (one-to-one correspondence). This is more difficult for preschoolers than simply rattling off a series of numbers. Counting the number of objects is based on the concept that each successive number is one more than the previous number, and that the final number they say represents the total number of objects.

Because preschool children frequently omit a number when they count above 10, their totals are often not accurate. Even when they touch or point to each object that they are counting, somehow they often skip one. There is no need to correct them. Let them try again. They will experience more success in this kind of counting if they are also **familiar with the objects being counted**. Counting the children in one of the learning centers gives them the kind of practice that appeals to them. In addition, they need all kinds of practice with one-to-one correspondence activities.

SETTING UP THE MANIPULATIVE/MATH CENTER

It makes sense to locate an activity area like this one as close as possible to an area promoting similar skills. Children using the Manipulative/Math Center are most likely to practice their skills on the computer, or vice versa. Children using computer programs featuring opposites, matching, and memory will also want to play the matching games in the Math Center. Furthermore, they will soon be deeply involved in all sorts of activities with numbers, supported by appropriate computer programs. The self-regulating method you have put in operation throughout your program will help children to select manipulative and math activities during the free-choice period.

The center itself should be large enough to accommodate four or five children comfortably. There should be a table with four or five chairs and floor space for children who prefer to sit on the floor while they work, sectioned off with material shelves or room dividers.

Manipulative and math materials are almost unlimited. Your shelves should feature many of the items listed in Table 5-1, including a section filled with collections for sorting and matching; containers of counting objects, such as Cuisenaire™

Table 5-1 Manipulative/Math Materials

Toy cars	Keys and locks	Picture dominoes
Seashells	Golf tees	Lotto cards
Buttons	Uncooked pasta	Color bingo
Bottle tops	Slotted wheels	Tic-tac-toe
Pebbles	Giant dice	Stacking blocks
Seeds	Shape blocks	Nesting cubes
Nuts	Color bricks	Snap blocks
Toy planes	Geoboards	Parquetry blocks
Toy animals	Peg-Boards	Bristle blocks
Abacus	Game boards	Cylinder boards
Lacing dolls	Computer games	Cuisenaire™ rods
Play money	Colored chips	Toy cash register
Boxes	Sectioned boxes	Egg cartons
Cards	Paper punches	Markers and caps
Rulers	Yardstick	Carpenter's rule
Balance	Stopwatch	Kitchen timer
Hourglass	Postage meter	
Puzzles	Zipping/buttoning frames	

rods; a shelf of table blocks or building sets; several sets of puzzles; a number of board games and counting games; materials for teaching particular concepts, such as shapes and colors; eye-hand-coordination activities such as stringing beads and buttoning boards; card games, lotto games, and dominoes; all kinds of counting books, as well as size, shape, and other concept books.

Be sure to label your shelves with illustrated and lettered signs for all of your materials. Not only will children become familiar with such symbolization, but they will also be able to see what is available and later return materials to their places with greater ease. Change some of the materials from time to time as interest wanes or as new concepts are being featured throughout the program. But be sure particular materials are available for a long enough time for most of your children to become deeply involved. Also have a bulletin board or an attractive wall space to display your children's math activities.

MATH-RICH ENVIRONMENT

In addition to the math materials and activities in the Manipulative/Math Center, be sure that the entire room is a math-rich environment. We often speak of "print-rich" environments that help children emerge into literacy. The same principle applies to math. **Make yours a math-rich environment** to help the children develop logical-mathematical knowledge.

How can you encourage children to use numbers? Throughout the classroom and throughout the year, have "authentic math" activities available, such as:

telephone numbers on cards and toy telephones

calendars with removable numbers

rulers and tape measures

numbered tickets to take for a turn

a bathroom scale

number sets and magnetic boards

toy clocks in the Dramatic Play Center

measuring cups and spoons for dramatic play and cooking

stepping-stone numerals for floor play

Then, be sure to **engage the children in authentic math problem-solving questions** as you interact with individuals and small groups throughout the day. How many giant steps will it take you to walk to the door? How much did your bean plant grow since you planted it? How can you find out? How many times will the phone ring before the answering machine clicks on? Which of the guinea pigs is biggest? How can you tell? How many napkins do we need for lunch? How many days until our Thanksgiving feast?

Toy phones engage children in words and numbers.

Children often imitate things the teacher says and does. When you hear children ask one another math-type questions, such as, "Guess how many cups it will take to fill the water table bucket?" you will know that your math-rich environment has really taken hold.

ACTIVITIES TO PROMOTE PHYSICAL DEVELOPMENT

The physical development promoted within the Manipulative/Math Center is small-motor coordination, which is principally concerned with strengthening finger and wrist muscles: picking up, inserting, fastening, unfastening, zipping, buttoning, lacing, turning, and screwing.

In addition to the commercial buttoning and lacing boards, Peg-Boards, and blocks, there are many excellent homemade materials and activities you should consider. **To strengthen muscles and provide a wonderful "counter," bring in several paper punches**. It may take two hands at first for your children to punch a hole in a 3-by-5 card, but this activity is such an intriguing challenge to young children that they will eventually become experts with one hand! Let them practice on cards of different sizes, shapes, and colors in the beginning.

Then, use the paper punches to count things in the classroom. **Paste a picture or draw an outline** of a cup, a dish, an animal figure, a doll, a dress-up dress, a dinosaur figure, and so on, **on each card**. Let children choose a card, go to the part of the room where the item is located, and punch the picture card for each item they count. Accuracy in counting is not the point. Young children are only at the beginning in developing the skill of one-to-one correspondence; that is, that there should be only one hole punched for each item. Any effort they make is acceptable. Later, as they develop both small-motor and counting skills, they will become more accurate. Children can sign (scribble) their names on each of the cards they punch. These **cards can then be displayed on a "punch board" in the area**, and later pasted in a child's personal scrapbook.

Next, **have picture-punching field trips** with small groups of children, each carrying a paper punch and a picture card. You can prepare the cards ahead of time with pictures cut from magazines and catalogs. The field trips can be short ones to an area near your building. If you are near a busy street, have a picture of a car or truck or bus on each card. Let children make one punch for each vehicle that passes by. If you are near a park, then have tree, bush, or flower pictures on each card. Use school-supply catalogs to cut out pictures of playground equipment for your cards. What other items can you think of?

Finally, print a number on each of the cards and let the children punch that many holes in the card. This is the most abstract activity of all. Save this activity for the time when you are introducing number symbols and using other number symbol activities such as computer programs, magnetic numbers, and counting books.

Children with hand or arm impairments can use Magic felt-tipped pens as their hole punchers. Be sure all of your activities allow for success with all of the children, even those with special physical needs. Do your children accept children with disabilities as a matter of fact? If you treat all of your children with the same care and concern, then the youngsters should reflect this behavior with one another.

Other small-motor counting activities involving real objects or real tasks include shucking peas or beans that will later be cooked for eating. Your children can learn to **open pea and bean pods** and then extract the peas and beans. Can they **count them**? If you cooperate with them in this activity you will eventually have enough to be cooked. If there are not enough individual vegetables for everybody, how about putting the vegetables in a soup or a stew?

Children also need opportunities to pick up objects between their fingers that are larger or heavier than peas and beans. Be sure to **have some kinds of knobbed materials on your manipulative shelves**. Puzzle pieces with knobs on one side give them that practice; Montessori-type graduated cylinders with knobs on the tops promote such small-motor coordination as well as ordering skills. These materials can be ordered through school-supply catalogs.

The mouse used to operate most computer programs also gives children a chance to develop small-motor strength as well as eye-hand coordination. Children must roll the mouse on a flat surface until its pointer (cursor) on the computer screen is on a desired object. Then they must click a button on the top of the mouse to activate the object, as described in chapter 4.

Puzzle pieces with knobs help the youngest children strengthen their fingers for picking up things.

Millie & Bailey Preschool, for example, is one of the most frequently used computer programs because of its wide range of challenging and fun math activities that combine music, speech, and sound effects with appropriate learning content. Children match shoes to three different-sized people using a mouse in the activity "Little, Middle, and Big." They experiment with the numbers 0 through 10 in "Build-a-Bug," and with patterns in "Bing and Bong." They use counting skills while operating a cookie-decorating jelly bean machine on the screen in "Cookie Factory," and then again with a large cash register in "Number Machine."

If you want to **make your own finger-strengthening materials that will promote color and shape concepts, make geoboards and Peg-Boards** for your children. You can make a geoboard from a 1-foot-square board with headless nails pounded in rows 1 inch apart. A set of colored rubber bands allow children to make all sorts of designs by stretching the rubber bands over the nails. Once they master this activity you can make simple patterns on graph paper cut to the size of the board using colored pencils in the same colors as the rubber bands. Make only one or two patterns on each sheet; for example, a red square, a blue triangle, and so forth. Let children put the graph patterns next to their geoboard and try to copy them with rubber bands.

Do the same with homemade Peg-Boards. Ask a lumber dealer for end pieces or scraps of Peg-Board. Cut them into individual boards of any shape, sand them down, and bring in sets of colored golf tees to fit in the holes. Later, make simple colored patterns on paper cut the same size as the boards. Can the children copy your paper patterns with golf tees on their Peg-Boards?

Although the physical development promoted within the Manipulative/Math Center is small-motor coordination, outside the center you should also consider movement activities that will promote large-motor skills. During creative movement sessions, **have children put on number necklaces or number vests from the math area and become those numbers**. If they are the number 3, for instance, they can twirl three times or jump three times when the action calls for it. Ask them to show you how the number 5 can dance to music with a beat.

ACTIVITIES TO PROMOTE COGNITIVE DEVELOPMENT
Number Games

Of the several cognitive concepts previously mentioned, it is numbers and counting that are discussed here. Make numbers personal and you will make numbers a hit in your program. Children already associate personally with numbers. They are a certain age: 3, 4, or 5. They can hold up the proper number of fingers to prove it. That is them—a certain number. If you **start with personal numbers**, you will quickly have the attention of your children.

Have sets of three-dimensional numbers in plastic, wood, or metal for them to handle. A parent with a jigsaw might be willing to cut out wooden numbers 0 through 9 for you, or they can be ordered from educational supply houses. Be sure that at least five copies of each number are made (or however many children are allowed in the Math Center). To introduce these particular numbers, you can trace around each number on a sheet of poster board. Let children try to **match the wooden number with their shape outlines**.

Another day, have small groups of children in the Manipulative/Math Center find their own personal number, their age. Have them choose a colored marker and trace around their own number on a paper. They can color in the number with crayons if they want. Let them make as many number tracings as they want; the first ones may not be very accurate. One of these papers can be signed by the child and displayed in the Manipulative/Math Center, and later taken home.

Although number symbols are abstract just as letters are, young children can learn their personal number name and number symbol just as they learn the letter names and letter symbols of their own names. Keep numbers personal like this and children will want to be involved with them. When they are able to sign their papers with the letters of their name, **they can also sign their age numbers**.

Another personal number for children is their house or apartment number. Do they know it? You can print the numbers on cards for them. Can they find the numbers from the set of three-dimensional numbers in the area? Maybe two children together can find their house numbers. When they have found them, you can **give**

them corresponding **peel-off numbers to stick on their cubbies** or wherever they choose. Other personal numbers are the children's telephone numbers. You may want to print them on a 3-by-5 card to be put on a ring and hung in the Dramatic Play Area for pretend play with telephones.

Counting Games

Before children experience actual counting of objects, let them **play number counting games, songs, chants, and fingerplays**. From such games, young children learn the names of numbers and their sequence, rather than how to count. Or make up your own number chants like the one at the beginning of this chapter. Let children help make number chants. They can substitute their own rhyming words for the words of the number chants they know.

Object Counting

Once children have become familiar with rote counting to 10, they may be ready to count objects. Such counting should always begin with concrete objects at first, before children use the computer or have counting stories read to them. Again, **make counting personal** and they will not only enjoy it, but also begin to understand it. Can they count their fingers on one hand? On two hands? Let them count their hands and their feet. How many shoes are they wearing? **Give them a peel-off number** sticker to put on each one: the numbers "1" and "2." They can also wear these numbers on the backs of their hands.

What else can they count in the classroom? Perhaps the number of fish in the aquarium, guinea pigs in the cage, plants on the windowsill, or puzzles in the puzzle rack (that's a hard one!). Let them put peel-off numbers on the objects they count. This is the time to **introduce number symbols at the entrance to each learning center**. Until now you may have been using a particular number of hooks, tickets, or necklaces as self-regulating devices for children to control how many can work in each center. Now you can also post the number symbol next to the hooks in each area. Have the children help you choose the correct number symbol.

Counting Books

Keep counting books in the Manipulative/Math Center. Children will look at them there and make the connection between books and counting activities. When you are in the area, read a counting book to the children who are interested. Some counting books are stories, but others just feature individual numbers like *123 Pop!* (Isadora, 2000).

Children are drawn to its exciting cover showing comic-book-like superheroes. Bold numerals on the right-hand top of each page start with 1 astronaut, followed by other in-your-face familiar figures (the "pop" refers to pop art). A giant hand with 5 ringed and painted fingers; 7 comic-book sounds explode: Bam! Pop! Splat!

Boom! Pow! Zing! and Blam! Just what children love. Also a double-spread page of 8 multiethnic superheroes and 18 hooting, squeaking, honking, hissing animals. There are 100 barking dogs (count 'em), 500 lightened skyscraper windows, 1,000 balloons, and 1,000,000 stars. Have children look for the wonderful patterns, if they haven't already pointed them out.

Another sure hit is the Farmer Brown story *Click, Clack, Splish, Splash* (Cronin, 2006) in which his unruly animals invade his house while he sleeps (1 farmer sleeping, 2 feet creeping) to empty his aquarium of its 10 fish, which they carry out to the pond and release in a grand countdown. Then there is the beloved *Chicka Chicka* alphabet book spin-off with a math counterpart: *Chicka Chicka 1 2 3* (Martin & Sampson, 2004). Its 20 numerals race each other to the top of the apple tree, only to be chased out by bumblebees until 0 saves the day.

Numbers can be beautiful in *Counting in the Garden* (Parker, 2005), with bugs and bunnies, dogs and dragonflies from 1 to 10 hiding among the flowers in polka-dot patterns. Can your children find the 9 inchworms?

Computer Math Programs

Preschool children do not seem to recognize numerals as early as they do letters, perhaps because they have had less experience with them. You can hope that your children will do better because they have played with three-dimensional numbers in the Manipulative/ Math Center. In computer programs that use the keyboard, children often cannot find the numbers on the top row. You may need to play a find-the-numbers game.

Most preschool programs, however, use a mouse to click on numbers or numbered pictures on the monitor. Here are some:

Adventure Workshop (Tots) Lego
     Simple number identity games
Blue's 123 Time Activities (The Learning Company)
     Counting game: Mother May I   Weighing game
     Shape & number card game   Cash register
Disney Learning Preschool
Disney's Mickey Mouse Preschool
     Opposites (Disney characters with cars)
     Cause and effect
Disney's Winnie the Pooh Preschool
     Classification (toys)
     Discrimination (photos)
Millie & Bailey Preschool (Edmark)
     Matching (shoe sizes)   Cash register
     Numbers game (Build-a-Bug)   Build a mouse house (shapes)
     Cookie Factory (counting; shapes; patterns)

ACTIVITIES TO PROMOTE LANGUAGE DEVELOPMENT

Language development involves words. Adults often **use seemingly simple words when talking with children about math concepts** without realizing children may not really understand even the simplest words: "more," "more than," "less," "less than," "few," "fewer than," or "one too many." How will you know what they understand? How can you help them learn meanings? Play some simple word games with them involving plastic foods, little dinosaur figures, or some other interesting items.

For example, pass out the items to three children at the table in the Math Center, giving uneven amounts to each child: three apples to Elena, two bananas to Ethan; four oranges to Tanya. Then ask questions such as: "Who has more pieces of fruit than Ethan?" "Who has more than Elena?" "Who has more than Tanya?" After working out these answers, one by one, ask Tanya to give some fruit to Ethan and to Elena. Then ask similar questions about who has more. Do the same with "less" and "less than," and "few" and "fewer than." If children are confused when you use a different word, play the game with the same word every day until they get it right. To follow up these concepts, read a book.

Just Enough Carrots (Murphy, 1997) tells the story of a rabbit family shopping in a supermarket with the little boy complaining that everyone has more carrots (and peanuts and worms) than they do, and he wants more. Pictures show "more," "same," and "fewer" for each item. If children enjoy the story, see if they can reenact it, taking the various roles with you being the mother.

In *So Few of Me* (Reynolds, 2006), Leo is a little boy with too many things to do, so he wishes "if only there were two of me." And there are! But that is not enough so he tries three, then four, five, six, and finally ten Leos. Isn't this finally enough? Ask the children how they would solve the problem. Then read on to find out how Leo does it. Many **other math words** that young children hear but may not understand are featured in picture books that, in turn, are good lead-in's or follow-up's to math activities.

Time words such as "second," "minute," "hour," are demonstrated in children's language in *A Second is a Hiccup* (Hutchins, 2007). **Large number words** are dramatized in the classic *How Much Is a Million?* (Schwartz, 1985).

ACTIVITIES TO PROMOTE SOCIAL DEVELOPMENT

Children can continue their exploration of number words as they operate the computer in "pairs." They can learn that a pair is "two" things together. They can look for other pairs in the room. **Put all of the shoes from your dress-up area into a sack for children to dump out and sort into pairs**. What else makes a pair in your classroom? A knife and fork, a cup and saucer, two mittens, two boots.

Do people come in pairs? What makes them a pair? How should the individual people in a pair act toward one another? A pair of children can also be called "partners." What do partners do together? Can they take turns? Can they share with one another? Can they walk down the hall or down the street with one another? This is a good time to talk about caring and cooperation. You may want to **read the humorous Chinese folktale** *Two of Everything* (Hong, 1993), about the little old man and little old woman who find a magic pot that creates two of everything that drops into it, including people. After the reading, your children may want to play their own "two of everything" game.

Sometimes people are grouped in threes. *One of Three* (Johnson, 1991) shows the littlest of three African American sisters being one of three in the store, on the street, in the subway, but sometimes only one of one at home.

ACTIVITIES TO PROMOTE CREATIVE DEVELOPMENT

Young children love to pretend. They take on the roles of the people they know or the people they have met as they play in the Dramatic Play Center. These activities, in turn, stimulate their creative imaginations as they make up pretend situations about the people around them. How do such activities involve mathematics? The dramatic play that children perform after a field trip, for instance, can include many number activities.

If children have taken a field trip to the post office, the teacher should put out props in the Dramatic Play Center that will stimulate "post office play": stamps, envelopes, a postage meter, letter carrier caps, a mailbag, and so on. Children can **pretend to weigh the letter on the meter** or balance scale. What numbers do the stamps have on them? What do these numbers mean? What numbers are in the addresses on the letters? What do these numbers mean?

After the children have visited a health clinic, they may want to play "doctor" and "nurse" in the Dramatic Play Center. In addition to the props you provide, such as a stethoscope, white coats (shirts), and other doctor paraphernalia, you **can bring in a bathroom scale and also a tape measure or yardstick**. Help children to weigh and measure one another, or let them pretend to do it. You can record the results on a chart. These are other "personal numbers" children will want to know about. Why is it important to be weighed and measured? What do the numbers mean? Discuss such concepts with the children.

The children may want to continue this clinic pretend play in the Block Center. **Put the postage meter or balance scale there for weighing the toy people**. You can make a chart to record these pretend weights as well. The heights of the block people can be measured with a tape measure or ruler, too, and recorded on still another chart. What else can children weigh and measure in your classroom? They may want to **weigh their dolls and the guinea pig, or measure how tall their bean plants have grown**.

Keep an eye open for the pretending that goes on in various areas of your classroom. There may be other opportunities for you to contribute math activities to dramatic play where appropriate. Are the children pretending to have races with the little cars in the Block Center? You can **bring in a children's stopwatch for them to time the races**. Children love to handle and operate such devices. If children express further interest in measuring time, bring in a three-minute "hourglass" egg timer, or put a toy clock with wooden hands in the Dramatic Play Center for hands-on exploration.

THE TEACHER'S ROLE IN THE MANIPULATIVE/ MATH CENTER

Talking About Math Concepts

Playing math games, doing math puzzles, and counting from 1 to 20 are not enough for young children to understand math. They also **need to think about and reflect on what they are doing**. They need to talk to each other and to the teacher about why they did what they did or why something turned out the way it did. As Kamii tells us in her classic book *Number in Preschool and Kindergarten* (2005), "Children do not learn number concepts with pictures. They do not learn number concepts merely by manipulating objects either. They build these concepts by reflective abstraction as they act (mentally) on objects" (p. 38).

She tells us about the world of difference between putting one napkin on each plate and thinking about the number of napkins in relation to the number of plates. Children can easily place a napkin for each empty plate they see, although they

Teachers need to elicit information about why children are doing what they are doing, or what they expect to happen.

often skip one. But a child who understands one-to-one correspondence will count the number of plates and get out that many napkins. When you ask each child how he figured out how many napkins to get out, the first one may tell you he got out a bunch of napkins, put one at each plate, and put the rest back. But the second one will tell you he counted how many plates there were and got out that number of napkins—showing he really understood one-to-one correspondence.

Teachers need to observe children carefully as they work and play in the Manipulative/Math Center with the idea of eliciting information about why children are doing what they are doing, and what they think about it. Commenting on what you see a child doing, often gets the child to tell you more about it. You can also ask open-ended questions such as "Why did you do it that way?" or "What did you think would happen?"

The more of these kinds of responses you gather, the more you will know about what the child is learning and how you can help him or her progress further.

Observing Developmental Levels

Teachers also need to keep careful track of individual children in this center in order to determine their developmental levels. What should teachers look for at the manipulation level, for instance? Children at this level will be playing around with the materials but not making or doing anything constructive with them. For example, they may dump out all of the little plastic bear counters, but not sort them by color or count them. They may put them back into the container and then dump them out again. They may get out puzzle pieces and scatter them around. The bag of hickory nuts and acorns you have collected for sorting by size into plastic cups may be poured out on the floor, or dumped into another container and carried away.

Teachers who see this behavior realize that it is the manipulation level, the children's first level of interaction with materials. Children need many such exploratory activities in order to discover what use can be made of materials. Teachers record such actions on the Child Interaction Form and write suggestions on the back of the form for helping such children progress to more mature levels of interaction.

Children who put together the snapping blocks, who string the beads, who make the puzzles, who pile up the stacking blocks, or who line up the dominoes— these children are most likely to be at the mastery level in their exploratory play. You may want to observe them closely to make sure. Are they using the materials in the ordinary way, or have they created their own games with them? Are they repeating the activity again and again? Most of your children will be playing at mastering the materials like this, but a few may have progressed beyond mastery to meaning: the level in which children apply their own creative ideas, using the materials in new and unusual ways. See Table 5-2 for other examples of interaction levels.

Whatever their level, give children time to use the materials you have provided. An "expert" at puzzle making may not have mastered bristle blocks at all!

Table 5-2 Manipulative/Math Activities: Levels of Interaction

Manipulation Level
Plays around with sorting, matching, counting objects Dumps out puzzle pieces Fills containers with counting items and dumps them out Gets out magnetic numbers and scatters them around

Mastery Level
Makes same puzzle over and over Sorts or matches objects again and again Strings beads or counts buttons for long periods Plays with cash register, math computer programs, abacus, or dominoes   with great concentration

Meaning Level
Makes up own game for computer program Uses counting or sorting games in creative ways Plays with dominoes, abacus, and cash register in creative ways Teaches others how to use computer games, stopwatch, balance, or other materials

RECORDING ON THE CHILD INTERACTION FORM

Children playing together in the Manipulative/Math Center may be at the same or at different levels of development as they interact with the materials. Careful observation and recording of children in the center can help teachers support children need assistance, as well as plan for individuals who are ready for more challenging activities. An example of such recording shows Lisa and Beth at work in the center one morning.

Lisa takes from the shelf a container of large, colored counting beads with holes in their centers and dumps them out on a nearby table. She sits down at the table and moves the beads around with both hands almost as if she is fingerpainting. She begins stacking them up but the stacks fall over, so she mixes them around on the table again with both hands. Beth comes into the center, watches Lisa, and then gets a board with stacking rods off the shelf. "This is how you do it," she declares. She sits down and begins to stack beads on each rod according to their color. Lisa tries to put beads on the rods but not according to their color. Beth dumps all of the beads off the rods and begins again. This time she refuses to let Lisa help. When she is finished, she dumps the beads off the rods and begins to stack them again. Beth gets up and leaves. A nearby observer records her findings on the Child Interaction Form (Table 5.3).

On the reverse side of the Child Interaction Form the observer notes her interpretation of this incident and suggests plans for the girls. This form will be

Child _Lisa, Beth_　　　　　　　　Observer _D.B._

Center _Manipulative/Math_　　　　Date _9/25_

CHILD INTERACTION FORM
With Materials

Manipulation Level　　　　　　　　　　　　　　　　Actions/Words

(Child moves materials around
without using them as intended.)

Lisa moves counting beads around on table. Tries to stack them (without rods) but they fall.
She mixes them around with both hands.

Mastery Level　　　　　　　　　　　　　　　　　　Actions/Words

(Child uses materials
as intended, over and over.)

Beth gets bored with rods; begins stacking beads by color; says, "This is how you do it." Dumps beads
and stacks them several times.

Meaning Level　　　　　　　　　　　　　　　　　　Actions/Words

(Child uses materials in
new and creative ways.)

With Other Children

Solitary Play　　　　　　　　　　　　　　　　　　Actions/Words

(Child plays with
materials by self.)

Lisa plays with beads by herself (as usual). Beth comes in and begins stacking beads on rods. She takes
over and does not let Lisa play. (Beth usually plays alone like this.)

Parallel Play　　　　　　　　　　　　　　　　　　Actions/Words

(Child next to others with same
materials but not involved with them.)

Cooperative Play　　　　　　　　　　　　　　　　Actions/Words

(Child plays together with
others and same materials.)

Lisa tries to put beads on rods that Beth is using but not by color; Beth dumps them off.

Table 5.3　Child Interaction Form: Math

collected at the end of the day along with any other observation forms and used in the daily and weekly classroom planning. The observer writes the following:

Accomplishments:

Lisa made the first move I've seen to play with another child by trying to stack blocks on Beth's rods.

Beth is at the mastery level of block-stacking play.

Needs:

Beth seems to need more practice playing at this level.

Beth also needs to become involved in playing with others.

Lisa needs to get involved with others, maybe be more assertive.

Plans:

Bring out more stacking materials and colored counters (nesting cubes, stacking blocks, colored chips).

Encourage Lisa to play with another child with these materials; maybe someone else at the manipulative level (observe to see who).

Ask Beth to show another child how to stack.

INTERACTING WITH CHILDREN IN THE MANIPULATIVE/MATH CENTER

Children often play with these materials on their own or parallel to other children seated at the same table. Your daily observations will help you to know when and how to interact with the children. If Tammy is still filling and dumping the parquetry blocks just as she did when the program began, you may want to sit beside her and ask what else she can do with the blocks. **It may take a question like this to get her thinking or to get her started doing something else**. Stay beside her for a while if it seems appropriate. You could play with a few of the blocks parallel to her. Try sorting out all of the red ones. Or stack up one of the shapes in a pile. Or make a simple design from them. If she is ready to try something different, she may enter your play, or start something similar and parallel to yours. If not, you can continue to observe. Your presence delivers an important nonverbal message to Tammy: the teacher cares enough about me to spend time watching what I do.

You may want to comment on what some of the other children are doing in the area in order to learn more about their thinking or what concepts they are dealing with. Rather than a direct question, it is often more appropriate to make a statement about their work: "Miguel, you are lining up many of the Cuisenaire™ rods of the same color." Miguel may respond in a totally unexpected way: "These yellow ones are carrot sticks and I'm going to feed them to my rabbit." But from this you realize Miguel has gone beyond merely sorting or counting to the meaning level of exploratory play with the Cuisenaire rods. Another day you may want to bring Miguel several Cuisenaire pattern sheets to build with: a more complex skill than many preschoolers can handle, but it may be a stimulating challenge to Miguel.

INTRODUCING A NEW ACTIVITY

Some manipulative/math activities are best introduced by the center itself with the children finding them on the shelves and figuring out how they work on their own. Others are better introduced by one of the teachers. If you know that your children have become really interested in a particular topic and want to go further with it, you may decide to introduce the new activity to a small group of children in this center. Later in the day or on the following days, other children can come into the center and be introduced to the new activity either by you or by the children who already know something about it.

For example, the children in one class became interested in measuring things because of a carpenter who had been working outside in the hall. They had watched him measuring the dimensions for a new door for the cafeteria. The teacher overheard some of them playing "carpenter" in the Block Center, building a structure that needed a new door.

The teacher decided to **introduce some measuring tools** in the Manipulative/Math Center. After five children had entered the area, he followed with a small metal box and a book. The children were used to having the teachers bring surprising new things like this into the various centers, so they gathered around him at the table with great anticipation. First **he read them** *I Love Tools* **(Sturges, 2006)**. The book shows simple pictures of all kinds of carpentry tools along with a boy, girl, mother, and father that use them to build a birdhouse.

Then he told the children that the metal box contained some of the tools pictured in the book. They of course wanted to know which ones. He asked them to guess. Some children said "hammer" or "screwdriver." But Tony asked to pick up the box so he could feel it. He rattled it around. Everyone watched and waited while he made his guess. Tony said, "It's not very heavy. Maybe it's a ruler." He was partly right. The box contained a flat ruler, a folding ruler, and a metal tape measure. The children were delighted because they knew they were going to get to use these "neat" tools. The teacher was delighted because of the way Tony had made his guess. He had really used a scientific method of inquiry rather than making a blind guess.

Afterwards, the children got to measure the door of their own classroom using each of the tools. Other children who watched the Manipulative/Math Center group do the measuring knew that their turn would come later that day or the next. The teacher added this box of tools to the manipulative shelf and put a label on it illustrating "measuring tools."

In this way the children in this classroom and in your classroom, too, can become excited about numbers: how to recognize them, what to do with them, and how they help us get along in our world.

IDEAS IN CHAPTER 5

1. *Promoting positive attitudes about math*

   a. Have children explore math as they do blocks

   b. Have fun with numbers

2. *Teaching math concepts*

   a. Give children playful opportunities to practice identifying shapes, sizes, and colors one concept at a time

   b. Give children time to learn. There is no hurry

   c. Talk with the children about what they are doing

   d. Learning about patterns helps children predict what will happen next

   e. Use familiar objects for counting

   f. Make your classroom a math-rich environment

   g. Engage children in natural math problem solving

3. *Promoting small-motor development*

   a. Strengthen finger muscles and provide counting practice by bringing in several paper punches

   b. Make "picture-punching" cards with a picture or outline on each

   c. Display cards on a "punch board" in the area

   d. Have "picture-punching" field trips

   e. Substitute felt-tip pens for paper punchers for children with special physical needs

   f. Have small-motor and counting practice from opening pea pods

   g. Have knobbed materials on manipulative shelves

   h. Make finger-strengthening materials like geoboards and Peg-Boards

4. *Promoting number concepts through personalizing numbers*

   a. Have children put on a number necklace or vest and "become" that number

   b. Start with "personal numbers" like age

   c. Match three-dimensional numbers to their outlines

   d. Have children sign their number age

   e. Use peel-off personal numbers on cubbies

5. *Promoting counting concepts*

   a. Play number counting games, songs, chants, and fingerplays

   b. Keep counting books in the Manipulative/Math Center

   c. Have a collection of dinosaur figures, dinosaur counting books, and dinosaur computer programs

   d. Play find-the-numbers game with computer keys

   e. Make counting personal with peel-off numbers on hands and shoes

   f. Put number symbol on entrance to every activity area when children begin learning number symbols

6. *Promoting math language, concepts*

   a. Talk with children using "more than" and "less than"

   b. Use time words and big number words like "millions"

7. *Promoting social development*

   a. Learn meaning of pairs/partners from shoe activity

   b. Read the Chinese folktale *Two of Everything*

8. *Promoting creative development through dramatic play*

   a. Bring in postage meter and weigh letters

   b. Have scale, tape measure, and yardstick to weigh and measure children

   c. Use postage meter to weigh toy people in Block Center

   d. Let children weigh dolls and the guinea pig, and measure plant growth

   e. Bring in a stopwatch or an egg timer to time little car races

9. *Teacher's role*

   a. Help children think and reflect about what they are doing

   b. Observe, sit beside a child, and ask appropriate questions

10. *Introducing a new activity*

   a. Introduce measuring tools

   b. Read the book *I Love Tools*

DISCUSSION QUESTIONS

1. What does math in the preschool involve?

2. How can you help your children develop positive attitudes toward math rather than math anxiety?

3. Why does math need to be manipulative in preschool?

4. What classification concepts should a preschool child learn? How?

5. What kinds of counting should children learn in preschool and how can they do it?

TRY IT YOURSELF

1. Set up your Manipulative/Math Center attractively with several activities, each to promote the skills of sorting, matching, one-to-one correspondence, seriation, numbers, counting, weighing, and measuring. In addition to the shelf materials, include books, computer games, and a bulletin board. (Or make a diorama of a Manipulative/Math Center.)

2. Do a counting activity based on a theme (animals, acorns, dinosaurs) with a small group of children. Include hands-on materials they can explore with, an appropriate book, and an activity in some other center of the room, such as Art or Dramatic Play.

3. Do a counting field trip with children using picture punch cards of objects to be counted.

4. Do a weighing or measuring activity with children, using real tools and recording the results.

5. Introduce a new math concept to a small group of children, bringing in a new activity or material for them to use.

REFERENCES CITED

Copley, J. V. (2000). *The young child and mathematics*. Washington, DC: NAEYC.

Gellens, S. (2005). Integrate movement to enhance children's brain development. *Dimensions of Early Childhood 33*(3), 14–21.

Hirsh-Pasek, K. & Golinkoff, R. M. (2003). *Einstein never used flash cards: How our children really learn—And why they need to play more and memorize less*. New York: Rodale (St. Martin's Press).

Kamii, C. (2005). *Number in preschool and kindergarten*. Washington, DC: National Association for the Education of Young Children.

Seefeldt, C. & Wasik, B. A. (2006). *Early education: Three-, four-, and five-year olds go to school* (2nd ed.). Upper Saddle River, NJ: Merrill/Prentice Hall.

Taylor-Cox, J. (2003). Algebra in the early years? Yes! *Young Children 58*(1), 14–21.

Other Sources

Cutler, K. M, Gilkerson, D., Parrott, S., & Bowne, M. T. (2003). Developing math games based on children's literature. *Young Children 58*(1), 22–27.

Edelson, R. J. & Johnson, G. (2003/2004). Music makes math meaningful. *Childhood Education 80*(2), 65–70.

Geist, E. (2001). Children are born mathematicians: Promoting the construction of early mathematical concepts in children under five. *Young Children 56*(4), 12–19.

Guha, S. (2002). Integrating mathematics for young children through play. *Young Children 57*(3), 90–93.

Murray, A. (2001). Ideas on manipulative math for young children. *Young Children 56*(4), 28–29.

Seo, K-H. (2003). What children's play tells us about teaching mathematics. *Young Children 58*(1), 28–34.

Thatcher, D. H. (2001). Reading in math class: Selecting and using picture books for math investigations. *Young Children 56*(4), 20–26.

Whitin, P. & Whitlin, D. J. (2005). Pairing books for children's mathematical learning. *Young Children 60*(2), 42–48.

Worsley, M., Beneke, S., & Helm, J. H. (2003). The pizza project: Planning and integrating math standards in project work. *Young Children 58*(1), 44–49.

Children's Books

Angelou, M. (1996). *Kofi and his magic.* New York: Clarkson Potter/Publishers.*

Angelou, M. (1994). *My painted house, my friendly chicken, and me.* New York: Crown.*

Cronin, D. (2006). *Click, clack, splish, splash.* New York: Atheneum.

Hong, L. T. (1993). *Two of everything.* Morton Grove, IL: Albert Whitman.*

Hutchins, H. (2007). *A second is a hiccup.* New York: Arthur A. Levine.*

Isadora, R. (2000). *1 2 3 pop!* New York: Viking.*

Johnson, A. (1991). *One of three.* New York: Orchard Books.*

Martin, B. & Sampson, M. (2004). *Chicka chicka 1 2 3.* New York: Simon & Schuster.

Murphy, S. J. (1997). *Just enough carrots.* New York: HarperCollins.

Parker, K. (2005). *Counting in the garden.* New York: Orchard Books.

Reynolds, P. H. (2006). *So few of me.* Cambridge, MA: Candlewick Press.

Schwartz, D. M. (1985). *How much is a million?* New York: Lothrup, Lee and Shepard.*

Sturges, P. (2006). *I love tools!* New York: HarperCollins.

Children's Computer Programs

From online Web sites listed at end of chapter 4

Note: Asterisk represents multicultural book.

BOOKS IN THE EARLY CHILDHOOD CLASSROOM

Your classroom should be filled with wonderful, warm, happy, exciting, and inviting books! Each of the learning centers needs a book nook or a book string with a kitchen clip at the end where children's picture books about the experiences happening in that area can be displayed: books about buildings in the Block Center, books about concepts in the Computer Center, books about counting in the Manipulative/Math Center, books about letters in the Writing Center, picture books about colors in the Art Center, books about songs in the Music Center, books about pets and plants in the Science Center, books about people pretending in the Dramatic Play Center, and books about running and jumping in the Large-Motor Center. This text offers suggestions in every chapter about specific books to use in each of the centers in order to support or extend the activities in progress.

But most important of all, your classroom should contain a wonderful, warm, happy, exciting, and inviting Book Center where individuals or small groups of children can gather and snuggle in for their favorite stories—to be read by you or looked at by them. The Book Center should be one of the most attractive learning centers in your classroom. A colorful shag rug with puffy pillows and a beanbag chair or bolster can invite your youngsters to "come on in!" and relax with a book.

"Can 3-, 4-, and 5-year-old children actually read?" you may ask. A few may be able to; most will not. That is not the point. The idea of locating books throughout the classroom and integrating them into every facet of the curriculum is to bring together children and books in wonderful ways. Children need to have good feelings about books. They can learn how important books are in the functioning of the classroom. They can

BOOKS

ACTION CHANT

"Come in, come in!"
  (Motion with hand)
Said the library door;
  I opened it wide
(Fling arms apart)
  And saw books galore!

Tall skinny books
  (Raise arms straight up)
Up high on the shelves;
  Little fat books
(Arms down and swinging)
  That stood by themselves!

I opened one up
  And sat down to look;
(Squat down)
  The pictures told stories
(Jump up)
  What a wonderful book!

The Book Center should invite children to gather and snuggle together for looking at their favorite books.

experience how enjoyable books are when they are sat down with and read from. They can see how beautiful picture books become when they are opened up and looked at.

Bringing together young children and picture books may be one of the most important services you perform for your youngsters, as almost every current study on children's learning points out. Research has shown that "reading regularly to young children significantly influences their understanding of what reading is all about as well as their later proficiency in reading" (Neuman & Roskos, 1993, p. 37). We can add that the more you read to young children or tell stories from picture books, the more children will want to be associated with books, and the more they will want to learn to read on their own.

Finally, both you and the children will find the book experience to be one of the most delightful activities you can do together. Snuggling up close to the teacher with a lovely book is a warm and wonderful way for both of you to express caring. The teacher's actions say to the child: "I am taking time out of a busy day to share something nice with you because I care about you." The child's actions say to the teacher: "I enjoy being close to you like this because I care for you, too."

EMERGENT LITERACY AND READING READINESS

Current research about how children learn to read, and why some don't learn very well, has made us change our minds about so-called reading readiness. We used to believe that children were not ready to learn to read until a certain age, say 6, or until various developmental processes, such as eye-hand coordination, had been completed. The best we could do for them was to give them reading-readiness activities such as ditto sheets and workbooks where they matched letters and sounds, or circled which pictures were the same or which were different.

Today we know that children are "ready" to learn to read almost at birth. Yes, that's right—birth! We have discovered that learning to read was not at all what we thought it was. Instead of learning a rigidly sequenced set of skills, children need to learn "print awareness"; that the words we speak can be written down, and that these printed words carry meanings. They need to encounter this print very early in life and have all kinds of interactive experiences with it. As Seefeldt and Wasik (2006) point out: "Making children aware of print in their environment by labeling common classroom objects, such as blocks and crayons, and labeling the different classroom areas such as the Dramatic Play and Art Center, creates a print-rich environment" (p. 211).

Children can also become aware of a print-rich home environment if you read them *Carlo Likes Reading* (Spanyol, 2001) about the giraffe who has tied printed signs to every item in his bedroom, his kitchen, his bathroom, and so forth. Ask your listeners to tell you the names of Carlo's items as you point to them, and then you read off the signs. Leave the book out where children can try to figure out the signs by themselves. But be sure to reread this book many times.

Children need to see and interact with "environmental print": the signs and symbols in everyday life, such as TV ads, fast food signs, supermarket products, gas station signs, cereal boxes, and DVD covers. They need to be exposed to books, reading, and storytelling as soon as they are old enough to be held on their mother's or father's laps. They need to see the adults around them reading books, magazines, and newspapers; writing letters, shopping lists, and notes to one another. They themselves need to be involved with "sending a card to Grandma," or "writing a letter to Santa Claus," or "telling Uncle Al the story about where the new kitten came from," or typing in their name in a computer game.

What has all this to do with learning to read? Through current research we have discovered that learning to read and to write are, in fact, developmental processes that emerge naturally in youngsters given the proper conditions and encouragement. Just as children acquire language naturally, they can also acquire literacy if their environment is full of written words, they hear these words spoken aloud, and an adult is around to help them make sense of what they see.

For learning to speak, children need to be exposed to people speaking the language. They, in turn, need to use language themselves in a developmental sequence over time until they have refined it. This is also true for reading and writing. For learning to read and write, they need to see and hear written print from books and other written material. Not every child emerges naturally into reading, but a good preschool program can give them a start. Then their emergence can continue to occur in kindergarten with teacher-directed activities as well as self-directed emergent ones. Some children's natural acquisition of literacy may not be terribly refined before age 7, but other children as young as age 4 may have taught themselves to read.

Kindergarten teachers are acknowledging the fact that every year a child or two enters their classes already knowing how to read. In checking with parents, they sometimes find that this fact is a complete surprise to the parents: Not only did the parents not teach their youngster to read, they did not even know the child could read!

How, then, did it happen? Their child was evidently exposed to a print-rich environment through which he picked up the necessary knowledge and skills to "crack the reading code" on his own. Perhaps there were older siblings whose reading motivated him to learn how. Seeing ads on television and hearing the words on the screen, going to fast food restaurants with signs he knew the meaning of, seeing familiar print on boxes of breakfast cereal, looking at magazine pictures with simple captions he could understand, being read to from familiar picture books, or playing games on the computer showing text along with spoken words—all of these print activities assisted his literacy to emerge naturally.

READING IN THE PRESCHOOL CLASSROOM

What do these findings mean for preschool teachers? Should you, in fact, begin teaching your children to read? No. Emergent literacy does not happen through formal teaching. It occurs in environments that are filled with print: signs, lists, records, charts, graphs, pictures, books, labels, stories, magazines, newspapers, computer programs, and food containers. It happens where favorite books are read by teachers to individuals and groups over and over, where books are available for children to look at on their own, and where children are encouraged to make up their own stories that are tape-recorded and written down. What you should be providing for your children includes four important items:

1. a "print-rich" environment
2. the freedom for children to choose books and activities
3. the time to become deeply involved so that books and activities become meaningful
4. reading to individuals and small groups on a daily basis

So important is this daily reading of stories to children that every investigation of how children learn to read mentions it. Their sense of story comes about by hearing stories and by being read to on a regular basis—perhaps no other finding in research is as well documented. From being read to and, afterward, looking at books on their own, children absorb other important details about the process of reading, such as:

1. Stories are written in horizontal lines of print.
2. You read lines of print from left to right.
3. Stories start at the top of the page and work down.

Thus, you could say that although you are not teaching children to read in a formal sense in preschool, both you and they are directly involved in their informal acquisition of reading skills.

Predictable Books

Predictable books are among the best and most effective kinds of books for emergent readers. These are books that feature repetitive language patterns. These patterns may be rhyming words or phrases, the cumulative adding on of characters or actions, or the answering of repetitive questions. We realize that mastery-level children are at the stage where repetition is necessary in order for them to learn. "Read it again, teacher," is a familiar refrain in every program featuring story reading. Preschool youngsters themselves also love to repeat rhyming words and phrases. They need to experience this repetition in order to learn.

Because predictable books directly involve the listeners in this manner, they are especially well suited to helping young children make the connection between spoken and written words. When such books feature the words of favorite singing games or fingerplays the youngsters are even more involved. Every preschool program should have several such picture books available.

Like predictable books, song lyrics contain features that help children to more easily make the link from oral to printed language. These song picture books are becoming increasingly popular and *available* as more teachers discover the powerful appeal that these books hold for learners—young and old (Barclay & Walwer, 1992, p. 76).

If your children know and love any of the following singing games or finger plays, it behooves you to have available the books that present such rhymes as stories with humorous illustrations. As you read the books together, you can stop and have the children say the next word or line as you run your finger under it. This means, of course, that you will be reading to individuals or small groups who will be as close as possible to the pages of any of the following:

> *I Know an Old Lady Who Swallowed a Fly* (Westcott, 1980)
>
> *On Top of Spaghetti* (Johnson, 2006)
>
> *The Lady with the Alligator Purse* (Westcott, 1988)
>
> *There Was a Bold Lady Who Wanted a Star* (Harper, 2002)
>
> *There Was an Old Lady Who Swallowed a Trout* (Sloat, 1998)
>
> *Mary Had a Little Lamb* (Hoberman, 2003)
>
> *Miss Mary Mack* (Hoberman, 1998)
>
> *Skip to My Lou* (Westcott, 1989)
>
> *The Itsy Bitsy Spider* (Trapani, 1993)
>
> *Fiddle-I-Fee* (Sweet, 1992)
>
> *The Wheels on the Bus* (Kovalski, 1987)

Children need to follow closely because some of the verses are different from the ones they know. These can be added to the singing you will be doing. Which comes first, the song or the book? Teachers who have tried both ways agree that children should have fun with the singing and the fingerplays first. Then the reading of the books can also become favorite activities.

Children are marvelous "meaning extractors." They come equipped with the curiosity to find out about their world and with their five senses with which to explore their world. The sensory input they receive from their explorations is then processed in their brains, where its meaning is extracted. Some children are better explorers than others. Some children are better "meaning extractors" than others. Literacy may thus emerge naturally in some children sooner than in others.

But we know that in order to support this self-directed process of learning, teachers must allow children the freedom to choose books and activities that interest them. Then they must allow children time enough to become deeply involved with the books. Finally, they must read children's favorite stories over and over. From such activities, children should be able to extract the following information:

1. how a book works

2. how a story goes

3. when to turn the pages

4. how print conveys messages

5. how illustrations help make sense of print

READING AT HOME

If children have been read to at home, they have already begun the process of learning to read. Morrow and Gambrell (2004) tell us: "There is a strong relationship between storybook reading in the home and beginning literacy development. Early readers come from homes where they have been read to frequently from the time they were only months old" (p. 5).

You will want to involve parents in all sorts of reading to their children. **Have a duplicate collection of paperback lending books for children to borrow** at the end of the day and return in the morning. **Invite parents to the Book Center to listen** with the children to your reading, **and then take a turn at reading themselves**.

If you have bilingual children, be sure to send home some bilingual books for parents to read to their children, perhaps in both languages. Invite bilingual parents to read such books to children in both languages in the classroom as well. Morrow and Gambrell say: "Preschoolers are likely to acquire English simply through immersion in an English-speaking classroom, something older children cannot do.

Invite parents into the Book Center to take a turn at reading to the children.

But it is important that they hear their own language as well" (p. 7). Bilingual books seem to be the best because both languages are available to be seen by children and read by both parents and teachers. Some English/Spanish books you might consider sending home include:

> *Amelia's Show-and-Tell Fiesta* (Chapra, 2004)
> *Carlos and the Squash Plant* (Stevens, 1993)
> *Drum, Chavi, Drum* (Dole, 2003)
> *The Empanadas That Abuela Made* (Bertrand, 2003)
> *I Love Saturdays y domingos* (Ada, 2002)
> *My Tata's Guitar* (Brammer, 2003)

Send home a newsletter with the names of the books and fingerplays that all the children are involved with, and give directions for making any of the book extension puppets, puzzles, and games you may be using in the Book Center.

Have a "book bee" for the parents to attend to become familiar with good children's books, and to make book games to take home for their children. Ask parents to send in the titles of books that they have read to their children at home, so you can keep track on a **"My Favorite Books" chart**. What other parent involvement book activities can you think of? How about **a field trip to the public library with parents**? Library cards can be issued to those families who do not have them.

SETTING UP THE BOOK CENTER

As already mentioned, make this area inviting! Do whatever is necessary to make it attractive so that children can't wait to become involved with books. **Use bright colors wherever you can**: on rugs, on pillows, on furniture, on the walls, and on the shelves. Put up book posters on the walls; colorful posters by favorite picture book artists are available in children's bookstores, from Demco (1-800-356-1200), the library supply company, or from the publishers. Use dust jackets from some of the books on your shelves. **Display book puppets, character dolls, book puzzles, and book games. Have a flannel board on the wall at the children's height or on a low easel. Have child-sized bookshelves** that display the fronts of your books. Also include a tape or CD player for children to use on their own as they look at their favorite books. Listening to a well-known book on a tape or CD while looking at the book is a wonderful independent activity for children.

Make this area comfortable. Because some children like to lie on the floor to read, provide soft, colorful rugs and pillows. Some children like to lounge on a window seat when they read; for these children put in a wooden bench, box, or ledge under a window, pad it with foam, and cover it with colorful upholstery material and pillows. Some children like to sit in chairs or rockers to read, so make room for child-size chairs and rockers, or perhaps a beanbag chair or two. **Inflated chairs, low wooden benches, sit-on foam animals, giant foam blocks, and upholstered junior couches are other popular seating devices**. One teacher we

Make the Book Center comfortable with beanbag chairs for children.

observed made her Book Center the most popular place in the room by putting in **an old clawfoot bathtub** that she painted, decorated with stick-on flowers, and filled with puffy pillows.

You may want a small round table with chairs in the area for displaying magazines and book-related games or puzzles. But if your area is a small one, it is often better to make room for comfortable floor reading space with cushions, rather than taking up the space with a table.

What about the adult readers? Make the area comfortable for yourself and other adult readers, too. An adult-size rocking chair is not safe for children, whose feet or fingers often end up under the rockers. You may be able to arrange, instead, for a donated couch or daybed. Be creative. Be different. Be daring with your Book Center!

What about the display of books? Be sure to have a good number and selection of picture books of all kinds. Display them on vertical shelves with the cover visible for easy selection by the children. Make sure they are in good condition; nothing is more discouraging to potential readers than books with torn pages and missing covers. The condition of such books makes a nonverbal statement you should not be making: that you do not take care of books. Remove such books or repair them.

It is not necessary to display all of the books you own at one time; but **have a core of favorites that is always on the shelves**. Children should be able to read a favorite book over and over. **Bringing in new books from time to time adds a new dimension and new interest to the area**.

There are other innovative ways to display books that may attract children to this and other areas. One is to fasten a **clothesline or rod** against the wall of the classroom from one end of the room to the other. **From this horizontal device hang several colored ribbons** for books in each of the learning centers. The colors of the ribbons can match the color code of each center. Tie one end of each ribbon to the rod or line and fasten a kitchen clip to the other end of each ribbon at children's eye-level. Then **clip the books you are using in each area to the ribbons**, where they can be displayed in an attractive yet space-saving manner against the wall. Children enjoy clipping and unclipping the books if you show them how—another good small-motor task. Can they also help choose which books to clip to each learning center ribbon every week?

BOOKS TO PROMOTE LANGUAGE DEVELOPMENT

"Don't all books promote language development?" you may wonder. Of course they do. All children's books use language in ways that children may never have heard before. But the books to be discussed in this section are the ones that support the theme of the Appropriate Practices Curriculum: that children develop various skills through three levels of interaction—manipulation, mastery, and meaning.

It is not difficult to understand how children learn to build with blocks first through manipulating them, then through the repetition necessary for mastery, and finally by applying their own meanings. It is easy to see how children can interact at these three levels with materials such as puzzles, Peg-Boards, and even computer programs. But it may seem strange that language development also occurs through this same interaction process. Nevertheless, it is true.

Strasser and Seplocha (2007) tell us: "As children listen to songs, nursery rhymes, poems and books with repetitive words and phrases, they begin to play with language" (p. 222). They actually learn language by playing around with sounds and words at the same three levels. From infancy, through toddlerhood, and into the preschool years, youngsters first play with the sounds of language. The "sound play" of young children equates with the "manipulation" level of interaction with three-dimensional objects.

Then the youngsters repeat over and over the sounds or words they especially like in interesting and funny patterns. This "pattern play" equates with the "mastery" level of interaction. Finally, youngsters apply their own meanings to words by using them in original ways. This "meaning play" is the most advanced and mature interaction of children with words; not every preschool child reaches this level.

Children's books can support these three important levels of interaction in youngsters' development of language skills. The books listed here have attracted children's attention and interaction at these three levels; many other similar books can offer the same opportunities for your own children's language development. Keep such language interaction levels in mind when you select books to promote your children's language development.

Sound Play

Young children play with words just as they play with blocks. Is this hard for you to believe? Then listen to your toddlers or preschoolers when they are lying down waiting to fall asleep. They often talk to themselves, murmuring sounds or words over and over. When they're awake, they often play around with similar sounds or words. If they stumble upon a funny one, they'll repeat it again and again, or make up similar words of their own to go along with it. If they hear you read a book with a word in it that tickles their funnybone, they'll break up with laughter and leave you wondering what was so funny. Some children mutter to themselves constantly just under their breath as they play. If you could turn up the volume, you might hear a sound chant or a word being played around with.

With this knowledge in mind, you will want to **have books available that feature interesting words or funny sounds**. One such classic picture book is Margaret Wise Brown's *Goodnight Moon* (1947). It is a simple story of a little bunny who says goodnight to all of the things in his room as it grows progressively darker.

The story contains one word that often sends children off into gales of laughter. Among the items the bunny says "goodnight" to are "a comb and a brush and a bowl full of mush." It is the sound of the word "mush" that children respond to so hilariously. If this is a favorite book for your youngsters, you will undoubtedly have to read it many times, just for them to hear the word "mush."

This might make a good "nap book" in your program if you read it after the curtains are drawn and the lights are turned down. Read it in a whispery voice to lull the children to sleep. You can extend the whispery singsong repetition if you also say goodnight to the things in your own classroom one by one. Perhaps the children will all be asleep before you finish.

Another classic with wonderful sound words is *Caps for Sale* (Slobodkina, 1968). A tree full of monkeys who steal the peddler's caps make the fascinating sound "tsz, tsz, tsz" every time the peddler shakes his finger at them. Your children will love to hear you say it, and love to repeat it themselves every time it occurs in the story. Here is a story they may also want to dramatize if it is a favorite. **Bring in some caps of various colors**, use them yourself in telling or reading the story to a small group, and then leave the caps in the Book Center **for them to use in their own dramatized version of the story**.

A third classic story with sounds that children enjoy hearing and repeating is Robert McCloskey's *Blueberries for Sal* (1948). Little Sal and Little Bear go off with their respective mothers to pick blueberries on Blueberry Hill, where they all get mixed up with one another before the day is over. The sound of "kuplink, kuplank, kuplunk" as Sal drops berries into her little tin pail is another favorite of children. **Bring in a little tin pail and let your children take turns dropping various items into it**. Ask them what the items sound like.

There are many more recent books featuring rhymes and sounds of different sorts that youngsters love to hear.

Cha Cha Chimps (Durango, 2006)
Fire! Fire! Said Mrs. McGuire (Martin, 2006)
Clink Clank Clunk! (Aroner, 2006)
Flip Flop Bop (Novak, 2005)
Dig Dig Digging (Mayo, 2002)
Mrs. McNosh Hangs Up Her Wash (Weeks, 1998)
Dooby Dooby Moo (Cronin, 2006)

Pattern Play

Once children have learned what to do with words, they begin playing with them at the next level of interaction by putting them into brief repeated patterns. Such word play is almost like a chant with one word repeated and another word rhymed, much like jump-rope rhymes. Children say things like "hamburger, ram-burger, lam-burger, sam-burger," to themselves over and over. Researcher Judith Schwartz

(1981) has found this to be the most frequent kind of language play she observed. It is almost a self-imposed language drill or practice of words and phrases. But, again, it is done playfully and spontaneously by the children, who often burst into laughter over the funny sounds of the words.

You can support this type of language interaction in your program with a delightful selection of **books that feature repeated rhyming words or phrases**. A wonderfully illustrated new rendition of the classic nursery tale, *The Little Red Hen* (Pinkney, 2006), has the hen asking all the animals for help in her quest to grow the wheat and bake the bread. The animals repeatedly reject her request, saying: "Not I," said the rat, "Not I," said the goat. "Not I," said the pig. Have your listeners join in once they catch on. They can become each of the animals if they want.

In *Snip Snap! What's That?* (Bergman, 2005), an alligator breaks into an apartment where three children live and threatens the children. Were the children scared? YOU BET THEY WERE are the repeated words that are shouted out on the pages whenever the question is asked. Your listeners can shout them too when you show them the pages of the book where these words appear.

Another "pattern play" book that children can't get enough of is a wonderfully wild modern version of the classic jump-rope rhyme *The Lady with the Alligator Purse* (Westcott, 1988), previously mentioned as a predictable book. The pattern here is the repeated phrase *in came the:*

> *In came the doctor,*
>
> *In came the nurse,*
>
> *In came the lady with the alligator purse.*

If you read this to your children, be prepared for all of them to want pizza for lunch the same as the lady with the alligator purse provides for everyone in the story. You might, in fact, **consider making pizza with the children as a follow-up to this book**. Bring in some big purses as well, and leave them in the Book Center to give children the opportunity of acting out this silly story. Children tend to memorize such rhymes spontaneously, once they have heard them repeated enough. Memory practice like this is another boost for emergent literacy.

A simple rhyming book with another comical pattern play is *Sheep in a Jeep* (Shaw, 1986). Five sheep jump in a jeep and take it for a rocky ride that will have your children making sheep and jeep rhymes after they finish laughing. If sheep are among the farm animals in the Block Center, you could **bring them into the Book Center along with one of your toy vehicles for follow-up play** after you read this book.

On the other hand, this book also lends itself to being converted for flannel board use because of its large colorful illustratons. Children enjoy doing follow-up activities with the books they like. To **make flannel or felt board characters**, scan or copy the pictures, cut out a picture of the jeep, the five sheep, the pigs, and the tree. Glue each to cardboard and sandpaper backing, and store them in a labeled manila envelope next to the felt board. Keep a second copy of the book in the envelope to be looked at when the children play with the flannel board characters. They may want to act out the original story on the flannel board or make up their own version.

To make your own flannel board, glue a square of felt from a hobby store or sewing center onto cardboard backing. This in turn can be mounted on an easel, the wall, or on a cardboard box whose sides are cut down as an easel. Children also like small personal flannel boards big enough for one child alone.

When children play with flannel board characters, they often like to hear the book being read. They can do this independently if you **tape-record your reading of the book** for playback on the cassette tape recorder located in the Book Center. As you record the story, don't forget to **include a sound cue every time you turn a page**, so the children will be able to turn the pages at the proper time when they use the tape and book on their own. Tapping a glass with a spoon makes a good page-turning cue. When they use the book and tape on their own, check to see if they are turning the page to keep up with the words in the book.

Meaning Play

Meaning play is the most sophisticated form of word play. Children who have truly mastered the rules for using words in the normal ways sometimes go on to applying their own meanings; that is, they try out new and funny ways of using words. They

Table 6-1 Book Activities: Levels of Interaction

Manipulation Level
Takes books off shelf, scatters them around Carries books, but doesn't look at them Looks at books upside down Uses books in playing, building Turns pages of books, sometimes several pages at a time
Mastery Level
Has favorite books, repeatedly looks at them Wants same story read again and again Knows words or phrases from story and repeats them
Meaning Level
Retells story from book, may pretend to read it Changes elements of stories (different names, endings) Makes up own stories, may scribble them or have them transcribed on paper   or printed on computer

try playing around with the meanings of words, using puns, mixing up words in sentences, and using synonyms and homonyms or words with double meanings.

Children go through the same 3-M levels of interaction with books as they do with other materials, although the process is often not as obvious because we are not looking for it. Table 6.1 lists some of the ways children can interact with books.

BOOKS TO PROMOTE SOCIAL DEVELOPMENT

Social development for young children involves the skills of getting along with others, including making friends, joining a play group, playing together in harmony, sharing toys, taking turns, and caring for one another. Books are an excellent means of reinforcing the caring theme of your program, that: 1) we care for ourselves, 2) we care for one another, and 3) we care for the things in our classroom.

Ellis, Gallingane, and Kemple (2006) agree when they tell us: "Researchers have found that children's stories, fables, and fairy tales have a profound effect on children's social skills when linked with their personal and social experiences" (p. 31).

In preschool, most friendships are fleeting or one-sided because children are still self-centered in their development, and more concerned with playing than making friends. But as psychologist Corsaro (2003) says: "You make friends by playing with other kids—as many as you can" (p. 69). Among the many children's books about friendship, the following are most popular.

Being Friends (Beaumont, 2002) is a story narrated in rhyme by one of the two girls who are best friends. They are each quite different but find activities they can share and enjoy together. Talk to your listeners about the things each of them likes to do. Can they be friends with someone who is so different?

Best Best Friends (Chodos-Irvine, 2006) tells the story of Clare and Mary who are best friends most of the day in preschool until Mary gets special treatment from everyone because it is her birthday, which upsets Clare and starts an argument. What would your listeners do if they were Clare or Mary?

Hunter's Best Friend at School (Elliott, 2002) shows two raccoon boys who are best friends. They dress alike, eat the same things, and play alike—until the day Stripe decides to cause mischief in school. Hunter reluctantly copies Stripe's antics, but feels terrible about it. Talk with your listeners about their own experiences with friends or playmates and what they would do in Hunter's case.

Another animal story, *That's What Friends Do* (Cave, 2004) shows one friend helping the other until the day they have a falling out. But that makes them so lonely they come back together again to wait, share, comfort, and care again for one another because that's what friends do. Do your children know other things friends may do?

Sharing is still difficult for many 3-, 4-, and 5-year-old children. Even at home, children have difficulty sharing as demonstrated by Gail in *Mine! Mine! Mine!* (Becker, 2006). Gail thinks her visiting cousin Claire is greedy because she wants to play with all of Gail's toys. Her mother tells Gail to watch how she shares all day long. Gail tries sharing at first with things she doesn't like, but finally agrees to try it out with her favorite things—tomorrow! How would your children handle it?

Your book collection must also contain many stories about children from various cultures. For children to become not only accepting but friendly toward youngsters of different races and ethnic groups, reading books featuring multicultural characters they can identify with is an excellent way to begin the process. The multicultural books in this text are labeled with at the end of each chapter.

Early childhood specialist Ramsey (1991) tells us:

> Children's books are a primary vehicle for this kind of teaching. By engaging children in stories, we enable our young readers and listeners to empathize with different experiences and points of view and experience a wide range of social dilemmas.... When children role-play situations and characters in a book, they learn how to perceive situations from a variety of perspectives and literally be "in another person's shoes." (pp. 168–169)

Some of the **multiethnic characters your children may enjoy meeting and role-playing through character dolls, puppets, or pretending** after reading their stories in the Book Center or Dramatic Play Center include:

Cassie, the African American girl who flies over New York City in her imagination in *Tar Beach* (Ringgold, 1991);

Rosalba, the Hispanic girl who also flies over New York City with her grandmother in *Abuela* (Dorros, 1991);

Anna and Juanita, the Anglo and Navajo girls who build a bridge together on the first day of school in *Building a Bridge* (Begaye, 1993);

Jenna, the contemporary Muscogee Indian girl who wants to jingle dance at the powwow, but doesn't have enough jingles on her dress and no time to make them in *Jingle Dancer* (Smith, 2000);

Yummi, the Korean girl who helps her grandmother get to know her American classmates in *Halmoni and the Picnic* (Choi, 1993);

Carlos, the Hispanic boy who won't wash his ears after work in the field until a squash plant starts growing there in *Carlos and the Squash Plant* (Stevens, 1993);

Ling Sung, the Chinese boy who can't seem to do anything right in his preschool until his cookies drop and break into pieces, which he picks up with inverted paintbrushes in *Cleversticks* (Ashley, 1991);

Luke the African American boy who wants to hit a home run like his hero Jackie Robinson, but the big boys won't let him play in *Luke Goes to Bat* (Isadora, 2005).

BOOKS TO PROMOTE EMOTIONAL DEVELOPMENT

Emotional development in the preschool classroom often involves children's learning to control negative emotions, such as anger caused by not getting their own way, or being blamed for something they didn't do; distress caused by becoming lost or being injured; or anxiety caused by being away from home or being separated from a loved one. There are many ways to help children overcome strong emotional feelings, such as helping them express their feelings in words, redirecting their aggressive actions, or helping them play with soothing materials such as finger paints, dough, or water. Reading appropriate books also ranks high as a technique to diffuse a tense situation or to overcome an emotional experience.

Children learn about how a little girl their age handles her anger in *When Sophie Gets Angry—Really, Really Angry* (Bang, 1999). When Sophie's sister grabs the toy gorilla Sophie is playing with, she gets so angry she trips and falls. That does it. Sophie explodes. But then she opens the door and runs—and runs and runs and runs until she can't run any more. Can your children identify with Sophie? What do they do when they get really angry?

When Katie Honors gets angry, she uses feet and fists instead of words against her little brother in *Sometimes I'm Bombaloo* (Vail, 2002). But when she is sent to her room to think about it she becomes Bombaloo, who wants to smash stuff not think. Her anger also runs out when something funny happens. Can your children identify with Katie? Lamme (1996) tells us that: "Book characters can be excellent role models for children, especially when students are encouraged to think deeply about the reasons for the characters' behaviors and decisions" (p. 415).

As you can see, simply reading a book is not enough. These two books especially call for talks with the children about handling anger. Children may want to identify further with Sophie or Katie by role-playing their situations. Have children take the roles and reenact the parts as you read the story. (Sophie can run around the classroom, of course, but not outdoors.) How do they feel afterward? Can they suggest other ways to handle the anger?

A humorous book that may diffuse feelings about taking the blame for something is *It Wasn't My Fault* (Lester, 1985). In this comical tale about Murdley Gurdson, who is always at fault for the unfortunate things that happen to him, a large bird's egg lands on his head. When he goes off to see whose fault this is, he meets a cumulative group of silly animals who eventually put the blame where it belongs, and end up at Murdley's house to scramble the giant egg for breakfast. **A fine follow-up for this story is for the children to help cook scrambled eggs**. Do you have an electric fry pan?

But what about feeling good about themselves? In *Wow! It Sure Is Good to Be You!* (Jabar, 2006), a little African American girl tells the reader that somebody, somewhere, is thinking about you and all the good things about you. As you go through this book, ask your small group of listeners which pages apply to any of them.

In *I'm Gonna Like Me: Letting Off a Little Self-Esteem* (Curtis, 2002), a little girl and boy take turns telling the reader all the things she and he like about themselves, even when they make mistakes or do something wrong. Again, ask your listeners how the various things apply to them. Would they like to make an "I'm Gonna Like Me" book about themselves? Help them get started in the Writing or Art Center.

THE TEACHER'S ROLE IN THE BOOK CENTER

It is up to the teacher to see that this important classroom area lives up to its promise in a self-directed curriculum. Three crucial tasks are involved:

1. providing a good selection of picture books appropriate to the children's developmental level

2. reading books to individuals and small groups daily

3. providing interesting follow-up book activities that children can become involved in

Providing a Good Selection of Appropriate Books

How do you make selections of books for preschoolers from the wide range of books available? It is important for you to **have a hands-on experience with the books you plan to order**; choosing them from catalogs is not good enough. Many fine picture books are just too sophisticated or too long for preschoolers. It is best to look at books in bookstores or a library and to try them out ahead of time if you can. Borrow books from the library and read them to your children. If the children respond well, you can consider purchasing them. Choose books that can be integrated into the curriculum just as you do with computer programs. Here are some **book selection tips**. Choose books that have:

1. simple illustrations in bright primary colors

2. brief texts that are easily read, so that the pages can be turned quickly

3. interesting characters that children can identify with

4. topics that can be integrated into different learning centers

Reading Books to Individuals and Small Groups Daily

A most important task for every team member of your classroom staff is to read books to children. As you move around the room during free-choice time, be sure to stop in at the Book Center. There is sure to be a single child or small group who would like to hear a story. Often the choice of book is theirs, but sometimes the teacher may have a new book in mind to introduce to the children.

Story reading traditionally has been done for the total group of children. The Appropriate Practices Curriculum suggests that **story reading,** in particular, **should be done principally with individuals and small groups of children**. It has proven more effective for each child to be as close as possible to the book and to the reader; then the book illustrations and the teacher's interactions with individuals can really make a difference. **Plan on reading to individuals and small groups at least once a day**.

Story reading should be done with individuals or a small group of children.

If you yourself are sometimes too occupied with children in the myriad of other activities going on simultaneously, then plan for other staff members to read on that day. Reading and storytelling with young children may be one of the most important of any activities you do with them. Volunteers can also help out. Check to see if there is a Foster Grandparents Program in your community that could help you.

Reading aloud to the children on a regular basis seems to be especially important in promoting independent readings. After children have heard a book read several times, they often gravitate to these same books in the library setting and pretend to read them. These emergent efforts represent meaningful attempts by children to act as if they were already readers. In a sense, they are beginning to grapple with the symbolic features of print long before they are able to read conventionally, say Neuman and Roskos (1993, p. 236). **How do you read a book aloud?**

1. Become acquainted with the book you are going to read.

2. Introduce the book to get the children's attention before you start.

3. Read with as much expression as you can muster.

4. Read the same stories over and over.

5. Involve the children with repeating words and guessing and what comes next.

6. Talk about what the children think about the story afterward.

Become acquainted with the book you are going to read before you read it. If it is a book your have on your shelves, be sure you are familiar with it because children may pick it up and ask you to read it. Read it through ahead of time—out loud, if possible. You may want to tape-record your reading of a book ahead of time, so the tape will be available afterwards in the center for the children to use on their own. As you familiarize yourself with the book, be thinking of how you can get the children involved in the story. The first time through you may not want to stop and interrupt the flow of the words, but on subsequent readings you may.

For example, in *Snip Snap What's That?*, an alligator story, a question is asked every few pages. (Were the children scared?) The answer "YOU BET THEY WERE!" is printed in large-font words that you can show your listeners and ask them to respond loudly every time the question is asked. As you leaf through the book *Being Friends* you note that the phrase "We both like being friends" is repeated at the end of every few pages. After the first time through, you might stop and ask children to say the phrase.

Introduce the book to get the children's attention before you start reading it. You need to decide ahead of time how you are going to do this. It is useless to begin reading if the children are not listening. Showing them the cover of the book and asking what they think it is about is a useful technique. The cover of *It Wasn't My Fault* shows Murdley Gurdson with a cracked egg on his head, a bird in the air above him, and three animals beside him looking guilty. You can tell the children the title of the book and then ask them what they think it will be about.

Reading to an individual or a small group gives everyone a chance to respond. This makes book reading interactive rather than just a passive listening experience. It also makes books much more personal. Using a book film or video is a passive experience for young children. Children need to be close to the book and close to the teacher to gain the most from stories. Unless they are interactive, films and videos are really an entertainment medium for children and have little place in the preschool curriculum where the goal is learning, not entertainment.

Another book introduction technique is to show the children the book, state what it is about, and then ask them how they think the main character is going to handle the situation. For example, the cover of the book *Sometimes I'm Bombaloo* shows Katie Honors holding a smiling mask part way over her red face. You can read the title, tell them the girl's name is Katie, and then ask what they think Katie is doing and why. Let everyone in the small group make a guess. Then read the book for them to find out.

Do the reading itself with as much expression as you can muster. If the story is funny, make your voice sound lighthearted. If it is spooky, make your voice low or whispery. Can you read each character's words with a different expression? Make your voice high for one character, low for another, and loud for a third. Tape-record your reading and play it back privately to learn what you sound like. Practice more than once until you get it the way you want it. Reading aloud should be a fun activity for both you and the children. You will know you have been successful when the children tell you, "Read it again, teacher."

Read the same stories over and over if your children like them. This is how emergent literacy develops. This is what they themselves do at the mastery level of their interaction. (Now you know why children are always asking for the same story over and over!) This is how children begin to understand the reading process—by relating words and print to the story they have become familiar with and the pictures they have seen. To become really familiar with a book, children need to have it read again and again. As Campbell (1998) notes: "Children like to hear stories again and again. It is not just enjoyment that they are getting from these readings; they also are getting new meanings with each reading, learning more new words, and acquiring new patterns of language" (p. 136).

Involve the children with repeating words and guessing what comes next. Children should be as much a part of the reading as you are. This will keep their attention and motivate them to want to hear the book again so they can repeat the exciting words. As Strasser and Seplocha (2007) point out: "As preschoolers, children should be active participants in picture book reading—chiming in on the refrain of predictable books, dramatizing stories they love, and reciting the text of books so familiar that they have been committed to memory" (p. 220).

Talk about what the children think about the story afterward. Reading a book to children and putting it back on the shelf is not enough. Children need to reflect on the story and think about what happened. Did the story turn out the way they predicted? Did the characters act the way they thought they should? How would the children have ended the story? Once children have participated in a story, they are usually willing to contribute to a discussion of it afterward. This helps you to know how much they understood of the story. It helps children to internalize thoughts and feelings, and to express themselves at a higher level.

Providing Interesting Follow-Up Book Activities for the Children to Become Involved with on Their Own

Throughout this text, children's book follow-up activities are included wherever possible. Use such suggestions as model activities that you yourself can design with your own books. In this way, you can adapt children's books to your own classroom and curriculum needs. Just as homemade games and materials are more useful than commercial games, so homemade book activities will serve you better than any commercial language kits you can buy.

As you select books for your Book Center, try to choose them on the basis of possible follow-up activities. **The pictures can be scanned and copied for puzzles, flannel board characters, board games, paper dolls, stick puppets, and counting games**. The books can be used as follow-up activities with computer programs, science projects, art activities, cooking, and block building. Be creative in your use of books. How can they be used in addition to reading or storytelling? When we realize that children create their own knowledge through interaction with materials in their environment, then we want books to be an active, and not a passive agent, in children's learning.

One of the delicious favorites for many children is *On Top of Spaghetti* (Johnson, 2006). They have already memorized the rhyming words of this song storybook because they know and love the song. Hilarious animal and people illustrations reenact its verses in the most surprising fashion—another huge attraction. Then there are the ridiculous words: "todwhacker," "fried fritter fricassee," "a-whooshed," "a-whizzin'," "bellyful," and that favorite of all time, "mush." So how can this book be a lead-in to other activities?

Cooking Center: **Cooking spaghetti and meatballs**
Dramatic Play Center: Setting up and **operating a pretend restaurant**

Choose books on the basis of possible follow-up activities.

Large-Motor Center: **Throwing and catching a "meatball"** (colored tennis ball); playing **"meatball toss"** into a bucket

Art Center: **Meatball stamping** using tennis balls and golf balls dipped in colored paint; drawings to illustrate children's stories

Music Center: **Singing book version of the song**, making up children's own version, and recording it

Writing Center: **Writing menus** for their restaurant; writing (dictating) their own exciting **"meatball" adventures**

Block Center: Building a pretend town

Science Center: Planting or **transplanting a real tree** outside to be called "Marvelous Meatball Tree."

Field trip: To a spaghetti restaurant

Ideas from this chapter can help to make your Book Center one of the most dynamic parts of the curriculum. If your children have truly made a real book connection, you can consider their experience with your Appropriate Practices Curriculum successful.

IDEAS IN CHAPTER 6

1. *Reading in the preschool classroom*

    a. Have daily reading of stories

    b. Use predictable books

2. *Promoting reading in the home*

    a. Have a duplicate collection of lending books for children to borrow at the end of the day

    b. Invite parents to the Book Center to listen and then take a turn at reading themselves

    c. Send home a newsletter with names of books children are reading and give directions for making book extension games

    d. Have a "book bee" for parents to make book extension games

    e. Have a "My Favorite Books" chart to keep track of books children have had read to them at home and in school

    f. Take a field trip to a public library with parents to help

3. *Setting up the Book Center*

    a. Use bright colors in the Book Center on rugs, pillows, furniture, posters, etc.

    b. Display book extension puppets, puzzles, games, and posters

    c. Have felt board on a wall at children's height or on a low easel

    d. Have child-sized bookshelves displaying fronts of books

    e. Have inflated chairs, benches, sit-on foam animals, giant foam blocks, or junior couches to sit on

    f. Have an old bathtub with pillows for a book-reading place

    g. Have a core of favorite books always on shelves, but add new books from time to time

    h. Hang books on colored ribbons from a horizontal rod or clothesline

4. *Promoting language development*

    a. Have books that feature interesting words or funny sounds

    b. Read *Goodnight Moon* in whispery voice and say goodnight to items in the classroom

    c. Dramatize favorite books like *Caps for Sale* by bringing in some caps

    d. Bring in a tin pail when you read *Blueberries for Sal* and drop items into it

    e. Have books that feature repeated rhyming words or phrases

    f. Follow up *Sheep in a Jeep* with toy sheep and a vehicle

    g. Make flannel board characters from paperback books

    h. Tape-record reading of book with a sound cue for turning pages

5. *Promoting social development*

    a. Role-play characters from multicultural books through puppets, character dolls, or pretending

6. *Promoting emotional development*

    a. Follow up *It Wasn't My Fault* by making scrambled eggs

7. *Selecting books*

    a. Have a hands-on experience first with books you plan to buy

8. *Reading books*

    a. Do story reading with individuals and small groups only

    b. Read to individuals and small groups at least once a day

    c. Become acquainted with the book you are going to read

    d. Decide how to introduce the book to get the children's attention

    e. Read with expression

    f. Read the same stories over and over

    g. Involve children in repeating words and guessing

    h. Talk about the story afterward

9. *Doing follow-up book activities*

    a. Scan book illustrations to cut up for puzzles, flannel board characters, board games, paper dolls, stick puppets, and counting games

    b. Do follow-up activities with *On Top of Spaghetti* in many centers

DISCUSSION QUESTIONS

1. Why is the bringing together of children and books one of the most important services you can perform for your children?

2. What is "emergent literacy" and how is it different from "reading readiness"?

3. How do children teach themselves to read before they go to school? Should this be promoted?

4. Should you teach reading in the preschool? Why or why not? If not, what should you do about reading?

5. What are "predictable books" and why are they important in the preschool classroom?

TRY IT YOURSELF

1. Set up your Story Center as described in this chapter, with rugs, pillows, bright colors, posters, games, puppets, and a core of good early childhood picture books, displayed attractively. (Or make a similar diorama.)

2. Read a book to a small group in the center that will promote their language development based on "sound play." Have a follow-up activity that extends the learning based on the book.

3. Use a book with children to promote their social development. Follow up with an activity based on the book in another part of the classroom.

4. Bring in several predictable books, tell what makes them predictable, use them with children, and report on the results.

5. Put an appropriate book in each of your learning centers. What books will you choose? How do you plan to use them? Report the results.

REFERENCES CITED

Barclay, K. D. & Walwer, J. (1992). Linking lyrics and literacy through song picture books. *Young Children 47*(4), 76–85.

Campbell, R. (1998). A day of literacy learning in a nursery classroom. In R. Campbell (Ed.), *Facilitating preschool literacy*. Newark, DE: International Reading Association.

Corsaro, W. A. (2003). *We're friends, right? Inside kids culture*. Washington, DC: Joseph Henry Press.

Ellis, S. M., Gallingane, C., & Kemple, K. (2006). Fiction, fables, and fairytales: Children's books can support friendships. *Dimensions of Early Childhood 34*(3), 28–35.

Morrow, L. M. & Gambrell, L. B. (2004). *Using children's literature in preschool: Comprehending and enjoying books*. Newark, DE: International Reading Association.

Neuman, S. B. & Roskos, K. A. (1993). *Language and learning in the early years: An integrated approach*. Fort Worth, TX: Harcourt Brace.

Ramsey, P. G. (1991). *Making friends in school: Promoting peer relationships in early childhood*. New York: Teachers College Press.

Schwartz, J. (1981). Child's experiments with language. *Young Children 36*(5), 16–26.

Seefeldt, C. & Wasik, B. W. (2006). *Early education: Three-, four-, and five-year-olds go to school* (2nd ed.), Upper Saddle River, NJ: Merrill/Prentice Hall.

Strasser, J. & Seplocha, H. (2007). Using picture books to support young children's literacy. *Childhood Education 83*(4), 219–224.

Other Sources

Al-Hazza, T. & Lucking, B. (2007). Celebrating diversity through explorations of Arab children's literature. *Childhood Education 83*(3), 132–135.

Beaty, J. J. & Pratt, L. (2007). *Early literacy in preschool and kindergarten: A multicultural perspective*. Upper Saddler River, NJ: Merrill/Prentice Hall.

Feeney, S. & Moravcik, E. (2005). Children's literature: A window to understanding self and others. *Young Children 60*(5), 20–27.

Kok, K. & Buzzelli, C. A. (2004). The moral of the story is … Using children's literature in moral education. *Young Children 59*(1), 92–97.

Lillestolen, S. R. (2006). "Teach me a story": A literacy legacy. *Dimensions of Early Childhood 34*(1), 23–27.

Ordonez-Jasis, R. & Ortiz, R. W. (2006). Reading their worlds: Working with diverse families to enhance children's early literacy development. *Young Children 61*(1), 42–47.

Children's Books

Ada, A. F. (2002). *I love Saturdays y domingos*. NY: Atheneum.*

Aroner, M. (2006). *Clink clank clunk*! Honesday, PA: Boyds Mills Press.

Ashley, B. (1991). *Cleversticks*. NY: Crown Publishers.*

Bang, M. (1999). *When Sophie gets angry—really, really angry*. NY: Blue Sky Press.

Beaumont, K. (2002). *Being friends*. NY: Dial.

Becker, S. (2006). *Mine! Mine! Mine!* NY: Sterling Publishing Co.

Begaye, L. S. (1993). *Building a bridge.* Flagstaff, AZ: Northland.*

Bergman, M. (2005). *Snip snap! What's that?* New York: Greenwillow Books.

Bertrand, D. G. (2003). *The empanadas that Abuela made.* Houston, TX: Pinata Books.*

Brammer, E. C. (2003). *My tata's guitar.* Houston, TX: Pinata Books.*

Brown, M. W. (1947). *Goodnight moon.* New York: Harper & Row.

Cave, K. (2004). *That's what friends do.* New York: Hyperion Books.

Chapra, M. (2004). *Amelia's show-and-tell.* New York: Katherine Tegen Books.*

Chodos-Irvine, M. (2006). *Best best friends.* Orlando, FL: Harcourt.

Choi, S. N. (1993). *Halmoni and the picnic.* Boston: Houghton Mifflin.*

Cronin, D. (2006). *Dooby dooby moo.* New York: Atheneum.

Curtis, J. L. (2002). *I'm gonna like me: Letting off a little self-esteem.* New York: Joanna Cotler Books.

Dole, M. L. (2003). *Drum. Chavi, drum.* San Francisco, CA: Children's Book Press.*

Dorros, A. (1991). *Abuela.* New York: Dutton.*

Durango, J. (2006). *Cha-cha chimps.* New York: Simon & Schuster.

Elliott, L. M. (2002). *Hunter's best friend at school.* New York: HarperCollins.

Harper, C. M. (2002). *There was a bold lady who wanted a star.* Boston: Megan Tingley Books.

Hoberman, M. A. (1998). *Miss Mary Mack.* Boston: Little Brown & Co.*

Hoberman, M. A. (2003). *Mary had a little lamb.* Boston: Megan Tingley Books.

Isadora, R. (2005). *Luke goes to bat.* New York: G. P. Putnam's Sons.*

Jabar, C. (2006). *Wow! It sure is good to be you!* Boston: Houghton Mifflin Co.*

Johnson, P. B. (2006). *On top of spaghetti.* New York: Scholastic Press.*

Kovalski, M. (1987). *The wheels on the bus.* Boston: Little, Brown.

Lester, H. (1985). *It wasn't my fault.* Boston: Houghton Mifflin.

Lester, H. (1992). *Me first.* Boston: Houghton Mifflin.

Martin, B. (2006). *Fire! Fire! Said Mrs. McGuire.* Orlando, FL: Harcourt.

Mayo, M. (2002). *Dig dig digging.* New York: Henry Holt.

McCloskey, R. (1948). *Blueberries for Sal.* New York: Viking.

Novak, M. (2005). *Flip flop bop.* Brookfield, CN: Roaring Brook Press.

Pinkney, J. (2006). *The little red hen.* New York: Dial.

Ringgold, F. (1991). *Tar beach.* New York: Crown Publishers.*

Shaw, N. (1986). *Sheep in a jeep.* Boston: Houghton Mifflin.

Slobodkina, E. (1968). *Caps for sale.* New York: Scholastic Press.

Sloat, T. (1998). *There was an old lady who swallowed a trout.* New York: Henry Holt.*

Smith, C. L. (2000). *Jingle dancer.* New York: Morrow Junior Books.*

Spanyol, J. (2001). *Carlo likes reading.* Cambridge, MA: Candlewick Press.

Stevens, J. R. (1993). *Carlos and the squash plant.* Flagstaff, AZ: Northland.*

Sweet, M. (1992). *Fiddle-I-Fee.* Boston: Little, Brown.

Trapani, I. (1993). *Itsy bitsy spider.* Boston: Whispering Coyote.

Vail, R. (2002). *Sometimes I'm Bombaloo.* New York: Scholastic Press.

Weeks, S. (1998). *Mrs. McNosh hangs up her wash*. New York: A Laura Geringer Book.

Westcott, N. B. (1980). *I know an old lady who swallowed a fly*. Boston: Little, Brown.

Westcott, N. B. (1988). *The lady with the alligator purse*. Boston: Little, Brown.

Westcott, N. B. (1989). *Skip to my Lou*. Boston: Little, Brown.

Note: Asterisk represents multicultural book.

CHAPTER 7 WRITING CENTER

LETTERS

I can say the alphabet
  A-B-C-D-E,

I can print the alphabet
  L-M-N-O-P,

I can write the alphabet,
  Watch me make a loop;

I can eat the alphabet
  When it's in my soup!

WRITING AS A NATURAL DEVELOPMENT

Just as learning to read can develop naturally with young children in a print-rich environment, so can learning to write. The new concept of "emergent literacy" discussed in chapter 6 refers both to reading and to writing as emerging naturally within children when they are surrounded by reading and writing activities at home and in the preschool and encouraged to interact with them playfully.

Why did we not know this about children before? If writing is truly a natural development, why did we fail to see it happening and encourage it to unfold naturally? And why do we still "teach" writing to children in the primary grades?

It is another case of "we see what we look for." In the past, adults assumed that children had to be "taught" to write. Therefore, we rarely paid attention to the pre-writing skills that young children have always displayed from infancy on. When children scribbled on paper, on frosted windows, or even in the mud, we dismissed it as nothing of real importance —merely something children always did before they could draw, just as babbling was something children did before they could talk.

Now we know better. It soon became obvious that the more researchers looked for evidence of emergent writing in young children, the more they found. First of all, they took a closer look at children's scribbling and discovered it was not all the same. Infants scribbled differently from toddlers. Toddlers scribbled differently from preschoolers. In fact, there seemed to be a definite progression from random scribbling, to controlled scribbling, to the writing of mock letters and words, and finally to real writing as children experimented and matured.

Furthermore, the children themselves realized what they were doing. They could even tell the difference between scribbles that were drawings and scribbles that were writing. Many could even read their scribble writing. Now we understand that just as babbling is a foundation for speaking, so scribbling is a foundation for writing. And both speaking and writing are different forms of the same basic urge found in all human beings: the desire to communicate, to make connections with one another. We now realize that if we expect this progression from scribbling to writing to occur naturally, we must nurture it in the home and in the preschool classroom. **We must fill the children's environment with examples of words, of print, and of written-down talk**. We must encourage and support any attempts at writing our children make, no matter how crude (Mayer, 2007; pp. 34–40).

Just as we display the children's art—even their scribbles and blobs so **we must also display the children's writing—even their scribbles and lines**. In addition, we need to provide a Writing Center in our preschool classrooms so that children will understand these new expectations of ours: that we count on them to make natural and playful experiments with writing, just as they do with art, blocks, and puzzles.

WRITING IN THE PRESCHOOL CLASSROOM

The print-rich environment discussed in chapter 6 applies in equal measure to a classroom where the natural development of writing is encouraged. Some examples of printed material that should be displayed throughout your classroom include:

Labels
on activity areas
on equipment shelves
on grocery items

Signs
for Block Center buildings
for building safety
for playground safety traffic signs

Children's names
on cubbies
on children's art, writing
on children's place mats
on children's stories
on attendance chart
on helper's chart

Charts
children's height, weight
growth of plants
weather

books read

recipes

menus

rules
activity schedules

Sign-up sheets
computer turns

art projects

uses of equipment

activities

outdoor play equipment turns

Bulletin board
notices

letters, invitations, thank-you notes

cards

directions

messages

Other
picture books

children's stories

Children's printed names should appear on their cubbies, their place mats, and on all of their work.

computer programs

self-regulating devices

maps

daily schedule

floor plan

first-aid kit

calendar

SETTING UP THE WRITING CENTER

This activity area should be located as close as possible to the Book Center and/or the Computer Center. Writing activities can then be stimulated by or spill over into these two areas as children become excited about written communication.

The Writing Center should contain a table and chairs—or better still, a child-sized desk. **A child-sized rolltop desk with pigeonhole compartments is a natural stimulus for writing.** Children are excited to be sitting at such a grown-up desk. You may need to have a sign-up sheet for turns at the desk as you do for turns at the computer. The compartments of such a desk should be filled with writing and printing tools and implements, such as the following.

Pencils: regular pencils, primary-size pencils, carpenter's pencils, soft colored pencils

Markers: felt-tip markers of various sizes and colors (water-soluble ink)

Pencil sharpeners: regular fastened-down sharpener; small hand-held sharpeners of different types

Paper clips: container of large paper clips

Stapler: child-size stapler and staples

Rulers: several wood and plastic rulers

Scissors: several pairs

Hole punch: several hole punchers and large brads for fastening

Rubber stamps: alphabet letters, rubber animal stamps, dinosaur stamps, flower stamps, etc.; address stamps, stamp pads of different color inks

The drawers of such a desk should be filled with the following.

Paper: blank typing paper, light-colored construction paper

Pads and tablets: small multicolor pads, writing tablets; pads with self-sticking pages

Notebooks: spiral notebooks, secretary's dictation notebooks, loose-leaf notebooks

Stationery: various kinds of notepaper and matching envelopes; regular white envelopes

Cards: 3-by-5 cards of various colors

Paste: rubber cement, glue, cellophane tape

Peel-offs: blank peel-off labels, peel-off stickers with pictures and designs, large peel-off alphabet letters, address labels

Stamps: cancelled stamps of various kinds

Small school-type desks or a table with several chairs can also serve well in the Writing Center. The area can be sectioned off with a shelf divider that contains **sets of alphabet letters**: plastic, wooden, magnetic, sandpaper, a sectioned box of movable alphabet letters, and sheets of peel-off letters of various sizes. Other materials can include: thick, soft, **colored sidewalk chalk and several individual chalkboards**; pencil box sets; alphabet books, and other picture books to motivate writing.

Chalkboards are fine, but the latest piece of writing equipment from Demco (1-800-356-1200) is a stand-up magnetic flannel board for letters on one side with a white marker board on the reverse.

Another of the shelves of the divider might hold several **small cases or backpacks for overnight lending, which contain a number of the writing tools and supplies** just mentioned. Children can borrow these cases and return them the next day, just as they do with your duplicate picture books. Children need to be involved with pleasurable writing activities at home as well as in the preschool. Parents may not be aware of their children's desire and need to communicate in writing at this early age. Circulating such writing materials into the home not only supports their children's interests but also affords you an opportunity to involve the family in a developmentally appropriate activity they may not be aware of (Love, Burns, & Buell, 2007; p. 18).

Filling your center with writing implements like this is no different than stocking your Art Center with painting supplies. It delivers a powerful message to the children: the teacher expects them to participate and experiment with writing activities on their own, just as they do with painting activities in the Art Center.

Another table in the area can feature a typewriter. Either a **primary typewriter or a regular adult typewriter** is preferred to a child's toy typewriter, which is often difficult to use. Old standard manual typewriters are often available at very reasonable prices from used office equipment dealers—or perhaps from a parent. How will children use it? Just as they use the computer, the youngsters will experiment with the typewriter until they get it to work the way it is supposed to. Then they will type—with or without paper—often in play or pretending activities, but sometimes typing real words or their names.

Another piece of equipment in the Writing Center that can be used with surprising results is **a sand table**. Children like to smooth out the surface of sand and use it for scribbling, writing, and printing letters and their names. Or they may stamp letters into wet sand from the wooden or magnetic alphabet letters on the shelf. They also can create scenes from the stories you have read or told them (Barbour, Webster, & Drosdeck, 1987). You may want to consider using a sand table for several months here in the Writing Center before shifting it to the Science Center for a completely different type of activity.

Have children make and decorate personal mailboxes from shoe or cereal boxes that are then stacked on one of the shelves in the center. You can print children's names on the end of the box that is cut to open. Have a large cardboard or wooden mailbox available as well. With your help, the child mail carrier for the day can collect and deliver mail from this box to the personal boxes.

The walls of the Writing Center should feature a variety of **colorful posters or pictures with labels**, a bulletin board for mounting children's writing or your messages to them, magazine pictures of children writing, and the alphabet letters from A to Z in upper and lower case. Book posters are appropriate here as well.

Depending on your wall space in the Writing Center, you may want **a wall hanging that contains letters**. Quilts, rugs, or children's bedspreads featuring the alphabet can be hung on the wall. Colorful carpeting with squares of alphabet letters can be ordered through school-supply companies. Flannel boards to be used with alphabet letters can be purchased or homemade.

Like the other learning centers in the classroom, the Writing Center is set up for children to explore and to play independently. We understand it is not appropriate for preschool teachers to give children formal instruction in writing. Instead, your program should encourage children to experiment with written symbols through play, just as they learned to talk by playing with sounds.

Learning to talk and learning to read and write begin as a kind of play for children. Play is how children make connections between their immediate personal world and activities in the larger social context of family and community. They begin by playing with speech sounds in ways that resemble nonsense syllables, and by playing with the implements and materials of written language. They may even use characters and plots from their favorite stories in their pretend play (Neuman & Roskos, 1993; pp. 48–49).

SCRIBBLING AND MOCK WRITING

All children everywhere scribble before they write, just as they babble before they talk. The earliest marks they make often occur before their first birthday, and are sometimes called "random scribbling." If infants are given writing tools, they will grip them in a fist and make marks on surfaces in a random manner without even watching what they are doing (Lamme, 1984). If adults in the vicinity show excitement in the scribbles or praise the youngsters for their efforts, they will continue with gusto. If, on the other hand, they are scolded or punished for marking up surfaces other than paper or chalkboards, they may discontinue their experiments with writing.

Even Mark Twain understood the importance of young children's scribbling and praised them for it. In a Christmas note to his little daughter Susy, in which he pretends to be Santa Claus, he writes:

My dear Susy Clemens: I have received and read all the letters which you and your little sister have written me by the hand of your mother and your nurses; I have also read those which you little people have written me with your own hands—for although you did not use any characters that are in grown people's alphabet, you used the characters that all children in all lands on earth and in the twinkling stars use; and as all my subjects in the moon are children and use no characters but that, you will easily understand that I can read your and your baby sister's jagged and fantastic marks without any trouble at all…. You will find that I made no mistakes about the things which you and the baby ordered in your own letters—I went down your chimney at midnight when you were asleep and delivered them all myself. (Salsbury, 1965, p. 46)

With practice and maturity comes control. By the time children have reached preschool age, they are usually able to do what is called "controlled scribbling." Here, children watch the marks they are making and place them where they want them on the paper. The scribbles generally take the form of circles, lines, dots, and splotches, although some scribbles are emerging into the basic shapes of circles, squares, triangles, and crosses. At this point scribbling often takes two different paths, one eventually becoming drawing and the other writing. Drawing scribbles are discussed in chapter 8, "Art Center."

As young children have more experience with print materials, they seem to recognize that writing occurs in horizontal lines, whereas art occupies whole spaces. Children in your class may thus begin making large scribbled art products

This child is using a marker board to do controlled scribbling, a precursor to writing and drawing.

that they identify as particular objects, with small linear scribbles underneath that they say "tells the story." They have progressed to the "named scribbling" stage.

At this point they will frequently ask an adult to write for them. They may want you to write down what their painting is about, to make a sign for their block building, or to write a note to their Mom. Sometimes they will scribble under or above your writing, or ask you to write underneath their line of scribbles. Often they will try to copy what you have written; encourage them in this endeavor. Copying seems to speed up the writing process for young children, whereas, tracing slows it down (Lamme, 1984). Nevertheless, because the development of writing is such a personal, as well as a spontaneous, affair for the young child, encourage each one to proceed as he or she is doing. If tracing alphabet letters appeals to the children, let them continue doing it.

At the same time, children are becoming aware of what real words look like and of the letters that make up words. At this point "letter awareness" begins to follow a parallel development with scribbling in children's progression into conventional writing.

Children who take pleasure in the fun of writing will now often fill pages with horizontal lines of scribbling. You soon recognize this as their "mastery" level of interaction, whereas, their earlier scribbling was certainly "manipulating the medium." Sometimes these children ask you to read their "writing" because they "can't read," and they believe that someone who can read should be able to decipher their "writing." You might respond by asking them what they think it says. Your Writing Center should appeal to children at this mastery level because of the exciting array of writing implements and writing surfaces you have provided for their use.

If you are keeping an eye on your children's writing products, you will eventually note that some of their linear scribbles are beginning to resemble letters, and that some may even resemble words. The children also may notice what is happening and share their discovery with great excitement if they know it will please you. They have arrived at the so-called mock letter and mock word stage in their progression into writing. To form mock words, they often separate their linear scribbles with a line or a period after each one. Some children even draw a circle around each mock word. It is not up to you to "correct" these spontaneous efforts. The children will eventually recognize how adults (you) divide lines of writing into words by leaving a space between each word.

Young children often fill pages with their mock writing. As they progress into the "meaning" level of writing development, they are more likely to tell you rather than ask you what it says. They are still scribbling, although their scribbles resemble conventional writing more and more—just as the "jargon" stage of young children's language development resembles real speech. For preschoolers this process of writing is much more important than any product they create. Nevertheless, they are usually pleased when you recognize their work and display it on a bulletin board. It is a motivation for them to continue writing.

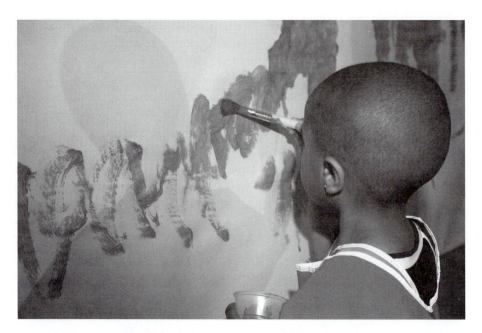

Eventually some of the children's linear scribbles may begin to resemble letters.

Think about it: have you ever displayed a page of a child's writing scribbles on the wall just as you do a child's artwork? Children extract important messages from what we do and what we do not do. They quickly understand what the adults in their lives consider important, as well as what is not important. If we want them to feel that writing is important, then we should display their pre-writing products.

LETTER AWARENESS

Letter awareness seems to follow a parallel development with print awareness in young children. In extracting this kind of meaning from their world, children first perceive print (writing) as lines (sentences). Later their perception becomes more refined as they recognize the divisions in the lines that are words. Still later they recognize that words are made up of letters.

The first letters they recognize are often those in their own names, because adults sign children's names on their work and encourage children to print their own names. In the beginning they often learn to make the first letter of their name and let that stand for their whole name. But soon they are printing their entire name, although not always in proper order, in conventional forms of letters, or in linear arrangement.

As with their early attempts at drawing, children's first printing of letters is a free-flowing sort of expression with letters of all sizes and shapes floating here and there on the page. A child named Kathy, for instance, may print a backward "K" somewhere on a sheet of paper. Then she may print a larger "a" somewhere else, maybe nowhere near the "K." She may not like the way that "a" turned out, so she makes another smaller one—or two. Then comes the "t." For this she turns her paper sideways where there is more room and makes a "t." The "h" she makes is up in the corner, and the final "y," which looks more like a "v," is down near the bottom of the paper. She has written her name!

Because you know that the process of writing her name is more important than the final product, you accept her effort with pleasure just as it is. She will eventually refine her writing skill by combining what she has learned about mock writing with what she is learning about alphabet letters. Little by little she will develop a sense of left-to-right progression, of linear writing, and of letter size, letter shape, and orientation.

If children are surrounded by letters, letter games, alphabet books, computer alphabet programs, and other letter activities, they will eventually learn to distinguish a number of alphabet letters. It is neither necessary nor appropriate to teach your children the letters of the alphabet in any formal sense. **Let them play around with letters, words, and writing** in your Writing Center and elsewhere in the classroom. If they ask you how to make a letter, show them. If they ask you the name of a certain letter, tell them. Thus they will teach themselves to recognize the letters they need to know as they use them playfully and seriously in the activities they pursue.

Emergent Writing in Preschoolers

1. Random scribbles

2. Controlled scribbles

3. Named scribbles

4. Mock letters and words

5. Real letters and words

WRITING ACTIVITIES TO PROMOTE COGNITIVE DEVELOPMENT
Alphabet Letters

For preschool children, the recognition and naming of letters are cognitive concepts related to their future reading achievement. Nevertheless, there is controversy regarding whether or not the "teaching of the alphabet" to preschoolers is appropriate. We realize that children can learn to read without knowing the alphabet. Why, then, should they have to learn it?

Preschool children want to and need to learn about letters. It is not necessary for them to memorize the names of the 26 alphabet letters in order. But it is important as they play with letters and learn the important ones for them to develop the following concepts.

1. Speech can be written down.

2. Such writing takes the form of words.

3. Words are made up of letters that have names.

Literacy emerges naturally with children whose lives are surrounded by print, and their recognition of single letters is a part of this spontaneous unfolding. Any *formal* "teaching of the alphabet" on the part of the teacher is as unnecessary as it is inappropriate. Children are going to learn about letters in spite of what adults do or do not do. As Green (1998) tells us: "Knowledge of all the letter names and forms is by no means a prerequisite to writing. Many children begin writing their names when they know only a few letter forms" (p. 226).

Make letters personal. Children definitely want to learn about letters so they can print their own names. Some children already know how to print their names when they enter your program, but most 3-year-olds are barely at the beginning of the writing process. They usually ask one of the classroom adults to sign their names to art products. **As you sign children's names, ask them to sign their own names, too**. It may be only a scribble, but that is how writing starts. You can tell the children that what they have written is their "personal script," and that what you have written is "conventional script."

They know that scribbling their names on an art product is not the same as printing their names with letters. As Kirk and Clark (2005) note: "A young preschool child typically recognizes and labels the initial letter of his own name first before recognizing and labeling other letters, and will make attempts to write his own name before acquiring general alphabet and word knowledge" (p. 139).

You can help by making name cards for children to copy, and by pointing out and naming the letters of their names. Can they find those letters anywhere else in the room? Think of other ways you can incorporate children's names in helping children learn the letters that are important to them. Bring in a set of alphabet blocks and see if the child can make her name from the blocks. **Take a photo of her block name** and mount it on the bulletin board in the Writing Center.

Read books that feature names. An old standby still in print is *A My Name is ALICE* (Bayer, 1984) containing names of critters from A to Z presented as pattern-play-type rhymes; for example, "My name is Alice and my husband's name is Alex. We come from Alaska and we sell ants. Alice is an APE. Alex is an ANTEATER." If the children like the book, have them participate with rhyming patterns of their own names. A more recent rhyming name story is the comical *Eleanor, Ellatony, Ellencake, and Me* (Rubin, 2003). A girl who starts out as Eleanor lets each member of her family try to give her a different nickname with different talents they think she should have. It is too much. She finally confronts them all and declares she is just plain ELLIE. What do your children know about nicknames?

Have children collect the alphabet letters they know. Bring in (or have the children bring in) empty tissue boxes for their alphabet letters. The boxes can be painted by the children and labeled with their names. You can **provide letter cards** for your children to use by taking an old set of playing cards, pressing them face down onto the sticky side of white contact paper, and cutting them out. Next take a sheet of large peel-off letters and transfer one letter to the white face of each card. Keep these cards in a shoe box for the children to select when they want. Even if they do not really know the letters by name, they will soon learn them if you interact with individuals, saying, "Oh, Daryl, look at all the alphabet letters you have collected! Do you know the names of any of them?" Children can also find their own letters for their box by cutting them out of old magazines that you provide for this purpose. Where else might they look for letters?

Some children may be interested in going further with letters than merely collecting them. You may see them copying the letters they know on a sheet of paper—over and over until the page is filled. Then they take another sheet and fill that one, too. Do you recognize what they are doing? Yes, once again they are interacting with materials at the mastery level. By now you probably realize that whenever you see young children doing something over and over again, they have advanced to the mastery level. Don't forget to display their letter sheets on the Writing Center bulletin board.

Next comes the meaning level. How do children spontaneously transfer meaning to the letters they know? At first they use one letter to stand for an entire word such as their name: "K" means "Kathy." Then they begin to use other letters to stand for words: "R" stands for "are," and "U" stands for "you." At this point they have begun to understand that letters stand for sounds as well as for words. Eventually they realize that letters can be put together to make up words. They may print "KY" to stand for "key" or "HS" to mean "house" in a kind of emergent spelling. Most children, however, reach this more advanced understanding at age 5 or 6.

Computer alphabet programs in the Computer Center should be used in conjunction with hands-on alphabet activities in the Writing Center. Some popular programs include:

Blue's ABC Activities	*Dr. Seuss's ABC*
Chicka Chicka Boom Boom	*Reader Rabbit: The Great Alphabet Race*
Curious George Pre-K ABCs	*School Zone Alphabet Express Preschool*
Disney Learning Preschool	*Zoboomafoo Animal Alphabet*

Several sets of 3-D alphabet letters should be available (e.g., wood, plastic, magnetic, sandpaper, and so forth) for matching and sorting games. You can make your own games by **tracing around a set of wood or plastic letters onto a poster board, and letting children try to match the letters to the outlines**. Youngsters love to stretch out on the floor with the poster board and the letters strewn about. This same activity can be created with magnetic letters that you trace on a metal surface such as a refrigerator door or a metal marker board. Children enjoy pushing the magnetic letters into place on this vertical surface so that they fill up the entire outline.

The computer program children still seem to like the best is *Chicka Chicka Boom Boom*, from the book of the same name by Martin, B. & Archambault, J. (1989) in which the alphabet letters themselves are the characters scrambling to get to the top of a coconut tree, all the time wondering, chicka, chicka, boom, boom, will there be enough room? When it gets too crowded, they all tumble down. Read the book to the children before using the CD-ROM. **Have the children play their own chicka-chicka game** by choosing one of your 3-D letters and climbing it up the tree when it is their turn. The best part, of course, is tumbling it down. They'll want to do it over and over using a different letter every time.

What about the tree? **Make your own coconut tree** by planting an inverted broom in a bucket of rocks and sand, and covering the top with green crepe paper streamers or something else appropriate. Last letter up gets to shake the tree and tumble down all the letters. You can also purchase a free-standing 20-inch tree and set of 26 letters from Lakeshore (1-800-778-4456) or Constructive Playthings (1-800-448-4115).

Alphabet books from your Book Center also need to spend time in the Writing Center. Fresh versions of this popular form of picture book come out in new editions year after year. However, some alphabet books feature glorious illustrations that turn out to be more of a showcase for an artist than a learning experience for young children. Others may be too difficult for preschoolers, or too simple. Borrow a few alphabet books from the library and **try them out with your children before you purchase your own**.

Superhero ABC (McLeod, 2006) is in a class of its own with its huge comic-book-like heroes. You know children will love it, but make sure you feel it is appropriate. The superheroes from Astro-Man (who has asthma) to Goo Girl (who shoots gobs of goo at gangsters) to the Zinger (who zanily zigzags through the Zero Zone) may not be for you. *Max's ABC* (Wells, 2006) may be more to your liking. It is the hilarious story of Max bunny's ants who escape from his ant farm and go looking for his birthday cake—right up his pants. Sister Ruby tries tricks of all sorts to get rid of the pesky bugs, but the only thing that works is the vacuum cleaner—until Max empties the bag.

Alphabet Under Construction (Fleming, 2002), which comes with a long border poster, shows a mouse building, carving, nailing, and pruning each separate letter; great ideas for you and the children to create in the Art or Woodworking Center. Did you know there is a dinosaur for every letter of the alphabet? The giant book *The Dinosaurs' Alphabet* (Fortey, 1990) depicts each one along with a comic verse and a large cartoon-like drawing on every page. Young children enjoy holding big books like this. They may not ever learn all these names, but the fun of rolling big words like this on their tongues makes up for it. Be sure you practice saying these names ahead of time.

Eating the Alphabet: Fruits and Vegetables from A to Z (Ehlert, 1989) is a wonderful, colorful, tasty expedition from "Apple" to "Zucchini." Each set of horizontal double pages contains an upper- and lower-case letter with several brightly colored fruits or vegetables to illustrate the letter. Using this book with small groups of children can lead into **a series of field trips to purchase one or two of the alphabet food items** each time you go. Take the book along to identify the fruit or vegetable you want. For example, the "Aa" pages show apricots, artichokes, avocados, apples, and asparagus. Be sure to purchase enough of the food item for

DeWayne's grandma comes in and reads an alphabet book.

everyone. The Writing Center children can then divide up and **serve the "letter food"** to the rest of the children.

For example, the children may want to create a "C" snack for everyone by cutting up carrots, celery, cucumbers, and cauliflower that they have purchased at the store; they can mix a dip made of sour cream and dried onion soup to serve with the vegetables. Thus, the abstract concept of letters becomes real to children when concrete, three-dimensional objects are involved like this. How else can you make letters come alive for children? What about **making alphabet soup**?

After all of this, what do you think? Do alphabet books really teach alphabet letters to preschool children? Wasik (2001) has this to say: "Alphabet books introduce the concept that the alphabet is comprised of a group of letters that all have different names and shapes. Children can see all the alphabet letters together. They can also hear that the letters have different names. With some alphabet books such as *Chicka Chicka Boom Boom*, the children learn letters as if they were characters in the book" (p. 37).

Be sure to send some of the story alphabet books home. But also encourage family members to come in and read their favorites to individuals and small groups.

WRITING ACTIVITIES TO PROMOTE PHYSICAL DEVELOPMENT

Small Motor

Young children learn to hold and control a writing implement on their own; you do not need to teach them how. They start in infancy with a "power grip" fist around the crayon or chalk, and later switch naturally to a "precision grip" using fingers and thumb. Your best help will come from the variety of writing activities and materials you provide in your Writing Center. Don't put out all of your writing tools at once. **Add a new one to pique the children's interest** every once in a while, **using a new activity to introduce it**. For instance, add colored chalk and small individual chalkboards; or **have a wet chalk activity** on finger-painting paper or grocery bags. The children can dip the chalk in a cup of water before writing on the paper, or they can wet the paper first instead of the chalk.

Another time have finger-painting itself. To encourage children to do personal writing, have them **finger-paint on small trays**. Their scribbled writing can be saved by pressing a sheet of paper onto it and rubbing. Still another time let them write in the finger paint with an implement such as a tongue depressor. Children can also **write with their fingers in trays of salt**. They especially enjoy erasing their marks by carefully shaking the tray.

What can they do with a pencil? Some children immediately want to scribble and write with one. Others prefer felt-tip markers. All of them enjoy another Farmer Brown book where the farmer goes on vacation and duck finds a pencil. No more typewritten notes to the house-sitting brother Bob in *Giggle, Giggle, Quack* (Cronin, 2002); only penciled notes demanding pizzas for cows, bubble baths for pigs, and TV movies for all. This is a fine book for re-enacting the story as you re-read it. Put out little pads and pencils for children to write or scribble notes.

WRITING ACTIVITIES TO PROMOTE SOCIAL DEVELOPMENT

The wonderful thing about writing is that it can be a social activity for young children. They all can write an invitation or a **thank-you note on a large piece of newsprint**, dictating to you the words they want on their note or writing the words themselves in scribbled "personal script" with your translation underneath. Then the children can sign their names and add a decoration if they want. The note can be folded and mailed in a large manila envelope. Children enjoy writing together like this. They tell each other what they are doing, ask each other for help, and compare notes.

Communal notes can be messages asking for permission to do something, thanking a parent or community helper for visiting, asking for information about a topic the children are pursuing, sending greetings to someone having a birthday, inviting people to come to a class picnic, thanking people for helping on a field trip, asking a high school student to come and play the guitar, thanking a librarian for the story hour she performed, or sending a get-well message to someone in the hospital. **Bring into the Writing Center all kinds of greeting cards** when this activity is in progress.

Children may want to write notes or messages to one another as well. They can help **make individual mailboxes from half-gallon milk cartons** covered with contact paper, or from painted shoe boxes or cereal boxes. Children will be motivated to write if you give them reasons for doing written communication. Write a note to each of them yourself at least once a week. Put it in their mailbox, and ask them to reply. This means you need your own personal mailbox, as well, to receive their answers. Read them a multiethnic book such as *Like Me and You* (Raffi, 1985), showing a child from a different country on each page writing, mailing, receiving, and reading pen-pal letters.

Another classic re-issued book is *The Jolly Postman or Other People's Letters* (Ahlberg & Ahlberg, 1986), in which the postman delivers real letters (inside the book) to storybook characters: the three bears, the Wicked Witch, the Giant, Cinderella, the Wolf, and Goldilocks. Do your children know these characters? How would they reply to the letters?

Another social skill that can be promoted through writing is turn taking. **Children can write their names to sign up for a turn** with the various activities in the classroom: a special toy, a piece of playground equipment, a book, the computer, and so forth. Put clipboards with pencils attached in the various areas of the classroom where turn taking is necessary. Have children write their names under one another's and cross them off when their turn is finished. Even if children are still scribbling in their own personal script, they can sign their name this way. They will be able to identify their own signature whether or not you can.

WRITING ACTIVITIES TO PROMOTE LANGUAGE DEVELOPMENT

Just as children acquire their language ability naturally by saying sounds first and then words, so they also acquire their writing ability by making letters first and then words. They start with "naming words" in writing, just as they do in language acquisition. They usually begin by printing their own name as previously mentioned. But in a classroom that features a Writing Center, some children will eventually want to write other name words as well.

Some children make long lists of words they know, printing or scribbling them under one another. They may want to meet another list maker, such as Wallace, a mouse-boy who makes to-do lists for everything in his life in *Wallace's Lists* (Bottner & Kruglik, 2004). His adventure at the airport to meet his friend Albert includes a stop at a gigantic list: the Arrivals and Departures board. But his shortest list is his Best Friend list: Albert.

Involve your listeners in making printed or scribbled lists of their own. Be sure to post them in the Writing Center. Another kind of list is a shopping list. Do any of the children help their parents make a list of things to buy at the grocery store? For your next cooking activity be sure children are involved in listing and buying the ingredients. Also read *Bunny Cakes* (Wells, 1997), the comical misadventure Max and Ruby experience in making birthday cakes for Grandma's birthday. Little Max keeps messing up Ruby's cooking, so she sends him to the store with a list of replacement items. He scribbles down the one ingredient he wants for his cake: Red-Hot Marshmallow Squirters. But the grocer can't read his scribbles until he finally draws a picture of the Squirters.

Journaling is another way the children can apply their new skills in writing. In many preschools these days, **every child has a blank notebook to be used to record his daily happenings**. Some children draw a picture like Max did and scribble a linear letter string under it. Others ask the teacher to write what they dictate. If you do this, be sure to have the child write or scribble her own words under yours. To motivate journal writing read *Diary of a Spider* (Cronin, 2005), *Diary of a Worm* (Cronin, 2003) or *Diary of a Fly* (Cronin, 2007) in which three dissimilar friends record humorous daily happenings from totally different points of view.

What **writing activities** can you involve children in **after a field trip**? Some may want to write a story of the trip, dictating it to you to write down. Afterwards ask them to write their own version under your words. Others may draw pictures of

This boy made a sign for the zoo without any help.

the trip and scribble captions under them. Still others may hurry to the Block Center to build structures experienced on the trip. These structures will need signs, you may suggest. Can anyone be the sign maker as in *The Signmaker's Assistant* (Arnold, 1992)? How about a sign for the zoo they have built?

WRITING ACTIVITIES TO PROMOTE EMOTIONAL DEVELOPMENT

To help your children control their negative feelings, you may be suggesting that they express their feelings in words rather than acting them out. Instead of striking out at another child in anger, for example, they can tell that child in words how they feel. Instead of becoming upset and crying when someone takes their toy, they can tell the person how they feel.

Another way that strong negative feelings can be diffused is to **write down the words expressing the feelings**. You may be the one writing down the words. Ask the child how he feels when he is upset, and write down a word or two. Sometimes children will seem to project their feelings into the actual words you write. They may even want you to write their "feelings word" on a card for a personal word collection. Then they can get it out and look at it when they feel that way again.

THE TEACHER'S ROLE IN THE WRITING CENTER
Observing Developmental Levels

Once the Writing Center is set up and equipped, the teacher needs to observe in an informal manner the children who are using the center, commenting on their involvement and encouraging them in their continuation of their activities. The teacher can also determine whether particular children are interacting with writing materials at the manipulation, mastery, or meaning level in order to support them with activities that will extend their learning.

In order to record observations on the Child Interaction Form, the teacher needs to be aware of what kinds of Writing Center activities can occur at the manipulation level, the mastery level, and the meaning level. Table 7-1 lists a number of possibilities. Because children's pre-writing activities tend to be individual in nature, most interactions fall under the "Solitary Play" or "Parallel Play" categories. The gathering of data on the Child Interaction Form helps the classroom staff plan for individuals as well as identify the kinds of new materials to be introduced in the Writing Center.

In addition to recording an individual child's interaction level, the teacher also needs to keep track of which children use the Writing Center regularly and which ones do not. The teacher's own presence in the center may bring in children who have not yet experimented with writing. Her attention to individuals may encourage them to attempt this new skill. She may also offer a direct invitation to

Table 7-1 Writing Center Activities: Levels of Interaction

Manipulation Level
Scribblings Playing with alphabet letters or blocks without regard to their names Playing with writing implements without writing Playing with stamping or printing materials without regard to meaning Playing with salt tray, sand table, or finger-painting without writing Making letters here and there on paper Playing around with computer alphabet programs with no control Playing with a typewriter without control

Mastery Level
Mock-writing the same words over and over again, sometimes in a list Filling a page with mock writing Making a list of words Writing/typing a letter, name, or word over and over Tracing letters over and over Matching 3-D letters, categorizing letters Stamping letters or pictures over and over Making letters, names, and words over and over on salt tray, or in finger-paint Playing with computer alphabet programs over and over

Meaning Level
Writing name scribble on paper, salt tray, sand table, or in finger-paint Printing name or words with letters Writing name or word on typewriter or computer Arranging alphabet letters or blocks to make name, words Stamping letters to make name, words Scribbling under drawing and telling what it says Making mock-writing sign, label Making mock-writing message Making mock-writing story and "reading" it back

a child who has not become involved. Perhaps the child can "write" a note to his mother or father about the block building he has constructed to go along with the digital photo he is taking home. Children are more often motivated to attempt a new activity when it relates to them personally.

Finally, sensitive teachers will keep their eyes and ears open to children's own ideas and suggestions, so that they can structure the Writing Center to better serve the needs of individuals. If they make the center fun for preschoolers, children will engage in writing activities with the same zest they bring to dramatic play or block building. Teachers understand that it is not their role to "teach" young children to write, but to set up a Writing Center to entice them to become deeply involved in writing activities on their own.

IDEAS IN CHAPTER 7

1. *Setting up the Writing Center*
   a. Fill the children's environment with examples of the children's writing and reading
   b. Display the children's writing, even their scribbles and lines
   c. Have a rolltop desk with pigeonholes to stimulate writing
   d. Provide sets of alphabet letters in wood, plastic, sandpaper, and magnetic materials
   e. Provide colored chalk and individual chalkboards
   f. Provide cases or backpacks of writing materials for overnight lending
   g. Provide a primary typewriter or a regular standard typewriter
   h. Have a sand table in the Writing Center
   i. Feature book posters with labels in the Writing Center
   j. Have an alphabet wall hanging, quilt, or rug in the Writing Center

2. *Promoting cognitive development*
   a. Let children "play around" with letters, words, and writing
   b. Have simple alphabet computer programs
   c. Trace around a set of alphabet letters and have children try to match the letters with their outlines
   d. Have alphabet books but check them carefully for their appropriateness for preschoolers
   e. Take field trips to purchase alphabet food items
   f. Create letter snacks for everyone
   g. Make alphabet soup
   h. Ask children to sign their own names, even if they are scribbles
   i. Make alphabet letters personal by using children's names in many ways
   j. Take a photo of children's names made from alphabet blocks
   k. Read books that feature names
   l. Have children collect alphabet letters
   m. Use playing cards, contact paper, and press type to make letter cards

3. *Promoting small-motor development*

   a. Add a new writing tool and a new activity to the Writing Center periodically

   b. Have a "wet chalk" activity

   c. Have children do finger-paint writing on small trays

   d. Have children write with fingers on trays of salt

4. *Promoting social development*

   a. Do a total group thank-you note on newsprint

   b. Bring in all kinds of greeting cards

   c. Make individual mail boxes from half-gallon milk cartons

   d. Have children "sign-up" to take a turn

5. *Promoting language development*

   a. Involve children in making lists

   b. Involve children in daily journaling

   c. Have children make signs after a field trip

6. *Promoting emotional development*

   a. Write down "feeling words" to help children diffuse strong negative feelings

DISCUSSION QUESTIONS

1. How can children teach themselves to write naturally? Should they?

2. What is the importance of children's scribbling, and why should we display it in the classroom?

3. Does it matter what materials and equipment you put in the Writing Center? Why? Give some examples.

4. What is the sequence for children's natural development of writing? How can you help them progress through it?

5. How do children naturally develop letter awareness? What support should you give?

TRY IT YOURSELF

1. Set up a Writing Center in your classroom with shelves full of writing tools, equipment, activities, computer programs, books, posters, a typewriter, and a bulletin board as described in this chapter. (Or make a diorama of one.)

2. Set up a print-rich environment in other areas of your classroom with labels, signs, children's names, charts, sign-up sheets, bulletin boards, and other print materials.

3. Do an alphabet letter activity with a small group as described in the chapter, using wood, plastic, or metal letters, books, a computer program, cards, or a field trip.

4. Do a writing activity with a small group as described in the chapter, involving the children's actually "writing" a story, a letter, a note, or something else.

5. Make an assessment of five of your children as to the level of involvement they display in writing or printing letters (i.e., manipulation, mastery, or meaning) and describe how you determined their level.

REFERENCES CITED

Barbour, N., Webster, T. D., & Drosdeck, S. (1987). Sand: A resource for the language arts. *Young Children 42*(2), 20–25.

Green, C. R. (1998). This is my name. *Childhood Education 76*(3), 130–135.

Kirk, E. W. & Clark, P. (2005). Beginning with names: Using children's names to facilitate literacy learning. *Childhood Education 81*(3), 139–144.

Lamme, L. L. (1984). *Growing up writing*. Washington, DC: Acropolis Books.

Love, A., Burns, M. S., & Buell, M. J. (2007). Writing: Empowering Literacy. *Young Children 62*(1), 12–19.

Mayer, K. (2007). Research in review: Emerging knowledge about emergent writing. *Young Children 62*(1), 34–40.

Neuman, S. B. & Roskos, K. A. (1993). *Language and literacy learning in the early years: An integrated approach*. Fort Worth, TX: Harcourt Brace.

Salsbury, E. C. (Ed.). (1965). *Susy and Mark Twain, Family dialogues*. New York: Harper & Row.

Wasik, B. A. (2001). Teaching the alphabet to young children. *Young Children 56*(1), 34–39.

Other Sources

Baghban, M. (2007). Scribbles, labels, and stories: The role of drawing in the development of writing. *Young Children 62*(1), 20–26.

Beaty, J. J. & Pratt, L. (2007). *Early literacy in preschool and kindergarten: A multicultural perspective*. Upper Saddle River, NJ: Merrill/Prentice Hall.

Hayes, L. E. (1990). From scribbling to writing: Smoothing the way. *Young Children 45*(3), 62–67.

Roskos, K. A. & Neuman, S. B. (1994). Of scribbles, schemas, and storybooks: Using literacy albums to document young children's literacy growth. *Young Children 49* (2), 78–85.

Schickendanz, J. A. (1999). *Much More than the ABCs: The early stages of reading and writing.* Washington, DC: National Association for the Education of Young Children.

Schickedanz, J. A. & Casbergue, R. M. (2004). *Writing in preschool: Learning to orchestrate meaning and marks.* Newark, DE: International Reading Association.

Strickland, D. S. & Morrow, L. M. (2000). *Beginning reading and writing.* New York: Teachers College Press.

Children's Books

Ahlberg, J. & Ahlberg, A. (1986). *The jolly postman or other people's letters.* Boston: Little, Brown, and Company.

Arnold, T. (1992). *The Signmaker's Assistant.* New York: Dial.

Bayer, J. (1984). *A my name is ALICE.* New York: Dial.

Bottner, B. & Kruglik, G. (2004). *Wallace's lists.* New York: Katherine Tegen Books.

Cronin, D. (2002). *Giggle, giggle, quack.* New York: Simon & Schuster.

Cronin, D. (2003). *Diary of a worm.* New York: Joanna Cotler Books.

Cronin, D. (2005). *Diary of a spider.* New York: Joanna Cotler Books.

Cronin, D. (2007). *Diary of a fly.* New York: Joanna Cotler Books.

Ehlert, L. (1989). *Eating the alphabet; Fruits and vegetables from A to Z.* San Diego: Harcourt Brace Jovanovich.

Fleming, D. (2002).*Alphabet under construction.* New York: Henry Holt and Company.

Fortey, R. (1990). *The dinosaur's alphabet.* New York: Barron's.

Martin, B. & Archambault, J. (1989). *Chicka chicka boom boom.* New York: Simon & Schuster.

McLeod, B. (2006). *Superhero ABC.* New York: HarperCollins.*

Raffi. (1985). *Like me and you.* New York: Crown.*

Rubin, C. M. (2003). *Eleanor, Ellatony, Ellencake, and me.* Columbus, OH: McGraw-Hill Children's Publishing.

Wells, R. (1997). *Bunny cakes.* New York: Dial Books.

Wells, R. (2006). *Max's ABC.* New York: Viking

Note: Asterisk represents multicultural book.

ART IN THE EARLY CHILDHOOD CLASSROOM

Young children seem to have a natural affinity for art just as they do for speaking and writing, if their environment is full of interesting opportunities. Art, like language, is a means of communication and self-expression for children. It is visual, though, rather than verbal, and involves the elements of line, shape, color, and texture rather than words.

Because young children have an inborn drive to communicate, they continually work at the development of this ability in every possible aspect. They coo, cry, babble, and finally speak. They scribble horizontally, play with letters, and finally write. In art they scribble, make shapes, combine shapes, and finally draw pictures. They experiment with colors and play around with textures. **If given a wide variety of materials as well as the freedom and time to discover how these work**, young children will teach themselves the art skills they need in order to express themselves. This communication can come from deep inside the children, revealing their uniqueness as few other classroom activities can do:

> Art has the role in education of helping children become more themselves instead of more like everyone else. Each child's inner existence calls for expression and takes pleasure in such expression. The arts can be the medium for this expression if children have access to materials, the time to explore them, and respectful encouragement in their exploration. (Clemens, 1991, p. 4)

Thus, art lends itself well to the activities of the self-directed learning environment, where children can choose their activities and pursue them in an independent manner. Nevertheless, in the classroom, adults must remember that the children are initially involved in a learning process rather than in creating an art product. Most 3- and 4-year-olds are not

PAINTING AND TALKING
ACTION CHANT

I'm a dabbler.
  Dabble-dabble,

With a paintbrush,
  Dabble-dabble,

On an easel,
  Dabble-dabbel,

Or the table,
  Dabble-dabble,

I'm a babbler,
  Babble-babble,

With a toy phone,
  Babble-babble,

On a doll bed,
  Babble-babble,

Or a table
  Babble-babble.

See me painting,
  Dabble-dabble,

Hear me talking,
  Babble-babble,

With the children,
  Babble-babble,

As I'm walking,
  Babble-babble,

I can't stop now,
  Babble-babble,

With my painting,
  Dabble-dabble,

'Cause my talking's,
  Babble-babble,

Got me fainting,
  Babble-babble,

Plop! (fall down)

"painting a picture" as they stand at the easel, wielding a paintbrush. They are instead "manipulating the medium" just as they did with blocks, computer programs, numbers, letters, and words.

They splash paint around on their paper, sometimes making a blob, at other times painting lines or circles. Just as you are about to hang up their "finished" work to dry, they may cover over the whole painting with brown. Why did they do that, you may wonder? The colors were so pretty before they covered them over. Then you must remind yourself that most of the children are not creating pictures but, instead, are manipulating the medium of easel paint. They are trying out brushes, colors, lines, and strokes to see what happens when they use them. As they gain control, they will advance to the "mastery" level of involvement, doing the same kinds of shapes or designs over and over. Finally, some (but not necessarily all) of the children will evolve to the "meaning" level of art development, and begin to paint identifiable objects and pictures.

Why do children draw, you may wonder? Edwards (2006) says: "Often children draw because they lack the words to communicate thoughts and feelings, and art provides a nonverbal language for expression. Drawing and painting allow very young children to feel, touch, hear, and see their world in ways that are a direct extension of themselves" (p. 153).

Most 3-, 4-, and 5-year-olds are not painting a picture as they stand at a blank sheet wielding a paintbrush; they are manipulating the medium.

THE DEVELOPMENT OF DRAWING SKILLS

All children around the world go through a similar sequence in the development of drawing skills. They begin with scribbles that they make on paper, table tops, walls, steamy windows, or even in dirt with a stick. Their first scribbles are purely motor expressions that they make one on top of another without even looking on. As children gain arm and hand control they will watch what they are doing and begin to control the placement of the scribbles on the paper.

Rhoda Kellogg, who collected thousands of children's drawings from around the world, was able to identify 20 basic scribbles and called them "the building blocks of art" (Kellogg, 1970, p. 15). From these scribbles, young children concentrate on a few favorite forms, repeating them over and over, often on top of one another as they master the use of brushes or crayons.

Shapes begin to emerge from the scribbles in the natural sequence of development. Kellogg identified six basic shapes in children's early art: the rectangle (or square), the oval (or circle), the triangle, the Greek cross (+), the diagonal cross (x), and an odd shape (Kellogg, 1970; p. 45).

By ages 3 to 5, children are not only repeating these shapes but often combining them one on top of another. It is intriguing to realize that these particular combinations are found not only in children's early art all over the world, but also in the rock drawings (petroglyphs and pictographs) of early man throughout the world. One of the forms, the so-called mandala, is a combination of a cross within a circle. Mandalas are commonly found on the walls of ancient caves, in early religious designs, and in the art of preschool children! What a universal human heritage our children are expressing in their natural development of drawing skills.

The sun is one of the next shapes to appear naturally in children's art, with the sun's rays evolving from the ends of a mandala cross whose lines perhaps protrude outside of the circle (although the cross itself no longer appears within the circle).

Next to evolve is the human, which is a sun with its rays becoming hair on top, arms on either side, and two legs coming out the bottom of the circle. The human's eyes appear as little circles or dots within the sun. Some children draw a nose or mouth as well, but some do not. All children everywhere seem to make their first humans this way with arms and legs attached to the head. Eventually, most children lengthen the two legs and place a horizontal line between them, making a more conventional body.

From ages 4 to 6, other recognizable objects appear in children's art, drawn from their minds and not from what they see. Thus, young children's houses, dogs, cars, and trees are quite similar. As you might expect, children next fill art papers with their repertoire of objects over and over until they have mastered them. You will recognize that they have reached the meaning level of their drawings when they begin telling you spontaneously what their pictures are about.

SETTING UP THE ART CENTER

To help children advance on their own through these levels of manipulation, mastery, and meaning, you can set up the Art Center of the classroom so that children can choose and use it easily. **Have at least one, and preferably two, easels available at all times**. Easels are among the most inviting and usable devices for stimulating children's independent involvement with art. Paints and brushes can be ready and waiting for children whenever they choose to paint. **Children can learn to take their own easel paper** from a shelf or a pad and attach it to the easel with clips. **When finished, they can hang their own papers to dry** over drying lines strung parallel on a homemade stand-up frame or from a commercial paint drying rack.

Commercial easels come in various types and sizes: the traditional free-standing two-sided easel, as well as the wall easel, table easel, and adjustable easel. **Attach a clipboard with pad and pencil to the side of each easel so that children can sign up when the easel is in use**.

For other kinds of art, the **paints available for child use should be on low shelves near the tables where they are to be used**. They can include: tempera paint of various colors in plastic jars or squeeze bottles, tempera markers with liquid paint and a flow-through brush on the top, watercolor sets in plastic boxes, and finger paints in plastic jars, along with brushes of various sizes, paint mixing jars, and sponges. Trays of white paint paper, colored construction paper, and glazed finger paint paper can be located on the same shelves easily available to the children.

Have a pan of clean water available for children to rinse brushes.

Keep materials in separate color-coded containers with illustrated labels on the shelves for easy selection and return by children. Because of space limitations, teachers in some programs prefer to roll out **art carts with shelves containing painting supplies**. Child helpers can assist in loading the carts for the day's activities.

The materials in the Art Center should be those available for free use by the children. It is not necessary to put out at the same time all of the art materials owned by the program. Instead, **add new materials from time to time, and retire the materials no longer used regularly**. Choose from among the materials listed in Table 8-1. Teacher's art supplies should be stored elsewhere.

Access to water is important for art activities. Locate the area near a sink, if possible, or arrange for pans of clean water and rinse water to be stored on a low stand for easy use by children.

Art activities can be integrated into the entire curriculum if materials from your other learning centers are included in this area. For instance, picture

Table 8-1 Art Materials

Tempera paints	Yarn	Scissor rack
Easels	Sequins	Masking tape
Finger-paints	Glitter	Transparent tape
Fluorescent paints	Pom-poms	Sponges
Watercolor sets	Feathers	Stampers
Tempera markers	Felt shapes	Stamp pads
Pastel crayons	Styrofoam shapes	Pottery clay
Wax crayons	Craft buttons	Clay bucket
Felt-tip markers	School paste	Clay boards
Colored pencils	School glue	Clay hammer
Colored chalk	Glue sticks	Rolling pins
Chalkboards	Rubber cement	Plasticine™
Easel brushes	White paper	Play dough
Hole punchers	Kraft paper	Cookie cutters
Peel-off shapes	Construction paper	Painting aprons
Paper doilies	Manila paper	Painting trays
Weaving loops	Glazed paper	Mixing jars
Weaving frames	Tissue paper	Drying rack
Pipe cleaners	Crepe paper	Aluminum foil
Tongue depressors	Newsprint	Cellophane paper
Corrugated paper	Food coloring	Wheat paste
Ribbon	Scissors	

books with colorful illustrations are especially attractive "lead-ins" to art activities, and should be available to children in both the Art Center and the Book Center.

BEAUTY AND AESTHETICS

The Art Center should also be the place where beauty and aesthetics begin. **An early childhood classroom should be both pleasing to look at and beautiful to be in**. We know that children appreciate bright colors and airy spaces. We realize that the adult staff also finds pleasure in beautiful surroundings. Let us then make our classrooms beautiful places to live and work in, beginning with the Art Center and spreading into the entire classroom environment.

A dull and gloomy environment puts a damper on happiness and joy. Although children themselves bring their own verve with them to the classroom, it is up to you to take advantage of their spontaneous delight by arranging the environment with beauty in mind. It is not necessary to go overboard with bright colors. Rather than painting your walls a bright yellow, for instance, you might consider a lovely light pastel color, which is more soothing, yet able to accentuate the colorful activity areas you arrange. Fresh wall paint may not be necessary (or possible if you are leasing your facility). Nevertheless, the walls can be cleaned and the activity areas made colorful.

Rolls of corrugated cardboard in a variety of hues **can color code your separate area walls** or be used as a bright baseboard throughout the room. Self-adhesive vinyl paper comes in a variety of solid colors for covering shelves, countertops, or tables. Matching curtains can be purchased or made. Homemade room dividers of folded packing crate sections can be covered with colored burlap. Make your own bulletin boards the same way out of cardboard and burlap with brown vinyl wood-print borders.

Do not overdo colors or clutter. Use your own sensibilities to decide how much color to use and how many materials to have available at one time. "Sensory overload," that overwhelming feeling of too many clashing colors or too much unnecessary material being displayed at one time, can affect both children and adults. Can you feel it when you walk into a room with too much clutter? Keep your decorating scheme simple but beautiful.

One bulletin board in the Art Center can display a changing array of the children's progress as they work through their artistic development from scribbles to identifiable designs. If your bulletin board has a light blue backing, then you might consider mounting the children's art on yellow or even pink backing paper. **Change the bulletin board backing from time to time**. Change your color scheme perhaps once or twice during the year. If you are using corrugated cardboard or self-adhesive vinyl this is not difficult to do. Children and adults alike respond well to variety if it is not overdone.

Picture-book posters can be laminated or mounted on cardboard backing and covered with clear food wrapping for display in any of the learning centers. This art from modern children's books is as impressive and beautiful as any in an art gallery. Posters of animal photos, flowers, trees, and outdoor scenes are also appropriate. NAEYC (National Association for the Education of Young Children; 1-800-424-2460) has posters of all kinds available, many of them laminated. Their yellow art poster with a child drawing says: "Encourage self-expression and art from the heart."

Talk to children about colors and natural beauty, starting with them personally. Mention how you like the colors of the clothing they are wearing. Wear attractive clothing yourself. **Bring in flowers, seed pods, and branches for attractive arrangements that you can discuss with the children**. Help them to see the beauty around them both within the classroom and outside. Did they notice the splash of red on the head of the house finch at the bird feeder? How many different shades of green can they see on the grass, trees, and bushes in the yard? Are there any colors like this in the classroom? Look out the window at the beautiful blue of the sky. How can they bring this color into the classroom to make their indoor environment more beautiful?

ART ACTIVITIES TO PROMOTE PHYSICAL DEVELOPMENT
Small Motor

The principal small-motor development you will want to promote through art activities is the holding of a brush, crayon, or drawing tool and controlling the marks it makes. This involves the development of arm, hand, and finger muscles as well as the eye-hand coordination necessary to make the tool do what you want it to do. In addition to the easel materials and other art supplies available for children's independent use, you will want to provide special activities that focus on holding implements and using them for drawing purposes.

An interesting way to begin is to **introduce a small group of children in the Art Center** to the little picture-book boy, Art, and the wonderful art he creates in *Art* (McDonnell, 2006). You can **make a stand-up cutout of Art** on a piece of cardboard by drawing a simple outline of Art and painting it blue for his pants and cap, red-and-white stripes for his shirt, and flesh color for his face. The story is quite simple with most of the pages filled with the art that Art makes. Read it slowly so everyone in the group gets a good look. Put out paintbrushes for the number of children and four containers of different colors of paint. Cover the art table with white paper and have the children swish the paint around on the paper in any way they want. Be sure to save and display the results.

Next time invite another small group to meet Art and his art. This time **put out spatter brushes and containers of paint for them to spatter** on the white paper covering the table. Finally, **cover the table with white paper again and put out Magic Markers for the children to scribble** all over the paper. Leave the book in the art center along with the brushes, markers, paint, and smaller sheets for children to use on their own. Talk with the children about the different paintings and what they like about them. Hang the paintings around the room.

Other small-motor art activities include tearing, folding, cutting, squeezing, spattering, pasting, and rolling out dough. Children enjoy **tearing up sheets of colored construction paper into pieces to be used in collages**. Let them keep a collage basket full of torn colored paper. Torn tissue paper, crepe paper, and colored aluminum foil can also be used. Have other baskets full of collections of items for collages such as Styrofoam shapes, colored pipe cleaners, feathers, seeds, pasta shapes, and pom poms. These can be pasted or glued to backing paper in free-form creations.

Preschoolers like to fold paper, too. Let them practice on small pads of colored paper. These folded papers can then be torn or cut and pasted on collages. Some children are skilled enough at cutting with scissors to cut off the corners of the folded papers, which turn out to be holes in them when opened up. If the papers are white, children may call them "snowflakes."

A fine multicultural book that can lead children into **making snowflakes and other cut paper objects** is *Pablo's Tree* (Mora, 1994). Every year on his birthday Pablo visits his adopted grandfather, Lito, who has made a surprise decoration for the live "birthday tree" he planted when Pablo was born. Your children may want to start the same tradition making decorations for a birthday tree you have in the classroom. Be sure to celebrate birthdays for everyone, even those who may be born in months when school is closed.

Let children learn to cut with scissors by having in your Art Center a basket or scissor rack containing forged steel school scissors rather than the blunt preschool scissors so often seen. Forged steel scissors are not only easier to cut with but also retain their sharpness. For safe use, **it is better to have sharp scissors than dull or blunt ones**.

Beginning cutters have better luck if you hold the paper tightly between your two hands while they cut. Let them **practice cutting with wrapping paper ribbon** that you hold for them. They can cut it **into confetti** for later use on greeting cards or collages. After you get them started, let one child be the holder and another child the cutter. Once they are able to coordinate their cutting they can practice cutting up sheets from colored pads into collage pieces or cutting pictures from old magazines or catalogs for the class scrapbook. Be sure to have a selection of magazines next to the scissor rack.

Children can also develop small-muscle strength by **squeezing plastic bottles of paint to make designs** on colored construction paper. Lines and squiggles of liquid color can cover the paper, or the paper can be folded and blotted together, making another kind of design altogether.

Children can practice cutting pictures from old magazines for the class scrapbook.

Large Motor

An interesting large-motor art activity suggested by Cherry in her classic book *Creative Art for the Developing Child* (1972) is **arm dancing with crayons to music**. Unroll a large sheet of butcher paper across the floor with enough room for several children kneeling side by side to make large arm movement scribbling to the rhythm of music you will play. Have each one scribble with a crayon while a lively or slow tape or CD is playing for a brief period. When the music stops, give each child a different crayon and play a different musical selection. Be sure the child is using her whole arm to move the crayon and not just her hand.

A variation of this activity **uses two arms with a crayon in each hand**. Using one arm the child increases her ability to control the use of muscles to scribble smoothly. Using both arms she develops bilateral coordination of the body. These exercises are especially helpful for a child with visual or auditory perceptual difficulties (pp. 53–54).

ART ACTIVITIES TO PROMOTE COGNITIVE DEVELOPMENT

The concept of color is a cognitive development that occurs in youngsters as early as 4 to 6 months of age (Richardson, Goodman, Hartman, & LePique, 1980; p. 123). Your concern in the preschool classroom is for children to learn to name and identify the various colors. This involves visual discrimination as well as knowing the names. Many preschoolers already recognize several colors. Others say the names of colors just as they say letter names of the alphabet, without really knowing what they mean.

In order for your children to put words and visual imagery together into a concept of color, **take one color at a time and let your children immerse themselves in it**. Because red is so bright and flashy you might want to start with red. Read *Who Said Red?* (Serfozo, 1988) to get things started. A girl and boy on a farm ask each other who said the various colors. As you read it, ask your small listening group what items they see around the room in the color being named.

Then **ask them to bring something red to the class** tomorrow. Bring something red yourself: perhaps red flowers. Put red paint in the easel jars and have red finger paint ready on one of the tables. Put out red Lego® bricks in the Manipulative/Math Center. Red toy fire engines can be parked in the Block Center for the children to use with their buildings. Put the book *Mighty Machines: Fire Truck* (Bingham, 1995) in the center for children to look through to find what other emergency vehicles are red. Do you have red plastic fire hats for children to wear?

In the Writing Center, red writing tools can be featured, such as felt-tip markers or colored pens and pencils. The children's scribbling can be mounted on red backing paper. Have red hats and shirts in the Dramatic Play Center. Color the water red in the water table. In the Music Center teach a color song. In the Book Center put out a different book, such as *Red Day Green Day* (Kunhardt, 1992), about a class whose teacher asks them to bring in various colored items for a different color day every week.

How long should you feature red? That will depend upon your children and your curriculum goals. After a week or so of red, you can continue with another color, perhaps green. You may decide to choose a particular color based on the season or a holiday.

The Computer Center should be stocked with at least one easy-to-use coloring program. *Curious George 3-Pack Collection* contains a disk called *Paint and Print Studio* that children enjoy using. They can choose from six scenes to do their coloring: zoo, circus, farm, home, downtown, and park. Several icons allow them to paint with an array of colors, spray paint, and draw with colored lines as in an Etch-a-Sketch®. It is more than just a coloring book, unlike so many programs for young children. After they have printed off the results, be sure to talk with them about theirs. What do they like about the colors they chose? Would they use a different color another time? What else did they do in the scenes?

After you have introduced all of the primary colors one by one, you will want your children to **experiment with mixing paint colors to make new colors**. Put out jars of two different colors in the easel trough, perhaps yellow and blue, and let the children experiment to see what will happen. Daubs of yellow and blue finger paint can be placed on finger paint paper on one of the tables before the children arrive. Children are always surprised and excited to see the color green appear.

Mixing various paints together is a wonderful way for your children to experiment with colors. The idea is not for children this age to learn which colors make green and which make purple, but merely to realize that new colors can be

Put out two containers of different colored paints on the art table for children to experiment with mixing paints.

made by mixing other colors together. Children can experiment with light or dark shades of a color by adding varying amounts of white or black to the color.

Bring in **food coloring for them to create new liquid colors**. A set of empty baby food jars in a tray can be half filled with water by you and a drop or two of different food colors added to each. Have several empty jars, a cup of clear water, and a squeeze bottle of a certain food color on the tray. One or two children can choose this color mixing experiment in the Art Center. On another day, use a different food color for the mixing. Using muffin tins half filled with different colors of water is another variation.

Different colors of light can be mixed, as well. Cover one flashlight with yellow cellophane and a second one with blue cellophane. Turn off the lights and close the curtains. Shine the lights on the ceiling and bring the two colors together. What happens? Green, of course. Other colored cellophane can be used another day with red and blue making purple, and red and yellow making orange.

Light has colors in it not normally seen by the children. **Bring in a prism and allow sunlight from a window to shine through it**. As the light passes through the prism it breaks up into the colors of the rainbow, which can appear on a nearby wall, a sheet of white paper, or wherever you direct the beam. Have the children take turns holding the prism in one hand and shining the rainbow colors on their other hand. What colors do they recognize?

The youngest children will then enjoy hearing the large book *Maisy's Rainbow Dream* (Cousins, 2003), in which Maisy Mouse dreams about each color of the rainbow. On the red page she dreams about a red ladybug. On the orange page, an orange fish. Then a yellow bee, a green leaf, a blue clock, indigo spots, a violet butterfly, and finally in rainbow land, all the colors. Some of the children may already be painting rainbows. You may want to start a rainbow book by collecting their work. They may want to turn their pictures into stories with a caption they will write or dictate.

ART ACTIVITIES TO PROMOTE LANGUAGE DEVELOPMENT

Did you know colors can talk? In Hubbard's clever book *My Crayons Talk* (1996), not only the colors but the giant crayons themselves capture the listener's attention immediately. A cartoon-like girl on the cover carries a life-size brown crayon in her arms while a purple crayon blasts off from the edge of the book. What do her crayon's have to say? Purple shouts yum, bubble gum. Red roars no, do not go. What do your children's crayons have to say? Children may want to **make up their own crayon-talk stories** after hearing these.

Stories

Cherry tells us crayons must not be neglected: "Crayons are important in the development of writing skills. The child can practice moving his arm, wrist, and lower palm rhythmically on a table top or floor, as he pushes a crayon back and forth and round and round. This prepares him for writing where similar, but more controlled motions are necessary" (p. 46).

Many legends feature stories of how birds or animals got their colors. *Rainbow Crow* (Van Laan, 1989) tells the Lenape Indian story of how the crow, who was once the most beautifully colored bird on earth, became Black Crow by his sacrifice of bringing fire to the earth. *The Legend of the Indian Paintbrush* (De Paola, 1988) tells the tale of Little Gopher and his Dream-Vision of bringing the colors of the sunset to earth in his buffalo-hide paintings; and of how his paintbrushes eventually grew into wildflowers. If you find such stories too complex for your youngsters, simplify them by telling them orally. Children are fascinated by such explanatory tales.

Another legend, this time from the Ila-speaking people of Zambia, is *Beautiful Blackbird* (Bryan, 2003) about the colors of the birds and how they got that way. A long time ago, all the birds of Africa were all the colors of the rainbow, each one a different color, the story goes. The most beautiful of all was blackbird. The other birds wanted to be black like blackbird, so at last he agreed to give them each a little of his color: a ring around the neck, or black dots or lines on the head, tail, wings, or back. They sang and danced the Slow Claws Slide as blackbird marked them all with his feather paintbrush.

Your children can **reenact this story** if they dance around in a circle to African music from a tape or CD, while one child acts as blackbird. Blackbird can mark each child who comes out of the circle with a black peel-off sticker until all have been marked. Then they all can recite the verse from the book, uh-huh! An excellent way to integrate art activities into music and language.

As the children look at the illustrations in the color stories you are reading to them, they may become interested in trying out the art ideas themselves. In the classic story *Swimmy* (Lionni, 1963), for instance, the artist does stampings of paper doilies to illustrate his "forest of seaweeds" that the little fish swims through. Your children may want to **put paint on paper doilies and press a white paper against them so that the imprint of the doily remains**. They can also roll over the paper with the rolling pins they use for play dough.

It is not necessary for children to tell you a story about their art products. Once you realize that most young children's paintings are the result of a process rather than a picture, your own comments about their art should be appropriate. Instead of saying, "Rachel, what a lovely picture of four suns! Do you want to tell me about it?" you might instead make comments about the child's efforts, such as: "Rachel, you really worked hard with colors this morning!" Or you might comment in terms of the art vocabulary you would like the children to understand: "Rachel, those yellow ovals you have painted are really bright! Did you notice the interesting pattern of circles and lines you drew?"

If the children want to talk about their art products, do not discourage them. However, the art can speak for itself; it is not necessary for the child to describe it.

Your **comments using art vocabulary words** such as *lines, shapes, colors, patterns,* and *textures,* as previously noted, may eventually become part of their own vocabulary. Once children understand that such things are more important to teachers than their telling a story about their art, they will begin to talk about their paintings in similar terms.

However, if any children want to tell or write stories about their drawings or have you write down their dictated stories, do not discourage this. Some children may really have painted a meaningful picture and want to tell a story about it. For many preschoolers, though, their finished products may have no story for them to tell at all, because it was the art process that was most meaningful to them.

ART ACTIVITIES TO PROMOTE EMOTIONAL DEVELOPMENT
Water Play

Art can be used to promote emotional development in young children in both direct and indirect ways. The direct, hands-on experiences involve using art as a therapeutic means for releasing negative feelings. When children are feeling out of sorts, **water play can be a very soothing art activity**. Put a pan of water on one of the art tables with a variety of small, thin, colored sponges nearby. Let the children soak the sponges and squeeze them out as much as they want. Then show them how the **sponges can be cut up into little pieces** with scissors **and used in collages** when they dry out, or be glued into sculptures or even a little pine tree. They may want to cut up a bucket full of sponges to play with in the water and later dry out for use in art projects like these.

Put several small pans of water on an art table with a set of food coloring containers, several empty pouring bottles, a small pitcher, several funnels, and eggbeaters. Have the same number of children as you do pans of water so that each can play with a pan of water, **experimenting with mixing colors, beating them up with an eggbeater, and filling and pouring colored water into bottles**. Because this is not a permanent activity that can be saved and displayed as it is, you may want to **take photos of the children's colored water play for a bulletin board display** or for a personal book they may be making. On the other hand, they may not want a picture taken if they are still not feeling up to par.

Dough

Dough, plasticine, and clay are also excellent therapeutic materials for releasing negative emotions. They can be **squeezed, pounded, rolled, punched, kneaded, pulled, and pressed** into various shapes. Each has a different tactile sensation, a different resistance, and a different degree of ease or difficulty in manipulating it. Thus each of these materials will give children a different experience as well as allow children to release tensions and work out emotions.

Use each of these materials one at a time at different times during the year, but be sure to try all of the various types with your children. Because play dough is easiest to make and use, many teachers limit art modeling material to dough. But dough is not the same as clay, and should not be substituted for clay. It is worth any time and effort you might expend to provide a real clay experience for your children.

Play dough can be made according to various recipes. Here is a favorite one:

2½ cups flour

½ cup salt

2 teaspoons alum

2 cups water

2 tablespoons cooking oil

Pour two cups of boiling water over the dry ingredients. Stir together and add cooking oil. When cool to the touch, turn the dough onto a lightly floured surface and knead with hands until smooth. Store in an airtight container. Do not refrigerate. For a larger group of children, double the recipe. In the beginning, you should **make the dough before the children arrive**. Give each child at the art table a chunk or ball of dough to experiment with. Let them **manipulate the dough with their hands at first**.

At another time you can add other implements such as little rolling pins and cookie cutters. But the initial experience is the time for them to have the opportunity of manipulating the medium without other concerns interfering. Let the children see what it feels like to squish it between their fingers, roll it into a ball, flatten it into a pancake, pull it to pieces, or knead it into different shapes. Remember, using play dough (like using paint) is a *process* for young children. Don't expect them to make something. Some may want to tell you what their dough shapes look like, and that is fine but not necessary.

The next time you make a new batch of dough, do it at the art table with a small group of children on hand to help measure, stir, and finally divide up the prepared dough for the number of children who will use it. **Have a recipe chart** that you have made, posted near the table for your helpers to see with the ingredients **illustrated with simple drawings** of cups, flour bag, salt box, water, and oil container. Don't use food colors yet. This is more effective later on when the children can make their own dough and experiment with colors.

Dough can also be purchased commercially as Play-Doh® or color dough, along with all sorts of clay cutters, clay hammers, clay presses, and cookie cutters in animal and alphabet shapes.

Swartz (2005) tells us: "Interactions with play dough allow children to express themselves in unique and creative ways. Play helps the very young child gain a sense of competence and in turn supports development of a healthy self-concept. Children often express pride in accomplishments when they use play dough in purposeful and meaningful ways (for example: 'Look, Sally! I made a tomato!'). Play dough, like water play, also serves as an outlet for children to expend aggression and act out their emotions by pounding on it" (p. 101).

Clay

Young children love to have their hands on natural clay (pottery clay), as well. It is an entirely different medium from dough. Buy it ready-mixed and keep it in an airtight container or plastic bag. Because it is water-based, it dries out when exposed to air. Keep it moist with a damp sponge, but if it gets too moist expose it to air again. A small piece of clay can be cut off the large lump with a wire or stout twine held in both hands and pulled through it. **Encourage children to work clay with their hands** in any way they want. At first it is dense and may be difficult to work with. But soon the children will be punching and poking it, twisting and rolling it into satisfying shapes. The children can set their shapes out to dry and then paint them with tempera paint if they want. Most take a week or two for them to dry. A new Air-Dry Clay by Crayola looks, feels, and performs like traditional clay but does not need to be fired.

Working with pottery clay is messier than dough, and some children are uncomfortable with this. Don't force them to use it, but show them how easily it can be brushed off like dust when it dries. Again, children will be manipulating the medium in their early efforts with clay, rather than modeling something. After they are used to working it with their hands, you can add other implements such as tongue depressors, large nails, forks, or the commercial clay hammers with different designs to be pounded in.

Plasticine

This material is sometimes called oil clay because of its oil base. It is denser than natural clay and does not dry out, although it can become hard. It has an entirely different feel from clay or dough. **Children can punch, poke, knead, roll, and model this clay just as they do the other forms.**

Finger-Painting

Another excellent **medium for releasing pent-up emotions in a nondestructive manner is finger-painting**. Children can stand over a table with their sleeves rolled up and get their whole bodies involved with the sweeping arm motions that may cover the entire tabletop with paint. Or they can sit quietly, spreading the paint around and around on a paper or tray in front of them. They can use both hands at once, fingers only, fists, palms, or sides of hands to make lines, swirls, circles, zigzags, handprints, and fingerprints. They can wipe out the lines they have made, mix two colors of paint together to make new colors, or draw a real picture.

If children want to save their finger-paint creations, they can do them on glazed art paper and hang them up to dry. Or they can press a sheet of paper onto their designs on the tabletop and make a rubbing of their art.

Hand-Printing

Hand-printing is another art activity that can promote children's self-esteem because the stamped results represent a personal and important part of each child. As a lead-in to hand-printing, read *I Call My Hand Gentle* (Haan, 2003), a simple book full of large-font words and colorful patterns. Multicolored, double-spread pages show what the author's hand can do: pick, hug, throw, hold, protect, hammer, write, and count; and what her hands do not do: steal, push, hurt, grab, or break. Talk with the children about what their own hands do or do not do.

Another book showing hands stamped around the outside of several pages is *The Colors of Us* (Katz, 1999), showcasing the many shades of skin we're in. Have your children place their hands flat on the table to take a close look at them. Is printing (stamping) a picture of their hands on paper the same as writing their names? What do they think?

One class felt it would be the same if they stamped their hands the right color. The teacher brought in a number of paint colors and had the children mix some in several shallow pans: umber, tan, cocoa, sand, toast, ochre, chocolate, sienna, brown, red, black, yellow, and white. It was not so easy to mix the exact color of each child's hand, but they came close. The children dipped their hands flat in one

Children dipped their hands in skin color paints and stamped them.

of the pans and then stamped it on two sheets of blank paper. Each child chose the best print for displaying on the "hand quilt" to be hung on the wall. The next best was put in a class scrapbook called "Our Hands."

Then the children wanted to trace around their hands and color them in using skin-colored crayons. These activities not only make young children stop and think about their hands in ways they never have before, but also appreciate their color.

Long ago many indigenous people also stamped their hands on flat canyon walls. In the *The Mud Family* (James, 1994), Sosi, an ancient Pueblo girl, creates her own mud figures down by the last pool of water to dry up before her family must leave the canyon. When a flash flood drowns her mud family, Sosi's father rescues the girl just in time. Then the whole family prints their mud handprints on the walls of stone behind their house in remembrance. You can still see such prints in Arizona, New Mexico, and Utah.

Artists

Children need to gain another kind of appreciation for the emotional side of art: that **art is also done by people called artists**; that artists have feelings about things; and that **they express** those **feelings in their art**. The world of pioneer American artist Georgia O'Keefe is portrayed in cut-paper collages of Georgia and her amazing paintings by Julie Paschkis in the children's picture book *Through Georgia's Eyes* (Rodriguez, 2006). Her giant red poppies almost pop off the page along with rusty red canyons and a white cow's skull. Georgia saw the world through different eyes than most people. Bring in postcards and prints of Georgia's flowers for the children to savor. Bring in bouquets of flowers, too. Have children investigate them with their senses: smell, sight, and touch. Some may want to **paint their own impressions**. Accept whatever they do.

Children may also want to meet an artist. Many communities have art clubs that can put you in touch with **artists you can invite to your program** to share their skills with your children. Newspapers often have an artist on their staff who might also agree to visit a classroom. The children's parents themselves may be artists or have contact with someone who is an artist.

ART ACTIVITIES TO PROMOTE SOCIAL DEVELOPMENT

As they do in other activity areas, the children can learn to share and to take turns with art materials. **Lessons in sharing can be planned** when the teacher puts out four art papers on the table but only one box of crayons or one bottle of glue that needs to be used by all. Children can also learn to sign up for turns at the easel or at the water table as previously noted.

Art also lends itself especially well to children's social development through group activities. Small **groups of children can do finger-painting** together on one large sheet of paper. A **group collage** or **a group mural** also can be made.

Several children can do a painting project together, such as painting a large cardboard carton to be a playhouse. Others can cut out pictures from magazines and paste them in a **class scrapbook**. Children working together like this learn to plan, to explain their ideas, to solve problems, and to cooperate.

ART ACTIVITIES TO PROMOTE CREATIVE DEVELOPMENT

All of the art activities mentioned in this chapter are designed to promote creativity in young children. Creativity is enhanced when children can accomplish things on their own, through their own choices and their own efforts. Teachers can provide the materials and occasionally some of the ideas, but then it is up to the children themselves to explore, experiment, and follow their own artistic notions. To assist children's development of creativity, teachers' best support is encouragement rather than direction.

Teacher-directed art may have a place from time to time when the goal is to help children learn to follow directions or to enhance their small-motor skills. Yet even then, free-choice art materials should always be available for those who want to pursue their own artistic impulses. Creativity connotes freedom—for both children and teachers. It is the underlying element of the Appropriate Practices Curriculum in a self-directed environment.

For instance, when the children are on the playground and the sky is full of puffy white clouds, you could call them together to look up in the sky. What do they see? Can they imagine different figures in the clouds? Listen to what they say. Some children will be more inventive than others. Take the book *It's Your Cloud* (Troiano, 2004) out with you and read it to anyone interested. A little boy and girl with wild imaginations see a beagle, a bagel, a butterfly, and many other figures on every page. Does this story spur your children to look at clouds more closely? Once back in the classroom, a teacher-setup activity **can invite them to create their own clouds** with shaving cream on a blue paper background.

THE TEACHER'S ROLE IN THE ART CENTER

Although the preschool teacher's primary role in the Appropriate Practices Curriculum may not be the traditional one of sitting at an art table with the children, directing them on how to cut out orange pumpkins or red hearts, the teacher is nevertheless responsible for what goes on in the Art Center. He needs to set it up in the first place with appropriate materials for the children's easy selection and return. Then he needs to observe individual children to determine at what level they are interacting with materials in order to support their further development.

Just as with Writing Center activities, children may pursue different types of activities in the Art Center at different levels of interaction (Table 8-2). In order to record these levels on the Child Interaction Form, the teacher needs to be aware of

Table 8-2 Art Center Activities: Levels of Interaction

Manipulation Level
Making random marks on paper Covering paper with color Making scribbles Swishing hands and fingers around in finger-paints Playing with paste, glue Playing with play dough, clay Playing with computer drawing program without control Scribbling on chalkboard Tearing, cutting paper randomly Playing with stamp pads and stamps

Mastery Level
Making shapes, lines, marks over and over with paint, crayons, markers, chalk Making shapes and designs in finger-paints Putting paste/glue on paper (sometimes on picture side) Making definite shapes with play dough over and over Cutting out play-dough cookies Making lines, shapes on computer drawing program; changing colors Tearing, cutting paper into many pieces Stamping pictures, designs on paper over and over

Meaning Level
Making sun with rays Making sun people with rays as arms, legs, hair Making animals, trees, flowers Making houses, rainbows, vehicles Pasting pictures Creating a named object with play dough, clay Making named lines, shapes on computer drawing program, or telling a story about a drawing Tearing, cutting paper and making a collage or named form Naming stamped pictures or telling a story

the kinds of activities that can occur in art at the manipulation, mastery, and meaning levels.

Once the teacher has identified the level of interaction for the different children in the Art Center and recorded it on the Child Interaction Form, he can use the information to promote the continued progress of the children. For Bianca, who is beginning to draw circles, lines, and crosses on the easel instead of her usual scribbles, the teacher might decide to encourage her in her mastery phase by providing colored chalk and a chalkboard as well. For Tyrone, who spends most of his time making cars from play dough, the teacher might decide to bring in another modeling medium such as clay or plasticine, or even wood.

Teachers' records will show not only the level of the children's interaction with materials, but also their favorite kinds of materials. Those who prefer to draw can continue drawing with crayons, markers, pencils, chalk, and paintbrushes as such materials are added to the center. Modelers can be encouraged to transfer their skills from play dough to clay to plasticine as the year progresses.

Art in the early childhood classroom can thus be an activity of great satisfaction for both children and teachers. If you are successful in your center setup, children can become deeply involved in activities that are highly meaningful to them personally. Art can become a wonderful means of communication and self-expression for them, a great promoter of a positive self-image.

For you, your observation of children at work in the process of art exploration and discovery can be just as meaningful. Young children have much to teach us if we are open enough to learn from them. Their fresh, new ideas, their inquisitiveness and experimentation, and their original uses of materials can give us new insights into the creative process and our role in supporting it.

IDEAS IN CHAPTER 8

1. *Setting up the Art Center*
    a. Give children a wide variety of materials and the freedom and time to discover how they work on their own
    b. Have at least one, and preferably two, easels available at all times
    c. Make it possible for children to get their own easel paper and hang finished papers up to dry
    d. Attach a clipboard with a pencil to the side of each easel for children to sign up for turns
    e. Have paints available on low shelves near tables where they will be used
    f. Have art carts that children help load with painting materials
    g. Add new materials from time to time and retire old materials
    h. Have access to water
    i. Integrate art activities into the entire curriculum
2. *Beautifying the classroom*
    a. Make the classroom pleasing to look at and beautiful to be in
    b. Color code Learning Centers with corrugated cardboard
    c. Do not overdo colors or clutter

    d. Change the bulletin board backing from time to time

    e. Picture-book posters can be mounted on cardboard and covered with clear food wrapping

    f. Talk to children about colors and natural beauty, starting with them personally

    g. Bring in flowers, seed pods, and branches for attractive arrangements and talk about them

3. *Promoting small-motor development*

    a. Introduce a small group of children to Art and his art

    b. Make a stand-up cutout of Art

    c. Cover art table with white paper for children to spatter paint with spatter brushes

    d. Have children scribble on white paper with Magic Markers

    e. Have children tear up sheets of colored construction paper for collage material

    f. Have children fold and cut paper

    g. Use sharp scissors rather than dull or blunt ones

    h. Practice using scissors by cutting ribbon into confetti

    i. Have children make snowflakes and other cut-paper objects

    j. Have children squeeze paint out of plastic bottles to make designs

4. *Promoting large-motor development*

    a. Have children arm dance with crayons to music

    b. Have children use two arms with crayon in each hand

5. *Promoting cognitive development*

    a. Introduce one color at a time and let children immerse themselves in it throughout the classroom

    b. Have children bring something of the same color to class

    c. Let children experiment with mixing paint colors to make new colors

    d. Let children try to create new colors with food coloring

    e. Mix different colors of light with flashlights and colored cellophane

    f. Bring in a prism and shine sunlight through it

6. *Promoting language development*

    a. Let children make up crayon-talk stories

    b. Have children reenact the story *Beautiful Blackbird*

    c. Have children "stamp" with paint-covered paper doilies

    d. Comment on children's art in terms of art vocabulary (lines, shapes, colors, patterns, textures)

7. *Promoting emotional development*

    a. Use water play as a soothing art activity

    b. Have children cut up colored sponges for a collage, sculpture, or Christmas tree

    c. Have children experiment with mixing and pouring liquid colors with eggbeaters and bottles

    d. Take photos of children's colored water play for a bulletin board or for personal books if they agree

    e. Use dough, plasticine, and clay as therapeutic materials for children to release negative emotions

    f. Make play dough before the children arrive

    g. Let children manipulate dough with their hands at first

    h. Use a simple illustrated recipe chart when children make dough

    i. Encourage children to manipulate clay with their hands at first; later add other implements

    j. Have children punch, poke, knead, roll, and model plasticine clay

    k. Use finger-painting as another medium for releasing pent-up emotions in a nondestructive manner

    l. Hand printing and tracing can promote children's self-esteem

    m. Have children learn that art is done by artists who express their emotions through their art

    n. Invite an artist to the classroom

8. *Promoting social development*

    a. Plan activities for sharing art materials

    b. Have children learn social skills through group finger painting, group collages, group murals, and group scrapbooks

9. *Promoting creative development*

    a. Create clouds with shaving cream on blue paper

DISCUSSION QUESTIONS

1. Why do young children seem to have a natural affinity for art?

2. Why do art activities lend themselves so well to a self-directed learning environment for children?

3. How and why are scribbles important in children's art development?

4. How does children's natural drawing of a human evolve from their drawings of suns?

5. Why do you think most children's spontaneous drawings of people, houses, trees, and animals are similar?

TRY IT YOURSELF

1. Set up the Art Center of your classroom as described in this chapter with easels, shelves full of materials children can choose and use, and at least one kind of material new to the classroom. (Or construct a diorama of an Art Center.)

2. Make your classroom beautiful to look at by following some of the suggestions in this chapter about colors, posters, etc.

3. Do an art activity with a small group of children that begins with your reading to them one of the children's books suggested in this chapter.

4. Set up a color-mixing activity for your children to discover on their own how colors can combine to make a new color.

5. Set up a clay activity for your children and observe what they do with it.

REFERENCES CITED

Cherry, C. (1972). *Creative art for the developing child.* Belmont, CA: Fearon.

Clemens, S. G. (1991). Art in the classroom: Making every day special.*Young Children 46*(2), 4–10.

Edwards, L. C. (2006). *The creative arts: A process approach for teachers and children.* Upper Saddle River, NJ: Merrill/Prentice Hall.

Kellogg, R. (1970). *Analyzing children's art.* Palo Alto, CA: National Press Books.

Richardson, L. I., Goodman, K. L., Hartman, N. N., & LePique, H. C. (1980). *A mathematics activity curriculum for early childhood and special education.* New York: Merrill/Macmillan.

Swartz, M. I. (2005). Play dough: What's standard about it? *Young Children 60*(2), 100–109.

Other Sources

Bakerlis, J. (2007). Children's art show: An educational family experience. *Young Children 62*(1), 88–91.

Isenberg, J. P. & Jalongo, M. R. (2006). *Creative thinking and arts-based learning: Preschool through fourth grade* (4th ed.). Upper Saddle River, NJ: Merrill/Prentice Hall.

Isbell, R. T. & Raines, S. C. (2007). *Creativity and the arts with young children.* Clifton Park, NY: Cengage Learning.

Riccio, L. L., Morton, K. C., & Colker, L. J. (2005). The SAIL effect: An arts-based charter school buoys children's learning. *Young Children 60*(4), 42–49.

Soundy, C. S. & Yun Qiu. (2006/2007). Portraits of picture power: American and Chinese children explore literacy through the visual arts. *Childhood Education 83*(2), 68–74.

Children's Books

Bingham, C. (1995). *Mighty machines: Fire Truck.* New York: Dorling Kindersley.

Bryan, A. (2003). *Beautiful blackbird.* New York: Atheneum.

Cousins, L. (2003). *Maisy's rainbow dream.* Cambridge, MA: Candlewick Press.

De Paola, T. (1988). *The legend of the Indian paintbrush.* New York: G. P. Putnam's Sons.*

Haan, A. (2003). *I call my hand gentle.* New York: Viking.

Hubbard, P. (1996). *My crayons talk.* New York: Henry Holt and Company.

James, B. (1994).*The mud family.* New York: G. P. Putnam's Sons.*

Katz, K. (1999). *The colors of us.* New York: Henry Holt and Company.*

Kunhardt, E. (1992). *Red day green day.* New York: Greenwillow Books.

Lionni, L. (1963). *Swimmy.* New York: Pantheon Books.

McDonnell, P. (2006). *Art.* Boston, Little, Brown and Company.

Mora, P. (1994). *Pablo's tree.* New York: Macmillan.*

Rodriguez, R. (2006).*Through Georgia's eyes.* New York: Henry Holt and Company.

Serfozo, M. (1988). *Who said red?* New York: Aladdin Books.

Troiano, J. (2004). *It's your cloud.* New York: Barnes & Noble Books.

Van Laan, N. (1989). *Rainbow crow.* New York: Alfred A. Knopf.

Children's Computer Programs

Curious George 3-Pack Collection: Paint & Print Studio

Note: Asterisk represents multicultural book.

MAKING MUSIC

ACTION CHANT

Can you whistle, whistle, whistle?
(Nod head)

Can you hum, hum, hum?
(Rock side to side)

Can you shake it like a thistle?
(Shake body)

Can you strum, strum, strum?
(Strum air guitar)

Can you tap your fingers lightly?
(Tap fingers)

Can you drum, drum, drum?
(Slap hands on knees)

Can you move around politely?
(Tiptoe in place)

Can you run, run, run?
(Run hard in place)

MUSIC IN THE EARLY CHILDHOOD CLASSROOM

Children are as attuned to music as they are to art. Music, too, is a medium for their communication and self-expression. Children enjoy moving to a beat and playing rhythm instruments. They take pleasure in using their voices as instruments, as well as making sounds with hands and feet.

Too often, though, music in the early childhood classroom is a passive or a controlled experience for children. It is a record, tape, or CD they hear being played. It is an instrument the teacher plays. Sometimes they learn to sing along to the music or move to the directions on the CD. But seldom do they have the chance to make their own music on their own terms in order to play around with tones and tunes and beats—in order to express themselves and their feelings in rhythm and melody.

The self-directed learning environment offers them this opportunity. The Music Center is set up for children's exploration. Materials are provided to give them experience in manipulating, mastering, and making their own meaningful music. The Appropriate Practices Curriculum gives them the freedom to explore on their own, and the time to get as deeply involved with music as they do with blocks and books and paints.

NATURAL MUSICAL DEVELOPMENT IN YOUNG CHILDREN

The elements of music that young children are involved with include *tone*, *rhythm*, and *melody*. The tone of a song has to do with its loudness or softness (dynamics), its shortness or length (duration), its highness or lowness (pitch), and its quality (timbre). Through maturity, exposure to sounds, and practice, children develop the ability to recognize and discriminate among tones and to imitate them, as well as to produce their own original tones in their singing and music making.

The rhythm of music has to do with its fastness or slowness (tempo), its pulse (beat), and its long and short or light and heavy accents (pattern). Melody has to do with a particular flow of tones in a certain rhythm. Children develop in their ability to recognize and to reproduce rhythm and melody in the same way that they develop tone: through maturity of physical, cognitive, and language abilities, as well as by being exposed to these elements of music and having a chance to try them out. This natural development follows a sequence somewhat similar to that of a child's acquisition of language skills. After all, speaking and singing seem to have a common origin, much like drawing and writing.

Birth to Six Months

Infants are aware of music from the beginning, as shown by their different responses to different kinds of music. Lullabies tend to calm them down, whereas lively music makes them more active. Infants themselves vocalize with crying that varies in pitch, loudness, and rhythmic patterns. They experiment with other sounds such as coos, gurgles, and squeals, and finally begin to babble by repeating long strings of sounds: "ba-ba-ba-ba" (Edwards, Bayless, & Ramsey, 2005). If someone is singing to them regularly, their vocalizing often sounds a bit like crooning, especially at naptime or bedtime. They are attracted to rhythmic sounds like the ticking of a clock, and to melodious sounds like musical toys. Tones of voice attract them, too, especially the voice of their primary caregiver (Jalongo & Collins, 1985).

In Howard Gardner's (1993) "theory of multiple intelligences," he describes "musical-rhythmic" as the earliest intelligence to emerge in humans. Hill-Clarke and Robinson (2004) add: "A child's first exposure to music is in the womb, hearing the repeated rhythm of the mother's heartbeat. For this reason, children, including infants, are naturally guided through their inner kinesthetic sense to move to basic beats and rhythms" (p. 92).

Six Months to Two Years

As they grow older, infants and toddlers show more awareness of musical sounds and will turn toward them and listen intently. Some may indicate what music they like best as well as what they do not like. They may move their bodies in response to music, rocking or swaying, and even clapping their hands, but not necessarily in time with the music. Some may attempt to imitate sounds, and as babbling becomes a favorite activity, it may resemble a song. Many infants prefer vocal to instrumental music at this age. Toddlers often seek out the sounds that please them most, including music on television programs. In addition, they will try to locate particular objects such as pots and pans or cups and bowls for sound-making activities (Edwards et al., 2005).

Two to Three Years

Toddlers may attempt to "dance" to music by bending knees, swaying, and swinging arms. They respond well to pattern repetition and can learn simple fingerplays. Two-year-olds may experiment with their voices, and often sing or hum at play. They may join in a favorite nursery rhyme or song and get many of the words right. They show increasing interest in listening to musical instruments and cassette tapes, and often enjoy making musical sounds on toy xylophones, drums, and tambourines (Edwards et al., 2005).

Three to Four Years

Their increased cognitive and language development gives 3-year-olds better voice control, rhythmic response, and mastery of song lyrics. They are beginning to

Some 4-year-olds love to dramatize songs, and even enjoy taking a turn to sing alone.

understand the basic musical concepts of loud-soft, and fast-slow. They may also love to dramatize songs or try out different ways to interpret songs rhythmically. Music has, in fact, become an important means for children to express and communicate ideas that are beyond their language abilities. They may spontaneously make up their own songs with repetitive words and a tune resembling ones they know (Edwards et al., 2005; Jalongo & Collins, 1985).

Four to Five Years

Children at this age are active listeners of music. Their attention span is longer, and, with encouragement, their desire to become involved in musical activities increases. They can sing complete songs from memory with greater pitch control and rhythmic accuracy because of their development of the concepts of high-low pitch and long-short tones. They are more responsive to group singing, and they may even enjoy taking a turn to sing alone. They can play many kinds of rhythm instruments often to accompany songs, and may even create tunes of their own (Edwards et al., 2005; Jalongo & Collins, 1985).

This is how children develop musical abilities naturally. All children everywhere progress through the same sequence of development, although their individual rates of progress may differ. Some children progress rapidly and may be singing whole songs at 2½ years. Others take their time and may not have developed much rhythmic or pitch accuracy even at age 5. It is not up to you to teach them how. Instead, children will continue their natural development if their preschool classroom is filled with music and happy sounds, and if the Music Center itself encourages them to participate in exciting musical activities (Table 9-1).

SETTING UP THE MUSIC CENTER

Music in the self-directed learning environment takes place not only in a designated activity center, but also in the entire classroom. The Music Center contains materials and activities for individuals and small groups to investigate sound, rhythm, and melody on their own. A large space in the classroom is also used for group singing games and creative movement. The other learning centers are eventually infiltrated with music and sound as the children bring new songs and rhythms with them into the Block, Dramatic Play, Art, and Book Centers, and as the teachers who visit these centers respond with their own personal music.

"Making music personal" should be the theme of your music activities. First of all, it needs to be personal in your own life. Do you enjoy music? Then **bring in records, tapes, or CDs of the music you enjoy to share with the children at appropriate times**. Soft music is appropriate at naptime. Rock music is appropriate at times when the children are actively engaged in the learning centers. Certain classical music may be appropriate at times when other moods are desired. Teachers may want to use their own cassette recorders to share this music.

Table 9-1 Natural Musical Development in Young Children

Birth to Six Months
Calm down to lullabies Become more active in response to lively music Vocalize with crying that varies in pitch, loudness, and rhythmic patterns Experiment with sounds: coos, gurgles, squeals Begin to babble: repeat a string of sounds May imitate crooning at bedtime Attracted to rhythmic sounds: ticking of clock, musical toys Attracted to tones of voice, especially caregiver's

Six Months to Two Years
More aware of musical sounds: turn toward them; listen intently Move bodies in response to music: rock, sway, clap Babbling becomes favorite activity May imitate sounds May prefer vocal music May seek out sounds that please them Look for and use sound-making objects (e.g., pots and pans)

Two to Three Years
Dance to music by bending knees, swaying, and swinging arms Respond to pattern repetition Can learn simple fingerplays Sing or hum at play Know words to nursery rhymes Play toy xylophones, drums, and so on

Three to Four Years
Have better voice control Know song lyrics Can follow rhythm Understand loud-soft, fast-slow Can dramatize songs May sing own words to familiar tunes

Four to Five Years
Listen actively to music Sing complete songs from memory Have better rhythm and pitch accuracy Respond to group singing May sing alone for group Play rhythm instruments to accompany singing May create own tunes

Have headsets available for individuals to listen to song storybooks in the Music Center or Book Center.

The Music Center itself should contain a **cassette recorder** for the children's use. Children can **learn to use it and not to abuse it**, just as they learned to do with the computer; a simple illustrated rules chart on the shelf near the recorder can tell them how. Both the Music and the Book Centers should have their own recorders, not only for prerecorded tapes, but also for recording the children's own productions. You may want a **clipboard nearby for children to sign up for use of the recorder. Have headsets available** if the tapes are for personal rather than group use.

Your Music Center should be set up to **promote** the following activities: **listening, sound exploration, rhythm, and music making**. Its contents will change as the children explore different elements of music. In addition to the cassette recorder and record or CD player, put the prerecorded tapes and blank tapes on a low countertop. The shelves in the center may contain sound-making materials, musical instruments, rhythm instruments, materials for children to make their own instruments, picture books with a musical theme, puppets and character dolls to go with the books, and hooks holding costumes, scarves, and other materials for creative movement. Illustrated labels will help children to choose and return particular materials to their shelves or hook spaces just as they do in the other activity centers.

You may choose **not to display all of your rhythm instruments at one time**. If the children are investigating drumming sounds, then drums and similar instruments may be the only ones out. On the other hand, you may be displaying materials on the shelves of your Music Center that have never even been associated with music. In addition to the shelves in your Music Center, you may choose to display instruments on a Peg-Board with hooks and an outline of each instrument drawn on the board so that children can match each instrument to its outline and return it to its place when they are finished. Some programs with limited space prefer to use a music cart (like the art cart), which can be rolled out and later put away.

MUSIC ACTIVITIES TO PROMOTE EMOTIONAL DEVELOPMENT

To make music meaningful for children, you should **make it personal for them** as well. Your musical activities can be centered around the things that your children respond to personally. This will not only attract their attention, but also help to promote their positive self-image. Thus, you might focus classroom music on themselves, by highlighting:

their names	their friends
their feelings	their pets
their toys	their homes
their clothing	their school
their food	their cars
their families	the school bus

For example, we know that young children are fascinated by shoes: their own shoes and everyone else's shoes. Children will often tell you they are wearing a new pair of shoes, whether or not they really are. This may happen because little children are so close to the ground that shoes are the first thing they notice about a person. With this in mind, you might **consider featuring shoes and "shoe music" in your Music Center**. This is not your everyday sort of musical activity, you may protest. But that is just the point: To make music meaningful for young children, you need to make it personal—and pleasurable. Why should you do the same ordinary "rhythm band" kinds of music activities when you have a world of intriguing things to choose from—when you have your own creative young children and their fascinating interests to tap into?

How, then, can you use "shoes" for music making? First of all, consider the elements of music you will be featuring in the Music Center and the classroom: listening, sound exploration, rhythm, and music making. What can you do with a shoe? Well, you can: try it, buy it, tie it, buckle it, Velcro™ it, hide it, walk in it, run in it, hop in it, jump in it, skate in it, dance in it, slide in it, stomp in it, tiptoe in it, tromp in it, work in it, play ball in it, flip-flop in it, climb tall in it, swim deep in it, fall down in it, play games with it, make art stamping with it, and read stories and sing songs about it. Remember, no matter what you do with a shoe, make "shoe music" fun for yourself as well as for the children!

Listening

Acquire a collection of shoes of all kinds and make a tape of shoe sounds for children in the Music Center to listen to and imitate. Following are some of the shoes you might collect:

regular leather tie shoes	bowling shoes
patent-leather buckle shoes	roller skates
ballerina slippers	ice skates
tap-dancing shoes	snowshoes
sneakers	swim fins
rain boots	cowboy boots
snow boots	motorcycle boots
work boots	high-heeled shoes
jogging shoes	slippers
basketball or football shoes	flip-flops
moccasins	crutches
stilts	sandals
golf shoes	

Take a blank tape, sit down at a table, and record some of these shoes walking, clumping, tapping, rolling, or whatever, on your table. You can hold a shoe in your hand (call it shoe #1) and clump it around. Have the same shoe make its same sound many times on your tape before you switch to the next shoe; remember, it may take your children longer than you think to match the sound with the shoe. It is not necessary to tape the sound of every shoe you have collected, only a representative few. When you have finished your tape, try it out on yourself to see if you can match the sound with the shoe. Make the tape over again if necessary, eliminating shoes that can't be identified easily.

Put the same shoes on your Music Center shelves, along with the "shoe music" tape, and **ask your children to guess what shoes made the sounds**. This should be a fun activity and not a test. Talk with children who are enjoying this activity on their own and congratulate them when they have guessed *one*. This is not a "right or wrong" activity—no activities should be "win or lose" in your classroom.

Rather than telling a child she has not identified any of the sounds correctly but the roller skate, you can congratulate her for guessing the roller skate and encourage her to try again and see what other shoes she can identify. Let her try each shoe itself with her hands on the table of the Music Center and have a partner play the tape while both listen to the sounds.

At the same time, bring books about shoes into the Music Center and read them to the children who are listening and trying to identify shoe sounds.

My Best Shoes (Burton, 1994) is a rhyming shoe tale on the days of the week, showing African American, Asian American, Caucasian, and Hispanic children strutting around in a different pair of shoes every day.

Red Dancing Shoes (Patrick, 1993) tells the story of a little African American girl and her dancing adventures in the shoes her grandma brings her.

Shoes from Grandpa (Fox, 1989) is a cumulative tale from Australia adding a new piece of clothing in a cumulative manner for the little girl whose grandpa has bought her boots.

New Shoes for Silvia (Hurwitz, 1993) tells the story of the red shoes Silvia, a girl from Central America, receives from her aunt in North America—but the shoes are too big. Silvia finds other fun uses for them, until at last her feet are ready.

Jamaica and Brianna (Havill, 1993) tells the story of an African American girl and her Asian American friend who have a conflict over new and old boots.

Mama, Do You Love Me? (Joosse, 1991) has an Inuit girl asking her mother this question in every situation she can think of, including if she put lemmings in her mother's mukluks (fur moccasins).

The Rainy Day (Milbourne, 2005) is about three children who don rain boots and go splish, sploshing in every puddle they can find.

Flip Flop Bop (Novak, 2005) is a story of what happens when all the children shed their socks and shoes for flip-flops in summer. They skip, hop, and bop everywhere all day long, until they finally come home exhausted and don their bunny slippers for bedtime.

Not so Fast, Songololo (Daly, 1985) shows a little South African boy shopping with his grandma for a pair of red sneakers.

Rap a Tap Tap: Here's Bojangles—Think of That! (Dillon & Dillon, 2002) tells the story of this famous tap dancer as he taps his way across the pages of the city in this wonderful rhyming celebration.

Dumpling Soup (Rattigan, 1993) celebrates New Year's Day in Hawaii with Marisa and her Hawaiian, Korean, Japanese, Chinese, and Caucasian relatives who leave their slippers, sandals, and shoes on the doorstep of Grandma's house, where the girl cousins play "shoe store."

My Shoes Take Me Where I Want to Go (Richmond, 2006) is a journey through the imagination with a girl who fantasizes about wearing sneakers as a basketball player, ice skates as a hockey player, sandals at the beach, flippers underwater, cowboy boots on horseback, and dancing shoes on stage.

Two Pairs of Shoes (Sanderson, 1990) is the story of Maggie, a Cree Indian girl, who has been given two pairs of shoes for her birthday: beaded moccasins and patent-leather. She loves them both, but now she needs to learn when and how to wear each pair.

Leave the books on the Music Center shelf for children to enjoy on their own. In the meantime, make a second tape or even a third one with other sets of shoes for children to match. Put the shoes for these tapes in separate containers in the Music Center for children to listen to.

Sound Exploration

Would children like to **make their own shoe music**? They can tape-record their own sounds of shoes from the shelf of the Music Center. Or they can take the tape recorder over to the Dramatic Play Center and tape-record children walking in the various kinds of dress-up shoes displayed there. (Be sure you have a wide variety of men's and women's shoes in stock.) Or they can tape-record the sounds made by the dolls walking in the Dramatic Play Center. Would they also like to tape-record the sound of their own shoes walking? They could say into the tape recorder: "This is what Keshawn's blue sneakers sound like," and then make the recording. Afterwards you might listen to the tape with them, talking about loud and soft sounds made by particular shoes.

The children may want to start a pretend shoe store in the Dramatic Play Center after hearing stories like *Dumpling Soup*, *Jamaica and Brianna*, or *Flip Flop Bop*. Or they may want to **record the way boots sound in the water table** or a shallow pan of water in the Music Center. Be sure to put enough newspapers on the floor for safety's sake.

If children in the Art Center want to get into the shoe act, you can plan a footprint session, in which children **make paint footprints on a large sheet of butcher paper** by placing washable paint on the bottoms of their sneakers or feet and stamping them on the paper. Or children may want to make footprints **in wet sand in the sandbox outdoors**. In this case, let children take off their shoes to make the prints. They can also make footprints music from the player you take out. Another wet footprint activity is having children step into a shallow pan of water and make footprints down the sidewalk.

Multicultural Recognition

These shoe activities not only make music personal for children, they also help children to recognize how all of us are alike (we all wear shoes), but at the same time different (our shoes may be different). Children from various cultures can be represented in your shoe activities whether or not they are in your classroom simply

Children may want to take off shoes to make prints in wet sand in the sandbox.

by your bringing in different shoes and reading some of the books mentioned. Books marked with a star (*) at the end of this chapter are multicultural. Preschool youngsters need to be exposed to the exciting multicultural mix of people that America offers to all of us. After reading the books, have children choose to be the characters and reenact the story as you read it again. They can see how it feels to be walking in the virtual shoes of the characters.

Mount pictures or posters of children from different cultures in the Music Center during your shoe activities. (See *Children of the World Poster Pack*, from Lakeshore.) Play CDs of music from around the world (see *Children of the World, Multicultural Children's Songs*, or *De Colores*) and have children tap or stomp their shoes. Children on crutches, in foot casts, or in wheelchairs can add their own special "foot-music" to the endeavor. Multicultural activities should be everyday occurrences and not special holiday events in the classroom.

Rhythm and Dance

Because each of the classroom activities needs to be integrated into all of the activity centers, you might start your shoe-rhythm activities in the Book Center by reading *Rap a Tap Tap: Here's Bojangles—Think of That!* about the famous tap-dancing man. Be sure to have a pair of tap shoes for your children to experiment with after you read this book. Perhaps some of the children or their siblings are taking tap-dance lessons. Could they demonstrate a tap-dance for the class? Or you might invite an instructor from a local dance studio to visit the class and demonstrate a dance.

Books are excellent lead-ins for music and dance activities. *Aunt Elaine Does the Dance from Spain* (Komaiko, 1992) is another fine shoe-tapping story in rhyme, about Katy's Aunt Elaine from Maine who becomes Elena from Spain when she puts on her costume and performs a Spanish dance. Katy gets lost backstage during a performance and stumbles into the wardrobe room where she too gets caught up in the Spanish excitement. Bring in fans, colorful scarves, and capes as well as Spanish guitar music to get your children moving to these rhythms.

Making music with shoes involves both music and dance. The teacher can **tape-record the children moving to any kind of music, wearing different kinds of shoes** at first. Use a second tape recorder and a record player or CD player for the music. What different ways can the children move? Can they slide, clump, tiptoe, stomp, hop, or raise up and down on their toes? Children with special needs who use a wheelchair, braces, or crutches can participate with their special "shoe sounds" being recorded, too. **Bring in a pair of children's crutches** and let all the youngsters try them out making "shoe music."

Special dances are another way children can make shoe music. CDs from Constructive Playthings or other educational supply companies can lead the way, such as *Children's Songs around the World* and *Multicultural Rhythm Stick Fun*, in which shoes instead of sticks can be tapped. Putumayo also features world music CDs from Barefoot Books: *Caribbean Playground*, *French Playground*, *Swing around the World*, and *World Playground*.

Another **shoe music activity is a group singing game called "Pass the Shoe"** (Figure 9-1). Children sit on the floor in a circle and sing the song. As they sing they pass a shoe from child to child around the circle. When the song stops, the child with the shoe must "do something," such as making a motion of some kind (e.g., patting the head or some other part of body, rubbing tummy, clapping hands, nodding head, waving hand, raising arms up and down). Everyone in the circle then copies this motion. Then the shoe is passed around again to the singing of the song, and the game continues in the same manner.

MUSIC ACTIVITIES TO PROMOTE PHYSICAL DEVELOPMENT

Other dance and whole-body-movement activities are discussed in chapter 12, "Large-Motor Center." In this chapter, we consider small-motor coordination activities involved in playing instruments. Most children love to make music. Whether they are blowing on toy horns or beating toy drums, young children tend to expend great energy in their production of sound. This is not surprising when we realize that those who love music the most are the music makers themselves. With youngsters at the preschool age it is even more important that they have the

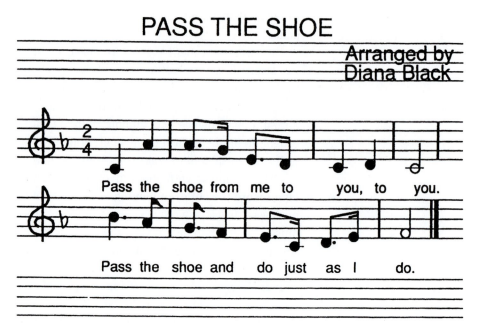

Figure 9-1 Pass the Shoe music

opportunity to make their own music rather than merely listening to the music someone else has made. Music for them is a means of expression that even their language cannot yet afford them.

Music promotes children's physical development when they respond physically to a beat, according to Neelly (2001). "Neural connections occur through the medulla, or brain stem, that stimulate the child's total muscular system" (p. 34). Give children the opportunity to get physically involved in your Music Center activities, first by making music with their hands and feet, and then by extending these skills to music making with instruments.

Start with clapping. **Can children clap to the rhythm of their names?** Be the leader with a small group of youngsters and let them all join in clapping to every syllable as the group says each child's name rhythmically: "My-name-is-Ko-mi-ko-what-is-your-name?" Another time have them clap to two different rhythms: "I-see-you-An-to-ni-o. (speed up) How-are-you-to-day?" Besides clapping hands, children can also sit in a circle and **slap their hands against their legs to a chant**. Use the chants at the beginning of each chapter to do slapping or clapping. The chant "Blocks" (chapter 3) asks the children to clap on the fourth line of every verse.

What other kinds of sounds can they make with their hands? They might ball their hands into a fist and **make pounding music** on the table or the floor to the beat of a song or to the chants they know. For the "Painting and Talking" chant (chapter 8) they could say the words on every other line and pound out the rhythm for "dabble-dabble" and "babble-babble." Can they make "knuckle music" as well?

Instruments

Rhythm instruments that can be played with hand beats include drums (bongo, conga, tomtom, Caribbean steel drum) and tambourines. There are many kinds, both commercial and homemade. Because your children may be too young to make complete drums with paper or skin heads, you can **collect empty coffee cans, salt, and oatmeal boxes** that they can paint and use **for tom-toms. The simplest homemade drum is an open coffee can covered tightly with a double layer of wrapping paper**, secured around the can with twine or a heavy rubber band. **Tambourines can be made from aluminum foil pie tins** with holes punched in the sides and Magic felt-tipped pen tops dangling on strings from the holes.

Tom-toms are beaten to music with two hands, whereas tambourines are usually held with one hand and beaten with the other. Talk to the children about "loud and soft" sounds, as well as "fast and slow" beats. Read them books about children like themselves who are natural drummers.

In *Max Found Two Sticks* (Pinkney, 1994), an African American boy named Max uses two sticks he finds to drum out his feelings on the steps of his apartment without using words. When a marching band comes by, the last drummer in line spies Max and tosses him his spare set of drumsticks. Have your interested children find a set of drumsticks in the classroom and tap out their own beat. Even paintbrushes or ladles will do!

It is important for young children to explore a single instrument at a time.

In *Drum Chavi Drum* (Dole, 2003), a Cuban American girl in Miami desperately wants to drum in the Calle Ocho Festival on her school's float, but everyone tells her girls can't drum. A Zorro mask and hat transform her appearance, and her flashing hands on the conga drums do the rest as she captivates the crowd. Read this bilingual book in both English and Spanish as you challenge the girls to drum like Chavi.

It is important for young children to **explore a single instrument at a time**, first on their own and then with a teacher. When children play all of the instruments in a rhythm band at the same time, all they hear is noise. Children can learn more about sound making and rhythm when they use the instrument alone or when they all use the same kind of instrument. Let them beat their hand drums to a variety of music: for example, marches, rock, rap, country, and folk music.

Other rhythm instruments played by hand shaking include: maracas, castanets, shekere, tic-tac drum, desert rainstick, hand bells, and jingle bells. Children can also **make musical shakers from margarine containers** filled with different items (seeds, paper clips, jingle bells). Put the various kinds of ingredients on the Music Center table in separate containers and let children try them out before making a final choice for their own shaker. Tape on the tops securely and let the children paint their musical shakers. Again, let children shake them to the beat of a variety of musical tunes.

Some instruments are played with sticks, including drums, wood blocks, bells, xylophones, and rhythm sticks themselves. Commercial drumsticks come with purchased instruments. Otherwise children can use pencils, Tinkertoy® sticks, wooden spoons, or dowels.

Other hand instruments include string instruments that you strum. Commercial guitars, ukeleles, and Autoharps are usually played by the teacher as accompaniment to singing. But **Autoharps can be strummed by a child** sitting next to the **teacher while the teacher presses the cords**. Have children try strumming with a felt pick, a plastic pick, or their thumb. How does each strummer sound? Which do they like best?

Homemade strumming instruments are more interesting to preschoolers. They can make their own from your collection of shoeboxes. Cut a 3-inch hole or heart in the top of each. Cut four small slots equidistant at either end of the top. String four rubber bands lengthwise around the box so that they go across the hole and are held in place by the slots.

The children will enjoy playing in a strumming band if everyone has a shoebox strummer. They can be strummed with a thumb or a tongue depressor. If children like their shoebox strummers they will want to hear you read and sing *The Banza* (Wolkstein, 1981), a folktale about Cabree, a little goat who must confront 10 hungry tigers with nothing but a "banza" (banjo). The banjo is magic, and the little goat sings a song that terrifies the tigers until they all flee. Can the youngsters strum along as you sing the song?

From all of these experiences come children's heightened interest in rhythm and music as well as a strengthening and coordination of the small muscles.

MUSIC ACTIVITIES TO PROMOTE SOCIAL DEVELOPMENT

One of the reasons music may be so enjoyable to young children is that it is so often a social experience. Everyone sings the same song together. Everyone plays the musical game in a group. That kind of togetherness makes music something special for all the children. To create such a feeling of togethernesss in your classroom, it is not necessary to begin with a music period where everyone leaves the activity centers and comes to the center of the room to learn a new song. Instead, you can infiltrate music into the entire classroom during the free-choice period by starting a song youself that everyone can sing while they continue to engage in their activity.

Choose a song you have sung together before, such as "The Alphabet Song," so that most of the children know the words. Children will join in as they hear others from other parts of the room singing. You and your coworkers can walk around singing to **encourage everyone to participate**. Do this spontaneous kind of singing whenever the mood strikes you, and you will soon have children also starting their favorite songs. In other words, it is not necessary to wait for a music period in order to enjoy singing. When people are happy they can express it any time in a song: "If You're Happy and You Know it, Clap Your Hands."

Neither is it necessary for you to be a performer in order to sing with the children. You remember that they are in the process period of their musical development. They are manipulating the medium of musical tones, pitch, rhythm, and melody. Some of them are mastering these musical elements by repeating them over and over. Only a few children will be at the meaning stage of music where they create a "product," that is, a song of their own.

If you find that you are uncomfortable singing, **ask a coworker to sing with you**. The two of you can then blend in with the children when they join in. If you make a mistake—laugh! Actually, there's no such thing as a mistake in music for you or your preschool children, only different ways of expressing yourself. Make music fun for yourself and the children. But whatever you do, *make music with the children!*

Singing can be a wonderful vehicle for so many facets of the educational scene. Everything from emotions to academics can be enhanced through music in general and singing in particular.... Many teachers shy away from singing with young children because of their own sense of musical inadequacy. This doesn't have to happen. With a little bit of background information, a set of criteria for selecting materials, and a plan of action, there is nothing to it! (Wolf, 1994).

One of the most delightful kinds of group music is musical **fingerplays**. Some are nursery rhymes put to music and finger movements; others are old favorites. You should **have a repertoire of these songs to sing during transition times** when children are waiting for something new to happen. The chants at the beginning of each chapter can be spoken or sung by you and the children. Music for most of these chants can be found in Appendix A.

Some of the most popular of the musical fingerplays have appeared in children's picture books, called song storybooks. Children can learn the words of the chant first; then do the motions, and, finally, sing the songs. What a surprise when they find the songs they already know in picture books! Read them to the children at first and then sing them together. Be sure to keep the books you are using in the Book Center or Music Center for children to "read" on their own. Can anyone read one to you? Here are some:

Fiddle-I-Fee (Hillenbrand, 2002)

I Love You a Bushel & a Peck (Loesser, 2005)

If You're Happy and You Know It (Warhola, 2007)

The Itsy Bitsy Spider (Trapani, 1993)

The Lady with the Alligator Purse (Westcott, 1988)

Miss Mary Mack (Hoberman, 1998)

Mary Had a Little Lamb (Hoberman, 2003)

On Top of Spaghetti (Johnson, 2006)

Skip to My Lou (Westcott, 1989)

The Seals on the Bus (Hort, 2000)

She'll Be Coming 'Round the Mountain (Emmett, 2006)

There Was a Bold Lady Who Wanted a Star (Harper, 2002)

The Wheels on the Bus (Kovalski, 1987)

The Wheels on the School Bus (Moore, 2006)

Children learn such fingerplay songs by singing them over and over with you as the leader. It is not necessary to use an instrument. Musical fingerplays are more pleasurable when done informally with everyone singing together and enjoying themselves. The children will let you know which ones are their favorites by asking for them again and again. In this case **it is easier for children to learn the words and actions when they are together in a group.** This could be at Circle Time or when they are waiting to go somewhere. Give children many experiences with musical fingerplays before you start musical games.

Most classrooms **use CDs or tapes for children's musical games.** Children listen for the directions on the CD and then follow them, with the teacher leading. Some are concept games involving colors, body parts, or numbers. Others are traditional circle games such as "The Farmer in the Dell" or "Skip to My Lou." Such games give children experience in listening and following directions. This is one kind of musical activity many young children enjoy, but it should not be the only one. In this case, the children are not the music makers but only the followers. Music is more meaningful and more pleasurable when children make it themselves, or when it has something to do with them personally.

Other musical games **involve children more directly when they make the music themselves by singing** rather than using a record. This means they must sing and perform the actions at the same time, a task more difficult for preschoolers than for older children. These are usually circle games where the children walk around a circle (e.g., "Ring around the Rosie"), move their bodies while standing in

Give children many experiences with musical fingerplays.

a circle (e.g., "Do the Hokey Pokey"), or sometimes sit in a circle (e.g., "Pass the Shoe").

Children who may be uncomfortable with any kind of music or group activities should not be forced to join in. Music is a wonderful socializer that may eventually entice shy children to join the group if they realize they are not being forced or singled out. You realize that your children are only at the beginning of their development of the social skills necessary for playing in a group, getting along with other children, sharing toys, and waiting for turns. Their refusal to join musical activities may have more to do with their shaky self-concept or social development than with their dislike of music. When they are more comfortable in the classroom and see how the others enjoy singing, they may join in.

Puppets

Such shy children (and even you) **may be more comfortable** in group singing or musical games **if they can hide behind something**. They (or you) can bring a hand puppet to the group, and let the puppet do the singing. In fact, one of the fun musical activities can be **a weekly puppet sing**, at which time each of the children make a simple sock puppet that they bring to Music Circle Time for singing. Have a basket full of socks that each child can select from. Let them put one hand in a sock and then stick eyes and noses on the curled over end of the sock from sheets of peel-off colored stickers of different kinds (e.g., circles, stars, triangles, smiley faces). They can name their puppets if they want. Another option is to have them make paper-bag hand puppets in the same way. Then have them sing the songs as their puppets would sing. You do it too.

MUSIC ACTIVITIES TO PROMOTE LANGUAGE DEVELOPMENT

Music activities to promote language development are involved chiefly with remembering and singing the words of the songs, making up new words to songs, and reading stories about music. Realizing that music in the preschool classroom needs to be personal in order to be meaningful to young children, you can focus your singing activities on people, places, and pets that have personal meaning to your children. Let's start with the children themselves.

Songs

Songs can be sung about their names, their families, their clothing, their pets, their favorite activities, and their favorite foods. Where can you find such songs?

You and the children can make them up. **Make up words to familiar tunes about things of interest to the children**. Some examples of songs made up about children's names and sung to familiar tunes include:

(To the tune of "Twinkle, Twinkle, Little Star")

Sarah, Sarah, there you are,

How I wonder where you are;

Show us now how you can run,

Then come in and have some fun;

Sarah, Sarah, there you are,

How I wonder where you are.

(To the tune of "Where Is Thumbkin?")

Where is Matthew, where is Matthew?

Here he is, here he is;

How are you this morning?

How are you this morning?

Come right in!

Come right in!

(To the tune of "Lazy Mary Will You Get Up?")

Alberto Morano, will you stand up?

Will you stand up, will you stand up?

Alberto Morano, will you stand up,

So early in the morning?

(To the tune of "Here We Are Together")

Here we have Samantha, Samantha, Samantha,

Here we have Samantha with a smile on her face;

Look this way and that way,

Look that way and this way,

Here we have Samantha with a smile on her face!

Use one song at a time, singing it over and over, inserting different children's names each time. Soon they will be familiar with the tune. You can also sing directions, a welcome, or some other message to the children in this way. Be sure to write down the basic words you use to a particular tune so that you remember them next time. Any of the songs named in this chapter can be used in a similar way. Children are delighted to hear their names used in a song. They will help you compose the words to a new tune if you ask them.

You can also make up games by using familiar songs and making up your own words. **Find out something about the children's pets**, for instance, **and then make up guessing-game songs**.

(To the tune of "London Bridge Is Falling Down")
> Someone I know has a dog, has a dog, has a dog,
> Someone I know has a dog, and his name is Sandy.
> Who do you think has a dog, has a dog, has a dog?
> Who do you think has a dog with the name of Sandy?

(To the tune of "Mary Had a Little Lamb")
> Someone has a pretty cat, pretty cat, pretty cat,
> Someone has a pretty cat by the name of Tiger.
> Who do you think has a cat, has a cat, has a cat?
> Who do you think has a cat, by the name of Tiger?

Be sure to make up a guessing-game song for every child in the class so no one feels left out. Use the same tune for everyone. If not all of them have pets, then choose something else of interest to a particular child (e.g., sneakers, a special toy, hairstyle, favorite food). If the singing game catches on, play it over and over until the children remember and can sing the words on their own.

The words to the action chants found at the beginning of each chapter as mentioned have been put to original music by D. J. Zeigler and are found in Appendix A. Try out these simple tunes with the children after they have had fun with the chants. **Print the words of the songs** you and the children are singing **in the newsletter you send home to the children's families**. If you don't have a newsletter, send home the words on a separate sheet, so families will know what their children are learning in school. Perhaps the children will want to sing the same songs with their families.

MUSIC ACTIVITIES TO PROMOTE COGNITIVE DEVELOPMENT

Music in the preschool classroom is perhaps more important in children's cognitive development than we ever realized. Current brain research tells us that early exposure to music greatly enhances the development of cognitive processes. As Davies (2000) points out: "Music synchronizes the right and left hemispheres of the brain. Researchers report that the left hemisphere analyzes the structure of music, while the right hemisphere focuses on the melody. The hemispheres work together when emotions are stimulated, attention focused, and motivation heightened. Rhythm acts as a hook for capturing attention and stimulating interest. Once a person is motivated and actively involved, learning is optimized" (p. 148).

Your children have been involved with cognitive activities in every aspect of music described thus far. The concepts of high and low, loud and soft, and fast and slow are ideas they have touched on with rhythm, sound exploration, instruments, and singing. In addition, they can explore these concepts by trying out various objects in their environment for sound. **Have children explore sound by tapping the objects in the classroom**. What kind of sound does each object make? Is it loud or soft? High or low? They can tape-record and listen to the results of their tapping explorations.

If such exploration has captured the attention of your children, **bring in a variety of empty glass containers and let children tap on them**. Is there a difference in sound? What is it? Why is it different? What will happen if you fill each of the containers with the same amount of water and then tap? Can the children predict the outcome? What will happen if you take a number of the same containers (e.g., glasses), fill them with different amounts of water, and then tap? Can the children help to make a graduated series of glasses with sounds from low to high by varying the amount of water in each?

Try the same kind of sound exploration with sand in the glasses instead of water. Can the children predict what will happen this time? This kind of experimentation is the same kind that scientists do when they want to find out about the properties of objects. It promotes high-level thinking skills in children.

MUSIC ACTIVITIES TO PROMOTE CREATIVE DEVELOPMENT

Creative development through music is promoted whenever the children are free to do their own musical activities, whether through making up words to songs, making "shoe music," singing and playing songs on their own, exploring sounds, experimenting with pitch, or making instruments. Another way you can promote creativity is to **integrate music with other areas of your classroom**, such as the Book Center or the Art Center. A number of professional artists actually paint to music. Your children can do the same.

Maurice Sendak is a well-known children's book artist who paints his illustrations to classical music. Because some of the stories in his books take place at night, it can be a magical experience for your children to listen to the stories being read while "night music" is played, and, later, for them to **manipulate "night" kinds of art materials while the same night music is played** again. Sendak's classic book *Where the Wild Things Are* (1963), in which Max makes mischief, is sent to bed, and escapes into a world of fantasy where he becomes king of all the wild things, can be read to the background music of Mussorgsky's *Night on Bald Mountain*.

Put out some dark materials in the Art Center at the same time; for example, sheets of black and white construction paper, white chalk, charcoal sticks, black pencils and felt-tip markers, black and white easel paint, or anything else the children might suggest. Play the same music as they experiment with the art materials. Again, we realize most of the children will not be painting a picture, but manipulating the medium of art materials that represent night.

Sendak's book *In the Night Kitchen* (1970) is another wonderful night story, this time about Mickey who falls out of his bed and into a fantastic kitchen where he gets covered with dough. **You can play Tchaikovsky's** *Nutcracker Suite* **as you read the story**, and again in the Art Center **as children make their own play dough**.

Owl Babies (Waddell, 1992), is another fine night story of three nervous baby barn owls covered with white down sitting up in a tree against the black book pages of night. Where is mother owl, they wonder aloud? You can play Mozart's *Eine Kleine Nachtmusik* ("A Little Night Music") as you read, and again when children experiment with "night" art materials. Perhaps they would like to try **cutting paper to be moons, owls, and snowflakes, or fence posts, trees, and shadows, and then pasting them into a collage**. Be sure to accept whatever the children are able to cut out, because most preschool children are not skilled at making real objects. *Francis the Scaredy Cat* (Boxall, 2002), *Night Shift Daddy* (Spinelli, 2000), and *Stellaluna* (Cannon, 1993) are other nighttime books children enjoy.

Can the children make their own night music? How would they do it? They might tape-record sounds they make with their voices and other materials: wind whistling, rain pattering, leaves rustling, footsteps clumping, and wings flapping. They can add their own musical accompaniment to these sounds with a little electronic keyboard or rhythm instruments. You can help children to respect the instruments in the classroom by using them musically and not running around with them, banging them noisily, or treating them roughly. From such activities they can learn that these instruments are not toys but real music makers for them to use creatively.

THE TEACHER'S ROLE IN THE MUSIC CENTER

Once again the role of the teacher in the Music Center may not be the traditional one of conducting a "music period" for the entire group. Instead, the teacher will set up the center as described in this chapter so that children can get involved in music on their own as much as possible. He will also interact with individuals and small groups in the center in order to stimulate their involvement in personal music listening experiences, sound exploration, rhythm experiments, singing, and music making in general. He will help them learn to record and play back their sounds, rhythms, and songs.

When classroom plans call for it, the teacher will bring in materials for making and using rhythm instruments. He will work both with individuals and small groups in the Music Center as well as the total group at Circle Time, promoting social musical experiences such as musical games, singing with puppets, and playing instruments.

Observing Development Levels

Observing children's interactions with music to determine whether they are at the manipulation, mastery, or meaning level is not as obvious with music as it is with blocks, for instance. Yet, sensitive observers are often able to record children's interactions when the youngsters are involved with materials such as rhythm instruments. Table 9-2 lists some of the typical interactions that can be expected for each level.

As teachers record their observations on the Child Interaction Form (Table 2-1, p. 36) they can begin to make plans for individual children. For children at the

Table 9-2 Music Center Activities: Levels of Interaction

Manipulation Level

Playing around with drums, rhythm sticks, shakers, tone blocks, triangles, and clackers in inappropriate ways
Using homemade tooters to blow air through, not making musical sounds
Snapping rubber-band strummers to experiment with sound or touch
Running mallets up and down xylophones, not striking separate notes
Banging on drums, tom-toms, and bongos

Mastery Level

Using drums, bells, triangles, and tone blocks in appropriate ways
Playing instruments over and over, almost as if practicing
Playing notes separately over and over on xylophone, and rubber-band strummer
Using mallets to strike bells, cymbals, drums, tone blocks, and triangles over and over
Swishing sand blocks together
Holding tambourine and tapping or shaking it
Rubbing rhythm sticks back and forth

Meaning Level

Playing single instrument appropriately to accompany own song
Beating drum in rhythm to music
Choosing and using particular instrument to make own music
Marching and playing instrument on own
Playing a melody on the xylophone
Playing a tape or record and accompanying music with instrument
Making up original ways to use bells, castanets, maracas, or tambourines
Humming real song through kazoo, cardboard tooter, or comb harmonica

manipulation level, they may want to leave certain intruments in the center for an extra amount of time until the children learn how to use them. Those at the mastery level can be encouraged to try their hand at mastering several different kinds of instruments. Children at the meaning level who are making music on their own might be motivated to tape-record their productions. Several children may, in fact, want to join forces to **record their own rhythm-band music**. Although music will remain a "process" for most of the children, some of those at the meaning level will want to preserve their accomplishments like this in the form of a tape recording.

Modeling a Love for Music

Music will fill the classroom at appropriate times if teachers encourage children to "sing while they work" by taking the lead themselves. Hum your favorite tunes. Whistle if you know how. Can the children also "Whistle While You Work" as the dwarfs did in *Snow White and the Seven Dwarfs*? **Play this music and see how many of the children can make whistling sounds**. In addition, you will use your repertoire of transition songs throughout the day. Finally, you will be playing records and tapes as background music to set the mood for reading certain books or working on special projects.

There will be a happy mood, indeed, in classrooms where teachers model their own love for music.

IDEAS IN CHAPTER 9

1. *Setting up the Music Center*
    a. Bring in records or tapes you enjoy to share with children at appropriate times
    b. Show children how to use and not to abuse a cassette recorder
    c. Have headsets available and also a clipboard for children to sign up for recorder use
    d. Promote listening, sound exploration, rhythm, and music making
    e. Display only a few of the rhythm instruments at one time

2. *Promoting emotional development*
    a. Make music personal for the children
    b. Consider featuring shoes and "shoe music" in your Music Center
    c. Acquire a collection of shoes, and tape-record what they sound like being walked in
    d. Ask children to guess what shoe made the sound
    e. Have children make their own "shoe music" and tape it

    f. Have a pretend shoe store in the Dramatic Play Center

    g. Record the way boots sound in the water table

    h. Have children make footprints on paper and in wet sand

    i. Invite a guest to demonstrate tap dancing

    j. Tape-record children moving to music while wearing different kinds of shoes

    k. Bring in a pair of crutches and tape the sound they make being used

    l. Play the circle game "Pass the Shoe"

3. *Promoting small-motor development*

    a. Lead the children in clapping out the syllables of their names

    b. Have a leg-slapping circle activity to a chant

    c. Have children make and then record their "pounding music"

    d. Collect boxes and cans for tom-toms

    e. Make drums from coffee cans and wrapping paper

    f. Make tambourines from pie tins

    g. Explore a single rhythm instrument at a time

    h. Make musical shakers from margarine containers

    i. Have children strum the Autoharp while the teacher plays

    j. Make shoebox strummers and have a band

4. *Promoting social development*

    a. Sing a familiar song, encouraging everyone to join in while working in the various activity centers

    b. Ask a coworker to sing along with you

    c. Make a collection of musical fingerplay songs to use during transition times

    d. Bring children together in a group to learn new songs and fingerplays

    e. Use CDs or tapes for some musical games

    f. Involve children directly in making music

    g. Do not force children to join in who are uncomfortable

    h. Shy children can hide behind some interesting object when singing

    i. Have a weekly puppet sing

5. *Promoting language development*

    a. Make up words to familiar tunes about children's names, families, clothing, pets, etc.

    b. Use one song at a time, singing it over and over and inserting different children's names

   c. Make up guessing-game songs about the children's pets

   d. Print the words of the songs you are singing in the parents' newsletters

6. *Promoting cognitive development*

   a. Children can learn the concepts of loud/soft, high/low, and fast/slow by tapping with objects

   b. Bring in glass containers, fill with water and then sand for tapping sounds

7. *Promoting creative development*

   a. Have children listen to stories and paint to music

   b. Play "night music" while children manipulate "night" art activities

   c. Have children listen to the *Nutcracker Suite* when Sendak's *In the Night Kitchen* is read and play dough is made

   d. Make a "night collage" after hearing the story *Owl Babies*

   e. Have children record their own rhythm-band music

   f. Have children try whistling after hearing the song "Whistle While You Work"

DISCUSSION QUESTIONS

1. Why do children seem to have a natural affinity for music?

2. What does it mean that music is often a passive experience for children in the preschool classroom? How can it become active?

3. How do children develop the ability to recognize and produce tone, rhythm, and melody?

4. How can the Music Center be set up to make music active and personal for young children?

5. How can you as a teacher model a love for music for your children so that they will participate and become involved in classroom music activities?

TRY IT YOURSELF

1. Develop and implement a series of personal music experiences for children based on their hands. Use the ideas described in this chapter about "shoe music" as a model. Record what happens.

2. Involve the children in making their own rhythm instruments to promote eye-hand coordination and fun with music. Record the results.

3. Teach the children some new songs in the informal manner described in this chapter. Also use a picture book that is based on the lyrics of a song or chant with the children. Record the results.

4. Help shy children to become involved in music by using puppets. Record the results.

5. Record on 3-by-5 cards the lyrics of all the songs you sing with children in your program. Then add cards with the lyrics you make up for personal songs about every child using a familiar tune as described.

REFERENCES CITED

Davies, M. A. (2000). Learning … the beat goes on. *Childhood Education 76*, 148–153.

Edwards, L. C., Bayless, K. M., & Ramsey, M. E. (2005). *Music a way of life for the young child* (5th ed.). Upper Saddle River, NJ: Merrill/Prentice Hall.

Gardner, H. (1993). *Frames of mind: The theory of multiple intelligences*. New York: Basic Books.

Hill-Clarke, K. Y. & Robinson, N. R. (2004). It's easy as A-B-C and do-re-mi: Music, rhythm, and rhyme enhance children's literacy skills. *Young Children 59*(5), 91–95.

Jalongo, M. R. & Collins, M. (1985). Singing with young children: Folk singing for nonmusicians. *Young Children 40*(2), 17–22.

Neely, L. P. (2001). Developmentally appropriate music practice: Children learn what they live. *Young Children 56*(3), 32–37.

Wolf, J. (1994). Singing with children is a cinch! *Young Children 49*(4), 20–30.

Other Sources

Barclay, K. D. & Walwer, J. (1992). Linking lyrics and literacy through song picture books. *Young Children 47*(4), 76–85.

Edelson, R. J. & Johnson, G. (2003/04). Music makes math meaningful. *Childhood Education 80*(2), 65–70.

Greata, J. (2006). *An introduction to music in early childhood education*. Clifton Park, NY: Cengage Learning.

Isbell, R. T. & Raines, S. C. (2007). *Creativity and the arts with young children*. Clifton Park, NY: Cengage Learning.

Jalongo, M. R. & Ribblett, D. M. (1997). Using song picture books to support emergent literacy. *Childhood Education 74*(1), 15–28.

Kemple, K. M., Batey, J. J., & Hartle, L. C. (2004). Music play: Creating centers for musical play and exploration. *Young Children 59*(4), 30–37.

Palmer, H. (2001). The music, movement, and learning connection. *Young Children 56*(5), 13–17.

Snyder, S. (1997). Developing musical intelligence: Why and how. *Early Childhood Education Journal 24*(3), 165–171.

Children's Books

Boxall, E. (2002). *Francis the scaredy cat*. Cambridge, MA: Candlewick Press.

Burton, M. R. (1994). *My best shoes*. New York: Tambourine.*

Cannon, J. (1993). *Stellaluna*. San Diego, CA: Harcourt.

Daly, N. (1985). *Not so fast, Songololo*. New York: Viking Penguin.*

Dillon, L. & Dillon, D. (2002). *Rap a tap tap: Here's Bojangles, think of that*! New York: The Blue Sky Press.*

Dole, M. L. (2003). *Drum, Chavi, drum*. San Francisco, CA: Children's Book Press.*

Emmett, J. (2006). *She'll be coming 'round the mountain*. New York: Atheneum Books.

Fox, M. (1989). *Shoes from grandpa*. New York: Orchard.

Harper, C. M. (2002). *There was a bold lady who wanted a star*. Boston: Little, Brown.

Havill, J. (1993). *Jamaica and Brianna*. Boston: Houghton Mifflin.*

Hillenbrand, W. (2002). *Fiddle-i-fee*. San Diego: Harcourt.

Hoberman, M. A. (1998). *Miss Mary Mack*. Boston: Little, Brown.*

Hoberman, M. A. (2003). *Mary had a little lamb*. Boston: Little, Brown.

Hurwitz, J. (1993). *New shoes for Silvia*. New York: Morrow.*

Johnson, P. B. (2006). *On top of spaghetti*. New York: Scholastic Press.

Joosse, B. M. (1991). *Mama, do you love me?* San Francisco: Chronicle Books.*

Komaiko, L. (1992). *Aunt Elaine does the dance from Spain*. New York: Dell.*

Kovalski, M. (1987). *The wheels on the bus*. Boston: Little, Brown.

Loesser, F. (2005). *I love you a bushel and a peck*. New York: HarperCollins.

Milbourne, A. (2005). *The rainy day*. Tulsa, OK: EDC Publishing.*

Moore, M-A. (2006). *The wheels on the school bus*. New York: HarperCollins*

Novak, M. (2005). *Flip flop bop*. Brookfield, CT: Roaring Brook Press.*

Patrick, D. L. (1993). *Red dancing shoes*. New York: Tambourine.*

Pinkney, B. (1994). *Max found two sticks*. New York: Aladdin Paperbacks.*

Rattigan, J. K. (1993). *Dumpling soup*. Boston: Little, Brown.*

Richmond, M. (2006). *My shoes take me where I want to go*. Minneapolis, MN: Richmond Studios.

Sanderson, E. (1990). *Two pairs of shoes*. Berkeley, CA: Oyate.*

Sendak, M. (1963). *Where the wild things are*. New York: Harper & Row.

Sendak, M. (1970). *In the night kitchen*. New York: Harper & Row.

Spinelli, E. (2000). *Night shift daddy*. New York: Hyperion Books for Children.*

Trapani, I. (1993). *The itsy bitsy spider*. Boston: Whispering Coyote Press.

Waddell, M. (1992). *Owl babies*. Cambridge, MA: Candlewick Press.

Warhola, J. (2007). *If you're happy and you know it*. New York: Orchard Books.

Westcott, N. B. (1988). *The lady with the alligator purse*. Boston: Little, Brown.

Westcott, N. B. (1989). *Skip to my Lou*. Boston: Little, Brown.

Wolkstein, D. (1981). *The banza*. New York: The Dial Press.

Note: Asterisk represents multicultural book.

PETS

ACTION CHANT

(March in place throughout),
Minnie's got a guinea pig

Tony's got a turtle,

Holly has a hermit crab,

Jackie's got a gerbil,

Aaron has an ant farm,

Baron's got some guppies,

Karen's got a kitten,

Now she wants some puppies;

Pets, pets everywhere;
  (March & clap)

What am I to do?

I don't need another pet,
  (Stop suddenly)

I've got you!
  (Point to someone)

SCIENCE IN THE EARLY CHILDHOOD CLASSROOM

Of all the activities in the early childhood classroom, few illustrate quite as vividly as does science the idea that young children acquire knowledge through self-discovery. Science, in fact, means *investigation* as far as young children are concerned. It is less about plants and animals, or weather and water, than it is about "finding out." How do preschool children find out about the world around them? Not through reading. Not through viewing a video. Not through listening to the teacher. Those are methods that somewhat older children may find helpful. But your youngsters learn most appropriately about their environment by interacting physically with the objects within it. It is a "hands-on discovery" approach that involves investigation with their five senses. In other words, for young children science is a *process of finding out*.

Conezio and French (2002) tell us in no uncertain terms: "Whereas many adults think of science as a discrete body of knowledge, for young children science is finding out about the everyday world that surrounds them. This is exactly what they are interested in doing all day, every day" (p. 13).

Children are born scientific explorers. From the moment they come into the world they use their senses to try out everything they come into contact with. Epstein (2007) tells us: "In science we want to capitalize on children's natural inclination to learn about their world, and involve them in scientific inquiry as they figure out how the world works. Children are naturally inclined to explore their surroundings. But they depend on us to give them a rich environment for inquiry and to develop their child-guided discoveries into a growing understanding of how science works" (p. 43).

SENSORY EXPLORATION

All children everywhere come well equipped for the task of investigating their environment. They bring with them into the world five wonderfully acute senses with which to explore: sight, sound, smell, taste, and touch. Infants put their senses to work almost immediately as they investigate every object, first with their mouths to see if it will supply them with food. Preschoolers often focus on the sense of touch: twisting things with their hands, and trying to take apart every new object they encounter. Even children with sensory handicaps, such as impaired vision, compensate for that lack by developing extra acute hearing or touch.

The Appropriate Practices Curriculum can lead your youngsters to successful scientific investigation of their environment if it taps into their natural mode of sensory exploration, and if it provides them with the opportunities and the tools to explore fascinating objects with each of their senses.

Sight

The sense of sight can be applied in several ways to your children's scientific investigations. First of all, they need to observe and notice things in their environment. If they are investigating water, for instance, they need to take a sweeping look to see what water is in evidence in their classroom environment. As you sit with a small group of children in the Science Center, **ask them what water they can see in the room**.

Children need to observe things closely in their investigations.

The children may name the water dripping from a faucet in the sink, the water in the aquarium, the water in the water table, the water in the guinea pig's dish, and the water in the toilet (someone is sure to say—although he or she may be challenged by another child who is quick to note: "You can't see it from here!"). Others may see the pan of water in the Art Center for rinsing paintbrushes, or the pitcher of water being used to make play dough. You will want to record this water list so that children can carry their water explorations even further.

As they investigate the visual qualities of water, children may want to **view water through a magnifying glass**. What other vision tools can they use to help them see water better? You can ask the children, "Would a pair of binoculars like these be good for viewing water?" Let them look through the binoculars, and then listen to their answers. Many of the children may not have seen binoculars before. But someone may reply, "You use binoculars to see water far away." That child may have used binoculars with his or her family. Perhaps a family member could be invited to **go on a water-viewing field trip** with the group.

Sound

Sound may be the next sense children will use, although this depends upon the object being investigated. "What sound does water make?" is a question you can pose to your small discovery group. Someone will be quick to tell you that it "splashes." What does a splash sound like, you may wonder aloud? There are different kinds of splashes, someone else may say, so you will need to **listen to water sounds up close**.

One of the children can turn on a faucet—first easy, and then hard. Have the children close their eyes as they listen. Can the youngsters hear the difference? Can anyone turn on the faucet so lightly that the water merely drips? You can **tape-record all of these different water sounds for later listening and sound-identification fun**. Someone else is sure to remember the book they listened to in the Book Center, *The Rainy Day* (Milbourne, 2005), about the children in their rain boots splish, splash, sploshing through the puddles. If it's rainy outside, be ready to have your children splash in their puddles, too.

Once children are caught up in the fascination of sensory investigation, there is no end to it. Someone will want to pour out the paintbrush rinse water to hear what kind of sound that makes. Put that on the tape, too. Record the bubbling of the water in the aquarium and the water sounds children are making at the water table. Can they **blow bubbles through straws in the water table**? Does the guinea pig's water make a sound when he drinks it?

What else can they hear if they listen quietly? Read *The Listening Walk* (Showers, 1991), about a little girl, her father, and her dog who go for a walk in which they do not talk but listen for all sorts of noises, including the sounds they make when they walk. Take your own children on such a walk. Bring a tape recorder along.

Smell

Children use smell all the time to help them identify and distinguish between the things in their world; all of us do. We often do not acknowledge our use of smell, and we often downplay its role because it is the polite thing to do. Research has shown us, however, that mothers can identify by smell alone which shirt out of several belongs to their own baby. Babies also have this ability regarding their mothers.

Your preschoolers will enjoy **sniffing at different kinds of water to see if there is a difference in the way they smell**. They may not find much of a difference with water in your classroom, although the aquarium water may smell of algae. Such an activity helps them learn that we can use smell to distinguish between different objects that look alike. **Take them on a water-collecting field trip** and let them smell pond water or river water. What other kinds of liquids can they identify by smell?

Taste

If something is edible, young children will want to try it. By ages 3, 4, and 5, they are not so likely to put everything new into their mouths the way babies do. Still, they will be interested in **trying out the various samples of water you provide to see if there is a difference in taste**. Obviously, you will be providing samples that are not harmful. Does bottled water from the supermarket taste different from tap water? This may be the time to experiment with taste changes of water by dissolving various flavored drink powders in it. The color changes too, the children may note. What happens when food coloring is dissolved in water? Does this change the taste as well as the color? Have them try different colors and find out.

Touch

Exploring a substance through touch can also be a stimulating experience for preschool children. **Pour a glass of warm water into one corner of the water table when no one is looking and ask them to find it**. Let different children continue this game on their own. What will finally happen to the water? Does anyone predict it will mix with the cooler water and soon feel the same? If so, you may have a child who is especially attuned to scientific thinking or sensory exploration. Challenge such a child with many opportunities to use this skill.

Attach a variable-spray nozzle to your water faucet and let children feel the spray at different settings. Can they use words that describe the different feelings of sprayed water (from a fine mist to a steady stream)? You may need to help out. **Let them use eggbeaters in the water table without soap bubbles**. Does the water feel any different before and after it has been beaten? Water lends itself well to such sensory activities, but the children can explore the sensory properties of all sorts of objects inside and outside the classroom.

Pour a glass of warm water into a corner of the water table and challenge a small group to find it.

A book for the children to hear, see, touch, but maybe not smell and taste is the simple story *Five for a Little One* (Raschka, 2006) about a bunny, outlined in black, with one fuzzy ear, who learns what each of the five senses means and how to use them. After you read it, keep the book in the Science Center as a reminder to children of how to explore with their senses.

CURIOSITY

In addition to the sensory apparatus that is their natural inheritance, young children also come equipped with a strong drive to find out everything they can about their world. We call this drive *curiosity*. Every child is born with it. Some children, however, seem to have a greater degree of curiosity than others. This drive to find out is equivalent in many respects to young children's other inborn drive: the drive to communicate. Youngsters acquire language naturally because of this drive. But they must hear language spoken around them in order to acquire their native tongue. They must be encouraged to speak, to imitate sounds, and to take part in conversations, if they are to become successful speakers.

In like manner, young children must be encouraged to explore their environment in order to acquire knowledge about it. Furthermore, they must not be continually discouraged from exploring if they are to preserve this precious sense of curiosity and wonder. At home it is possible that some children are scolded if they touch things. In the classroom when such children act in an out-of-bounds manner, it is often because they are too severely restricted at home.

Other children who show no curiosity at all about the new things around them in the classroom, may also have learned this behavior from being too restricted at home. If this is the case, then you should consider **talking with parents about how children learn through exploration** and how they might explore things in fun ways at home. You should also think of delightful ways to reawaken children's natural curiosity in the classroom. This drive in young children to find out needs to be nurtured and encouraged.

> Exploring is fun. Discovering is fun. A problem solved is fun. Laughing, squealing, joyously shared science is a goal worth seeking for yourself and for children. People learn best when they enjoy. (Holt, 1989, p. 12)

You can start by being an exploring behavior model for the children yourself. Pretend you know little or nothing about the objects in your environment. How would you go about using your senses to explore things? Join in with the children in the great adventure of discovering the life around them. You, too, can be a scientific investigator!

SETTING UP THE SCIENCE CENTER

To be successful in enticing all of the children into the Science Center, you should set it up based on topics of real interest to them. As you did with music, you should **make science personal**. Focus the children's scientific explorations on themselves and their nearby world, and you will attract their attention and interest. That means you will be investigating such topics as:

The children themselves
their bodies
their clothing
their food, drink
their shadows

The children's pets
dogs, cats, fish, birds, rabbits
insects, snakes, gerbils, guinea pigs
hermit crabs, frogs

The schoolyard and nearby parks
trees, grass, flowers, dirt, stones
birds, insects

The weather, seasons
wind, rain, clouds, sun, snow
fall, winter, spring, summer

You will be **stocking** your Science Center **with all kinds of tools for investigating things**, for measuring things, for containing things, for collecting things, for recording things. Table 10.1 shows lists of items you may want to include.

One of the shelves in your Science Center should contain **a collection of books on the topics you are investigating**. As new topics emerge during the year, additional books will be added. The books can be storybooks you will be reading to the children, as well as information books for yourself and the children with illustrations the children will enjoy looking at. You can start with books about:

Trees	Amphibians	Sun
Flowers	Snakes	Stars
Animals	Shells	Rocks
Birds	Insects	Water
Butterflies	Clouds	Air

The center itself will need shelves for containing the tools you will be using; a bookcase or shelves for the books; display space for collections on shelves or countertops; work space on a table; **space for an aquarium, a terrarium**, an ant farm, or **animal homes** for gerbils or a guinea pig; and soil in containers for growing seeds and cuttings. All of the items in the Science Center will be marked with illustrated labels for easy identification by the children.

Children can take care of fish on their own in the Science Center aquarium.

Table 10-1 Science Materials

For investigating:	
Gooseneck lamp	Plastic tubing
Stool magnifying glass	Straws
Hand magnifying glass	Sponges
Binoculars	Filter paper
Incubator	Screen
Mirrors	Sieves
Prism	Funnels
Hammer	Sponges
Tweezers	Scissors
Flashlights	Magnets

For measuring:	
Balance	Stopwatch
Postage meter	Spring scale
Folding ruler	Twine
Tape measure	Yardstick
Wind-up ruler	Hourglass

For containing:	
Margarine cups	Cigar boxes
Plastic trays	Shoeboxes
Plastic jars	Adhesive tape boxes
Plastic bottles	Egg cartons

For collecting:	
Paper bags	Pouches
Plastic bags	String bags
Jars, boxes	Backpacks
Collecting nets	Dippers

For recording:	
Cassette recorder and blank tapes	Twine, string
Digital camera	Cellophane tape
Notebooks, pads, writing tools	Scissors
Chart paper	

THE SCIENTIFIC METHOD

Because young children come prepared to explore and investigate things with all of their senses, it is easy to channel their energy along the lines real scientists use in their research.

1. Pose a problem or a question about something.
2. Guess or predict what will happen if …
3. Conduct the investigation.
4. Observe, record, collect.
5. Draw conclusions.
6. Record the results.

For example, suppose Angelina comes in one snowy winter morning with something exciting her dad has told her on the way to school: that every snowflake is different—there are no two snowflakes that are alike. Can that be true? Angelina and four other children want to investigate that idea scientifically. The teacher sits down with them in the Science Center and talks about how they can find out. **The teacher listens to what the children have to say and jots down their ideas.**

Doug thinks it can't be true because nobody in the world could look at every snowflake. Angelina thinks her dad is right because he is always right. Lori doesn't know. Jonathan wants to go outside and get a bucket of snow and bring it inside and look. The teacher poses the question: What will happen if we bring a bucket of snow inside? Will we be able to see the snowflakes? Will we be able to tell if they are different? The children think they will, so they bundle up, go outside, and get a bucket of snow.

Back in the classroom it is soon obvious that they have a mass of snow that is beginning to melt, but no snowflakes. Where are the snowflakes? What do they look like? Before the children can take off their winter wraps, Jonathan exclaims: "I see a snowflake! It's on Angelina's scarf! And there's another one!" But before the other children get a chance to look closely, the snowflakes have melted into the scarf. Now what to do?

After talking it over with the teacher, the children come to a new conclusion: you can't see snowflakes by bringing snow inside because they are so small, and they melt right away. So they decide to look at them outside. "You have to catch snowflakes when they are falling," announces Jonathan, "because on the ground they are all mashed together."

"You can catch them on my scarf," suggests Angelina. But what about the other children who have no scarves? How can they catch any snowflakes? "Is there some kind of dark cloth in the room that they can take outside to catch snowflakes?" wonders the teacher. The children scurry around to look. Doug comes back to the Science Center with three personal-sized flannel boards from the Book Center.

"Will we be able to see the snowflakes we catch when they're so small?" asks the teacher? The children say that they will be able to see them, but they wonder if they will be able to tell if they're different because they are so small. They decide that each child should also take a magnifying glass outside to look at the snowflakes. Out they go again, armed with their scientific investigating apparatus. This time **each child catches snowflakes and looks at them through a magnifying glass**. The children have to come under the shelter of the eaves so that the falling snow doesn't cover their boards or their glasses. They exclaim over the beautiful shapes of the snowflakes. They really are different!

Back in the classroom, the four children **discuss their investigation with the teacher**. When they have made their conclusions about whether it is true that each snowflake is different, **the teacher gets out the tape recorder and a blank tape and the children report their findings**.

Angelina says:	"The snowflakes I saw were all different."
Lori says:	"I saw a lot of pretty snowflakes."
Jonathan says:	"My snowflakes were in clumps so I couldn't tell."
Doug says:	"My snowflakes were different, but nobody can see all the snowflakes in the world."

The teacher marks on the outside of the tape "Snowflake Research: 12/13." Perhaps some of the other children will want to continue this investigation.

The teacher then gets out a picture book about snow, such as Robert Frost's poem *Stopping by Woods on a Snowy Evening* (1978) and reads it to the children. They love Susan Jeffers's snowy illustrations, especially the jewel-like snowflakes on the page that says, "and downy flake." Angelina notes that they are all different. Jonathan likes it that the old man makes angel's wings in the snow just like the wings on the birds in the picture. Lori likes the fact that the grandpa takes seeds to the birds in the woods because there are no seeds on the trees in the winter. Doug wishes he was there to feed the man's horse like the children in the picture. Angelina also says she didn't know horses had blankets like the one the man put on his horse. (The teacher hadn't noticed this!) All of the children wished they could have a ride in a horse sleigh like the one in the book. The teacher decides privately to look into such a possibility for a field trip.

The children spend a great deal of time looking at this book, even after the teacher has read the single line or two on every other page. Suddenly Doug discovers that there are animals hidden in the woods on the page where the man has made a snow angel. Then they all have to look. The teacher says that Susan Jeffers, the artist, likes to hide animal outlines in her pictures. The children find seven rabbits and a deer (although Doug says one of the rabbits is really a squirrel). On another page they find two rabbits, two deer, *one* squirrel, one blue jay, and a mouse. (The teacher hadn't noticed the mouse!) This book quickly becomes a favorite of everyone in the class. The teacher says she will try to bring in another of Jeffers's books with hidden animals [such as *Brother Eagle, Sister Sky* (1991) and Doolittle's *The Forest Has Eyes* (1998)—both with hidden Indian faces].

Then they all want to cut out snowflakes in the Art Center, so the teacher goes over with them to show them how to fold and cut the paper (see Chapter 8).

Notice how this entire science activity about snowflakes was totally spontaneous. It occurred because the teacher was listening to what the children had to say, and then followed up on their intense interest with questions. Teachers who listen to their children, who take seriously the questions children ask, and who are willing to risk going in the direction of the youngster's interests, even when they don't know the answers, soon find that science activities become the most popular ones in the classroom. Everyone wants to get involved, and all have their own ideas about how to investigate the topic.

You may find that: "To be a naturalist, all you need are curiosity, joy of exploration, and a desire to discover firsthand the wonders of nature. Young children are natural naturalists. Adults take a little longer" (Galvin, 1994, p. 4).

SCIENCE ACTIVITIES TO PROMOTE COGNITIVE DEVELOPMENT

The cognitive concepts most appropriate for preschool children to investigate involve the properties of objects (their shape, size, color, texture, sound, and odor); the actions of objects (how they move, react, balance, stand up, grow, and eat); and the similarities and differences between objects. **Preschool children need not be so concerned about "why" things are the way they are, but rather "how" they look, act, and interact**; and especially how the things they see relate to them.

For example, when Alonzo hears his favorite Ezra Jack Keats's story *Whistle for Willie* (1964), he wants to know about jumping off your shadow like the boy Peter does in the story. (Old books like this are still available in paperback or through www.amazon.com.) The children talk with the teacher about shadows. Does everyone have a shadow? Can you run away from your shadow? This teacher does not know all the answers, but he invites the small group over to the Science Center, where he closes the blinds, puts a sheet of white paper on the wall, and turns on the gooseneck lamp. He shines the light on each child's upheld hand so **every child in the group can make a shadow of his hand on the paper**.

Someone discovers that they can make the shadow bigger than their real hand. The children are fascinated. Everyone has to try it to see how big they can make their hand shadows. The teacher places the lamp up high on a shelf and aims it so a child's shadow shows up on the floor. Can you jump away from your shadow like Peter does in the book? Everyone wants to try it.

Can you jump away from your shadow like Peter does in the book?

The children are most interested in the fact that shadows can be bigger than they themselves are. They all want to draw pictures of their hands showing them bigger than they are. It's hard to trace around the big shadow of a hand unless the child holds it very still. Jonathan holds his hand like a monster's! Some of the children want to color in their hands so they take them over to the Art Center.

The teacher realizes he has struck a common cord of great interest for the children, and decides to extend the experience. The next day he brings in another Ezra Jack Keats's book, *Dreams* (1974), and reads it to the group of children who made their hand shadows. It illustrates the story of Roberto who brings home a paper mouse he has made in school and places it in the open upstairs window of his apartment building. When Roberto is awakened in the middle of the night by a dog chasing a cat, he looks out to see what is happening and accidentally knocks the paper mouse off the windowsill. It tumbles down the side of the building making weird gigantic shadows from the street light as it falls, scaring the dog away.

The teacher also understands that his role as facilitator in preschool science activities is to listen to the children's comments and questions, and to set up the Science Center for them to explore things of great interest to them or to help them find the answers to their questions. One thing leads to another in preschool science, he realizes; thus it is his job to **listen and then follow the children's lead—especially when their interests take them in a direction that seems an appropriate area for study**, whether or not he has planned for it.

Again the children are delighted. This time they want to make Roberto's mouse. The teacher is prepared and has brought in sheets of gray construction paper that he helps them twist into a cone fastened by cellophane tape. They look at the picture of the paper mouse in the book and decide to make the head and nose by bending down and taping the pointed top. Then they make pink ears and tape them onto their cones. Black dots for eyes and whiskers complete their mice.

Once again the teacher closes the blinds and hangs a white sheet on the wall. The gooseneck lamp is shined on the sheet while one child at a time climbs up on a chair in front of the lamp, holds his mouse up high, and lets it drop. Yes. The mouse really does make tumbling shadows. The children try getting up closer to the light and then closer to the sheet to make the shadows bigger and smaller. Later, one of the teacher's assistants brings in Robert Louis Stevenson's classic book *A Child's Garden of Verses* (1957) and reads his famous poem: "My Shadow."

The children's study of shadows does not end there. **One of the parents reads** in the parents' newsletter **about the class's experiments with shadows** and **volunteers to come in and show the children how he makes shadows of animals with his fingers**. The teacher covers over the opening of their puppet theater with a sheet and shines light on it from the back. The parent holds his folded fingers up in back of the sheet while the light throws their shadow onto the screen. The children seated in front are entranced. They all want to try making finger animals. Soon they are holding up animal figures from the Block Center, and, later, cutouts of their own.

Meanwhile, the children continue to look for and find shadows of all kinds of things inside and out. They are excited about outdoor shadows of themselves, the trees, and the playground equipment, made by the sun. "You have to have light to have shadows," declares Alonzo. The teacher is delighted, for he realizes that their curiosity has indeed been piqued by their investigation of shadows, and that can, in turn, lead them in other exciting directions.

This teacher **continues to listen to the children's questions and comments to help** him **lead the class in an appropriate science direction**. He finds that one topic usually leads to another topic over the course of the year. Some of the cognitive concepts this class explores include: How much rain falls when it rains? (They make a rain gauge.) Why do earthworms come out of the ground when it rains? (They start a terrarium with earthworms in it.) What other things live under the ground? (They start an ant farm.)

SCIENCE ACTIVITIES TO PROMOTE EMOTIONAL DEVELOPMENT

Whenever classroom activities are **focused on children personally, they help promote the children's positive self-concept**, thus making them feel good about themselves. A favorite personal science activity that one classroom often conducts as a yearlong project is an **"adopt-a-tree"** experience. The schoolyard is a large one with many maple and oak trees and several pine trees. This teacher has each one of the trees located and labeled with a color-coded circle on a large newsprint chart. Early in September each child chooses a tree to be his or her adopted tree for the year. The teacher takes a picture of each adopted tree with its child standing next to it. The chart is then mounted on the wall along with the tree/child photos next to the proper tree-circle.

The children make a special visit to their trees once a week, after which different things happen, depending upon the children, their questions, and the direction their interests take them. Some of the tree activities include:

Choosing tree, introducing self, hugging tree

Talking about taking care of tree, how trees help us

Naming of each tree by its child

Doing a sensory study of the tree: (close eyes)

What can your nose tell you about your tree?

What can your fingers tell you about your tree?

Looking at tree close-up (with magnifying glass, with cardboard tube "viewer")

Looking at tree from distance with binoculars

Making adopted tree scrapbook

Making bark rubbings

Collecting leaves, needles, twigs, fallen branches

Making leaf rubbings

Pressing leaves and displaying in clear food wrapping

Comparing leaves from different trees; from same tree in different seasons

Identifying tree in tree book

Collecting nuts, seeds, pinecones

Counting, sorting, weighing seeds and cones

Making seed collage

Taking photos of trees in different seasons

Looking for living things in the tree

Squirrels/nests

Birds/nests/holes/eggs

Insects/spiders/webs/wasps/nests

Caterpillars/cocoons

Fungus/moss/lichens

Activities about squirrels, birds, insects, caterpillars

Hatching butterfly or moth from cocoon or chrysalis

Making bird feeders

Putting out seeds, suet, peanut butter for birds in winter

Putting out string, yarn, strips of cloth for nests in spring

Tape-recording sound of wind in tree, birds' songs

Doing creative movement to tapes of wind in trees

Making popcorn strings to decorate trees at Christmas

Reading stories about trees

Making up stories about personal trees

Planting seeds from tree

Collecting things around tree in different seasons

Thanking tree for giving shade, seeds, homes for animals and birds, air for people to breathe, beauty

When a baby bird falls out of a nest in Jessie's tree, a whole new science activity begins. They put the baby bird in a box lined with cotton and leaves, and wonder what to feed it. But the teacher next door, an Audubon Society member, tells the children it is better to put the bird back where they found it so the mother can come and take care of it when they are gone. She tells them it is a baby robin. They watch out the window and, sure enough, some time later the mother robin comes and gets her baby into a nearby bush. The next morning it is gone. This teacher tells the children that parent birds know best about baby birds. It is very difficult for people to raise wild birds.

Then the children remembered the story of Stellaluna, the baby fruit bat that falls from its mother's breast when an owl attacks, and lands in a bird's nest. They get out the book *Stellaluna* (Cannon, 1993) and ask the teacher to read it once more about how the mother bird makes the baby bat behave like a bird by eating bugs and sleeping right-side-up in a nest—until she is finally rescued by her mother bat. Other children get out the DVD *Stellaluna* and play the find-the-animals game or listen to an oral reading of the book on the computer. They had already heard it so many times, they almost knew it by heart.

Baby animals being separated from their mothers? Was that something the class should pursue? Yes, said the children. They remembered about the three scared baby barn owls in the book *Owl Babies* (Waddell, 1992). It was a favorite story they loved to reenact with little owl Bill squeaking out: "I want my mama!" on every other page.

It is certainly an emotional theme, decides the teacher. Since he likes to begin new activities with a new book as a lead-in, the teacher searches for one and finds *Bats* (Gibbons, 1999), a paperback book with whole-page illustrations and a few lines of text at the bottom. The book is factual and tells everything a person needs to know about these creatures. Are they ugly? Some of their faces are ugly to us but must be beautiful to other bats, say the children. They want to make tracings of some weird bat faces and wear them as masks in their dramas: the tube-nose fruit bat with two little tubes sticking out of its face; the Jamaican fruit bat with leaf-like shapes sticking out of its nose, and the epaulet bat that looks like a dog.

The Art Center is soon busy with some **children making brown paper bat wings and masks**. Other children cut out baby bats: long brown ovals with two paper clips for feet, which they hang upside down on thumbtacks all over the classroom. Then the children **make up a game called "Find the Baby Bat"** in which the room is darkened, night music is played, and two children at a time wearing masks and bat wings go around the room trying to gather up as many baby bats as they can before the music stops. The Writing Center takes up the bat challenge, too, with children dictating to a teacher, or **printing, scribbling, and drawing their own versions of "Diary of a Bat,"** based on the Cronin (2003) book *Diary of a Worm* that they love. The Music Center also joins this integration of ideas with children making up bat songs to "Mary Had a Little Lamb" and "Where, Oh Where Is Little Baby Bat?" (*Paw Paw Patch*).

Do other mother animals lose their babies, the children want to know? The teacher eventually finds them the tender true story of Owen, in *A Mama for Owen* (Bauer, 2007), about a brownishgray baby hippo in Africa who loses his mother in a flood. After his rescue when Owen looks for his mother in the long grass, he spies a large brownishgray form. It is the very old tortoise, Mzee, and he becomes Owen's new mother.

One by one, other appropriate books appear on the scene, are read by the teacher, enjoyed by the children, and integrated into the learning centers.

Is Your Mama a Llama? (Guarino, 1989); mother and baby animals

Does a Kangaroo Have a Mother, Too? (Carle, 2000); mother and babies

I Love It When You Smile (McBratney, 2005); mother and baby kangaroo

Panda Whispers (Owens, 2007); fathers and baby animals

Alligator Baby (Munsch, 1997); mixed up baby zoo animals

Sammy, the Classroom Guinea Pig (Berenzy, 2005); lonely guinea pig

Patches Lost and Found (Kroll, 2001); lost guinea pig

When the classroom guinea pig, Whiskers, escapes and is lost, these last two books become a great hit with the children. Nicolas finally lures the animal out from behind a cabinet with a piece of lettuce. Everyone cheers.

Whiskers, the classroom guinea pig is rescued by Nicholas and put into an enclosure.

SCIENCE ACTIVITIES TO PROMOTE SOCIAL DEVELOPMENT

One teacher noted that many of the science activities pursued by her children were individual projects, such as the "adopt-a-tree" experience. She felt that science could be socially oriented as well, so she watched for an opportunity to **involve small groups of children in a learning experience that would call on their social skills**. She wanted individual children to be involved with other children so that they would have to take turns, wait for turns, and help one another. Care for the environment and for one another had been a theme in the classroom throughout the year. However, sometimes young children forget about others when they want something for themselves. The teacher decided to start with **teams of two children each**.

Because the children showed a great deal of interest in looking for insects around their trees, she felt that **a pets-in-a-jar project might be a good one to help children learn to work together**. The teacher brought in **enough jars for every two children** to have one. She also provided **one collecting net** (an aquarium fishnet) **for every team of two children**. She and her assistants each took **one trowel or small digging tool and a magnifying glass that the children could borrow and return**.

Before they went outside on an insect-collecting field trip, the teacher read *The Icky Bug Alphabet Book* (Pallotta, 1986) to the whole group, a book that had become a favorite of individuals in the Science Center since their interest in insects had begun. The large, realistic whole-page illustrations by Ralph Masiello gave the children a good idea of what certain insects looked like. The teacher talked about the fact that **these pictures were "larger than life," and that the insects the children find might be much smaller**. The youngsters had already seen non-stinging ants around their trees and now knew just where to look for them.

In addition, the teacher **talked to the children about teams and teamwork**. A team of two children would be working together to collect insects. Each team would have one collecting jar and one collecting net. They would need to take turns. What would they put in their jars besides insects? The children came up with some ideas: grass, sticks, leaves, bark, dirt. One child said: "Whatever the bug is on." "Don't forget to put the cover on the jar so your bug doesn't get out," another child reminded the others.

The children decided ahead of time that **they would keep the insects for only a day or so** to look at them inside, but that then **they would let them go so they wouldn't die**. Again the teacher and children talked together about care for our environment and care for each other.

The collecting expedition was a great success. Children are closer to the ground than adults, and seem to have an eye for tiny things that adults sometimes overlook. They found a number of large black carpenter ants, small brown ants, a spider, a cricket, several caterpillars, a ladybug, a cocoon under a piece of bark, a small dark beetle, and a little toad.

Back in the classroom they talked about where each team had found its insect (or amphibian) and how they collected it. Only one team had trouble sharing during the collecting: Brad said that Alex had grabbed the net out of his hand; Alex replied that the toad would have gotten away if he hadn't acted so quickly. Now he said, "Sorry," to Brad. The teacher fastened netting over the jars so that the creatures would have air but couldn't escape. Some of the children wanted to keep their collections for a few more days, so they talked about putting in appropriate food (leaves, crumbs) and water (a damp piece of sponge). They learned that their toad would eventually have to have insects to eat, so they let it go. They decided to keep the caterpillars and the cocoon, to see whether the caterpillars would make cocoons and whether the cocoon would hatch into a butterfly or moth. They also decided that the particular jars they kept would belong to the whole class and not just to the team that had collected the insects.

After the children had let their collections go free, they wished they had something in the jars to look at again. The teacher suggested collecting more ants, this time to make an ant farm. They had been talking about ants and how they lived in a "colony" underground, and how each ant had a certain task to perform to help the colony. They talked about how people do the same thing when they live together in a city or town.

Instead of having teams of children this time, each with one jar of ants, she told the children she would bring in two large gallon jars and that they could **sign up to work with other children on one of the two ant farms**. One of the adult staff members worked with each group of children to make their ant farms. Before they went outside, they **discussed what the tasks would be to make an ant farm**.

1. Put a block in the middle of the jar to force the ants to tunnel against the glass so that their tunnels can be seen.

2. Fill the jar about half full of dirt.

3. Find an anthill or opening in the ground and dig up the ants. Be sure to get white ant eggs, ant cocoons, and wriggling larvae in addition to the ants. Look for an ant larger than the rest who is the queen. Put all of these in the jar.

4. Put a piece of wet cotton on top for moisture.

5. Cover the top of the jar with fine netting and tie it tight.

6. Bring the jar inside and tape a piece of black construction paper around the outside of the jar for a few days to encourage the ants to build their tunnels against the outside of the glass where it is darkest, but where you will be able to see them best when the paper is removed.

7. Add drops of water when the cotton dries out, but not too much or it will get moldy.

8. Keep the jar away from direct sunlight or the radiator.

9. Feed the ants every other day by putting bits of food on a piece of cardboard and removing old food. Try different things like bread crumbs, cereal, pieces of vegetable or fruit, a spoon of honey. Don't overfeed.

10. Be sure to find the queen. If the queen is not in the jar, the ants will tunnel for awhile, but the colony will eventually die.

Before they went outside, the children decided which children would perform what task. "Just like the ants!" said one girl. After the ant farms became active, the children **took turns feeding the ants and reporting on what was happening**. They named the colonies "Underground City" and "Tunnel City."

The teacher brought in new books about ants to read from time to time. One of the favorites was *Ant* (Hawcock & Montgomery, 1994), a simple but fascinating fold-out and pop-up book containing a realistic cardboard ant mobile for the children to hang up. They learned from this book that ant colonies have graveyards, garbage dumps, nurseries, and pantries, so they tried to locate these in their ant farms. On the other hand, *Find Anthony Ant* (Philpot & Philpot, 2006) was a fun counting book with the song "The ants came marching one by one ..." Children are challenged on every two pages to decide why Anthony stopped and what he was doing in the underground maze at the bottom of the pages. All in all, the ant project was a highly successful social affair for many weeks.

SCIENCE ACTIVITIES TO PROMOTE LANGUAGE DEVELOPMENT

Talking about science projects; learning new names of things and new words to describe things; listening to stories about science topics; making up stories about plants, animals, birds, and insects; talking about who will do a certain task: all of these are science activities that promote language development in young children. Perhaps the scientific activity most directly related to language, however, is **recording the results of the children's explorations**.

The results can be recorded in several ways. Children can discuss the conclusions they make about their project, and then each one can **tape-record** aloud what he or she learned. For growing things that youngsters want to keep track of (including themselves), children can **make simple charts** where heights are recorded with lines and labels. Another satisfying activity may be **keeping a journal** about their study, just like scientists do.

For instance, each of the children in the adopt-a-tree project kept a **"tree diary."** The teacher would write down the date and then the children would scribble in their notebooks, make drawings, or dictate to the teacher what to write after they had made their weekly visit to their trees. When children did not know what to say, the teacher prompted them with open-ended questions such as, "What did your tree look like today?" Most entries were quite simple: "My tree looked cold," or "wet." But one said (through dictation to the teacher): "The leaves are starting to come out. They are all curled up." Children pasted photos of themselves and their trees in these diaries as well.

The children also wanted to **keep two group journals for the two ant farms**. They **took turns making entries**; some children had things to say every day. Later, children often looked back over these notebooks and made comments about them to other children, their teachers, and their parents. Photos, drawings, and cutouts from magazines also found their way into these journals. One child exclaimed: "We made a real book!"

SCIENCE ACTIVITIES TO PROMOTE CREATIVE DEVELOPMENT

Creativity involves new and original ways of seeing things and doing things. The Science Center is yet another classroom area where this sense of originality can bloom. Young children already bring with them the spirit of wonder and natural curiosity to explore, experiment, and find out. Those who do not can be encouraged by you as a behavior model to wonder about things and try to find out why: why leaves fall off the trees in the autumn; why the ocean is blue but sometimes gray; why it gets dark at night.

One teacher was so impressed with the insects, spiders, butterflies, dragonflies, and snails that her children were able to find on the grounds around the building, that she started a fascinating "what if …" activity with them. She knew that **making science as personal as possible would help make these creatures come alive** for the children. So, what if **each child pretended to be one of the creatures** he or she had collected? What would he look like? What would she eat? Where would they live? Children love to pretend, and pretending to be a certain living creature could be supported by every learning center in the classroom.

The children accepted this new challenge with gusto. They wanted the Art Center to help them make a costume for them to look like their creature; the Writing Center to help them write a story about it; the Music Center to help make up a song or rhyme about their creature; the Dramatic Play Center to help them act out a scenario about their creature; and the Book Center to find a good book about it. The teacher searched and found the perfect series of paperback books to respond to all their needs: the Backyard Books by Allen and Humphries that ask the readers if they are a … whatever. Following are the books this class used:

Are You a Butterfly? (2003)

Are You a Dragonfly? (2002)

Are You a Ladybug? (2000)

Are You a Snail? (2000)

Are You a Spider? (2000)

The very simple text is illustrated by bright pictures of each creature, its parents, how it grows and changes, what it eats, and other important facts. Once each child chose the creature he or she wanted to be, the teacher read them the story—more than once. From then on it was up to the children how they wanted to dramatize their creature. The children "dragonflies" made up a fingerplay that they chanted as they unfolded paper wings, put on antennas, and flew away.

Dragonfly, dragonfly,	*Dragonfly, dragonfly,*
Eat and grow,	*Whir and sway,*
Dragonfly, dragonfly,	*Dragonfly, dragonfly,*
Don't be slow.	*Fly away!*

The "spiders" made a web for themselves with a squeeze bottle of glue and silver glitter on black paper. Then they brought in a figure of Spiderman to climb on their web. The "ladybugs" hid ladybug magnets on metal objects around the room for other children to find. The "dragonflies" found them all! The "butterflies" made beautiful butterfly wings and danced around to music. The "snails" crawled around with a balloon on their backs for a shell, and pipe cleaner antennas on their heads. Everyone loved being the creatures and wanted the books read again each time they put on their creature costumes.

Being creative like this means exploring, experimenting, and manipulating in a playful and original manner. If you have no books, simply take a small group of children at a time outside and **let them lead the way**. What catches their attention? What makes them excited? What questions do they ask? It is the process of exploration itself that is important in the development of creativity. **Give children the freedom to explore and enough time to get deeply involved**. But most important of all: let the children lead the way.

THE TEACHER'S ROLE IN THE SCIENCE CENTER

Although it is true that young children learn science concepts through self-discovery, the teacher's role is nevertheless a crucial one. Self-discovery could hardly take place if the teacher was not deeply involved in:

1. setting up the Science Center so that children can use it easily in their investigations

2. listening carefully to children's comments and questions to help decide what direction the children's explorations might take

3. trying to arouse children's curiosity in the world around them by bringing into the Science Center intriguing objects—displays of natural beauty; appropriate books; guessing games about science objects; and animals, insects, birds, and fish

4. assisting children in exploring with all five senses

5. helping children use the scientific method

6. helping children record their results

7. extending science opportunities in new directions whenever appropriate

8. making science interesting to young children by making it personal

Because teachers understand that science is a process for finding out, they will involve the children in trying to find out all they can about themselves and the things in their environment. Yet when children bring in outside interests they have heard about, teachers also take note of these and try to integrate them into the Science Center or other activity centers. For example, children who are excited about the space shuttle may want to hear stories about it in the Book Center or make a clay space shuttle in the Art Center. Or they may want to pretend to be space explorers in the Dramatic Play Center.

However, not all of the children are ready to glean meaning from science projects like this; they may be at the manipulation or mastery levels of learning, rather than at the meaning level. It is important for teachers to observe children in the Science Center working with materials and to record their actions on the Child Interaction Form. Then teachers can interpret these data by indicating "Accomplishments," "Needs," and "Plans" for individuals and groups. Table 10.2 shows some possible interactions in the Science Center.

From these data, teachers can make plans for activities in the Science Center. For instance, if most of the children are playing around with the measuring implements, the teacher may want to postpone the actual measuring of the room until the children have taught themselves to use the implements. If children are just beginning to master their use of the balance, the teacher may want to provide them with other collections of items to balance: nails, nuts, buttons, counters, and stones.

When children begin to take the lead in science exploration by bringing in interesting items or suggesting places to go and things to see, teachers will realize that their science curriculum has really caught on. They then need to take the role of

Table 10-2 Science Center Activities: Levels of Interaction

Manipulation Level
Playing around with magnifying glasses, magnets, prisms, rulers, balances in inappropriate ways
Using a magnifying glass for an eyepiece
Using a magnet for a toy gun
Looking through the wrong end of binoculars
Pulling out wind-up ruler and snapping it back
Filling up collecting bottles, boxes, bags with items and dumping them out
Knocking on the side of an aquarium or terrarium to see what will happen
Collecting piles of leaves or seeds and throwing them
Shining a flashlight in other people's faces

Mastery Level
Using magnifying glasses, magnets, prisms, rulers, balances appropriately
Lining up stones, shells, and so on, and observing one at a time through magnifying glass.
Pulling out wind-up ruler, measuring something, and rewinding it, over and over
Piling up items on balance until they balance, dumping them off, and repeating action
Picking up nails with magnet, taking them off, and repeating action

Meaning Level
Looking at insect through magnifying glass and telling what it looks like or what kind it is
Displaying shells, stones, seeds in a collection and telling something about them
Looking through binoculars, focusing on something, and describing what is seen
Measuring something and describing results
Making up story or book about adopted tree
Identifying bird, fish, insect, or butterfly, and finding its picture in book

follower, listening carefully to the comments and questions of these energetic explorers and supporting their boundless curiosity with new paths of wonder that they all can follow.

IDEAS IN CHAPTER 10

1. *Using the sense of sight*

   a. Ask children what water they see in the room

   b. Have children view water through a magnifying glass

   c. Go on a water-viewing field trip

2. *Using the sense of sound*

   a. Have children listen to classroom water sounds

   b. Tape-record all of the different water sounds for later listening and sound-identification fun

   c. Blow bubbles through straws in the water table

3. *Using the sense of smell*

   a. Have children smell different kinds of water to see if there is a difference in the way they smell

   b. Go on a water-collecting field trip

4. *Using the sense of taste*

   a. Have a water-tasting session with bottled water and tap water

5. *Using the sense of touch*

   a. Pour warm water into a corner of the water table and have children find it through touch

   b. Put a spray on your faucet and have children feel it

   c. Have children use eggbeaters in the water table without soap

6. *Reawakening curiosity*

   a. Talk to parents about how young children learn by exploring their environment

   b. Be an exploring behavior model yourself for the children to see

   c. Make science personal for the children

7. *Setting up the Science Center*

   a. Stock the Science Center with tools for investigating things, measuring things, collecting things, and recording things

   b. Supply a collection of books on topics to be investigated

   c. Have space for an aquarium, terrarium, and animal homes

8. *Promoting the scientific method of investigation*

   a. Listen to what children have to say about snowflakes and jot down their ideas

   b. Catch snowflakes outside on a dark cloth and view them with magnifying glasses

   c. Talk about children's findings and conclusions and then tape-record them

9. *Promoting cognitive development*

   a. Concentrate with children this age on *how* things look and act rather than *why* they are the way they are

   b. Make a shadow of a child's hand on white paper on the wall

   c. Have children try to jump away from their shadows

   d. Write about children's science investigations in the parents' newsletter

   e. Invite a parent to demonstrate how to make animal shadow pictures with hands

   f. Listen to children's comments and questions about things and then follow their lead in setting up science activities

   g. Use the children's present interests as a lead-in to another topic with some connection to the first

10. *Promoting emotional development*

   a. Focus science activities on children personally to help improve their self-image

   b. Have each child adopt a tree for the year

   c. Follow children's interest in baby animals being separated from their mothers

   d. Make paper bat wings and masks

   e. Play game "Find the Baby Bat"

11. *Promoting social development*

   a. Involve small groups of children in a science activity that calls on their social skills

   b. Have a team of two children do a "pet-in-a-jar" project, each team with one jar and one net

   c. Lend a trowel and a magnifying glass to the children

   d. Talk about the size of insect pictures in books, in case they are "larger than life"

   e. Talk to children about teams, teamwork, and their tasks during the collecting field trip

    f. Talk to children ahead of time about letting their insects go after a few days

    g. Two groups "sign up" to make an ant farm

    h. Discuss what tasks are necessary to make an ant farm

    i. Take turns feeding ants and reporting on what is happening

12. *Promoting language development*

    a. Record results of science exploration by tape-recording and making charts, journals

    b. Keep a "tree diary"

    c. Keep a group journal for the ant farms, having the children take turns making entries

13. *Promoting creative development*

    a. Read books to stimulate curiosity

    b. Make science personal

    c. Have children be one of the creatures they collected

    d. Give children freedom and time to explore on their own

DISCUSSION QUESTIONS

1. Why does preschool science illustrate so vividly that young children acquire knowledge through self-discovery? Give examples.

2. How can children explore the world around them through each of their senses? Give examples.

3. In what ways can you help children who have been restricted at home to regain their sense of wonder and curiosity?

4. What is the scientific method and how can it be applied specifically to an object or an idea preschool children want to find out about?

5. What should you do if you don't know the answers to questions the children ask about science topics? Should you answer every question the children ask? Why or why not?

TRY IT YOURSELF

1. Set up the Science Center in your classroom with tools for investigating things, for measuring things, for containing things, for collecting things, and for recording things as discussed in this chapter. Or bring in all of the tools and demonstrate how they will be used.

2. Do an activity with a small group of children that encourages them to explore with one or more of the five senses. Be sure to include children who speak little English and children with special needs. Record the results.

3. Read a picture book to a small group of children to stimulate their interest in a personal science topic, and come prepared to follow up on this interest with materials or a project they can do. Record the results.

4. Write down the questions and comments you hear children making about the scientific investigating they are doing, and then make and write out plans to extend this activity based on the children's comments.

5. Invite parents to go along on a collecting trip and record the results in one of the ways mentioned in this chapter.

REFERENCES CITED

Conezio, K. & French, L. (2002). Science in the preschool classroom: Capitalizing on children's fascination with the everyday world to foster language and literacy development. *Young Children 57*(5), 12–18.

Epstein, A. S. (2007). *The intentional teacher: Choosing the best strategies for young children's learning.* Washington, DC: National Association for the Education of Young Children.

Galvin, E. S. (1994). The joy of the seasons: With the children, discover the joys of nature. *Young Children 49*(4), 4–9.

Holt, B. G. (1989). *Science with young children.* Washington, DC: National Association for the Education of Young Children.

Other Sources

Buchanan, B. L. & Rios, J. M. (2004). Teaching science to kindergartners: How can teachers implement science standards? *Young Children 59*(3), 82–87.

Charlesworth, R. & Lind, K. K. (2007). *Math & science for young children* (5th ed.). Clifton Park, NY: Cengage Learning.

Helm, J. H. & Katz, L. (2001). *Young investigators: The project approach in the early years.* New York: Teachers College Press.

Klein, A. (1991). All about ants: Discovery learning in the primary grades. *Young Children 46*(5), 23–27.

Lind, K. K. (2005). *Exploring science in early childhood: A developmental approach* (4th ed.). Clifton Park, NY: Cengage Learning.

Rockwell, R. E., Sherwood, E. A., & Williams, R. A. (1983). *Hug a tree, and other things to do outdoors with young children.* Mt. Rainier, MD: Gryphon House.

Seefeldt, C. & Galper, A. (2002). *Active experiences for active children: Science.* Upper Saddle River, NJ: Merrill/Prentice Hall.

Simon, S. (1975). *Pets in a jar: Collecting and caring for small wild animals*. New York: The Viking Press.

Warner, L. (2003). Planning effective classroom discovery centers. *Dimensions of Early Childhood 31*(1), 22–27.

Worth, K. & Grollman, S. (2003). *Worms, shadows, and whirlpools: Science in early childhood classrooms*. Portsmouth, NH: Heinemann.

Children's Books

Allen, J. & Humphries, T. (2000). *Are you a ladybug?* Boston: Kingfisher.

Allen, J. & Humphries, T. (2000). *Are you a snail?* Boston: Kingfisher.

Allen, J. & Humphries, T. (2000). *Are you a spider?* Boston: Kingfisher.

Allen, J. & Humphries, T. (2002). *Are you a dragonfly?* Boston: Kingfisher.

Allen, J. & Humphries, T. (2003). *Are you a butterfly?* Boston: Kingfisher.

Bauer, M. D. (2007). *A mama for Owen*. New York: Simon & Schuster.

Berenzy, A. (2005). *Sammy, the classroom guinea pig*. New York: Holt.

Cannon, J. (1993). *Stellaluna*. San Diego, CA: Harcourt.

Carle, E. (2000). *Does a kangaroo have a mother, too?* New York: HarperCollins.

Cronin, D. (2003). *Diary of a worm*. New York: Joanna Cotler Books.

Doolittle, B. (1998). *The forest has eyes*. Shelton, CT: The Greenwich Workshop.*

Frost, R. (1978). *Stopping by woods on a snowy evening*. New York: E. P. Dutton.

Gibbons, G. (1999). *Bats*. New York: Holiday House.

Guarino, D. (1989). *Is your mama a llama?* New York: Scholastic.

Hawcock, D. & Montgomery, L. (1994). *Ant*. New York: Random House.

Jeffers, S. (1991). *Brother eagle, sister sky*. New York: Dial.*

Keats, E. J. (1964). *Whistle for Willie*. New York: The Viking Press.*

Keats, E. J. (1974). *Dreams*. New York: Collier Books.*

Kroll, S. (2001). *Patches lost and found*. Delray Beach, FL: Winslow Press.

McBratney, S. (2005). *I love it when you smile*. New York: HarperCollins.

Milbourne, A. (2005). *The rainy day*. Tulsa, OK: EDC Publishing.

Munsch, R. (1997). *Alligator baby*. New York: Scholastic.

Owens, M. B. (2007). *Panda whispers*. New York: Dutton's Children's Books.

Pallotta, J. (1986). *The icky bug alphabet book*. Watertown, MA: Charlesbridge Publishing.

Philpot, L. & Philpot, G. (2006). *Find Anthony Ant*. New York: Random House.*

Raschka, C. (2006). *FIVE for a little one*. New York: A Richard Jackson Book.

Showers, P. (1991). *The listening walk*. New York: Harper/Collins.

Stevenson, R. L. (1957). *A child's garden of verses*. New York: Grosset & Dunlap.

Waddell, M. (1992). *Owl babies*. Cambridge, MA: Candlewick Press.

Note: Asterisk represents multicultural book.

WHO AM I?

ACTION CHANT

(Make own motions)
Let me see—
I am Wonder Woman on TV;

I am a dancer on the stage,
I am a rock star—all the rage.

Today I'm the mother who pours
the milk,
Yesterday, a princess dressed in silk;

Tomorrow I don't know what I'll do—
Do you?

DRAMATIC PLAY IN THE EARLY CHILDHOOD CLASSROOM

Dramatic play is one of the most complex kinds of play that young children engage in—and perhaps the most important. In dramatic play or socio-dramatic play, as it is sometimes called, young children use pretending to investigate their world. They engage in "make-believe," creating pretend roles for themselves, pretend places for their roles to be enacted, and pretend situations to respond to—all done spontaneously, without an adult's direction.

Edwards (2006) tells us: "sociodramatic play is also described as play that involves social role-playing with others and refers to children's pretend play when two or more children assume related roles and interact with each other" (p. 192).

It is difficult for many adults to understand the why's and wherefore's of dramatic play among young children because it is such a brief phenomenon—coming to a peak around ages 4, 5, and 6, and fading away after age 7. Most adults have long forgotten their own foray into the world of make-believe, and are a bit suspicious of anyone—even a young child—who engages in fantasizing. Isn't that some kind of escape from reality? Is it really healthy for young children to pretend to be someone other than themselves?

It is not an escape from reality for young children, and yes, it is healthy for young children to pretend to be someone else. Pretending for young children before the age of 7 is a necessary prelude to the life of reality that they will be leading. Imagining and pretending are creative tools all children are endowed with in order to investigate the world around them. Through pretending to be someone else, they find out what it is like to be themselves. Through pretending to be somewhere else, they find out what it is like to be where they are. A real paradox, but true.

Play researchers Dorothy and Jerome Singer report: "Over many years of observing children in free play, we have found that those who engage in make-believe, what Piaget calls symbolic play, are more joyful and smile and laugh more often than those who seem to be at odds with themselves" (Singer & Singer, 1990, p. 64). If they are girls, they often try on the roles of mother, baby, sister, aunt, grandma, nurse, doctor (sometimes), teacher, or female superheroes. If they are boys, they often try on the roles of father, brother, uncle, doctor, policeman, repairman, fireman, race car driver, or male superheroes such as Superman or Spiderman.

"Wait a minute," says the adult mind, "aren't those roles rather sexist?" They may indeed be sexist according to an adult frame of reference, but you must remember that young children are not operating in an adult frame of reference. These are the spontaneous roles young children may choose for themselves in order to investigate their world. The girls, after all, are exploring their perceived female roles to find out what it is like to be a girl or a woman. Yes, some girls do try out the perceived male roles of race car driver or Batman, just as some boys try out perceived female roles. Teachers of young children should accept any role that young children want to try so long as it is not one of violence or does not cause harm to anyone.

What can young children possibly learn by pretending, you still may wonder? The answer is that so much is gained through dramatic play in every aspect of child development that a listing of possibilities seems the only way to approach the question. From participating in dramatic play, young children can learn:

> ### In social development:
> *Cooperation*
>
> *Sharing*
>
> *Social roles*
>
> *Prosocial values such as honesty, service, loyalty, truthfulness*
>
> *How to gain entrance to a group*
>
> *How to wait your turn*
>
> *How to be a leader*
>
> *How to deal with a strong leader*
>
> *How to negotiate*
>
> *How to deal with people you disagree with*
>
> ### In cognitive development:
> *Concepts such as work, pay, order, time*
>
> *Concepts of travel, transportation, construction*
>
> *Concepts of illness, doctors, emergencies*
>
> *Roles of family members, workers*
>
> *Problem solving*

Abstract thinking

Planning

In language development:

How to carry on a conversation

How to speak as a different character

Meanings for and use of many new words

How to express feelings in words

Use of words as a substitute for actions

In emotional development:

Positive self-concept

How to express strong feelings in acceptable ways

How to control negative tendencies

How to deal with conflict

In physical development:

Mastering of certain motor skills (running, jumping, climbing, tricycle riding)

Pouring, mixing

Putting on and fastening garments, shoes

In creative development:

Divergent thinking

Novel solutions to problems

New ideas, plots, characters

Children who are able to engage in dramatic play with others learn to be co-operative and flexible. They soon realize that in order to keep the play flowing smoothly they may need to compromise, take an alternate approach, accept someone else's ideas, or accede to another child's wishes. For egocentric young children who are often used to having their own way, the joy of the play itself seems to make most sacrifices worthwhile.

Dramatic play allows children to be whomever they choose. Boys and girls can be boss, drive a car, soar through the air, come in late, eat what they want, and command other people—as long as they can negotiate these roles with the other players. Thus, for young children who are obviously controlled by adults in their real lives, dramatic play offers a powerful outlet for their feelings of helplessness in the adult world around them.

Because they "play around" with new ideas and novel solutions to problems, children who engage in such pretending are able to develop abstract thinking, creativity, flexibility, the ability to communicate, and the ability to get along better with their peers. Of course, not every child takes easily to dramatic play. But children who engage in highly elaborate kinds of imaginative play seem to reflect higher levels of development, and there is evidence that a high fantasy predis-position in children is linked to creativity (Garvey, 1977, p. 97).

SETTING UP THE DRAMATIC PLAY CENTER

This area of the classroom is somewhat different from the other activity areas. Rather than being an area of shelves full of materials and of tables for use in investigating the materials, the Dramatic Play Center is more like a stage setting for children's spontaneous pretending. Because many of their roles center around home and family, **there should be a family area available to stimulate such role-playing**.

The traditional kitchen area with child-sized stove, refrigerator, sink, table, and chairs is still considered one of the most appropriate settings for dramatic play. Other props in this area can include: a full-length mirror, a cradle or baby's bed, two telephones, an ironing board, a high chair, and a doll buggy. A corner storage area for child-sized broom, mop, dustpan, bucket, and vacuum cleaner add other possibilities to the roles. **Cups, pots and pans, and cooking utensils can be hung on a Peg-Board with an outline or cutout of each item** for matching and returning to its place by the children. A variety of cutlery can be stored in a plastic container or drawer with dividers to give children an additional opportunity for sorting and classifying. Plastic food—fruit, vegetables, and even pizza—is available if you choose to use commercial props. Be sure to include Mexican, Chinese, Japanese, and Italian plastic foods from educational supply companies; also include a diversity of baby dolls, boy and girl dolls, and adaptive equipment for dolls with disabilities.

Dress-up clothes can hang separately on hooks; hats can hang on Peg-Boards or a hat tree; purses, belts, wallets, shoes, jewelry, and other dress-up items can have shelf space with illustrated labels so that children can see what is available and return items easily when they are finished. The dress-up clothes themselves should include both men's and women's clothing: dresses, skirts, tops, slacks, shirts, jackets, and vests. (Teenage sizes are easier for young children to manage.) Also include multicultural dress-up clothing from companies like Lakeshore, which provides Mexican faida and blusa; Ghanian dashiki and kuku; Vietnamese ao dai; Japanese happi coat; Guatamalen toto and camisa; and Nigerian iro, buba, and gele.

Outfits and hats in children's sizes for construction workers, mail carriers, doctors, nurses, chefs, police officers, firefighters, astronauts, pilots, and veterinarians are also available. If you cannot afford all of these, at least purchase the hats. Other props include crutches, braces, eyeglasses, doctor's bag, and construction workers tools. **A second "room" in the Dramatic Play Center can be a sort of generic sitting room** with chairs and perhaps a child-sized couch or bench around the outside. A table with a lamp (no bulb or cord) and a telephone are useful. Some low shelves with various props may help to divide this area from the kitchen. A pull-out counter or a folding play screen with a counter is another valuable addition. This area can serve as the setting for an infinite number of play situations if it is flexible. For example, it can become a:

- Doctor's office
- Shoe store
- Bus or train (or terminal)
- Supermarket
- Repair shop
- Science museum
- Barber/beauty shop
- Post office
- Business office
- Ticket office

- Bank
- Gas station
- Restaurant
- Theater
- Laundromat
- Hospital
- Fire station
- Airport
- Zoo or pet store
- Check-out counter

Additional props in the area will vary with the kinds of pretending the children and you wish to pursue. Bring in (or **have parents contribute**) a number of **empty shoeboxes, bags, and old shoes when you set up a shoe store**. Be sure to have a

Having a loft in the room gives children room to expand their imaginations.

toy cash register for any store setup. Children can help collect empty food boxes, cans, and jars for a supermarket. The typewriter from the Writing Center can be used for an office setup.

If the size of the classroom does not allow for this second dramatic play space, consider having a loft. Children use both the loft and the area under the loft for pretending. Some classrooms build their own lofts with ladders, steps, or climbers for getting up and down. Greenman (2005) says: "And, of course, lofts or platforms are fun; children literally get high. They survey the world from a different vantage point, one that may allow them to look adults in the eye. Children have the opportunity to explore the world from a different angle" (p. 228). Having a loft in a classroom presents inventive children with a whole new perspective for their pretending. Can it be a fort? A castle? A pirate ship? A space ship? An observation tower? A clubhouse?

Pretending with miniature objects such as figures of people and animals, miniature dolls, dollhouse equipment, and cars, trucks, and trains may take place in other areas of the classroom. However, the Dramatic Play Center focuses on roles and plots the children choose to investigate spontaneously using full-scale materials.

DRAMATIC PLAY ACTIVITIES TO PROMOTE SOCIAL DEVELOPMENT

Before young children can participate in spontaneous dramatic play, they need to have reached a certain level of social development that will allow them to become involved in this cooperative play. Child development specialists have noted that young children seem to go through a sequence of social behavior categories based on their maturity and experience with other children. The sequence begins with unoccupied or onlooker behavior and progresses through solitary play, parallel play, and finally reaching cooperative play as described in chapter 2.

These social behaviors are observed when children engage in dramatic play as well as the other activities of the classroom. Sometimes children are onlookers or solitary players because they are ill at ease in the classroom setting. This is often the case with 3-year-olds who are more used to a home setting and adult association than they are to a classroom with a lively group of peers. Sometimes children are onlookers or solitary players because they are immature and have not yet developed the cognitive and language skills that allow them to pretend with a group. Other times children resist joining group dramatic play because they simply don't know how. They have not had the experience of taking on a role and pretending with other children. Or they don't seem to know how to gain access to a group of experienced players.

The activities you provide in your Dramatic Play Center can help such children become involved in pretending with others. In addition, children from culturally diverse groups can also become integrated into classroom activities. Although this will be spontaneous dramatic play on the part of the children, you can help set up the play through the props you supply and the initiating activities you provide. Isbell and Raines (2007) tell us:

> In drama, children interact and communicate to create a community of ideas, images, and actions. As they adjust their action in response to the group, children gain skills in negotiating and collaborating. Working in a group continually requires the child to participate in cognitive, social, and emotional exchanges. Drama facilitates social development because it requires interaction, negotiation, and cooperation. (p. 248)

Dramatic play based on a travel theme is something personal that appeals to most of the children because they have traveled in a car, a bus, or a train (or subway). It **is also an especially attractive activity for newcomers or non-English speakers because they can participate easily as passengers, undemanding and nonspeaking roles for beginners**.

To initiate such an activity, you can invite a group into the Dramatic Play Center and **read them a book about travel on a vehicle** such as a school bus. *Bus Stop, Bus Go* (Kirk, 2001) is a simple story with a bright yellow school bus stretched horizontally across every two pages as it stops to pick up its children passengers. They speak simple but exciting words in cartoon balloons. Listeners need to sit close to see the wild action down the aisle as toes get stepped on, Tommy's gerbil gets loose, and everyone tries to catch it with pieces of lunch food.

Or read *The Little School Bus* (Roth, 2002), another simple bus book in which a different animal dressed as a school child gets on the bus at every stop in rhyming cumulative lines (goat in a coat, pig in a wig, etc.). If the children would like to have their own school bus, ask them how they might set it up. **A driving bench** (stationary bench with a steering wheel at one end) **can put the driver up front with a row of chairs for passengers lined up one behind the other**. As the children take roles and set up the school bus activity, you can invite one or two onlookers to join the play as passengers with you. Shy children sometimes become involved in group play if the teacher joins too. "Come on, Marisa and Jose, let's get on the school bus before it leaves." **You can stay with the play until the players feel comfortable, and then extract yourself**. Although it may be tempting for you to stay longer because it is so enjoyable playing with the youngsters, remember that children gain most from dramatic play when they do it on their own.

If the children enjoyed the school bus activity, they may want to take their bus to the beach for a picnic on another day. Read *Me First* (Lester, 1992) to get them started. You will remember that this story is about Pinkerton, the pushy little pig who always has to be first, even when his Scout troop goes to the beach. Have picnic props ready for the children to take with them on their pretend bus: bags, towels, hats, sunglasses, and a picnic basket for the pretend food.

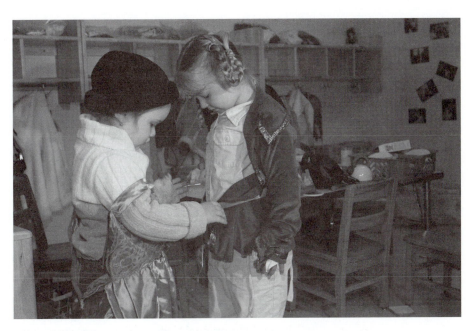

These children are getting ready for their imaginary trip on the bus.

Or you can suggest that **they pack a bag before they go on their trip**. Be ready by having bag props available for everyone: airline bags, book bags, athletic bags, or backpacks, and of course the clothes in the Dramatic Play Center. The non-English-speaking participants can now do something more than merely sit on one of the "bus" seats if they have to pack a bag. You may even hear English words from them before the play is finished—or words in their language from the other riders. Talk to the children afterwards about the story and what happens when someone always tries to be first.

LEADER AND FOLLOWER ROLES

Other social roles in dramatic play involve being a leader or following the lead of someone else. In order to begin dramatic play and keep it going, leadership is necessary. In dramatic play it is not up to you to appoint a leader. You will want one or more leaders to emerge spontaneously from the group, who will then set the stage for the play by suggesting the theme, determining the roles (sometimes assigning the roles), and filling in the details of the play as it progresses. A leader is usually accepted by the group and is generally retained by them as long as the play goes smoothly or the leader is not too demanding. A common sequence in preschool dramatic play might go as follows:

Emily: Let's play "school bus." I'll be the driver.

Rosa: No. You were the driver yesterday. It's my turn to be driver.

Emily: Okay. But I'm going to be the next driver. *Rosa sits down on driving bench and "starts bus" with a loud "Br-r-r-room-m-m."*

Rosa: We're ready to go. Get the children on the bus. Tell them to hurry.

Emily: I'm not the teacher. She sits down in a chair behind Rosa. Sarah, you be the teacher and get the children on the bus.

Sarah: I'm a passenger. *She sits in a chair behind Emily.* I'm going to the mall today to go shopping.

Rosa: You can't go to the mall. This is a school bus. You're going to school. *Makes motor noises.*

Sarah: You better hurry or we'll be late to school.

Emily: Sit down in your seat, little girl. You have to sit down when the bus is in motion. If you don't sit down, I'm going to report you. *Sarah, who has remained seated all the while, now giggles. Then she stands up, and then quickly sits down when Emily turns and gives her a scowl.*

Typical of leadership roles in dramatic play, in this scenario more than one leader has emerged, and negotiation has to take place in order to settle who will be "driver." The original leader, Emily, agrees to wait until her turn comes to be driver. But she will not agree to take an assigned role as "teacher" (so she says), although she quickly acts as a teacher once Sarah has joined the play. In this brief play segment Sarah has accepted a follower's role and agrees to most of the ground rules set by both Rosa and Emily.

It is obvious from this typical drama that leader and follower roles are not all that distinct among preschoolers. To be effective and to keep the play going, leaders must practice a give-and-take style of leadership in which they recognize the feelings of others in the group and compromise when necessary. The most successful leaders are those who can perform both leader and follower roles with ease, who can accept the ideas of others (yet have novel ideas of their own), and who are fun to play with. Some children seem perfectly happy being followers as long as they are not dominated too forcefully by the leaders (Trawick-Smith, 1988, pp. 53–54).

Through many experiences in playing together, children learn what works best in their particular group and how far they can go. When a leader becomes too demanding and uncompromising, the play simply disintegrates and the players leave. When you consider the practice for real life experienced by child players in these spontaneous dramas, it becomes obvious that dramatic play has a vitally important role in the lives of young children.

INTEGRATING DRAMATIC PLAY

Although it is not necessary to initiate dramatic play by reading a book, some teachers have found that it is a fine way to integrate dramatic play into other learning centers. The children who enjoyed the bus-driving scenario were attracted

Children lined up animal figures in the Block Center to drive block vehicles.

to the sounds the "drivers" like Emily made. The teacher, who had been collecting driving books, found the perfect book to support this interest. *Who Is Driving?* (Timmers, 2007) showed a row of four different dressed-up animals lined across the left page and a driverless vehicle on the opposite page, with the words "who is driving …" the fire engine, the fancy car, the race car, the tractor, the convertible, the jeep, and the airplane on the following pages. The children had to guess which of the four animals would be the driver when they turned the page.

This was a cognitive game in which the main clue was how the driver-to-be was dressed. Some children caught on immediately, but others guessed blindly, and then in subsequent readings guessed from memory. But the children really loved the sounds each of the drivers made and were soon copying them in their dramatic play driving scenario: vroooom; putt-putt-putt; takke-takke-tak. They kept the line of chairs and driving bench set up for many days and played their own game with the driver making one of the vehicle noises from the book and the riders guessing what kind of vehicle they were riding in. This game then spilled over into the Block Center with block vehicles and animal figure drivers, into the Music Center where children's vehicle noises were tape-recorded and listened to, and into the Manipulative/Math Center where the teacher and children made lotto cards cut out of car dealer's catalogs.

SUPERHERO PLAY

Many children enjoy taking on the roles they see performed in television cartoons, espcially those of the so-called superheroes such as Batman, Superman, Wonder

Woman, Spiderman, or whoever happens to be the featured star of the moment. Many preschool teachers are not especially happy with the prospect. They feel that too often superhero play disintegrates into rowdy rough-and-tumble play that is not appropriate indoors in the preschool classroom. The question is twofold: Should superhero dramatic play be allowed in the preschool classroom? If so, what can young children gain from it?

The gains should be considered first. Cartoons teach children some very basic values that our society espouses: who is good and who is bad; what do good people and bad people do that makes them good or bad; and what happens to you if you are good or bad. Cartoons deal in stereotypes. The characters are simple one-dimensional figures who are either all good or all bad. The superhero is a good character who is usually good-looking, strong, loyal, helpful, unselfish, ready to fight against evil, and always the winner. The bad character is generally evil-looking, strong, selfish, disloyal, underhanded, sneaky, always challenging the good character, and eventually the loser.

Cartoons like this play the same role fairy tales did in an earlier time; they are not supposed to be true-to-life. Instead, they teach values in a very exaggerated and forceful manner. Hoffman (2004) tells us: "In superhero play, children don't just mimic adult activities, they become larger-than-life characters that help them explore their fears, hopes, and passions" (p. 5). If children can learn such prosocial values from superhero play in the Dramatic Play Center, then perhaps you should consider it.

Does such play really have a place in the preschool classroom? If it can be kept from getting out of hand, if its inherent violence can be downplayed and controlled, the answer may be "yes," or at least "perhaps." Of course, children are going to attempt superhero play whether or not it is allowed, because it speaks to something deep within them. Think of yourself as a young child. Were you attracted to such cartoons? Are your own children attracted to them? Then you realize that superheroes are powerful symbols, indeed, to young children. When you understand that such symbols can represent positive values in our society, you may want to consider allowing superhero dramatic play in the classroom if it can be controlled and directed into prosocial channels.

Children's play researchers have noted that dominant themes in pretend play often include: capture and rescue, submit or vanquish, and attack or flee (Kostelnik, Whiren, & Stein, 1986, p. 5). With this being the case, the superhero play is not so far off base. But why do some of your children want to play the role of the bad guy? What can they learn from being Dracula, Darth Vader, or the Joker? They know already that these evil characters are going to be defeated by the superheroes. However, think about being little, helpless human beings controlled by big powerful adults and you may have the answer. Yes, young children want to try the negative roles, too—the ones that challenge the good guys, because they, too, want to challenge their adult "keepers." They realize that these "bad guys" are not going to win; they do not want them to win. Children want us, the teachers and adults in their world, to put limits on negative behavior—their own and the bad superheroes.

If you decide to admit superhero play to your classroom, you need to **channel it in the direction of prosocial learning with restrictions and limits**. When it occurs, you can sit down with the children and talk with them about their superheroes. What are some of their humane, prosocial traits that can be admired? They are loyal to their friends, they are unselfish, they help the underdog, and they stand up against evil. Can children be like that? How?

Do people have to use violence and fighting to bring about good things? How else can a person who wants to be a superhero behave? How should pretend superheroes behave in the classroom? What should they avoid doing? What should happen when things get out of hand? If you can talk with your children about values and behavior, and if you can establish limits ahead of time about what is allowed and what is not allowed, then it is possible that superhero play can help your children learn to practice prosocial helping behavior.

Reading a book such as *Kapow!* (O'Connor, 2004) in the Book Center can stimulate such a discussion. Illustrated with comic-book-like child characters who talk in comic-book balloons, it takes place in the home of the little boy "American Eagle," dressed in cape, cap, boots, and gloves, and his bad-guy brother the "Rubber Bandit." While helping his friend "Bug Lady" stop the Rubber Bandit from robbing the "First National Bank" their play gets out of control and they knock over a bookcase. Their mom is just happy no one is hurt and it ends with the children volunteering to clean up the mess. This book, too, calls for a discussion of how these characters behaved and what your children would do in this case.

Can children with disabilities be superheroes? Of course. Just as with all of the activities you set up, a child in a wheelchair, for instance, can choose to be Dragonboy and swoop up and over everything using the pair of paper dragon wings you have made. Read him and anyone else interested *If I Had a Dragon* (Ellery & Ellery, 2006) about Morton who decides to get a dragon for a pet.

All of the children should have the opportunity (but not be forced) to be superheroes. Think of capes or easy-to-make headbands with horns or halos or giant feathers or huge ears they can wear to create characters with magic powers. Provide a basket full of superpower articles such as power bracelets (from thrift stores), magic buttons, badges, medals, old watches, or an old cell phone spray-painted gold (Hoffman, 2004, p. 103). But Edwards (2006) reminds us: "Help children with visual impairments know when, where, and how to participate by giving hands-on narrated tours of objects in the environment beforehand" (p. 210).

DRAMATIC PLAY ACTIVITIES TO PROMOTE EMOTIONAL DEVELOPMENT

As with other activities in the self-directed learning environment, children learn social roles more effectively when they do them on their own. Dramatic play is not always smooth and happy. Often there is haggling and disagreement. Teacher intervention may solve problems temporarily, but children learn best how to control emotional outbursts and to interact with peers on their own, rather than having an adult solution imposed.

One of the most common types of conflict in dramatic play at this age involves children trying to get their own way. Young children are at an egocentric level of their cognitive development, in which each one of them acts as if he or she is the center around which everything revolves. Because not everyone in a group situation can have his or her own way, there is great potential for disagreement and conflict during dramatic play. This also means that there is a great potential for children learn to resolve emotional upsets as well.

We have already noted that the most effective leaders find ways around this conflict in order to keep the players appeased and the play going. Some children are unable at first to allow another person's desires to take precedence over their own. Why should they? After all, their feelings are the ones that count, they may believe. They seem unable to see things from another child's point of view. Isenberg and Jalongo (1993) tell us:

> When children become someone else, they learn the behaviors and feelings of that character or role, as well as how people affect other people. Role enactment enables children to develop their *perspective-taking ability*. Even very young children may glimpse insights that help in understanding people, and therefore, in living. (p. 142)

That is the point of dramatic play: to see things from another character's point of view. Children who insist on having their own way and who are unable to accept another child's position soon find themselves on the outside of the play. A noisy conflict does not seem to resolve anything, they find. It may bring the teacher down on the group, with her own solution. But when the teacher leaves, the children are on their own again, and they may refuse to play with the children who get their own way through argument or bullying.

On the other hand, **children** left to themselves **are often able to work out very creative solutions to conflict**. When the disagreement centers around a desirable role and who will play it, negotiation and give-and-take enter the picture on the part of experienced players. As with Emily and Rosa, they work out the problem of who will be the driver without resorting to arguing or refusal to play. Other children learn how to negotiate and compromise by watching how experienced players handle problems. Then they find out what works and what does not work by trying out negotiations themselves.

Teachers can best **help children to consider various solutions to dramatic play conflicts with activities conducted outside the Dramatic Play Center**. For instance, they can **read stories centered around play confict, and talk with the children** afterward about **how the conflicts were resolved**. For instance, every time Bootsie comes to visit and play with the narrator of *Bootsie Barker Bites* (Bottner, 1992), she manhandles the poor narrator and scares her to death pretending to be an angry dinosaur ready to eat her alive. Finally the little girl learns to stand up for herself, and when Bootsie next walks into her room the girl is dressed as a paleontologist with trowel and bones ready to hunt for dinosaurs and dig up their bones. Talk with your small group of listeners about how they would resolve such a play conflict. Do any of them notice how grotesque shadows are used to scare the girls?

Some youngsters, strange as it seems, want to be babies in their role play. They may be children who are having inner emotional conflicts over leaving home and coming to preschool. Ramsey (1991) has this to say: "Children's play provides an outlet for emotional tension and an opportunity to resolve emotional conflicts. For example, a child who is torn between being independent and dependent may enact the role of the bad baby. At the same time, common emotional concerns facilitate peer interactions. As one child begins to enact the misbehaving baby, the other child seems to know instinctively how to play the irate mother (p. 25).

In the book *What Shall We Play?* (Heap, 2002), the conflict among Martha, Matt, and Lily Mae involves what they are going to play. Right away Lily Mae wants to play fairies; but Matt wants to play trees and then wibbly-wobbly Jell-O; and Martha wants cars and then cats. Matt's ideas are accepted by all three. Martha's ideas are also accepted. But Lily Mae's idea is totally ignored until the end when they all finally play fairies and fly. Ask your child listeners why they thought this happened, and why the children did not seem to argue or fight over the solution. What would they have done if they had been Lily Mae?

Dramatic play thus offers children many opportunities to resolve emotional problems, both with their peers and within themselves. As they take on some of the roles discussed here, children learn not only how to control behavior unacceptable to others, but also to accept themselves.

DRAMATIC PLAY ACTIVITIES TO PROMOTE COGNITIVE DEVELOPMENT

Some of the problem-solving methods mentioned previously could just as well come under this heading of cognitive development. Children need to be cognitively mature in order to see things from another person's point of view or to problem solve in the manner suggested under section Emotional Development. They also need **practice in problem solving in real situations in order to discover what works and does not work**, as just suggested. Obviously, child development occurs in a holistic manner, with a particular curriculum activity contributing to many aspects of development.

Isbell and Raines (2007) point out that: "In drama, children interact and communicate to create a community of ideas, images, and actions. Through improvisational activities, young children begin to adjust to the responses of the group. They develop the ability to think on their feet" (p. 248).

Another important contribution that dramatic play can offer in promoting children's cognitive development is in helping them understand concepts or general ideas about their world and how it works. **Dramatic play can serve as a follow-up to field trips** the children take, helping them to conceptualize and understand new things they experienced on the trip.

After a field trip to a fire station, children can dress up as firefighters in a dramatic play scenario.

A field trip to the fire station is one that many preshool programs take. Children see the trucks, the ladders, the hoses, the cherry-picker crane for tall buildings, the alarm bells and sirens, the firefighter's boots, coats, and hats, and sometimes a Dalmatian dog mascot. When they return to the classroom they need to talk about the things they have seen. Perhaps **photos of children on the fire trucks have been taken** that can be placed in the Dramatic Play Center. **The teacher can read a fire station book to stimulate more discussion and thinking about the field trip.** Finally, fire station **props can be placed in the Dramatic Play Center for the children to use** in taking roles and pretending about their experience.

There are several books that help children understand the roles of the firefighters they met. *Firefighter Frank* (Wellington, 2002) is a simple story with cartoon-type characters showing a day in the life of a firefighter. *Firefighters A to Z* (Demarest, 2003) is an alphabet storybook with a large, realistic picture on each page illustrating an alphabet letter in firefighting terms. Children like this book for the realism it shows. On the other hand, *Even Firefighters Hug their Moms* (MacLean, 2002) shows a little boy at home playing the roles of firefighter, police officer, emergency medical technician, construction worker, helicopter pilot, train conductor, astronaut, and garbage-truck driver. Children love this book because of the creative ideas it illustrates for converting common household items into wonderful play props.

After reading these stories, you can put out fire station props such as several fire hats from educational-supply houses or paper fire hats from party-supply stores, a fire chief's cap, a bell, some boots, raincoats, and a short piece of hose. If the children have seen a Dalmatian at the fire station, you may want a stuffed Dalmatian prop as well. **Children can use the driving bench and chairs for their fire truck** if they want, or they can make up their own plot.

DRAMATIC PLAY ACTIVITIES TO PROMOTE LANGUAGE DEVELOPMENT

Every role-playing situation the children are involved with provides them with opportunities for language development, as they listen to the conversation around them, participate in the give-and-take of negotiations, and speak for the character they are portraying. As Garvey (1977) has noted: "Carrying out the make-believe is largely a matter of communication" (p. 86). Children involved in dramatic play often have to speak not only for their own character but also for other pretend characters. If they are leaders they have to give directions, plan for action, add new details, and explain the plot line or its changes to other players as they go along. As the Singers (1990) note: "One of the characteristics of this talking out loud is that children, to some extent, hear their own vocalization. In other words, in the absence of adults who talk directly to the child, the child's own words during make-believe play provide an ongoing source of verbal stimulation" (p. 141).

Because almost every kind of pretending affords children opportunities for speaking and listening, it is important that preschool programs **allow enough time** for **children to become deeply involved in dramatic play**. Garvey's research reveals the following types of pretend action to be most popular:

- treating/healing
- averting a threat
- packing
- taking a trip
- shopping

- cooking
- dining
- repairing (of car)
- telephoning (pp. 92–94)

Props make a difference in dramatic play. For example, if there are no telephones in the center, there will be little telephoning. To promote this type of conversational language production, **you need two telephones or cell phones** for children to call and answer with. Some programs have pretend telephone booths as well. However, children derive as much or more pleasure from **making their own classroom phone booth from a large cardboard carton**. They may want to visit a real phone booth to try it out before making their own.

Written language should also be visible in the Dramatic Play Center. The print-rich environment discussed earlier needs to occur here, too. **Have real calendars on the walls**. Have real **phone books and a notepad near the toy telephones**.

It is important to have phones in the Dramatic Play Center.

Have a magazine rack for **magazines and newspapers** (back issues are fine for this make-believe setting). Children can pretend to read and write. Someone can pretend to be the newspaper deliverer and bring the daily paper to the housekeeping area. Look around your own home. What other written language is visible that children could use in their pretend play?

Can **children make up stories about their dramatic play episodes**? To motivate this sort of storytelling, read to a small group of children a book such as *Just Another Morning* (Ashman, 2004), in which a little boy narrates his typical day—all imaginary—from the moment he wakes up "in a zoo" (a bed full of stuffed animals) to his travels through a "desert" (sandbox) and wrestling with a "spitting snake" (water hose).

Don't forget to include picture books with multiethnic characters such as those in *Amazing Grace* (Hoffman, 1991) about the African American girl Grace who loves to hear stories and act out every story she hears, sometimes when they are still going on. She gives herself the most exciting parts such as Joan of Arc, Anansi the Spider, Peg Leg Pete the pirate, and Aladdin. If there is no one around, she plays all the parts herself. What imaginative worlds can your children see in the book illustrations? What other worlds can they invent? They can tell stories to the tape recorder about their own dramatic play adventures.

DRAMATIC PLAY ACTIVITIES TO PROMOTE CREATIVITY

Most dramatic play episodes call on children's creativity to get them started and keep them going. If you want to stretch their imaginations even further, take the children on a wild and wonderful safari around the classroom. What wild animals can they see? None? You may need to read them a book about a real safari. One that many children enjoy is *We All Went on Safari: A Counting Journey through Tanzania* (Krebs, 2003). Ten Massai children, accompanied by an adult, walk in a straight line across every two scenic pages of this wonderful African story, noticing and counting different animals in their habitats. Arusha counts one leopard; Mosi counts two ostriches, and so on, all in rhyming lines. Your children will want to get out the African animal block figures and match them with the pictures.

Take this same group of children on a similar trek outside the building another day. Have them pack a bag or backpack to take along. Then proceed slowly and cautiously with yourself as the leader. Now what kinds of animals or other imaginative creatures can you see in the shapes of the bushes and trees? **Pretend to see elephants in the school yard, tigers in the bushes, and parrots in the trees**. What exciting incidents can occur? You might have to hide behind a tree if a rhino charges! Phew, a narrow escape! Watch out for the monkeys in the trees! They are throwing fruit!

If your safari is a success, you will want to invite other small groups on other days until everyone has had a chance. Then on the next repeat trip, encourage the children to join the pretending. What fabulous creatures do they see? To motivate the children to make up more of their own creative adventures, read similar stories based on imaginative plots.

Can your children make up wild stories of their own about the giant guinea pig that bursts its cage or the block tower that grows by itself right up through the ceiling? **Creative pretending helps children develop their imaginative powers**, which in turn strengthens their ability to play pretend roles with others in the Dramatic Play Center.

THE TEACHER'S ROLE IN THE DRAMATIC PLAY CENTER

Just as the Dramatic Play Center itself consists of two separate parts—a housekeeping/family area and a generic sitting room area—so the teacher's role in the center is twofold. The teacher must set up the family area in a permanent way to entice children to enact the roles they are most familiar with: that of mother, father, brother, sister, baby, and grandparent. Thereafter, he will be observing children to see which ones participate in cooperative group play, which ones play parallel to a play group (perhaps waiting for an opportunity to join it), and which ones are solitary players, doing their pretending apart from the group. In addition, the teacher will be observing the levels of interaction the children demonstrate.

Observing Interaction Levels

Do young children "manipulate the medium" in dramatic play as they do in art, in music, in writing, with blocks, and with other new materials? In other words,

Here is a solitary player in the housekeeping area.

do they go through the stages of manipulation, mastery, and meaning? The answer seems to be a guarded "yes," although dramatic play is such an all-encompassing and complex endeavor that we realize many factors are at work in children's pretending. If children's pretending involves physical objects, then we can apply the "3-M formula."

When young children first begin to pretend and play roles at around the age of 2 or 2½, they play bits and pieces of roles such as putting the baby doll in bed and putting a blanket over it; then taking the doll out of the bed and repeating the action. Other play bits may include picking up a broom, sweeping the floor, and putting the broom back; then repeating this action. Or getting out the dishes and setting the table, then putting the dishes back, over and over. Where do their actions originate? They often observe what is going on around them and repeat bits of it. They are highly influenced by props. Props dictate their play (Wellhousen & Crowther, 2004). If they see a broom, they will sweep the floor. If they see a baby doll, they will put it to bed.

They don't seem to be able to get beyond these limited actions, perhaps because they are as yet developmentally unable to conceptualize the roles more fully. Even coaching on the part of other more mature children has little effect. Instead, the younger children play the same "bits" over and over again in the same way, as if they were practicing them—just like children at the mastery level of interaction.

On the other hand, children ages 3 and 4—who are developmentally more mature than 2-year-olds but who have not done such pretending before—show definite tendencies, first to manipulate the materials by playing around with them, and later to use the materials in a more mature fashion. They may first use an object like a stethoscope, for instance, to blow into or shout into as if it were a microphone rather than a doctor's examining instrument. Their involvement with children who are more experienced with dramatic play eventually helps them "correct" such inappropriate actions, and they are finally able to master their roles with props.

Eventually, they may use props not only as they were meant to be used, but also by applying their own meaning in purely original ways. For example, this may mean pretending that a flashlight is an implement for sending out a magic laser beam. Children at the highest level of fantasy do not need real objects at all for their dramatic play, but can create imaginary objects out of thin air. As play researcher Garvey (1977) has noted:

> We have seen that, in the early stages of play with objects, pretending is tied to the perceptual or physical properties of objects. It seems to be the case, however, that once a child reaches a level of cognitive maturity that permits him to operate with roles and plans, he becomes less dependent in his pretending on the real properties of objects. (p. 96)

Teachers can record such observational data on the Child Interaction Form. If a group of children together are engaged in a dramatic play episode, then all of their actions and dialog can be recorded on the same form. Plans for individuals can then be formed based on interpretation of the data as recorded under "Accomplishments," "Needs," and "Plans" for the various children. Table 11-1 shows some possible interactions in the Dramatic Play Center.

Facilitating Dramatic Play

Sometimes dramatic play disintegrates or gets out of hand. If children seem unable to solve a problem themselves (but have been given enough time to try), teachers then have a third role to play: that of facilitator. As such, they have several options. They can:

1. redirect the play

2. extend the play

3. take roles in the play themselves

4. stop the play and talk to the children in terms of the class's "caring theme"

If they choose to *redirect* the play, teachers can suggest to the players another direction to take with their pretend situation. For example, if the doctor play has gotten out of hand with children fighting over the stethoscope or who is going to give shots, teachers can say something like, "It is time for the doctor's office to close for the day. He needs to pack up his bag and go home. He'll have to call a taxi because his car is broken. Is there anyone here who drives a taxi or can fix a car?"

Table 11-1 Dramatic Play Activities: Levels of Interaction

Manipulation Level
Gets out many props but does not use them Plays around with props in inappropriate ways Picks up props and carries them around Does not usually dress up

Mastery Level
Pretends by playing familiar routines Plays same role or plot over and over Uses same prop or dress-up clothes realistically Uses same dialog again and again

Meaning Level
Plays different roles in new ways Includes many details and much dialog to sustain plot Pretends with props in creative ways Can pretend without props

On the other hand, teachers may choose to *extend* the play by inserting an exciting new idea that bypasses the trouble with the stethoscope but keeps the play going. For example, they might say: "Here are the four new laser scopes you ordered, doctor [gives "doctor" four cylinder blocks]. The hospital would like you and your assistants to try them out on your patients, and see if you can look right into their bodies with them to find out what their sickness is. These laser scopes are a new invention, and you are the first medical people to use them. Be careful with them, as they are very fragile."

You need to know your children and how they respond to suggestions in order to decide how to salvage dramatic play that has gotten out of hand. If you *take a role* in the play yourself, children will generally either calm down or leave the play. If the play resumes in a peaceful manner, you can excuse yourself the same way you inserted yourself.

Sometimes it is necessary to stop the play: if children are so out of control that they cannot take suggestions for redirecting or extending the play, then teachers may need to step in. This is the time to *talk calmly but firmly* about the three-part "caring" theme emphasized by the program: that in this classroom we care for ourselves, we care for one another, and we care for our surroundings and materials. "Luke, I can't let you hit Andy. In this classroom we care for one another. We do not hit others. If you feel angry, you need to tell Andy how you feel. If you are too angry to talk, then you need to leave the Dramatic Play Center until you feel better."

If everyone is involved in the turmoil, you may need to stop the play and calm them down right then and there by reading an appropriate book. "This sounds like a squabble over getting a shot. Lots of patients have problems with getting a shot. Maybe you do, too. Listen to this story about Filbert MacFee and the magic animal crackers he uses to avoid getting a shot."

This Is a Hospital, Not a Zoo! (Karim, 1998) tells the hilarious tale of how Filbert avoids everything the nurses and doctors have in store for him by turning into an animal—or two, or many. Or read *Froggy Goes to the Doctor* (London, 2002), which tells the tale of the little boy frog who goes for a check-up and turns the tables on the doctor. You need books like these available for such disruptive situations, because you are aware of the kinds of conflicts that commonly occur among preschool children.

Children who lose control should not be punished or talked to harshly. Instead, they need to learn from the situation in a calm, nonjudgmental manner. If you demonstrate to children that you care for them and will help them to stay in control, they will be better able to resolve their own dramatic play conflicts when the time comes.

Dramatic play can indeed be an exciting experience for the children and for you, too. As they try on various roles and begin to learn what real life is about, you can watch their progress from the sidelines. You will be able to observe which children can conceptualize complex ideas, which ones know how to resolve conflicts peaceably, and which ones are the creative youngsters who propose original solutions to the problems of life in the Dramatic Play Center.

IDEAS IN CHAPTER 11

1. *Setting up the Dramatic Play Center*
   a. Have a family area available to stimulate family role-playing
   b. Cups, pots and pans, and cooking utensils can be hung on a Peg-Board with an outline or cutout of each item for matching and classifying by the children
   c. Hang dress-up clothes separately on hooks; hang hats on Peg-Boards or a hat tree; store purses, belts, wallets, shoes, and jewelry on shelves with illustrated labels
   d. Have a second "room" in the Dramatic Play Center as a generic "sitting room" for use in different play themes
   e. Have parents contribute empty shoeboxes, bags, and old shoes for a shoe store setup
   f. Use a toy cash register for any store setup
   g. Consider having a loft for two extra rooms

2. *Promoting social development*
   a. Dramatic play on a travel theme can include shy children in the undemanding role of passengers
   b. Initiate school bus play by reading a theme book and setting up a school bus with a driving bench and chairs
   c. Invite onlookers to join the travel play with you as passengers
   d. Extract yourself from the play when the players feel comfortable
   e. Have the children pack a bag before they take their pretend trip
   f. Have the driver make vehicle noise and children guess the vehicle
   g. Channel superhero play in a prosocial direction with limits

3. *Promoting emotional development*
   a. Help children deal with dramatic play conflicts with activities conducted outside the Dramatic Play Center
   b. Read stories centered around play conflicts and discuss with the children how the conflicts were resolved
   c. Give children real practice with their ideas of resolving conflict in dramatic play

4. *Promoting cognitive development*

    a. Give children practice in real play situations to discover what works and what does not work for them

    b. Have dramatic play serve as a follow-up to field trips

    c. Stimulate field trip follow-up play with photographs in the Dramatic Play Center and theme stories

    d. Read books related to a field trip

    e. Put out field trip props for use by the children

    f. Use the driving bench and chairs as a fire truck

5. *Promoting language development*

    a. Allow time enough for children to become deeply involved in dramatic play

    b. Have two telephones in the Dramatic Play Center

    c. Make a phone booth from a cardboard carton

    d. Have calendars on the wall, phone books and notepads near the phones, and magazines and newspapers in the family area

    e. Have children make up stories about their dramatic play episodes

6. *Promoting creative development*

    a. Take children on an imaginative safari around the building

    b. Pretend to see elephants in the yard, tigers in the bushes, and parrots in the trees

    c. Motivate creative play themes by making up stories featuring imagination

DISCUSSION QUESTIONS

1. Why is dramatic play in the early childhood classroom considered by many to be one of the most important kinds of play young children can engage in?

2. Girls and boys often take on pretend roles that seem sexist to adults, but this is not really the case. Why?

3. How do children learn cooperation and being flexible through dramatic play? Be specific.

4. The spontaneous leader and follower roles that emerge in dramatic play sometimes lead to an important kind of conflict. Why is this conflict important and what can children learn from it?

5. How should teachers deal with superhero play that gets out of control?

TRY IT YOURSELF

1. Set up the Dramatic Play Center to include a family/housekeeping area with appropriate props as described in this chapter and a second "sitting room" area for other play themes.

2. Observe and record the levels of social play that your children demonstrate, according to Parten's levels (see chapter 2).

3. Help onlookers or solitary players become involved in dramatic play by inviting them to share an undemanding role with you. Be sure to include children with special needs.

4. Record several episodes of dramatic play that give evidence of leader and follower roles.

5. Take children on a field trip and follow it up with dramatic play activities using appropriate props and a story. Record the results.

REFERENCES CITED

Edwards, L. C. (2006). *The creative arts: A process approach for teachers and children.* Upper Saddle River, NJ: Merrill/Prentice Hall.

Garvey, C. (1977). *Play.* Cambridge, MA: Harvard University Press.

Greenman, J. (2005). *Caring spaces, learning places.* Redman, WA: Exchange Press.

Hoffman, E. (2004). *Magic capes, amazing powers.* St. Paul, MN: Redleaf Press.

Isbell, R. R. & Raines, S. C. (2007). *Creativity and the arts with young children.* Clifton Park, NY: Cengage Learning.

Isenberg, J. P. & Jalongo, M. R. (1993). *Creative expression and play in the early childhood curriculum.* New York: Merrill/Macmillan.

Kostelnik, M. J., Whiren, A. P., & Stein, L. C. (1986). Living with He-Man: Superhero fantasy play. *Young Children 41*(4), 3–9.

Ramsey, P. G. (1991). *Making friends in school: Promoting peer relationships in early childhood.* New York: Teachers College Press.

Singer, D. G. & Singer, J. L. (1990). *The house of make-believe.* Cambridge, MA: Harvard University Press.

Trawick-Smith, J. (1988). "Let's Say You're the Baby, OK?" Play leadership and following behavior of young children. *Young Children 43*(5), 51–59.

Wellhousen, K. & Crowther, I. (2004). *Creating effective learning environments.* Clifton Park, NY: Cengage Learning.

Other Sources

Bodrova, E., Leong, D., Hensen, R., & Henninger, M. (2000). Imaginative, child-directed play: Leading the way in development and learning. *Dimensions of Early Childhood 28*(4), 25–30.

Brokering, L. (1989). *Resources for dramatic play*. Carthage, IL: Fearon.

Hatcher, B. & Perry, K. (2004). Seeing is believing: Visible thought in dramatic play. *Young Children 59*(6), 79–82.

Jones, E. & Reynolds, G. (1992). *The play's the thing: Teacher's roles in children's play*. New York: Teachers College Press.

Children's Books

Ashman, L. (2004). *Just another morning*. New York: HarperCollins.

Bottner, B. (1992). *Bootsie Barker bites*. New York: G. P. Putnam's Sons.

Demarest, C. L. (2003). *Firefighters A to Z*. New York: Aladdin Paperbacks.*

Ellery, T. & Ellery, A. (2006). *If I had a dragon*. New York: Simon & Schuster.

Heap, S. (2002). *What shall we play?* Cambridge, MA: Candlewick Press.*

Hoffman, M. (1991). *Amazing grace*. New York: Dial Books for Young Readers.*

Karim, R. (1998). *This is a hospital, not a zoo!* New York: Clarion Books.*

Kirk, D. (2001). *Bus stop, bus go*. New York: G. P. Putnam's Sons.*

Krebs, L. (2003). *We all went on safari: A counting journey through Tanzania*. Cambridge, MA: Barefoot Books.*

Lester, J. (1992). *Me first*. Boston: Houghton Mifflin.

London, J. (2002). *Froggy goes to the doctor*. New York: Viking.*

MacLean, C. K. (2002). *Even firefighters hug their moms*. New York: Dutton Children's Books.

O'Connor, G. (2004). *Kapow!* New York: Simon & Schuster.

Roth, C. (2002). *The little school bus*. New York: North-South Books.

Timmers, L. (2007). *Who is driving?* New York: Bloomsbury Publishing.

Wellington, M. (2002). *Firefighter Frank*. New York: Dutton Children's Books.*

Note: Asterisk represents multicultural book.

JOHNNY IS A JUMPER

ACTION CHANT

Johnny is a jumper,
See him hop-hop-hop;
(jump in place three
times)

Bonnie is a bumper,
See her bop-bop-bop;
(jump forward three
times)

Phillip is a flier,
See him loop-the-loop;
(turn in place, arms
outstretched)

I can go still higher,
Watch me fly the coop!
(run away, flapping
arms like wings)

LARGE-MOTOR ACTIVITIES IN THE EARLY CHILDHOOD CLASSROOM

Running, jumping, and climbing are large-motor skills closely associated with young children—the very essence of early childhood, most people readily agree. Striding, gliding, and galloping are locomotor skills that young children seem to accomplish almost without effort. Whirling, twirling, and bending are whole-body movements that preschool youngsters perform with verve and vigor.

Is it true that all young children are so skilled and so energetic about body movements? Do all preschoolers participate in large-motor activities with such ease and excitement? Poest, Williams, Witt, and Atwood (1990) tell us: "Many educators believe that children will automatically develop fundamental movement skills when they are ready. This is only partially true. Maturation provides a young child with the ability to perform a specific movement skill at a very low level of performance. It is only with continuous practice and instruction that a child's level of performance will increase" (p. 4).

We are beginning to realize that our society is becoming sedentary. More people are spending more hours in activities that require little movement—watching television, playing video games, sitting at a computer. Young children reflect the attitudes and practices they have experienced in their environment. They learn a great deal from older sibling and adult role models. Failing to exercise enough creates health problems as they mature, including obesity.

In addition, many children's free movement is being restricted as city streets and parks become unsafe. Where, then, are children to practice the skills of running, jumping, and climbing? Today, more than ever, the early childhood classroom must provide such activities. The preschool program is being called upon to guarantee young children their birthright of growing up with strong and healthy bodies.

The Large-Motor Center in an early childhood classroom thus takes on an importance it may not have had before. As a crucial component of the self-directed learning environment, it must be set up to appeal to children's own interests in motor skills. As an essential element in the Appropriate Practices Curriculum, it should include child-initiated activities to enhance development of particular large-motor skills. The center should also be available for children's daily use, just as the other classroom learning centers are.

Outdoor time needs to complement the daily program, but not substitute for large-motor activities within the classroom.

What about an outdoor playground or an indoor gymnasium? They also play an important role in children's development of large-motor skills because there are many running, jumping, climbing, balancing, swinging, sliding, and riding skills that cannot be practiced freely in the classroom. Outdoor and gym time need to complement the daily program wherever possible, but they do not substitute for large-motor activities within the classroom. Children need in-class large-motor experiences on a daily basis.

In the developmental scheme of things, the focus should be on large-motor skills for preschool children. These skills are the foundation for much of the rest of the child's development. Parents and teachers alike want that foundation to be a strong one. We know that competency in movement is important for children now and in the future, since the ability to move affects children socially, emotionally, and physically. Children who score significantly below normal in the area of motor development are not likely to be included in the games of their more highly skilled playmates. They are also likely to experience problems in the area of peer relationships and self-esteem (Poest et al., p. 5).

SETTING UP THE LARGE-MOTOR CENTER

The Large-Motor Center of the preschool classroom should contain equipment and materials to promote the development of many physical skills, such as:

walking	leaping	climbing
running	crawling	creative movement
galloping	creeping	throwing
jumping	balancing	catching
hopping	bending	

Flexible equipment is best. A multiuse climber is as important indoors as outdoors. A junior-gym or house-gym that includes a ladder going up to the fenced-in platform on top, and a slide going down, provides challenges for several children at a time in using the large muscles of the arms, legs, feet, hands, and torso. These gyms come in a variety of sizes and configurations. Some have a section with a tunnel attached to the climbing platform through which a child crawls to go down the slide. Some have a door or crawling hole at the base. Most are made to fold up for easy storage.

House-climbers or lofts also serve as dramatic play areas, where children can play on top and underneath the platform as well as on the ladder and sides. A smaller, solid-wall version of the house-gym has steps going up to a platform with railings, a wooden slide going down, and a crawling hole underneath. Vinyl and foam-filled floor mats should be placed under and around such climbing equipment to cushion falls.

Some programs prefer large, hollow, heavy-plastic climbing cubes with holes in the tops and sides. **Children can** (with your help) **create their own climbing-crawling-sliding apparatus** if the Large-Motor Center contains a set of snap-together or push-together materials. Modular sets contain walls with circular openings, steps, slides, railings for platforms, tunnels, and ramps. One contains a tunnel, slope, bridge, and stair blocks that securely join together in different configurations. Rugged plastic play cubes with a slide that flips over to become steps is popular. Two cubes can be connected with inner platforms that convert to become a crawl-through tunnel.

The advantage of snap-together climbing materials is their versatility in size and function: you can adapt such climbers to your particular space. Even a small Large-Motor Center can accommodate a climbing cube. Programs with small spaces often omit climbers because they believe they have no room for them. With the new plastic snap sets or cube climbers, almost any program has room for this important piece of equipment.

Other climbing materials include large vinyl foam-blocks in several colors and in a variety of shapes (square, round, and ramp) that can be pushed together and held in place with Velcro fasteners. All of these materials can be purchased through educational supply houses.

Many preschool programs do not extend their classroom large-motor facilities much beyond the climbing equipment mentioned here. The Appropriate Practices Curriculum, on the other hand, fills the Large-Motor Center with a variety of activities at particular "stations" within the center. These stations are discussed under each of the skills to follow. In addition, the center can **display pictures of children** involved in climbing, crawling, jumping, and running. If you do not have a source for such pictures, take them **from a play-equipment catalog**, enlarge them on a copy machine, and mount them attractively on the walls of your center. Or take digital photos of your own children as they climb, crawl, or slide. Enlarge them and mount them in the center.

ACTIVITIES TO PROMOTE SPECIFIC LARGE-MOTOR SKILLS

Walking

All preschool children surely know how to walk, don't they? Take a look, and you will note that not all of your children walk the same. Depending on their size, their center of gravity, their development, and their personalities, children walk in many different styles and with different degrees of ability and confidence. Many taller, more mature girls stride along like adults. Younger children, who still retain some of the top-heaviness of toddlers, may walk with less agility. Some children seem more awkward in their movements than others. Physically impaired children may have locomotor difficulties.

Thus, your Large-Motor Center should at all times feature materials and activities to promote walking—a basic skill for all human beings. Walking comes in different forms. Your children should be able to: step, tiptoe, tread, tramp, hike, stroll, saunter, march, prance, stride, strut, clump, shuffle, trudge, slide, and glide. Keep your activities personal and fun for the children, and everyone will want to become involved.

For instance, you can motivate walking activities by reading a book such as *Funny Walks* (Hindley, 1994), with pictures and text of children and animals doing their funny walks. Children should enjoy the comical words as much as the pictures: *skitter, dawdle, bumble in bunches*. One picture shows a guinea pig in a duck-footed waddle and then a streak. Then the story invites the children to try their own funny walks.

Where can children walk inside the classroom? In the Large-Motor Center itself they can **walk up and down steps if you have commercial equipment such as a "rocking boat"** that inverts to steps, or a step-and-slide climber, or a nursery gym with steps. It is not necessary, though, to purchase commercial equipment. Creative teachers can devise all kinds of walking activities. For instance, **children can walk or march in place when you lead them in action chants** such as those at the beginning of each chapter. Change the words to fit the action. Johnny in this chapter's action chant can be a "walker" rather than a "jumper." Use the names of your children to make it more personal.

For an always-available walking activity that children do on their own, you can **designate one area of the center as the Walking Rink and section it off with a rope attached to a circle of chairs**. Not only does such an area promote walking, but it also controls large-motor movement that might otherwise get out of hand in a small classroom with some exuberant walkers! Your rink can be a circle large enough for several children if you have sufficient room. Remember that you don't need to provide for the entire class at once in any of the learning centers. Bring in a child-sized "walker," not only for children with physical disabilities, but also for everyone to try in the Walking Rink.

Children can take a ticket (from an envelope attached to the rope or the wall) **that designates what motion they will perform** within the rink: red tickets for walking, blue for jogging, yellow for hopping, purple for tiptoeing, and green for using the walker. Have a stick-figure drawing of the motion on each ticket. Children can then perform their motion inside the area of the rink and return the ticket when they are finished. How long they stay in the rink is up to the children. If you **mount a chart with their names** on the wall in the area, **they can put a peel-off colored sticker after their name each time they do an action**. Children love to fill up the chart with as many different colored stickers as possible!

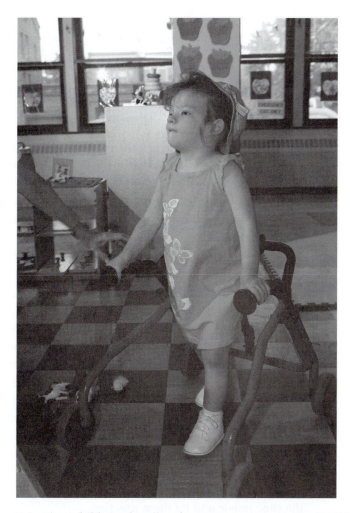

Bring in a child-sized walker for everyone to try in the Walking Rink.

Another week, **use the Walking Rink for animal walking**. Have tickets with animal pictures on them: elephants, ducks, cats, dogs, deer, rabbits, or kangaroos. Let children move as they think these animals would move. Or read a book to initiate animal movements such as *Move!* (Jenkins, 2006), with its large, realistic illustrations of a rabbit, monkey, jacana (bird), whale, armadillo, crocodile, snake, praying mantis, roadrunner, spider, penguin, and polar bear.

Children also love to imitate dinosaurs. They seem to have a special attraction to these extinct giants. To get your youngsters started with dinosaur movements, read *Dinosaurumpus!* (Mitton, 2002) or *Saturday Night at the Dinosaur Stomp* (Shields, 1997), where triceratops bomps, diplodocus tramples, and tyrannosaurus rex stomps. Don't be fooled by the so-called difficult names: young children love to roll them around on their tongues. Some children want to **cut out and color their** own paper "dinosaur feet" with three toes that they fasten on top of their shoes with tape. At this time you should also be featuring miniature toy dinosaurs in the Block Center, "dinosaur music" in the Music Center, and dinosaur software in the Computer Center. If you don't have music, use drum beats.

Clements and Schneider (2006) note that: "Teachers who favor the imitative approach in movement-based learning recognize the importance of fostering the young child's imagination. They realize that many preschooler children become easily frustrated and develop anxiety that inhibits further participation unless a model is available to duplicate or copy. This is especially true if a child has no concept of how to perform a physical task" (p. 10).

What if your children want to continue their walking fun outside the Large-Motor Center? Can they do their high-stepping elsewhere? They can if you **cut out footprints from colored contact paper and make a walking trail around the room** with them. Make the footprints the same colors as your tickets and place the footprints as they would look for walking, jogging, hopping, and tiptoeing. The children can help.

Children enjoy skating and skiing as well. The Walking Rink activities can include these gliding, sliding skills during one of the winter months. **Bring pairs of double unit blocks from the Block Center to be used as skates or skis**. Preschoolers can balance on a pair of blocks and slide along the floor. Wax the blocks if they are not slippery enough. Bring in some ski poles from children's toy skis or have the children use a pair of brooms from the Dramatic Play Center as ski poles.

Children can go on hikes or go mountain climbing in the Walking Rink if they want to stretch their imaginations even further. **Have them fill up backpacks** to wear as they hike. Have walking sticks in the Large-Motor Center to add to the drama. What other walking activities can you or the children dream up? What about walking with crutches? **Bring in a pair of children's crutches as you did for the shoe music and let them practice**.

Running/Galloping

Children need to practice the skill of running indoors as well as out. Once again, you can promote (yet control) the activity if you provide a special space for it. **Have a Running Pad (a doormat or some other rubberized nonskid mat)** in the Large-Motor Center where children can run in place. This can be one of several stations in the center where children take a ticket and do the exercise required, just as they do with the Walking Rink. Mount a chart of children's names nearby and let them paste a peel-off sticker on the chart after they do their running in place on the mat. Be sure everyone has a chance to get a sticker.

If you have the space, consider having a Running Ring. This ring can be the Circle Time circle if you have a circle marked on the floor. It can also be a circle in the Large-Motor Center marked off by a length of rope looped through the backs of chairs that are formed into a circle, as you did for the Walking Rink. The size is immaterial: it can be big enough for one, or for three or four. You would probably not want space for more within the classroom itself. Children especially like this type of circle because it allows them the freedom to run in the classroom, yet controls the area within which they can run. They can help you set it up, even on a daily basis if need be.

Like swimmers swimming laps, **the children can run "rings"** around the *inside* of the circle. They can keep track of their own rings, **and take a number from the basket you provide that tells the number of rings they have run**. Thus a large-motor activity can promote cognitive skills as well, although accuracy in counting is not the point at this stage of children's development.

How else can children move in the Running Ring? How about **galloping on a horse around the track**? For this kind of movement you may want to supply your riders with several stick horses. They are available commercially, or you can make your own from a child-sized mop or broom. The galloping movement is as close as many preschoolers will come to skipping—a more complex skill not expected of children younger than 6 or 7 years old.

Try to discourage horse races in the ring because of their potential win–lose element—fine for horse races, but destructive for the preschoolers who lose. (All of the children who participate in your galloping ring are winners!) Why else would someone ride in a ring if not to race? What about a horse show? Children can help make their own stick horses and then show them off in the ring.

What about a rodeo? For inspiration, read to a small group of interested participants the book *White Dynamite and Curly Kid* (Martin & Archambault, 1986). It is the spine-tingling adventure of the wild ride of a rodeo bull rider, Curly Kidd, on the bull White Dynamite, as his little child Lucky Kidd looks on. Lucky Kidd tells the story with wonderful rhyming words on the full-color pages of the book, keeping readers and listeners on the edge of their seats until the ending surprises everyone: Lucky Kidd is a girl! **Can children make stick bulls** (like stick horses) **for a pretend rodeo**? What kinds of movements would a rodeo bull make? What about **a bucking horse**? This type of activity is especially appropriate where rodeos are a part of the children's culture.

Children can perform in the Running/Galloping Ring for any number of weekly or monthly events: **a motorcycle rally** with children riding stick motorcycles they have made; **a car show** with children driving stick cars; **a kangaroo hop** with children seeing how far they can jump (two feet together) around the ring; **a camel trot** with riders "crossing the desert." The only limits to "ring running or galloping" are your and the children's imaginations.

Don't forget to **bring the large wooden riding vehicles into this area** for at least one day a week as well. If you do use riding vehicles or even trikes inside, be sure to read *Mike and the Bike* (Ward, 2005), a great bike story for young children that comes with a CD narrating Mike's adventures. Don't worry, girls, there's one for you, too. Read *Sally Jean, the Bicycle Queen* (Best, 2006), narrated by Sally Jean herself. Don't forget to provide bicycle helmets even for pretend play—children love them.

Jumping/Hopping/Leaping

Here is another station for the Large-Motor Center: **have a Jumping Pad where children can jump up and down**, two feet together on some kind of pad or cushion. The station can be sectioned off with chairs, rope, or merely masking tape and a sign. Some teachers tape a hula hoop to the floor with cutout footprints inside to show where jumping can take place. The Jumping Pad can be located inside the Running Ring if space is a problem.

More elaborate kinds of jumping can take place in the Large-Motor Center if you make proper arrangements. If you read children the book *Jump, Frog, Jump* (Kalan, 1981), be prepared to **have a Frog Pond** with a lily pad, a log, a net, an

Children jump on jumping pads when they hear a signal.

island, and a basket. These can be made by marking out the various areas on the floor of the center with masking tape; or better still, by using a series of nonskid vinyl mats for the pad, the log, the net, the island, and the basket. Let children jump from one pad to the other as you read this cumulative tale. If you cannot locate the book, make up your own frog-jump tale.

Another wonderful frog-jumping book is *Hop Jump* (Walsh, 1993), about Betsy, the frog who gets bored with just hopping and jumping. She begins to experiment with other kinds of movements by watching the tree leaves float down in the fall. Soon she is leaping, turning, and twisting. "It's called dancing," she says. Finally, the other frogs come to watch, and soon all but one are dancing. With you as the leader, can your children's hopping and jumping movements turn into dancing? Try it and see.

Is bouncing the same as jumping? It is in the comical book *Bounce!* (Cronin, 2007). A comic-book dog leads the listeners through everything from a rabbit's hip-hop and a frog's ker-plop to ball bouncing and puddle bouncing and roller skate bouncing (no). Have your listeners try to reenact this story as you reread it.

Jumping skills can also be promoted by having a **Basketball Jump Station** in the Large-Motor Center. Bring in a free-standing children's basketball basket for use with a sponge or foam ball that is light and not bouncy. This is not a basketball game, but a jumping station. Again, place a chart with children's names nearby where they can put a colored sticker next to their name after they have completed the basketball jumping. Have everyone who tries it give themselves a sticker.

Once again there is a wonderful book to read: *Hoops with Swoopes* (Kuklin, 2001) shows cutout photos of a real woman's basketball star, Sheryl Swoopes, as she jumps, catches, steps, and shoots. Simple large-font words bounce across the pages as Sheryl Swoopes shoots hoops. Your girls will want to pick up the ball and get started.

Children can also hop on one foot and then the other if your activities encourage this movement. **Have a Hopping Pad** as yet another station in the Large-Motor Center. Some teachers prefer a footprint hopping trail made of self-sticking colored vinyl footprints mounted on the floor. For children who have difficulty hopping on one foot, have them hold onto the back of a chair while they practice.

Leaping activities can occur in the Large-Motor Center if you tape off a section of the area for such an activity. Because leaping is a skill that carries a child across a space from one side to the other, make leaping inviting for children by giving them something intriguing to leap across. You can designate Leapfrog Lodge as a station where a different kind of leaping activity takes place each week. One week, tape securely to the floor a section of blue poster board to serve as a "river" that the children must leap across, taking off on one foot and landing on the other. Children can also leap across pretend mud, sand, or snow.

Again, put up a name chart for colored stickers. Check to see that everyone has stickers after his or her name in all the stations. This should not be a win or lose situation. If a child does not have many or any stickers, help the child to perform and give themselves a sticker for his or her effort.

Balancing/Bending

Children can practice the skills of balancing and bending in the Large-Motor Center if you **set up a Balancing Bower** as a station. Again, on a weekly basis include a particular balancing or bending activity for them to practice on their own. One week, have **a balance beam or a walking board** as a bridge across a taped-down blue poster board "river" for children to cross by walking forward, sideways, and backward. They might try to carry a little suitcase as they walk across the balance-beam bridge. Another time they can try carrying a little bucket in each hand as they cross the bridge.

Read to a small group at a time *Tightrope Poppy on the High-Wire Pig* (Bardham-Quallen, 2006), the rhyming story of a little pig who knows she can be a star on the high wire when the circus comes to town. She practices balancing on fences and railings and never thinks of falling. But when she first steps out on the circus high wire, she does fall—and more than once. She's ready to give up until her mom e-mails her saying "some dreams take lots of trying." So she tries again—and finally succeeds. What do your listeners think about it? Do any of them feel like Poppy? Would they now like to reenact the story as you reread it? Who wants to be Poppy? You can **set up your Balancing Bower as a circus ring** and give everyone a chance on the "high-wire" balance beam set on edge.

For a bending activity, **place a pole or broom between two chair backs and have children "duck under the fence."** Another week, have objects (e.g., pebbles) at the bottom of a bushel basket that children have to bend over to retrieve. Another bending activity can be **a pick-up-chips or put-down-chips game** in which children take a container of colored plastic chips and bend over to place them on self-sticking vinyl stepping-stones of the same color as the chips. When they have finished placing all the colored chips on the proper stepping-stone, they can go around and pick up the chips for the next child, thus giving the first players a second bending experience.

Each week you can substitute a new bending activity for the children. For instance, **try "panning for gold" with gold-painted pebbles** that you place here and there on the floor of the station. They can use a pie pan to collect their gold. You can also base your activities on topics the children are pursuing in other centers of the classroom. When they are reading about dinosaurs or playing dinosaur computer games, for example, **have a dinosaur food-gathering expedition** in which children must bend over to collect in a basket or bucket the cutout pieces of food you have scattered here and there around the floor of the Balancing Bower. Such activities should lead you and your children into devising similar creative experiences based on curriculum interests and needs.

Crawling/Creeping

Although we often use the words interchangeably, *crawling* refers to the movement of propelling the body forward with arms and legs when it is flat on the floor, whereas *creeping* refers to the forward body movement done on hands and knees with the body raised above the floor. Your Large-Motor Center can afford children an opportunity to develop these skills if you **set up a Crawling Chamber as a station**. In addition to the crawling spaces provided by commercial climbing equipment, you can purchase fabric tunnels that are collapsible and easily stored, as well as vinyl pad tunnels. A **creeping/crawling trail** through the classroom can stand on its own or be **part of an obstacle course that takes children under tables**.

Many teachers prefer to make their own crawling/creeping materials. **A large cardboard carton can be cut out with an opening at each end** large enough for children to crawl through. **Call it a cave or a car tunnel**, and have the children help you paint it an appropriate color. **Tunnels can also be made of pairs of adult-sized chairs** laid down opposite one another with their backs touching to serve as the roof of the tunnel. Cover the chairs with a blanket for a more interesting effect. Children can pretend to be bears creeping into their dens or cars driving through a tunnel in the mountain. **Sing a song together when children creep and crawl**. How about "The Bear Went *Under* the Mountain"?

If your program is in a large city, take the children on a subway field trip, and then **make a subway tunnel** in your Crawling Chamber upon your return. The children can be the cars of the subway train as they creep through the tunnel. Another week they can be explorers crawling through a mountain cave. Still another week they can be scuba divers "swimming" through an underwater cave or exploring a shipwreck. For added interest, place some objects (such as gold pebbles) inside the "tunnel" or a "ship" for the children to discover. A tent too small to stand up in also promotes creeping/crawling movements, as does a **homemade card table "tent"** with a blanket over it for the walls.

Cross-lateral movements like creeping and crawling are important not only for strengthening children's muscles, but also for promoting brain development. Pica (2007) notes that: "creeping and crawling activate both hemispheres of the brain in a balanced way. Because they involve both eyes, ears, hands, and feet, as well as core muscles on both sides of the body, both hemispheres and all four lobes of the brain are activated. This means that cognitive functioning is heightened and learning becomes easier" (p. xii).

We remember that creeping is a young child's first efficient form of locomotion. If you find that any of the children are having difficulty with this "cross-lateral crawling" they should be given many opportunities to practice. Do not point out children who need extra help, but include them in a small group of children who listen to a story about a tunnel and then reenact the story by creeping through a

A creeping/crawling trail through the classroom can stand on its own or be part of an obstacle course that takes children under tables.

tunnel you have set up. Such a story can be *All Aboard the Dinosaur Train* (Lund, 2006), in which huge dinosaurs ride on top of the train cars through a tunnel; or *All Aboard* (Ray, 2002), in which a little African American girl and her toy rabbit, Mr. Barnes, take a train ride to Florida to visit her grandparents, going through a long dark tunnel at one point.

Climbing

Climbing activities are popular with children because of the excitement they offer and with teachers because of the variety of children's large-motor skills they promote. Children exercise arms, hands, shoulders, legs, and feet, as well as perform bending, twisting, balancing, pushing, and pulling skills. The commercial climbers, waffle blocks, and foam blocks previously mentioned are popular in classrooms that can afford the space and monetary commitment. However, homemade climbing materials can be just as effective, and perhaps more appealing to the children if they have a hand in setting them up.

Add a Climbing Corner as a station in the Large-Motor Center. **Plastic milk crates** that are used for storage **can also be used for climbing**. Place them on the floor open side up, and tie them together in a long line or a maze for children to climb in and out of one by one like an obstacle course. Play peppy music as the children perform their crate climb.

A small **closet** can also serve as a Climbing Corner by **removing the door and fastening rungs across the door opening or inside the closet from bottom to top**, with a pad covering the closet floor to cushion jumps.

Large hollow blocks really belong in the Climbing Corner rather than in the Block Center. Children can build child-sized huts, forts, steps, and walls, climbing up and down and in and out of their structures.

Throwing/Catching

Children ages 3 through 5 are at the beginning of their throwing/catching skills. Some still use two hands to throw an object, just as they did as toddlers. Others throw one-handed in a pushing movement. Children need practice in throwing objects both overhand and underhand in order to develop this complex skill. If you **use lightweight, nonbouncing objects** such as beanbags, sponge balls, yarn balls, foam balls, and perforated plastic balls in a confined classroom space, you afford children the opportunity to throw as hard as they want. **Set up a Throwing Booth** as a station in the Large-Motor Center to encourage children to practice this skill on their own.

Place a small table or low counter for holding the throwing objects two or three yards from the wall. Place a target against the wall. Make it something colorful and interesting: a tall, flat cardboard carton painted with a clown face with a wide open mouth (a large hole) to fill with "food"; a bright basket or plastic hoop fastened to the wall; a small bucket standing on the floor against the wall; a hanging sheet of cardboard with several large holes outlined with colorful circles.

Have children stand behind the counter to throw the balls or beanbags into the target. Children can sign up for turns, take a ticket, or wait at the counter for a turn, thus giving them yet another opportunity to practice social turn-taking skills.

Your Throwing Booth can become a feed-the-animal experience whenever you are featuring animal activities in the other learning centers. Put "animal food" (beanbags) on the counter of the Throwing Booth and have an animal "mouth" against the wall for them to throw the food into. A circle with animal ears, eyes, nose, and a large hole for a mouth drawn on a cardboard carton can serve as the animal for the children to feed. Beanbags can be thrown overhand or underhand into the mouth. Homemade beanbags can be made of banana-shaped pieces of yellow cloth filled with dry beans and sewn together to represent bananas for a monkey; green beanbags can be catnip for a cat; white beanbags can be bones for a dinosaur, alligator, or dog.

Catching is often a more difficult skill for preschoolers than throwing, because their reflexes are not as developed as they will be by the time they reach kindergarten. Nevertheless, preschool children appreciate the opportunity to practice catching as well as throwing if you **set up a Catching Coop station for two children to use together**. To help them control their catches in the beginning, have each

Bouncing/catching of a large beach ball is a good option for your Catching Coop station.

child wear a catching mitt on the non-throwing hand, made by sewing or gluing a strip or two of Velcro to the palm of a regular mitten. Glue strips of the other half of the Velcro to a foam ball. Commercial Velcro gloves are also available.

Children can throw the ball to one another or up at a target on the wall, trying to catch it when it comes down. The two children will also be practicing the social skills of give-and-take, as well as language skills as they talk with one another during the activity. Bouncing a large beach ball and catching it is another option.

Creative Movement

We tend to think of creative movement activities as promoting only physical and creative abilities. But Benzwie (1987), in her descriptively illustrated book *A Moving Experience: Dance for Lovers of Children and the Child Within*, has a more holistic notion: "Movement, the heart and soul of nonverbal communication, expands our awareness, heightens our sensitivity, and enhances our verbal skills." She also says: "Art has movement, movement can be art, a sculpture in space and time" (p. 123).

Creative movement can and should occur in various parts of the classroom: perhaps in the Music Center, as children explore with their bodies the sound and movement of wind or rain; perhaps in the Circle Time circle, when the whole class moves creatively to "dinosaur stomp" music. Creative movement can also be an individual large-motor activity at a station in the Large-Motor Center.

Fasten a hula hoop to the floor or place masking tape down in a small ring in a space that you designate as the **Dancing Ring**, Locate two Dancing Rings next to each other if you want two individuals to practice dancing movement at the same time.

What will the dancers do? If you read a story to a small group about a certain type of movement or dance and then place a tape player near the Dancing Ring, one or more children can try doing dancing movements to music while staying within the ring. Read the bouncy, rhyming book *Twist with a Burger, Jitter with a Bug* (Lowery, 1995), and you should have your Dancing Ring dancers doing every kind of movement imaginable to a mambo, a rap, a tap dance, a polka, the twist, a jitterbug, a boogie, a hula-hula, and a rumba.

Or you might read the animal dancing book *Cha Cha Chimps* (Durango, 2006), where the rhino shakes it, the cobra does the limbo, the lion does a jitterbug, the cheetah sambas, the hippo does the hokey pokey, the giraffe does the tango, the meerkat macarenas, the zebra Irish clogs, the ostrich does a polka, and the chimps do a cha-cha-cha.

Don't force any of the children who do not show an inclination to dance. But you might read them *Giraffes Can't Dance* (Andreae, 1999), where Gerald Giraffe longs to dance at the Jungle Dance, but all the animals make fun of him because he is so clumsy. He sneaks away to gaze at the moon, listen to the swaying grass, and

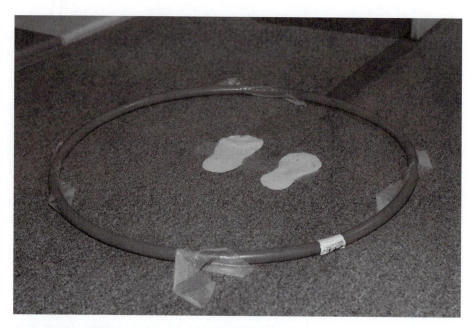

Fasten a hula hoop to the floor for a Dancing Ring.

soon he is swaying too—and dancing! One by one the other animals come by and are astonished to see Gerald dancing. He tells them that we all can dance when we find music that we love.

Dancing Ring movements are especially well suited to children in wheelchairs who may be able to move only the upper part of their bodies. Whether or not a child with such a physical impairment is a class member, you can put a chair in the Dancing Ring and **have each of the children try upper body "dancing" to music as they sit in the chair**. What other creative movement ideas can you think of for an individual to perform within the Dancing Ring? Ask the children.

Props such as a hat, cap, crown, feathers, cape, paper wings, flags, streamers, or a "jet-pack" may be all that children need to **motivate them to move to the music** you provide for the Dancing Ring. Try a new "dance" every week with new music, and soon this station will become one of the most popular ones in the Large-Motor Center. Once they have tried it, children enjoy the challenge of dancing in one spot within a ring. In addition, such an activity promotes creativity as children invent their own movements to go with the music and the props.

THE TEACHER'S ROLE IN THE LARGE-MOTOR CENTER

Most classrooms obviously do not contain space enough for all of the stations described to be set up at the same time, nor should they be. One or two stations at a time are the most your children can use to best advantage. How will you know which to provide of the ones described?

Walking Rink	Balancing Bower
Running Pad	Crawling Chamber
Running Ring	Climbing Corner
Galloping Ring	Throwing Booth
Jumping Pad	Catching Coop
Basketball Jump	Dancing Ring
Leapfrog Lodge	Frog Pond

The particular stations you set up will depend upon the needs and interests of the children, based on your observations. As you do in each of the other learning centers in the classroom, you will be observing individual children to determine their large-motor abilities. In this case, manipulation, mastery, and meaning are not practical observation points because the focus is on children's physical skill development rather than on their interaction with materials.

Observe individuals on the playground, in the gymnasium, and in the classroom, recording on note cards their ability, first of all, to walk and run with ease and confidence. If some of the children exhibit developmental lags in these areas, set up stations in the Large-Motor Center to promote these skills. As children progress in these abilities, other stations can be added and the original stations put aside for the time being. Keep a station in use for as long as children show a need for developing the particular skill.

In addition to taking into account children's developmental needs, **your rationale for including particular stations can involve the children's own interests, as well as the integration of large-motor experiences with other classroom activities**. The Throwing Booth is a popular station in some classrooms because certain children like to throw. The Frog Pond may become the focus of jumping activities because of the live frog in the Science Center terrarium. The Riding Ring may increase in popularity when a rodeo or car race comes to town.

How long should a station remain set up in the Large-Motor Center? This is a teacher's judgment call. As long as the station is serving the needs of the children and the curriculum, it can remain. But because we realize that young children learn best when they are challenged by activities slightly above their abilities—and that young children participate more frequently when activities and materials exhibit some novelty—you will want to **add intriguing new stations to the Large-Motor Center when interest in present activities begins to lag. Keep track of the names and numbers of children using the various stations on a daily basis**. Use this information at the weekly planning sessions to determine when to add or eliminate a station.

On the other hand, **do not eliminate a new station just because few children are using it**. If there is a need for a Jumping Pad, for instance, but few children are using it, then **it is up to you and your staff to stimulate children's interest** in jumping. Make the Jumping Pad into the surface of the moon and read them a book about it.

> *Astronaut Piggy Wiggy* (Fox & Fox, 2001)
>
> *Hedgie Blasts Off* (Brett, 2006)
>
> *If You Decide to Go to the Moon* (McNulty, 2005)
>
> *Zoom! Zoom! Zoom! I'm Off to the Moon!* (Yaccarino, 1997)

Because gravity is less on the moon, the children can bounce and take long leaps just like astronauts. See how high the children can jump up and down or from one crater to another. Have them help you make astronauts' helmets out of gallon ice cream containers covered with aluminum foil and everyone will want a turn to jump on the moon. **Transform your Jumping Pad into the surface of the moon** by marking off a large circle with small circular chalk craters or rubber mats here and there inside it. Children enjoy engaging their imaginations in this way, and your Jumping Pad should take on a new life when everyone tries "moon jumping"!

Thus, it is up to you and your children, based on their interests and needs, to determine which activities you will include in your Large-Motor Center and when to change them. Physical skills in young children do not develop overnight. Give your children the time and the opportunity to try out the various large-motor skills. If the activities you provide are interesting enough, children will happily take the time to practice each of these skills.

IDEAS IN CHAPTER 12

1. *Setting up the Large-Motor Center*
   a. Provide flexible, multiple-use equipment
   b. Have children create their own climbing-crawling-sliding apparatus
   c. Mount pictures enlarged from toy catalogs of children involved in large-motor activities

2. *Promoting walking*
   a. Have children practice walking up and down steps on equipment such as a "rocking boat"
   b. Lead children in walking or marching-in-place activities with action chants
   c. Set up a Walking Rink station in the Large-Motor Center with chairs and a rope or tape on the floor

    d. Have children take colored tickets for walking, jogging, hopping, or tiptoeing

    e. Mount a name chart on the wall for use with peel-off stickers

    f. Use the Walking Rink for "animal walking"

    g. Cut out dinosaur feet to tape to their shoes

    h. Make a walking trail around the room with contact paper cutouts

    i. Children can skate and ski on unit blocks

    j. Children can go on hikes in the Walking Rink wearing knapsacks

    k. Let children practice walking with crutches

3. *Promoting running*

    a. Set up a Running Pad in the Large-Motor Center

    b. Have a Running/Riding Ring as a station

    c. Have children run rings and take a number that corresponds to the number of rings they have run

    d. Have children gallop around the ring on stick horses

    e. Try to discourage "horse races"

    f. Have a rodeo with stick bulls or bucking horses

    g. Have a motorcycle rally or car show

    h. Have a kangaroo hop or a camel trot

    i. Bring large wooden riding vehicles to this area

4. *Promoting jumping, hopping, leaping*

    a. Set up a Jumping Pad as a station

    b. Have a Frog Pond for jumping

    c. Set up a Basketball Jump station

    d. Have a Hopping Pad station or a hopping trail

5. *Promoting balancing, bending*

    a. Set up a Balancing Bower station with a balance beam or a walking board

    b. Place a pole between two chair backs for ducking under

    c. Set up the Balancing Bower as a circus ring

    d. Have a pick-up-chips bending activity

    e. Pan for gold in the Bending Bower

    f. Gather dinosaur food in the Bending Bower

6. *Promoting crawling, creeping*

   a. Have a Crawling Chamber as a station

   b. Have a large cardboard carton or pairs of chairs as a car tunnel

   c. Sing a song as children creep through the tunnel

   d. Make a subway tunnel

   e. Have a tent or a card table tent with a low opening

7. *Promote climbing*

   a. Add a Climbing Corner with plastic milk crates as a station

   b. Remove the door of a small closet and fasten rungs across the opening

   c. Keep large, hollow blocks in the Climbing Center

8. *Promoting throwing, catching*

   a. Set up a Throwing Booth as a station with lightweight, non-bouncing beanbags and balls

   b. Have a feed-the-animal beanbag activity in the Throwing Booth

   c. Set up a Catching Coop for two children to use together

9. *Promoting creative movement*

   a. Set up a Dancing Ring as a station for creative movement

   b. Have children do creative movement sitting in a chair or a wheelchair

   c. Use props such as hats, caps, crowns, feathers, capes, etc., to stimulate creative movement

10. *Changing the Large-Motor Center*

    a. Observe individual children to determine which stations to set up

    b. Other stations can be set up based on the children's interests and curriculum activities

    c. Add new stations when interest in present activities begins to lag

    d. Keep track of numbers and names of children using stations on a daily basis

    e. When particular stations are necessary but are not being used, stimulate children's interest in them by reading an appropriate book

    f. Transform your Jumping Pad into the surface of the moon

DISCUSSION QUESTIONS

1. As children develop large-motor skills naturally, what can you do to increase their level of performance?
2. Why should we include a Large-Motor Center within the classroom if an indoor gym and outdoor playground are available?
3. What kinds of large-motor equipment are best for the center? Why? Give examples.
4. How can "stations" be used to promote large-motor skills? How can you decide which stations to use?
5. How can children's picture books be used to promote large-motor development? Give examples.

TRY IT YOURSELF

1. Observe each of the children in the class, on the playground, or indoors in the Large-Motor Center to determine whether they walk and run with ease and confidence.
2. Set up the Large-Motor Center to include two stations to promote two different skills as described in the chapter. (At least one station should feature walking or running if your observations show this as a need.)
3. Read a book to stimulate children to pursue the activity at one of the stations you have set up.
4. Observe and record the numbers and names of children using the stations in the Large-Motor Center on three different days.
5. Add a large-motor activity for children with special physical needs, and have everyone participate in it.

REFERENCES CITED

Benzwie, T. (1987). *A moving experience: Dance for lovers of children and the child within*. Tucson, AZ: Zephyr Press.

Clements, R. L. & Schneider, S. L. (2006). *Movement based learning: Academic concepts and activity for ages three through eight*. Reston, VA: National Association for Sport and Physical Education.

Pica, R. (2007). *Moving and learning across the curriculum* (2nd ed.). Clifton Park, NY: Cengage Learning.

Poest, C. A., Williams, J. R., Witt, D. D., & Atwood, M. E. (1990). Challenge me to move: Large muscle development in young children. *Young Children 45*(5), 4–10.

Other Sources

Gellens, S. (2005). Integrate movement to enhance children's brain development. *Dimensions of Early Childhood 33*(3), 14–21.

Javernick, E. (1988). Johnny's not jumping: Can we help obese children? *Young Children 43*(2), 18–23.

Pica, R. (2006). Physical fitness and the early childhood curriculum. *Young Children 61*(3), 12–19.

Sanders, S. W. (2002). *Active for life: Developmentally appropriate movement programs for young children.* Washington, DC: National Association for the Education of Young Children.

Sanders, S. W. (2007). Physically active for life: Eight essential motor skills for all children. *Dimensions of Early Childhood 34*(1), 3–10.

Children's Books

Andreae, G. (1999). *Giraffes can't dance.* New York: Orchard.

Bardham-Quallen, S. (2006). *Tightrope Poppy on the high wire pig.* New York: Sterling Publishing.

Best, C. (2006). *Sally Jean the bicycle queen.* New York: Melanie Kroupa Books.

Brett, J. (2006). *Hedgie blasts off.* New York: G. P. Putnam's Sons.

Cronin, D. (2007). *Bounce!* New York: Atheneum.

Durango, J. (2006). *Cha cha chimps.* New York: Simon & Schuster.

Fox, C. & Fox, D. (2001). *Astronaut Piggy Wiggy.* Brooklyn, NY: Handprint Books.

Hindley, J. (1994). *Funny walks.* New York: BridgeWater Books.

Jenkins, S. (2006). *Move!* Boston: Houghton Mifflin Company.

Kalan, R. (1981). *Jump, frog, jump.* New York: William Morrow.

Kuklin, S. (2001). *Hoops with Swoopes.* New York: Hyperion.*

Lowery, L. (1995). *Twist with a burger, jitter with a bug.* Boston: Houghton Mifflin Company.*

Lund, D. (2006). *All aboard the dinotrain.* Orlando, FL: Harcourt.

Martin, B., Jr. & Archambault, J. (1986). *White Dynamite and Curly Kidd.* New York: Henry Holt.

McNulty, F. (2005). *If you decide to go to the moon.* New York: Scholastic Press.

Mitton, T. (2002). *Dinosaurumpus!* New York: Orchard Books.

Ray, M. L. (2002). *All Aboard!* Boston: Little, Brown and Company.

Shields, C. D. (1997). *Saturday night at the dinosaur stomp.* Cambridge, MA: Candlewick Press.

Walsh, E. D. (1993). *Hop jump.* San Diego, CA: Harcourt Brace.

Ward, M. (2005). *Mike and the bike.* Salt Lake City, UT: Cookie Jar Publishing.

Yaccarino, D. (1997). *Zoom! Zoom! Zoom! I'm off to the moon.* New York: Scholastic Press.

Note: Asterisk represents Multicultural book.

SAND IN THE EARLY CHILDHOOD CLASSROOM

Children love to play in sand. They love to run their hands through it, pour it, dig in it, and fill up containers. Many classrooms have sandboxes on the playground, but nothing in the classroom, unless they empty their water table and fill it with sand occasionally. It is **not necessary, however, to have free-standing sand or water tables**. Both sand and water are important enough to include both in the classroom at the same time. **Large plastic dishpans can be set on tables** near shelves where sand or water toys are stored. For sand, many teachers provide safety goggles to keep sandy fingers out of eyes. If you need to limit the number of children using the sand table at a time, put up a sign with the appropriate numerals or stick figures, along with sand table necklaces for them to wear. Sand, of course, is more than just an entertainment medium for children.

Hogben and Wasley (1996) tell us: "Sand is a versatile medium that allows for the development of creative abilities, imagination and appreciation, and awareness of a natural material. The nature of sand encourages exploration and experimentation, leading to concept formation. Equipment and materials provide opportunities for children to dramatize, dig, tunnel, scoop, mold, fill, pour, carry, load, and more" (p. 91).

ACTIVITIES TO PROMOTE MOTOR SKILLS

Filling/Dumping

Filling buckets or pans with sand and then pouring or dumping them out are activities that come naturally to children when they play with sand. This, of course, is a *manipulative* skill promoting eye-hand coordination, but one that children at more advanced levels find very satisfying, as well.

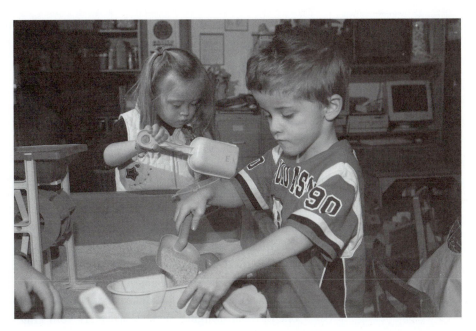

Sand encourages exploration and experimentation, leading to concept formation.

What children do with sand depends on the materials you provide: buckets, pans, scoops, spoons, shovels, trowels, spatulas, funnels, molds, sifters, sieves, hoppers, and more. For specific activities keep special tools on hand.

For example, **sand tables can be used as excellent follow-up activities after a field trip to a construction site. Read construction-theme books** to a small group at a time and then put out a box of construction-type materials for them to recreate or reenact their trip.

B Is for Bulldozer (Sobel, 2003) shows two boys watching a bulldozer, dump truck, excavator, forklift, grader, front loader, and a work crew constructing an amusement park.

Construction Countdown (Olson, 2004) shows dump trucks rolling down a road, earth movers scraping up a load, bulldozers reshaping the ground, payloaders moving dirt around, graders leveling the land, rollers packing down the sand, concrete mixers turning, backhoes scooping up gravel, and skidloaders hauling rocks. The last double-page spread shows a gigantic sandbox and children playing with all the toy construction trucks.

I'm Dirty (McMullan & McMullan 2006) is a story narrated by a big backhoe loader about the dirty work he enjoys performing all day as he clears a lot full of trash, fills in a hole, and smooths out the lot. Put a number of these toys, plus a funnel, a sieve, and a hopper for sifting sand, on a shelf next to the sand table. The children wearing sand table necklaces can then choose their materials and get to work What they do with the toys is up to them. They can follow the leads of the stories in the books or make up their own construction stories. It is important to record what they are doing, with digital photos, to be used later for stories they may want to tell or have taped or written down.

Molding

A few children may have learned to mold sand using beach buckets during trips to the beach. But most children may need your help to get them started. After all the children have had a sufficient opportunity for free play with sand at the sand table, you might propose that they **take an imaginary trip to the beach,** or a real field trip if that is possible. **As a lead-in, read to a small group at a time a beach or ocean book** such as: *Beach Day* (Roosa, 2001) about a little boy, girl, toddler and their parents who spend the day at the beach, swimming, digging in the sand, playing ball with the other children, and, finally, building a big sand castle with a moat. The children make towers on their castle using sand molds from their sand buckets, and the toddler makes a star sand mold.

Have the children look closely at the castle builders in the book. Do they see one of them bringing buckets of water? Your children may also have to **wet the sand table sand in order for it to be molded** in a bucket, cup, or other container. The physical skills of filling the bucket with damp sand, patting it down firmly, and holding and turning over the bucket quickly to prevent spilling may need to be practiced many times to get it right. Once children understand what they have to do to make molds successfully, they will soon be producing rows and rows of towers. You remember that this is their *mastery* level at work. When they begin telling stories about their towers or castles they have reached the *meaning* level of exploratory play.

ACTIVITIES TO PROMOTE COGNITIVE SKILLS

Concepts

Teachers need to be aware of other activities in the classroom that can be integrated into activities in the sand table. The children themselves in one classroom pointed out that Max in the book *Bunny Cakes* (Wells, 1997) was making an earthworm birthday cake for Grandma's birthday, while his sister Ruby was doing what they were doing at the time: making a real birthday cake. Some wanted to borrow the **measuring cups to make their own earthworm cake at the sand table.** This started a whole new activity of guessing how many cups of sand it would take to fill the coffee can mold that was to be used for Max's cake. They compared that to cups of flour for their real cake.

When some of the beads from the Art Center used for decorating Max's cake got lost in the sand, the children had fun sifting through the sand to find them. One boy used a magnet and actually found a metal bead. What else could be buried in the sand?

The next day the teacher had them **search for treasure** (nuts, nails, screws, and beads) **in the sand using several magnets**. This led to learning about metals and nonmetals.

When dinosaurs were featured in several of the learning centers, the teacher read the children *Bones, Bones, Dinosaur Bones* (Barton, 1990) about dinosaur hunters looking for and digging up dinosaur bones. **Into the sand went the small plastic dinosaurs** from the Block Center along with slotted spoons for digging and toy trucks for carrying the dinosaurs they found to the museum they constructed in the Block Center. One thing always seems to lead to another when children and teachers stay alert to the possibility of integrating their activity into other learning centers.

ACTIVITIES TO PROMOTE LANGUAGE SKILLS

Children learn to understand and use words such *heavy/light*, *empty/full*, and *tall/ short*, in comparing their sand structures. They also learn terms describing the placement of their molded towers such as *beside, behind, next to*, or *in a row*.

Although a great deal of sand play is usually of a solitary nature, **when children are involved in measuring, comparing, molding towers, and digging for treasure** or dinosaur bones, **they quickly revert to conversation** with the other workers. They describe what they are doing to one another, ask each other questions, and make comments about each other's structures. **Telling stories about their structures** or the results of their treasure hunts also becomes a popular activity. **Some want their stories tape-recorded** and transcribed. Others

When children are playing as close together as they are at a sand table, they are forced to interact socially with the children playing next to them.

want their **structures photographed**, captioned by them, and put into the class scrapbook.

ACTIVITIES TO PROMOTE SOCIAL DEVELOPMENT

When children are playing as close together as they are at sand tables, they are often forced to interact socially with the children playing next to them. Because they are so intent and deeply involved in their own activity, they seem to accept what is happening with the other players. Taking turns and waiting for a turn does not seem as difficult for them as it sometimes becomes in other endeavors.

Because it is more difficult to build a castle out on the playground without having it knocked down by other children, the idea of building a small castle in the classroom sand table caught on in one class. Using small container molds to build their towers, they all contributed to the structure. It became a focal point in the classroom, and soon everyone wanted to build a castle when it was their turn at the sand table. The teacher's contribution was more sand in the table and papers on the floor to catch the spills.

She noted that the small group of four children who listen to a story usually come together as the same group at the sand table to reenact the story or create similar structures. Thus **stories also seem to be a catalyst for children to form sand table social groups** in order to carry out a group action.

ACTIVITIES TO PROMOTE EMOTIONAL DEVELOPMENT

Children enjoy the feel of sand sifting through their fingers and of pouring sand out of containers. When children become upset or out-of-sorts you should consider **setting up a private sand tub** apart from the others for them to play in until they feel better. You can even **add some of the little block figures** of people, animals and vehicles for them to create a world of their own (Beaty, 2006, p. 87).

Some teachers also **make sand available for children's relaxation on a tray** rather than in a tub. Wheat (1995) tells us: "The very process of working with the sand tray regularly has helped some children work through sadness, anger, and disappointment and finally return to the group in a relaxed state of mind" (p. 82).

ACTIVITIES TO PROMOTE CREATIVE DEVELOPMENT

Children need time to explore and experiment with sand and sand toys at first. This, we understand, is the *manipulation* level of sand play. When they start building rows of towers over and over they have progressed to the *mastery* level. Finally, some of them may arrive at the *meaning* level where the ditches they dig and mounds they pile up have a purpose. The sand they sift through a hopper or a sieve may be for a construction site. As with the block buildings they create, they begin to name their molded sand towers.

Most preschool children do not reach this level of play at the classroom sand table. They are content to fill and dump, to pour sand through a funnel, or to grind it through a hopper. For teachers who want sand play to promote creative development in the children, they will need to add other elements: books and props.

Books, as noted earlier, add a story element that can be reenacted in the sand table by those who are interested. Appropriate props help children not only recreate these stories, but also to create stories of their own. **Little figures of block people**, for instance, are especially helpful in opening children's minds to the possibility of **creating miniature dramatic play episodes**. Some of the props might include:

Dinosaurs, trucks, small containers, figures of people

Race cars, spatulas, small containers, figures of people

Construction vehicles, hopper, sieve, figures of people

Planes, space vehicles, small containers, figures of people

Farm animals, fences, figures of people

Jungle animals, sticks for trees, figures of people

Stand a set of the props separately on a nearby shelf for at least a week at a time and watch what use the children make of them. Label the shelf: "For Sand Table." Listen unobtrusively for stories the children may make up as they play. Ask if they would like to **photograph their scenario**. Ask if they would like to **tell a story about what their figures are doing** and have it tape-recorded. Ask if they would like to have a book read about the topic. When children use figures of people in their sand play they are more likely to make up dialogue for the characters. Children's creativity at the sand table can blossom if they have this kind of support and the freedom to pretend.

TEACHER'S ROLE AT THE SAND TABLE

In addition to the suggestions already mentioned, it is up to the teacher to keep the area safe by:

1. using only sterilized sand

2. changing the sand regularly

3. cleaning the sand daily by sifting out unwanted materials

4. keeping broom, dustpan, and garbage can nearby for children's help in cleanup

5. providing safety goggles where necessary (Wellhousen & Crowther, 2004, p. 86).

Teachers should also observe and record data on the Child Interaction Form (Table 2-1, p. 36), making sure to add any creative uses the child may make of the sand and props. While allowing children the freedom to use the sand table on their own, teachers should nevertheless keep track of what is going on and make encouraging comments about what individual children are doing from time to time. Teachers should talk with the children when it is time to change the props, to get their input in what they would like to do next. Teachers should also keep track of what new ideas have blossomed at the sand table that can also be integrated into other learning centers of the classroom.

WATER IN THE EARLY CHILDHOOD CLASSROOM

Children love to play with water just as they do with sand. More classrooms, in fact, have a water table than a sand table. Wellhousen and Crowther (2004) tell us: "Water is a magical medium. For centuries, water has been used to soothe, relax, teach, enjoy, and sustain. Water play is a wonderful medium to use with children. It is familiar as children are in contact with water every day. They drink it, wash, play, and bathe in it" (p. 66).

The table itself can fit into almost any location in the classroom. But like a sand table, it should be **near a shelf where water toys can be stored** so that children see what is available for them to use on their own. Give them plenty of time for free exploration. Children seem to be mesmerized by the sight, sound, and feel of water splashing. Watch how they pour it over and over.

It is **not necessary to have a free-standing water table**. Large plastic pans can serve just as well. Place them on a table near the water toy shelf; or hang the toys from a Peg-board™ along with four plastic aprons for four children at a time. No need

Children are mesmerized by the sight of water splashing.

to fill the pans or table to the top. **A few inches of water can be just as much fun** for the children and will keep them and the floor fairly dry. In order to avoid squabbles over favorite toys, **have more than one of the egg beaters and large plastic basters on hand**. Other toys can include: plastic bottles, squeeze bottles, pitchers, hoses, funnels, and eye droppers. These toys can later be exchanged for the ones you will be using for special activities.

ACTIVITIES TO PROMOTE MOTOR SKILLS

The small-motor skills of **filling a pitcher and emptying it** are satisfying actions for all children at a water table. They will do it over and over, until someone decides to **fill up all the plastic bottles**. Then these will be emptied and filled—but with some difficulty until someone discovers using a funnel. Children also learn to **fill up small squeeze bottles under the water and then squirt them out**, following the rule of squirting only inside the water table: this is wonderful for strengthening finger muscles.

Another small-motor skill involves **making bubbles in water. Challenge children to find more than one way to do it**. Some will splash or twirl their hands. Others will make bubbles by squirting the squeeze bottles under water, squirting the basters under water, or beating the eggbeaters in the water as fast as they can. After each of your four water table workers has tried everything, ask them what will happen if you **add a little liquid soap**. Bubbles galore!

Another day put liquid soap in the water and have the children bubble it up for **washing the baby dolls, doll clothes, or plastic dishes**. Have a separate pan with clear water for rinsing. Children can squeeze out the clothes and dry them on a drying rack or the hangers you bring in. The dishes and dolls can be dried with towels: more good small-motor exercise.

ACTIVITIES TO PROMOTE COGNITIVE CONCEPTS

As with all of the activities you set up at the various learning centers, the Water Table should be included when the children are **exploring the concepts of floating and sinking**. Have a **basket of materials on hand that will float or sink**: Styrofoam, corks, wood pieces, pencils, pieces of paper, magnets, nails, stones, small toy trucks, figures of people, plastic water toys. Talk about floating and sinking. Ask children to guess what each item will do: float or sink. Children who understand the concepts of *up* and *down* sometimes get confused and say, "The nail floated down," or "The cork sinked up." Bring in different items from time to time and let the children experiment.

Talk about boats and how they float. Would the children like to make their own sailboats? Put out pieces of Styrofoam, toothpicks, glue, and little squares of white or colored paper to be cut for sails. Can the children figure out how to **stick**

the toothpicks into the Styrofoam to make a boat? Most can cut their own sails and glue them onto a vertical toothpick mast. If they would like to **hold a regatta**, have them take turns blowing their boats across the water table. Be sure to take photos of the Styrofoam navy for the children's scrapbooks. This activity may continue for many days as each group of four children makes its own boats and sails them.

ACTIVITIES TO PROMOTE EMOTIONAL DEVELOPMENT

Water in the classroom has always been considered therapeutic. You can **help a distressed child squeeze away her bad feelings with sponges of different sizes** or a baster, or by filling plastic bottles and pouring them out, or by turning an egg beater to make bubbles, or simply by swishing her hands around in the water (Beaty, 2006, p. 86). If the large water table is too much for a distressed child to manage, fill a smaller tub with water and set it aside for her to play in until she feels better.

ACTIVITIES TO PROMOTE CREATIVE DEVELOPMENT

As with sand play, water play can best promote creative development through children's dramatic play of making up or acting out their own scenarios or stories from books. Children who have been to **an aquarium or sea world park, may want to convert the water table** into such a park using figures of vinyl sea creatures such as whales, dolphins, sharks, rays, turtles, octopuses, seals, lobsters, and fish from educational supply companies or toy stores. Home aquarium stores also have plastic underwater figures including scuba divers and hard hat divers.

An **excellent book as a lead-in for converting the water table to a sea aquarium is** *My Visit to the Aquarium* (Aliki, 1993). A big brother narrates the story of taking his little brother and sister to a large public aquarium. They walk under a tropical coral reef, see a giant kelp forest where a scuba diver feeds large fish, visit a huge shark pool, and finally the pool where dolphins and beluga whales leap, dive, whistle, and splash. After reading this book **put out your fish and marine creature props for small groups of children** to play with at the water table. Try to catch their conversations. Are any of them pretending to be divers or attendants at an aquarium? Would any of them like to **tell their story to the tape recorder for others to hear** later?

A pretend trip to the beach is another occasion for creative water play. Read to a small group at a time *Seashells by the Seashore* (Berkes, 2002) about how Sue and her brother Ben collect shells along the seashore for their grandma's birthday. Not only is it a counting book as they collect 12 different shells, but also a shell identification guide with a cardboard tear-out sheet showing all 12 of the shells and more together. **Bring in seashells and place them in the water table for the children to collect and identify**, making this a cognitive activity as well. Can they match each shell with one from the book? Some children may not yet understand that this is how you learn the name of each shell.

Another wonderful book for a hilarious pretend activity is *When an Elephant Comes to School* (Ormerod, 2005), showing what happens when an elephant tries out every activity in a preschool classroom. Just imagine what it does with water and sand.

Have children choose to be a pretend elephant and act out this story. Use your own imagination and other picture books in your collection to plan other fun activities at the water table.

TEACHER'S ROLE AT THE WATER TABLE

As with the sand table, the teacher must also make sure the water table is safe. This means changing the water every two to three days to discourage the growth of bacteria, and leaving the table uncovered at night (Coughlin *et al.* 1997, p. 318). The table and toys should also be disinfected at least once a week. It is also important to have children wash their hands before they engage in water play. The area around the table needs to be kept dry to prevent slipping. Some teachers place rubber mats on the floor.

Be sure to observe each child as he or she plays in the water table using the Child Interaction Form. A great deal of parallel play usually goes on as the children pursue solitary activities while standing close to one another. Listen for and record conversation whenever you can. Children should play undisturbed most of the time, but occasionally you can comment on what they are doing or ask them a question or two. You may want to discuss possible new activities at the table to get their input on curriculum ideas.

WOOD IN THE EARLY CHILDHOOD CLASSROOM

Of all the learning centers discussed in this text, the Woodworking Center is the one most frequently omitted in many early childhood classrooms. Yet children seem to love wood. If you watch them in the Block Center you will see them moving wooden blocks around, picking up armfuls, and building with great abandon. Perhaps, it is the teachers who are not so enamored of woodworking. If teachers view pounding and sawing as something foreign that they would rather not be involved with, then a woodworking area will probably not be a part of their curriculum. Teachers in the know, however, have this to say about woodworking:

"Working with wood is a great adventure! With all the varied attributes—types, textures, weights, colors, and smells—wood offers children a total experience with opportunities to explore, discover, and create. As they hammer, saw, sand, glue, and paint wood, children develop fine and gross-motor skills—improving their coordination and control. Best of all, woodworking is physical fun that is endlessly challenging!" (Feeney, 1991, p. 24).

You need to take these words to heart and be sure to include a Woodworking Center in your classroom. To start out, you will **need hammers and nails of different sizes. Small adult hammers are best**. White pine, spruce, and poplar are

Woodworking is physical fun that is endlessly challenging.

soft woods that children can hammer into most easily. **Some teachers prefer using ceiling tiles instead** of wood at first because children have better control over hammer and nails with this softer substance. This is especially important for children with limited muscular strength. Children can also pound nails more easily through leather and foam boards (Beaty, 2008, p. 90).

Not every program can afford a workbench, but children can still have the experience of pounding if teachers provide them with tree stumps. **Children can pound nails in the tops of the stumps over and over**. After this mastery level of self-directed discovery, some may even pound their nails into designs.

The **woodworking area needs to be away from the main traffic lanes** in the classroom; perhaps in a corner or somewhere the pounding will not bother the children who are involved in quieter activities. **Children should wear safety goggles**, and love to, because it is such an adult thing to do. **Tools and equipment can be stored on a nearby shelf or hung on a Peg-board against an outline of their shape**. Most programs limit the woodworking area to two children at time.

ACTIVITIES TO PROMOTE MOTOR DEVELOPMENT

Pounding a nail with a hammer into a board or stump takes well-developed eye-hand coordination. Children need to learn to hold the hammer properly, hold the nail straight, and bring the hammer down firmly on top of the nail. Nails with broad heads are best. Once children learn how, they can practice to their hearts' content. **When the top of a stump has been completely covered, it can be sawed off and used again**. Put several slices of tree stumps on a table with a towel underneath to absorb the sound, and let children pound nails for the fun of pounding and the practice of eye-hand coordination. Although using a saw promotes large muscle development, most preschool children do not have the strength or coordination to use one.

As a lead-in to hammering read *I Love Tools!* (Sturges, 2006), the story of a boy and his sister who help their mother and father build a house for a bluebird. The boy uses a ruler and a square to measure the size while his father saws the boards. A hammer pounds a nail and then pulls it out again. A chisel and mallet make a groove and a drill drills a hole. They glue the parts, twist them together with a clamp, and then sand the wood smooth—all in rhyme. An outline of each tool appears on the end pages. **Have your children make their own outlines of the tools they use**, which can be gathered together **for a class book about tools**.

Reading a book is, of course, fine, but not necessary to motivate children's hammering, for as Leithead (1996) points out: "As soon as children are old enough to grasp a hammer, few can resist the urge to pound nails" (p. 17).

ACTIVITIES TO PROMOTE EMOTIONAL DEVELOPMENT

Pounding nails into wood has another use in an early childhood classroom. It is an **excellent method for letting off steam harmlessly when a child is upset** or out-of-sorts. Let him or her pound out their frustrations. They can help themselves to nails, a hammer, and pieces of wood to pound together. Or they can pound nails into a stump. Sometimes **playing appropriate music on a cassette or CD player to accompany the pounding will help children release tension**.

Being able to use adult tools like this also gives children a sense of accomplishment and increases self-esteem. As they become more adept at using the tools, they may even **create a simple product such as a boat or car—another boost for their self-esteem**.

ACTIVITIES TO PROMOTE CREATIVITY

Once children have completed the mastery level of self-discovery by pounding nails into stumps over and over, some of them may progress into the meaning stage. This is where creativity comes into play. This is where they begin making simple objects and naming them. Be sure to have plenty of wood scraps on hand of different sizes and shapes, as well as pieces of leather, bottle caps, spools, cardboard cutouts, and other materials that can be pounded together to represent something.

Some children like to make their own props to create or reenact a story. A truck to carry dinosaur bones in the sand table may consist of a piece of wood with spool wheels. A rocket ship to Mars may be a vertical piece of wood with smaller vertical pieces hammered to each side. A boat for the water table may be a triangular piece of wood with a square cabin on top. Once a few children begin creating objects, many more will want to try it. Be prepared.

TEACHER'S ROLE IN THE WOODWORKING CENTER

Safety should be the main concern of the teacher in the woodworking center. Be sure the center is not in the main traffic area and is sectioned off with shelves or a table. Tools should be hung on a Peg-board or kept separately on a shelf when not in use. You **may need to demonstrate the use of a tool and remain in the center** while the children try it. It is not necessary to stand over the children whenever they are in the center, but you should keep an eye on what is happening. **You should model and reinforce the idea that tools and nails must be picked up and put away after use**. Children can help you check the floor for spilled nails and wood scraps. You may also want to **contact a parent who is a carpenter** or who makes things with wood to come in and demonstrate his or her skill.

You can help and **support beginners and children with special needs**, so that they too have a chance to participate successfully. It may mean bringing in materials other than wood for them to pound on. In addition, you or a staff member should be observing and recording children's use of the Wood Center on the Child Interaction Form. Children can sign up to use the Wood Center or take one of the two necklaces you provide. Be sure to **take photos of each child's work** in the center, whether it is pounding nails in a stump or making an object. Mounted photos of children's work or products can stimulate other children to participate in the Woodworking Center. In addition be sure to **observe and record each child's use** of the Woodworking Center on the Child Interaction Form.

IDEAS IN CHAPTER 13

1. *Setting up the sand center*
   a. Not necessary to have free-standing sand or water tables
   b. Large plastic dishpans can be set on tables

2. *Promoting motor skills*
   a. What children do with sand depends on materials you provide
   b. Sand table is an excellent follow-up of field trip to construction site, beach
   c. Use wet sand for molding towers

3. *Promoting cognitive skills*
   a. Use measuring cups to make cake at sand table
   b. Search for treasure using magnets
   c. Bury plastic dinosaurs in sand and search for them

4. *Promoting language skills*
   a. Involve children in activities to promote conversation
   b. Tell and tape-record stories about their structures

5. *Promoting social development*
   a. Use stories as catalyst to form social groups

6. *Promoting emotional development*
   a. Set up private sand tub for upset children
   b. Use sand trays for children's relaxation

7. *Promoting creative development*
   a. Use books and props for creating dramatic play episodes
   b. Stand set of props on shelf for at least a week at a time

8. *Setting up water play*
   a. Set up water table near shelf where water toys are stored
   b. A few inches of water is enough
   c. Have more than one of favorite toys

9. *Promoting motor skills*
   a. Fill pitchers, plastic bottles, squeeze bottles
   b. Make bubbles in water
   c. Wash baby dolls, clothes, and dishes

10. *Promoting cognitive concepts*

    a. Explore concepts of floating, sinking

    b. Make boats out of Styrofoam

11. *Promoting emotional development*

    a. Have upset child squeeze away bad feelings with sponges

12. *Promoting creative development*

    a. Convert water table to aquarium

    b. Read book; put out marine creature props

    c. Put seashells in water; children identify them

    d. Read and act out elephant story

13. *Setting up Woodworking Center*

    a. Use stumps for pounding

    b. Use small adult hammers, ceiling tiles

    c. Children should wear safety goggles

    d. Store tools on Peg-board or nearby shelf

14. *Promoting motor development*

    a. Practice hammering on top of stump

    b. When top is covered, saw it off

    c. Read *I Love Tools!*; make outlines of tools

15. *Promoting emotional development*

    a. Have upset children pound to let off steam

    b. Play appropriate pounding music

    c. Create simple products; boost self-esteem

16. *Promoting creativity*

    a. Make own wooden props to reenact story

17. *Teacher's role in Woodworking Center*

    a. Demonstrate uses of tools

    b. Model and reinforce rules for using materials

    c. Contact parent who is a carpenter

    d. Support beginners and children with special needs

    e. Take photos of each child's work

    f. Observe and record children in center

DISCUSSION QUESTIONS

1. If you had a choice of having a sand table or a water table, which would you choose and why?

2. How can you prevent children's activities at the water table from getting out of hand?

3. How can you best promote creativity in sand or water play?

4. How would you deal with a parent who is upset because the children are using adult hammers?

5. What can children learn from pounding nails into a stump?

TRY IT YOURSELF

1. Observe each of the children using sand, water, or wood and record their actions on the Child Interaction Chart. How would you interpret this data?

2. Read one of the books suggested to motivate pretending at the water table; put out appropriate props and record what happens.

3. After a field trip put out a tub of sand, appropriate props and books, and record how the children pretend about the trip.

4. Bring in two tree stumps, several hammers, nails of different sizes, and observe and record how children use the center.

5. Have children trace the woodworking tools and dictate a story about them.

REFERENCES CITED

Beaty, J. J. (2008). *Skills for preschool teachers*. Upper Saddle River, NJ: Merrill/Prentice Hall.

Beaty, J. J. (2006). *50 early childhood guidance strategies*. Upper Saddle River, NJ: Merrill/Prentice Hall.

Coughlin, P. A., Hansen, K. A., Heller, D., Kaufman, R. K., Stolberg, J. R., & Walsh, K. B. (1997). *Creating child-centered classrooms: 3-5 year olds*. Washington, DC: Children's Resources International, Inc.

Feeney, L. (1991, April). The wonders of working with wood. *Pre-K Today*. Scholastic.

Hogben, J. & Wasley, D. (1996). *Learning in early childhood: What does it mean in practice?* Education Department of South Australia: Hyde Park Press.

Leithead, M. (1996). Happy hammering … a hammering activity center with built-in success. *Young Children, 51*(3), 12.

Wellhousen, K. & Crowther, I. (2004). *Creating effective learning environments*. Clifton Park, NY: Cengage Learning.

Wheat, R. (1995). Help children work through emotional difficulties—Sand trays are great! *Young Children, 51*(1), 82–83.

Other Sources

Cherry, C. (1972). *Creative art for the developing child*. Belmont, CA: Fearon.

Diffily, D., Donaldson, E., & Sassman, C. (2001). *The Scholastic book of early childhood learning centers*. New York: Scholastic Professional Books.

Isbell, R. (1995). *The learning center book*. Mt. Rainier, MD: Gryphon House.

Seefeldt, C. & Galper, A. (2002). *Active experiences for active children*. Upper Saddle River, NJ: Merrill/Prentice Hall.

Children's Books

Aliki (1993). *My visit to the aquarium*. New York: HarperCollins.

Barton, B. (1990). *Bones, bones, dinosaur bones*. New York: HarperCollins.

Berkes, M. (2002). *Seashells by the seashore*. Nevada City, CA: Dawn Publications.

McMullan, K. & McMullan, J. (2006). *I'm dirty*. New York: HarperCollins.

Olson, K. C. (2004). *Construction countdown*. New York: Henry Holt & Company.

Ormerod, J. (2005). *When an elephant comes to school*. New York: Orchard Books.

Roosa, K. (2001). *Beach day*. New York: Clarion Books.

Sobel, J. (2003). *B is for bulldozer*. San Diego, CA: Harcourt.

Sturges, P. (2006). *I love tools!* New York: HarperCollins.

Wells, R. (1997). *Bunny cakes*. New York: Dial Books for Young Readers.

PLANNING FOR SOMETHING TO HAPPEN

There is an old cliché that states, "If you want something to happen you must plan for it to happen." Furthermore, you can add, "if you want something wonderful to happen with the children in your classroom, then you must make wonderful plans." This statement is true. Although your program can proceed without a great deal of formal planning once you have set it up, you cannot expect particular results to occur unless you have made plans for them to occur. Setting up your classroom into the 13 learning centers described in the previous chapters is the foundation for such ongoing planning. They address the principal theme of the Appropriate Practices Curriculum: "Let the environment do the teaching."

Now it is up to you, your staff, and your children to plan particular activities for children, based on their needs and interests, that will promote their development of physical, cognitive, language, social, emotional, and creative skills. Such planning is not a chore, but a challenge: the directions for a marvelous learning adventure that you and the children can pursue together. Making such plans with staff members and children can be as exciting as carrying them out.

MAKING PLANS PERSONAL FOR CHILDREN

In each of the 13 learning centers, we have focused on young children and their interactions with materials, activities, and other children. We have observed individual differences in children's interactions and discussed activities that can help them proceed through manipulation, mastery, and meaning levels as they create their own knowledge through exploratory play. At all times we have noted that the key to success in helping youngsters develop and learn has been "making learning personal."

LEARNING LADDER
ACTION CHANT

(Hold up fingers)

Lets's climb up the ladder,
  One step up;
Where we start won't matter,
  Two steps up;
Every rung goes higher,
  Three steps up;
What if we should tire?
  Four steps up;
There are friends to go up,
  Five steps up;
They won't let us slow up.
  Six steps up;
Now the air is clearer,
  Seven steps up;
Look, the top is nearer!
  Eight steps up;
Oh, we're up so high now!
  Nine steps up;
Maybe we can fly now!
  Ten steps up: Whee-ee-ee!!!

Making plans with staff members can be as exciting as carrying them out.

Once again, in curriculum planning we must focus on the personal aspects of planning for children. Children ages 3, 4, and 5 years old respond best to materials and activities that speak to them personally. The overall curriculum must also speak to children at this personal level. Then they will respond at a personal level and become deeply involved in their own learning in the self-directed learning centers you have provided.

The most successful curriculum plans will be those that begin with the child and branch out in various directions. They will include the child's family, friends, pets, neighborhood, community, and, finally, the natural environment surrounding the child. You will need to write out these plans in a simple, straightforward manner for you and your staff to visualize and discuss as you create the plans.

Do this preliminary planning together at a planning session early in the year before the children come. To **begin your plans with a focus on the child**, take a sheet of newsprint and write the words "The Child" in the center. Then, in a clockwise circular manner around "The Child," list the principal personal influences in a child's life. You might decide on the previously mentioned influences: family, friends, pets, neighborhood, community, and natural environment as the most important. Under each of these topics, make a list of subtopics relating to each that you may wish to pursue during the year.

Be sure that all of the staff members contribute their own ideas to this diagram. Take time to discuss each idea in this preliminary planning session. Cross off and add to the diagram as necessary. This is only a beginning: nothing should be etched in stone.

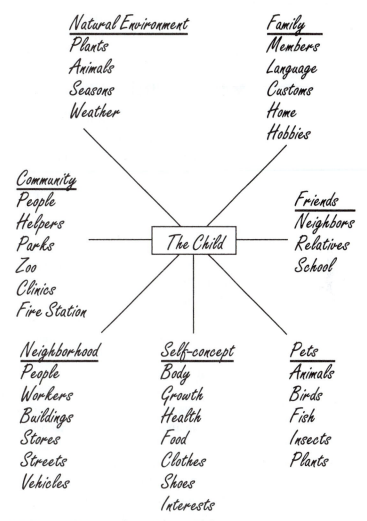

Figure 14-1 Personal Curriculum Content Web.

What you have created is a **web of personal curriculum content**. Every item on this web should relate to the child in a personal manner (see Figure 14-1). Such a web can be the basis of curriculum planning for the entire year. Any of the items on this web can be converted to a curriculum theme that will be meaningful to children and useful to your planning. Each item, in fact, can be the theme of its own web.

Using webs like this in curriculum planning is an effective way for the entire staff to contribute to short-range and long-range plans. Not only are such webs practical devices in the curriculum planning process, but the creators of these webs—you and your staff—can see at a glance how the activities being planned can relate to one another and to the children. As Workman and Anziano (1993) tell us: "Semantic webbing, especially the integration and *connections* among webs, may become the central feature of any curricular approach. Developmentally appropriate activities and outcomes for children result from teachers responding to the children's interests" (p. 4).

MAKING INTEGRATED PLANS

The next step for you and your staff is to choose a theme from the personal content web. At the beginning of the year, you may decide to select from the topic "Family" because of its familiarity to the children. On the other hand, some programs prefer to start with "The Neighborhood" because children need and want to learn about the new place where they will be staying during the day.

Whatever theme you select, this topic and its subtopics can carry the program for several weeks, depending on how much detail you and the children want to go into. As the year progresses you and your staff (and even the children) will be selecting other themes that seem appropriate from the personal content web, again depending upon the children's needs and interests.

How will you integrate this topic and its subtopics into your curriculum? Gestwicki (2007) says: "Integrated curriculum includes the various subject matter disciplines—such as science, mathematics, social studies, the arts, technology, and literacy—in common activities, rather than as separate branches of knowledge" (p. 67).

Such a curriculum works well in the learning centers of the self-directed learning environment.

To integrate the chosen theme into all 13 of the learning centers, you should next **create another curriculum web with the particular theme at the center of the web**; have your staff members contribute ideas to it. For example, **a curriculum web based on the theme "The Neighborhood" should begin with those words written at the center** of the newsprint. **Around the outside place the names of each learning center**. Under each learning center, have staff members brainstorm ideas for activities that will support such a theme. List the ideas as they are expressed. Afterwards you can discuss the various ideas and refine the list together by adding or deleting activities. Your *Learning Centers Web* based on "The Neighborhood," showing 10 of your learning centers may look something like Figure 14-2.

IMPLEMENTING PLANS

Once the theme has been selected and the activities for each learning center decided on, the room can be arranged to support the theme. Often a new theme begins with a special activity in one or more of the centers. In this case, the teacher in charge of the Block Center plans to take a different small group of children on a brief field trip around the outside of the building every day for the first week until all the children have had a turn. On another week small groups will go on a brief walking field trip

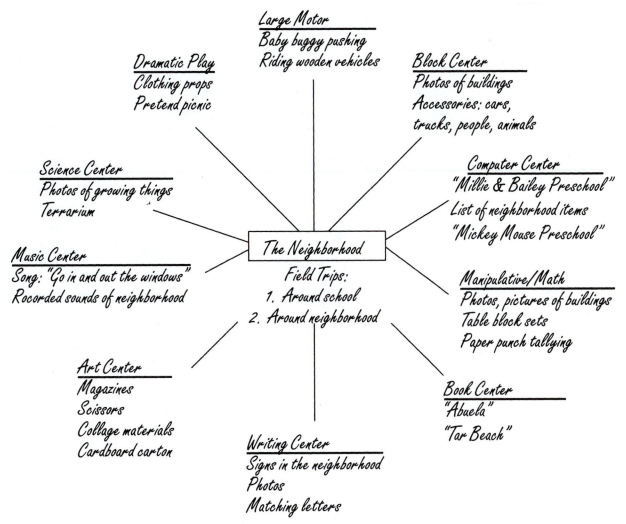

Figure 14-2 Learning Centers Web.

around the neighborhood. For both trips they will take with them a camera to record the sights and a tape recorder to record the sounds of the neighborhood.

In the Block Center, a display of pictures of buildings from magazines and then the photos of buildings taken on the field trips may stimulate children's block building. Accessories will include items that relate to this neighborhood, such as miniature cars, trucks, emergency vehicles, people, community helpers, animals, and street signs. Your neighborhood may look different and need different accessories.

Many of the children are not, of course, at the mastery or meaning level of building, especially at the beginning of the year, so they cannot be expected to build representations of buildings. Nevertheless, the idea that the buildings they observe

Some children will try building; others will observe.

in the neighborhood can be represented by blocks is an appropriate concept for them to consider. Some will try their hand at building. Others will observe or merely line up the blocks.

Other learning centers can contribute to the neighborhood theme in a variety of ways.

Art Center: Have scissors and magazines available at some point during the month. Children may want to tear or **cut out pictures like the things they have seen in the neighborhood**. They can paste together a collage of the neighborhood pictures. Another week, you can bring in a large cardboard carton, cut out a door and a window, and then put out paints for the children to paint their house.

Music Center: The children can sing a song about their house or their neighborhood. Make up the words to a well-known melody such as "Go In and Out the Windows."

Go round and round the building,
Go round and round the building,
Go round and round the building,
As we have done today.
Go up and down the sidewalk,
Go up and down the sidewalk,
Go up and down the sidewalk,
As we have done today.

They can make motions with hands and body, or move around in a circle or in a follow-the-leader line.

Book Center: Books about buildings can be read by the teachers to small groups of children during the month. A book such as *Tar Beach* (Ringgold, 1991) or *Abuela* (Dorros, 1991), which shows a bird's-eye view of the buildings in New York City, can be reread and talked about.

Writing Center: The children in this center can go outside with the teacher and **look for signs in the neighborhood**. The teacher can write down the words on the signs spotted by the children or take photos of them. Back in the Writing Center the teacher can **print these signs on poster board**. Children can try to find and match the letters on the signs from their sets of magnetic letters or alphabet blocks.

Manipulative/Math Center: Let children **build houses and other buildings from sets of table blocks**, such as Legos or bristle blocks. Be sure to take a photo of their buildings along with the builders for display in the center. Another day they can look out the window and tally the cars they see with a paper punch.

Science Center: This center can challenge the children to **find out what growing things are in the neighborhood**. If it is a city neighborhood the children may see plants growing in someone's window, trees in a park, a dandelion in a sidewalk crack, or weeds on a vacant lot. Photos can record the findings. Children's questions and comments can help lead the teacher in charge of this center to particular follow-up activities, such as making a terrarium.

Dramatic Play Center: This center can feature people the children see in the neighborhood. Bring in clothes and props and have a neighborhood get-together for children to dress up like the people they have seen: the mail carrier, police officer, street cleaner, taxi driver, or housepainter can **have a pretend neighborhood picnic** in the center.

Large-Motor Center: What kinds of movements did the children discover on their field trip around the neighborhood? Was someone walking a dog? Riding a bike? Driving a truck? Pushing a baby stroller? **The Walking Ring can feature baby-stroller pushing** for a few days—or riding on large wooden vehicles. Drivers of the vehicles can wear a truck driver's cap or a taxi driver's hat.

ADVANTAGES OF CURRICULUM WEBBING

As new needs or fresh ideas emerge from the staff or the children, new learning center webs can be created, from which an ongoing curriculum can be developed. Using curriculum webs like this makes planning an active, and interesting part of the everyday program. **Everyone, including the children, can have a say in the creation of a new web**. Webs are simple, easy to do, and flexible. There are no time constraints to limit how long a topic should be pursued. Staying with a theme long enough for children to gain understanding of concepts may take an unpredictable amount of time. But when themes do not work out, a new theme from a new web can easily replace it.

Webs like this need to be saved in order for teachers to have a record of what activities worked and what did not work with various groups of children. Teachers who use such curriculum webs as a part of their planning process have this to say, according to Workman and Anziano (1993): "The possibilities inherent in a webbed curriculum are virtually limitless. Each time a teacher or a child creates an interesting question or sees a relationship that he is interested in pursuing, the follow-up exploration can be documented and added to enrich the repertoire of possibilities for other children and teachers at other times. It becomes possible to document curriculum as it emerges uniquely with each group of children and teachers" (p. 9).

CHILD INPUT INTO THEME PLANNING

Themes like this can evolve from the children's own interests as they build with blocks, take field trips, try out new ideas, or ask questions about topics of interest. **Teachers in the various centers must listen carefully to what the children say and the questions they ask**. Teachers must ask children open-ended questions about the activities and jot down the children's answers. For example, Tiffany in the Block Center wants to know: "Why doesn't the new bridge fall in the river?" She is asking about the new bridge being built over a nearby river that they saw on their neighborhood field trip.

The teacher realizes that her ideas about bridge building come from an adult point of view. She asks the other children in the center what they think the reason is. Most of the children do not have an idea, but Gerald says: "It's on posts." Mikey adds: "Wires hold it up." From this discussion the teacher decides to change her plans for the Block Center for the rest of the week, and let the children experiment with their own bridge building.

The children are excited about trying to build their own bridges across a pretend classroom river. It is their suggestion to make a river out of blue paper. Then the children can try out building-block bridges across it. A number of the children are at the meaning stage of block building: they will be trying out various block configurations, from long quadruple blocks to shorter blocks on several pillars. Even children at the manipulation level may end up lining up blocks across the blue paper.

The teacher reads the book *Building a Bridge* (Begaye, 1993) to help get them started. This story prompts them to discuss whether one person should build a bridge or whether several people should build one together like the two girls in the book. They decide to do it both ways. The teacher, meanwhile, decides to continue the bridge-building theme for at least another week, perhaps longer, until all of the children have had a chance to try out their building skills. She takes pictures of each group's block bridge and mounts them in the Block Center. Later she will take small groups to visit the real bridge construction site from time to time and bring back reports about its progress to the class.

At the next staff planning session, the Block Center teacher suggests that the **staff members and children together make a curriculum web about bridges,** and brainstorm ideas for the other learning centers. Figure 14-3 shows what the web eventually looks like.

One of the teachers wonders if this plan contains too much about bridges in every learning center. Perhaps some of the centers should do other things. The children say no. Tiffany wants next week to be called "Bridge Week." Everyone votes for Tiffany's idea. This sends the teachers scrambling over the weekend to find books and materials to be used in their bridge activities. They are even able to locate one of the bridge construction workers who agree to come in during his lunch hour and talk about his work on the new river bridge.

From their own bookshelves the teacher finds two more books with bridge references: *The Three Billy Goats Gruff* (Galdone, 1973) and *Tar Beach* (Ringgold,

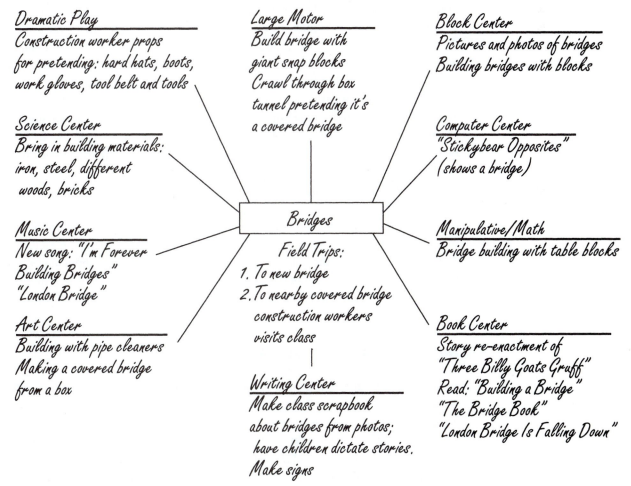

Figure 14-3 Learning Centers Web: Bridges.

1991). In Tar Beach Cassie, a little African American girl, flies over the George Washington Bridge in her imagination. Then the teacher finds the best one: *The Bridge Is Up!* (Bell, 2004), a simple story about a drawbridge that stops traffic, one vehicle after another, when it is up. Children have fun reenacting this book taking on the roles of bus, car, bike, truck, motorcycle, bulldozer, and tractor. Two other children become the bridge that stops the traffic when it is up and lets it go when it is down.

Another staff member brings in books with bridge themes from the public library: *The Bridge Book* (Carter, 1992), a nonfiction picture book with black-and-white drawings about bridges around the world, and *The Random House Book of How Things Were Built* (Brown, 1992), about famous buildings and bridges around the world.

The children quickly find pictures of the first Ironbridge in England and how it was built from the ends out to the middle, and the Golden Gate Bridge, with its gigantic cables and towers. There is even a picture in *The Bridge Book* of a covered bridge and a story about why it was built that way. The teacher reads the words that go with the pictures. This book ends with the words: "No two bridges are the same. Every bridge tells its own story; the story of the people who built it and the people who use it."

This statement prompts the children to decide to make two books of their own: one about the bridge being built across the river in their neighborhood and one about the bridges children are building in the classroom. They will dictate stories about each of the photos they have taken and put them together in their own bridge books. "Don't forget to tell about the people who use them," Tiffany reminds the children who are dictating their stories.

Be aware that once you have involved the children in planning, you need to follow through on many of their suggestions. However, let them know that not every suggestion can be followed, if this is the case. They may want to vote on which suggestions are most important to them. What an exciting experience it is for them to have input into their classroom's operation! As Casey and Lippman (1991) note: "Planning is a very important part of being successful both in school and throughout life. It has been shown that even children as young as three can be planners" (p. 52).

MONTHLY PLANNING SESSIONS

Set aside time for the staff to plan for the month ahead. A particular afternoon can be selected, such as the last Friday in the month. This is the time for the entire staff to gather and talk over what has occurred with children and activities over the past month, and to make plans for the next month. Many programs find that having **one staff member in charge of a particular learning center for a month at a time** works best.

Early childhood programs often have two or three staff members per classroom: a teacher, an assistant teacher, and an aide or volunteer. When this is the case, the

The monthly planning session is the time to discuss what works and what does not work.

learning centers can then be divided up, with **each adult in charge of four centers for a month at a time** and one of the teachers keeping an eye on a fifth center. Being in charge of a center means setting it up for the day and observing (often from a distance) to see that things progress smoothly. It does not mean that the adult must spend most of the class time within the learning center, because it is actually more appropriate for children to interact with materials and one another on their own.

In programs where space is at a premium, **learning centers can be combined to save space** and still provide separate activities for the children. For example, the Computer Center can be combined with the Manipulative/Math Center or with the Writing Center. The staff member who is the computer expert should **share** this **expertise with other staff members**, so that they, too, can help children enjoy computer activities. In another arrangement, the Book Center can be combined with the Writing Center.

Staff members can choose or be assigned to the centers. The lead teacher may decide to start out the year with the Block Center and its field trips around the neighborhood. Other staff members can then brainstorm and add ideas to the learning center web about how their particular learning centers will support the neighborhood theme week by week. Flexibility should be the key word. Some plans will be completed sooner than others. Not every plan works successfully. Some need refinement. Some need rethinking. The monthly planning session is the time to discuss such issues. Then when children come up with their own plans, these, too, can be integrated into learning center activities.

PLANS FOR INDIVIDUALS BASED ON 3-M OBSERVATIONS

The basis of your planning for individual children is the 3-M observations you and the staff have been making of children's interactions with materials and with one another in the learning centers. You have recorded information about the children's three levels of activity interaction (manipulation, mastery, and meaning), as well as their three types of social interaction (solitary play, parallel play, and cooperative play). Now you must record interpretive information on the back of the Child Interaction Form under the headings: "Accomplishments" and "Needs." Only then will you be able to fill in the third item on the form: "Plans." In order to make plans for individual children that will satisfy their observed needs, you must interpret the data you have recorded on the front of the form.

INTERPRETING RECORDED INFORMATION

The children's levels of interaction, along with their actions and words, are the basis for information recorded on the reverse side of the form under "Accomplishments." Next on the reverse side of the form comes "Needs." It is here that the observer must **interpret the data in order to determine a child's needs**. In addition to the recorded data, the interpreter should use knowledge of the child's ordinary behavior in the classroom.

For example, Leslie is 4 years old and has attended this particular program for the last 3 months. She spends a great deal of time in the Science Center with the animals. She watches the fish in the aquarium, making comments or asking questions about them. She feeds the guinea pig, helps clean out its cage, and likes to pick it up and carry it around. She is the one who named it "Whistler" for the noise it makes. However, everything she does in the Science Center is by herself.

The teacher checks on the data recorded about Leslie in the other centers, and asks the other staff members about Leslie's interactions. The teacher finds that Leslie enjoys painting at the easel in the Art Center; plays by herself in the Dramatic Play Center, often dressing the dolls, feeding them, and taking them for a ride in the baby stroller; and plays table games by herself in the Manipulative Center. Leslie has never been observed playing in the Block Center, the Computer Center, or the Writing Center. She sometimes looks at books by herself in either the Book Center or Science Center.

The teacher decides to put together a cumulative record of Leslie's interactions for purposes of interpretation and planning. After reviewing previously recorded data about Leslie and talking with other staff members, the teacher completes the Child Interaction Form shown in Table 14-1.

From these data the teacher makes the following interpretation on the back of the Child Interaction Form.

Child _Leslie W._   Observer _D.B._
Center _Dram. Play, Manip., Story, Art, Sci._   Date _9/15 – 11/15_

CHILD INTERACTION FORM
With Materials

Manipulation Level   Actions/Words
(Child moves materials around
without using them as intended.)

Mastery Level   Actions/Words
(Child uses materials
as intended, over and over.)

Dram. Play: Dresses and feeds dolls; rides dolls in buggy.
Manip.: Plays lotto, pegboard, number matching games.
Story/Sci.: Looks at books, esp. animal stories.
Art: Paints at easel—lines, circles, scribbles. (Fills many sheets.)

Meaning Level   Actions/Words
(Child uses materials in
new and creative ways.)

Sci.: Watches fish in aquarium. Asks, "What's that one's name? Can I feed him?" Feeds guinea pig,
talks to it; cleans cage; carries guinea pig around; names it "Whistler" for the noise it makes.

With Other Children

Solitary Play   Actions/Words
(Child plays with
materials by self.)

Plays by self in Art, Sci., Dram. Play, Manip. and Story Centers; talks to fish, guinea pig,
dolls and teachers; seldom talks with other children.

Parallel Play   Actions/Words
(Child next to others with same
materials but not involved with them.)

Did one group art project —painting a cardboard carton to be used for house in Dram. Play, but
worked parallel to others without talking.

Cooperative Play   Actions/Words
(Child plays together with
others and same materials.)

Participates in group singing, finger plays and circle games when led by teacher; sometimes talks
with other children during these games; knows words to songs and games.

Table 14-1   Child Interaction Form.

Accomplishments:

Strong interest in animals, animal stories, animal names; in painting; in matching games; in feeding animals and dolls; in looking at books.

Speaks in expanded sentences to teachers, animals, sometimes dolls; articulates clearly.

Is at mastery level in dramatic play, matching games, and art; at meaning level in science and animal activities.

Needs:

To interact with other children, talking to and playing with them.

To try out activities in Block, Computer, and Writing Centers.

To advance to meaning level in art, dramatic play, and math games.

PLANNING FOR THE INDIVIDUAL CHILD

In making plans for an individual child like Leslie, the teacher takes into consideration both her accomplishments and her needs. Then the teacher lists possible activities that will use Leslie's interests and accomplishments to help her fulfill her needs. To involve Leslie in playing with other children, for instance, the teacher decides it might be helpful for her to start with one other child. If this interaction works, the teacher will watch to see whether she makes connections with other children as well, whether the teacher needs to help her get involved in group activities, or whether Leslie needs more time to feel comfortable in the classroom.

The teacher then proposes on paper several ideas that will be discussed at one of the daily summary sessions or weekly planning sessions, and that may be implemented in the days to follow.

Plans:

1. Change classroom Job Chart to teams of two children instead of only one child for each job; add jobs of "feeding fish" and "washing doll clothes" to chart along with jobs of "feeding Whistler," "cleaning Whistler's cage"; two children will need to sign up for each job and work together.

2. Suggest that Leslie learn to play the computer program *The Tortoise and the Hare* along with a computer partner. If she likes using the computer, she might like the CD-ROM *Stellaluna*. Books are also available for both.

3. Bring in books *Sammy, the Classroom Guinea Pig* (Berenzy, 2005) and *Patches Lost and Found* (Kroll, 2001) for Leslie to look at with a friend.

4. Suggest that Leslie take a photo of Whistler with the class camera and make her own book about him in the Writing Center with the teacher's help.

WEEKLY PLANNING SESSIONS

Plans for Leslie as just noted will more likely be discussed and agreed upon at the weekly planning session. Then they will be implemented for as long as necessary. The Child Interaction Form will be returned to a Weekly Planning Folder for its results to be discussed next week. Did the plans work out? Is Leslie interacting with at least one other child? Should the plans continue to be implemented for another week or should other ideas be considered?

Planning sessions like this not only provide the opportunity for the entire staff to have input on the accomplishments and needs of individual children, but also to **make an ongoing evaluation of the plans for individuals**. Are the plans working out? Should they be continued? Are new plans necessary? The staff looks back at the needs of the child as indicated on the Child Interaction Form. Then they decide if these needs are being addressed by the plans. If not, new plans are made for the child.

LEARNING GOALS FOR INDIVIDUALS

Some programs prefer to make long-range plans for individuals in each of the classroom learning centers. After the child has been in the program long enough for the staff to become acquainted with him or her, the teachers look over recorded data on the child and decide on a set of learning goals. These are referred to at the monthly planning sessions that follow, and added to or changed as the year progresses. A sample set of "Learning Goals for Joel," dated October 1, reads as follows.

Block Center:

Joel is at the manipulative stage; help him progress to mastery of block building.

Computer Center:

Find program that Joel can "master"; pair him with child who knows program.

Manipulative/Math Center:

Can he count with counters rather than just playing with them?

Book Center:

Help him learn to sit still through a whole story.

Writing Center:

Interest him in using this center; he has not used it so far.

Art Center:

Interest him in using this center; he has not used it so far.

Music Center:

Joel listens, but does not participate in songs; help him become involved.

Science Center:

Joel shows great interest in insects and animals, but doesn't stay still long enough to accomplish projects; help him work with a partner on an insect project.

Dramatic Play Center:

Joel seems to avoid this center; involve him with a partner playing the role of a scientist or a jungle explorer; his language skills need developing; more practice in conversation.

Large-Motor Center:

Joel loves to run in the Running Rink; give him many experiences; have him help others to accomplish running games.

Learning Goals such as these are kept in Joel's folder from month to month. They **are shared with staff members at planning sessions and with parents at parent conferences**. The goals are then updated when appropriate at the monthly planning sessions. Thus the program stays responsive to the needs and interests of individuals throughout the year.

THE TOTAL GROUP: CIRCLE TIME

Is there any place for a total group activity within the self-directed learning environment? Yes, definitely. **It is important for individual children to feel a part of the total class** as well. Your plans should call for **activities that lend themselves to the performance of the entire group of children** together, such as songs,

Research has shown music to be one of the most successful circle-time activities.

fingerplays, storytelling (not book reading, which is better done in small groups), musical games, creative movement and dancing, large-motor games, and circle time.

Because "circle time" itself provides the framework for any or all of these activities, many programs schedule a daily circle time within which such activities can take place. **If circle time** is scheduled at the beginning of the daily sessions, its purpose is to **welcome the children and help them make the transition from home to school**, as well as to **introduce them to the activities available** in the various learning centers. If scheduled in the middle of the day, circle time often serves as a change of pace to speed things up or slow them down, and to **help children focus on what comes next**. Circle time at the end of the day helps children to recall what they did, to **clarify any questions or concerns** they might have, and to help them **make the transition from school to home** with a goodbye song or chant.

Whenever it is held, circle time should be planned to help the children focus their attention and interest on the activities at hand. Research has shown that the most successful circle-time activities are stories and music; the least successful is show-and-tell (McAfee, 1985). Whatever is planned, it should **start with a high-interest activity that involves the total group**, thus engaging everyone's attention. **Then a calming activity** such as a fingerplay or a story can slow things down and help to focus the children's attention on what individuals have to say.

In the Appropriate Practices Curriculum, this sort of total-group activity can help to pull together at the end of the day all of the separate activities performed by individuals and small groups in the learning centers, as children volunteer to report on what they have accomplished during the day. Children also can give the teachers information about the activities that interested them most. This interchange thus helps to **summarize the day's accomplishments** for both children and teachers. Teachers should make note of such comments for use during the daily summary session.

DAILY SUMMARY SESSION

At the end of each day, the staff briefly **evaluates the activities in the various learning centers**. Were they carried out successfully by the teachers and the children? **How did the children respond? Should there be any changes for the next day? Activity ideas and changes are noted on file cards** that are **placed in a file box to be used in weekly and monthly planning sessions**.

The use of activity file cards captures the spirit of the moment, encourages creative ideas, and helps curriculum planning to be a challenge for the teachers, not a chore. **For ideas that work especially well, some staff members award themselves a "Good Job" sticker on their cards**, calling attention to activities they may want to use in the future. Because each staff member has direct input into daily, weekly, and monthly planning, each tends to give more time and energy in making such plans. Ideas also blossom when each staff member is responsible for what happens on a daily basis in his or her particular learning center.

IN CONCLUSION

Look back again to the first chapter of this text. What were your own expectations for gaining information, ideas, and applications about an Appropriate Practices Curriculum? Have you met them? Make a list of ideas you would like to apply from each of the chapters. Talk to your coworkers and have them add their ideas. Then start with one learning center and one child observation at a time as you begin to implement the new ideas.

When you develop excitement about the activities you and your coworkers have proposed, the whole program takes on a new life. The Appropriate Practices Curriculum thus applies to staff members as well as to children. And when **teachers are enthusiastic about the curriculum, the children reflect the same zest about their learning**. The classroom thus becomes a stimulant for everyone, and the ripples of excitement started by self-direction spread out into the lives of each child and each teacher involved.

IDEAS IN CHAPTER 14

1. *Making yearlong plans*

    a. Discuss overall topics with staff at the beginning of the year

    b. Begin your plans with a focus on the child

    c. Make a "personal curriculum content web" diagram that includes topics about the child and his or her environment

2. *Deciding how learning centers can contribute to "The Neighborhood" theme*

    a. Make a second web that includes topics about the neighborhood under each learning center

    b. Print signs in the Writing Center found in the neighborhood

    c. Build buildings with table blocks in the Manipulative/Math Center

    d. Discover on a field trip what growing things live in the school neighborhood

    e. Have a pretend picnic in the Dramatic Play Center for "people in the neighborhood"

    f. Feature baby-stroller pushing in the Walking Ring

3. *Having children contribute to theme planning*

    a. Have teachers listen to questions children ask and provide answers

    b. Have children and staff members make a curriculum web together

4. *Conducting weekly and monthly planning sessions*
   a. Set aside time to plan for the week or month ahead
   b. Have *one* staff member in charge of particular learning centers for a month at a time
   c. Have each staff member in charge of four centers at a time
   d. Combine certain learning centers if space is a problem
   e. Share expertise with one another (e.g., computer expertise)

5. *Making plans for individuals based on 3-M observations*
   a. Base planning for individual children on 3-M observations
   b. Use child's interests and accomplishments to help fulfill his or her needs

6. *Conducting weekly planning sessions*
   a. Do an ongoing evaluation of plans for individual children
   b. Develop learning goals for individuals to be shared with staff and parents

7. *Conducting circle time*
   a. Help children feel a part of the total group
   b. Have activities that lend themselves to total group involvement
   c. Use circle time to help children make the transition from home to school, to introduce new activities, to clarify activities, or to make the transition from school to home
   d. Start with a high-interest activity that involves the total group, followed by a calming activity

8. *Conducting daily summary sessions*
   a. Spend time at the summary session at the end of the day to share information about children and to plan for the next day
   b. Evaluate the various activities in the learning centers
   c. Note changes on Daily Schedule File cards
   d. File cards by subject in a file box at the end of the week
   e. Award yourself a sticker on your cards for outstanding activities
   f. Be enthusiastic about the curriculum, and children will reflect the same attitude

DISCUSSION QUESTIONS

1. Why should you plan for something to happen if the learning centers are already set up?

2. How do you make plans personal for children?

3. How can curriculum webs help staff members have direct input in planning?

4. How can a curriculum web be the basis for planning for the entire year?

5. How can each learning center be integrated into the curriculum plans?

TRY IT YOURSELF

1. Make a curriculum web by yourself on the theme "The Family."

2. Make a different curriculum web with other staff members and children on the same theme. How are the two webs different? How are they the same?

3. What can you do if your plans do not work out well, and the children seem more interested in an idea of their own?

4. How can each of the learning centers contribute to the theme "Children's Pets"?

5. Attend a weekly or monthly planning session and write out plans for an individual child based on observations recorded on the Child Interaction Form and interpreted by you.

REFERENCES CITED

Casey, M. B. & Lippman, M. (1991). Learning to plan through play. *Young Children* 46 (4), 52–58.

Gestwicki, C. (2007). *Developmentally appropriate practice: Curriculum and development in early education* (3rd ed.). Clifton Park, NY: Cengage Learning.

McAfee, O. D. (1985). Circle time: Getting past "Two Little Pumpkins." *Young Children* 40(6), 24–29.

Workman, S. & Anziano, M. C. (1993). Curriculum webs: Weaving connections from children to teachers. *Young Children* 48(2), 4–9.

Other Sources

Jones, E. & Nimmo, J. (1994). *Emergent curriculum*. Washington, DC: National Association for the Education of Young Children.

Seefeldt, C. (Ed.). (1999). *The early childhood curriculum: Current findings in theory and practice*. New York: Teachers College Press.

Seefeldt, C. & Wasik, B. A. (2006). *Early education: Three-, four-, and five-year-olds go to school*. Upper Saddle River, NJ: Merrill/Prentice Hall.

Wortham, S. C. (2006). *Early childhood curriculum: Developmental bases for learning and teaching*. Upper Saddle River, NJ: Merrill/Prentice Hall.

Children's Books

Begaye, L. S. (1993). *Building a bridge*. Flagstaff, AZ: Northland.*

Bell, B. (2004). *The bridge is up*. New York: HarperCollins.*

Berenzy, A. (2005). *Sammy, the classroom guinea pig*. New York: Henry Holt.*

Brown, D. J. (1992). *The Random House book of how things were built*. New York: Random House.

Carter, R. (1992). *The bridge book*. New York: Simon & Schuster.

Galdone, P. (1973). *The three billy goats Gruff*. New York: Clarion.

Kroll, S. (2001). *Patches lost and found*. Delray Beach, FL: Winslow Press.

Ringgold, F. (1991). *Tar beach*. New York: Crown.*

Note: Asterisk represents Multicultural book.

Chapter 1   **COME IN**

Chapter 2   **TEACHER**

D. J. Zeigler

Good mor-ning tea-cher, how do you do, good mor-ning tea-cher,

I'm fine too; good after-noon tea-cher I want to state, good

Af-ter-noon tea-cher I feel great!

Chapter 3   **BLOCKS**

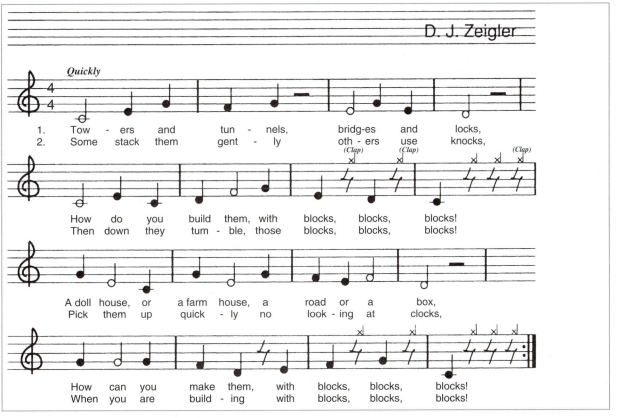

D. J. Zeigler

Quickly

1. Tow - ers and tun - nels, bridg-es and locks,
2. Some stack them gent - ly oth - ers use knocks,

(Clap) (Clap) *(Clap)*

How do you build them, with blocks, blocks, blocks!
Then down they tum - ble, those blocks, blocks, blocks!

A doll house, or a farm house, a road or a box,
Pick them up quick - ly no look - ing at clocks,

How can you make them, with blocks, blocks, blocks!
When you are build - ing with blocks, blocks, blocks!

Chapter 4   **COMPUTER**

D. J. Zeigler

Disk in the disk drive shut down the door

Turn on the mon-i-tor feet on the floor

Boot up the pro - gram what will we see
(Spoken)

Pro-gram is **ready!** "Press a - ny key."

Chapter 5   **NUMBERS**

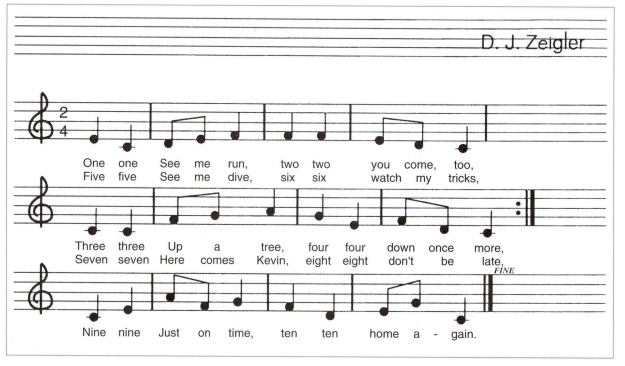

D. J. Zeigler

One one See me run, two two you come, too,
Five five See me dive, six six watch my tricks,

Three three Up a tree, four four down once more,
Seven seven Here comes Kevin, eight eight don't be late,
FINE

Nine nine Just on time, ten ten home a - gain.

Chapter 6   BOOKS

D. J. Zeigler

Come in Come in said the li-bra-ry door; I
O-pened it wide and saw books ga-lore. Tall skinny books up
high on the shelves, lit-tle fat books that stood by them-selves. I
O-pened one up and sat down to look, the pic-tures told sto-ries what
won-der ful book!

Chapter 7   LETTERS

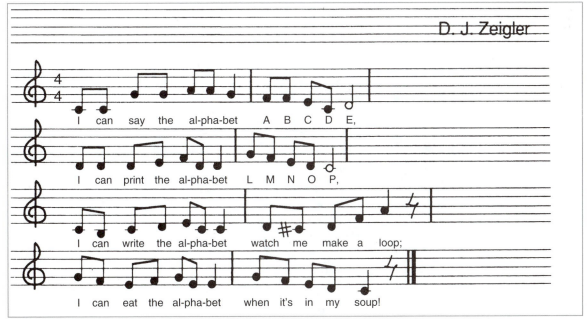

D. J. Zeigler

I can say the al-pha-bet A B C D E,
I can print the al-pha-bet L M N O P,
I can write the al-pha-bet watch me make a loop;
I can eat the al-pha-bet when it's in my soup!

Chapter 9   **MAKING MUSIC**

D. J. Zeigler

Can you whis-tle, whis-tle, whis-tle? can you

Hum hum hum? can you shake it like a this-tle? can you

Strum strum strum? can you tap your fin-gers light-ly? can you

Drum drum drum? can you move a-round po-lite-ly? can you

Run run run?

Chapter 10   **PETS**

D. J. Zeigler

Min-nie's got a guin-ea pig Ton-y's got a tur-tle,

Hol-ly's got a her-mit crab, Jac-kie's got a ger-bil,

Aa-ron has an ant farm, Ba-ron's got some gup-pies,

Ka-ren's got a kit-ten, now she wants some pup-pies;

Pets, pets ev-ery where what am I to do?

I don't need an-oth-er pet I've got you!

Chapter 11   **WHO AM I?**

D. J. Zeigler

Who am I, let me see, I'm won-der wo-man on T - V

I'm a dan-cer on the stage, I'm a rock star all the rage; to-

day I'm the mo-ther who pours the milk,

Yes-ter-day a prin-cess dressed in silk, to - morrow I don't know what I'll do,

I don't know - do you? *(Spoken)*

Chapter 12   **JOHNNY IS A JUMPER**

D. J. Zeigler

Johnny is a jum-per see him hop - hop - hop;

Bon-nie is a bum-per see her bop - bop - bop;

Phil-ip is a fli - er see him loop-the - loop,

I can go still high - er watch me fly the coop!

Chapter 14   **LEARNING LADDER**

Assessing Young Children's Progress Appropriately	www.ncrel.org
Better Brains for Babies	www.fcs.uga.edu
The Center on the Social & Emotional Foundations for Early Learning	www.csefel.uiuc.edu
Child Care Information Exchange	www.childcareexchange.com
The Children's Music Web	www.childrensmusic.org
Consumer Product Safety Commission	www.cpsc.gov
Institute for Early Learning Through the Arts	www.wolftrap.org
International Child Art Foundation	www.icaf.org
KidsHealth	www.kidshealth.org
Mind in the Making	www.mindinthemaking.org
National Art Education Association	www.naea-reston.org
National Association for Bilingual Education	www.nabe.org
National Association for Sports & Physical Education	www.aahperd.org
National Coalition for Parent Involvement in Education	www.ncpie.org
National Safe Kids Campaign	www.safekids.org
Read Write Think	www.readwritethink.org
Reading Is Fundamental	www.rif.org
Reggio Emilia	www.reggioemilia.com
Teaching Strategies	www.teachingstrategies.org

INDEX